# PORRIDGE: THE SCRIPTS

# PORRIDGE: THE SCRIPTS

DICK CLEMENT AND IAN LA FRENAIS

EDITED BY RICHARD WEBBER

headline

First published in 2002

By HEADLINE BOOK PUBLISHING

10 9 8 7 6 5 4 3 2 1



Cataloguing in Publication Data is available from the British Library

ISBN 0 7472 5546 6

Typeset in Sabon, Helvetica Light and American Typewriter by Letterpart Ltd
16 Bell Street, Reigate, Surrey
Printed and bound in Great Britain by Mackays of Chatham plc, Chatham, Kent
Text design by designsection, Frome, Somerset

HEADLINE BOOK PUBLISHING
A division of Hodder Headline
338 Euston Road
London NW1 3BH

www.headline.co.uk
www.hodderheadline.com

# CONTENTS

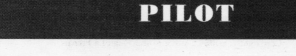

## PILOT



## 1 SERIES ONE



## 2 SERIES TWO

# FOREWORD

Fletcher was an easy character to play and I didn't have to think too much about it, which is fortunate. I think much of that is because there was a lot of me in Fletch; there was also plenty of my father, too. Although the character was a Cockney and I was born in Oxford, he was working class and I could relate to him.

Although he was out for everything he could get, being a wide-boy, he was a likeable chap. You always need charm in a character, even if you're playing an old tramp, and I think Fletcher possessed a lot of that.

Working on the show was such a delight, particularly as everyone worked so well together. When it came to rehearsals we'd race through them with ease. We'd often start at ten and be finished by one, simply because we all knew what we were doing. Obviously I was carrying a lot of the responsibility on my shoulders but I never received anything but total support from the rest of the team; you knew no one was going to let you down, ruin a gag or bit of timing.

I feel I owe much to *Porridge*. It was probably the best and most important show I did.

RONNIE BARKER 2002

# INTRODUCTION

The first time Ian and I ever sat down to write together was in a pub in the Old Brompton Road. I don't remember any discussion about who should do the actual scribbling, but it was me. This tradition continued and when asked about it we used to answer that it was because my calligraphy was more legible than Ian's. It is, but I don't think that is the entire reason.

The essentials haven't varied much over the years. We write *together*. Other collaborators work by e-mail or split the script up and say, 'You do that scene, I'll do this one.' If it works, fine, but it's not the way we do it. We discuss everything. It starts with the story. What's the main thrust and where are the juicy scenes? Inevitably, while we're kicking ideas around, some dialogue occurs to us. I suppose we're doing a form of actors' improvisation. So we step into character and throw out a line and a response may occur and if it's any good we incorporate it when we do the actual writing.

A tape recorder might sound like a good idea for this stage of the process. I think we even bought a couple over the years but the batteries ran out, or we forgot to switch them on and then the thought of wading through all the discarded drivel in search of a forgotten gem was too daunting and time-consuming. We jot down anything we really like and then it's time to write 'Fade In'.

Everything is debated, alternatives considered, choices made. And as I'm always the one with the pen in my hand – here's the hidden agenda – I have the power to choose my version over Ian's if it is a split vote. But if he doesn't like it when he sees it on the page and raises the red flag, back it goes. Or maybe we find a compromise, another line, another word.

We switched to a computer a few years ago. Ian stared at the grey cube on the table with deep suspicion. When I started to tap the keys he was appalled. 'You're not going to do that *while we're writing*?' I certainly was, because the alternative was transcribing everything at the end of the day after he'd gone home. He grudgingly got used to it after a while, won over by the obvious advantages of instant print-outs and corrections, though it was a year before he walked round to my side of the table to take a look at the text on the screen.

Somebody once said that writing is all about re-writing. It's certainly true in our case. Bang the words down on paper then polish, edit, tighten and improve. With an original screenplay everything is carved as if from a new block of granite. Every character, every setting needs to be discovered. It's different with a television series. Once the actors have played the characters a few times, their voices are in your head.

If I wanted to conjure up Fletcher, I imagined him sitting in his cell and somebody bursting in to tell him that an asteroid was due to hit the earth in three days. I can hear his response now: 'Oh yes?'

Just two words. But spoken with the infinite scepticism of a man who believes nothing until he sees it with his own eyes. A small thing in itself but a great clue to character. He's wary, protective of what's his and determined to let no man make a sucker of him.

We wrote the first series of *Porridge* when we were rehearsing the stage musical *Billy*. It was a very happy time. One show was written on our knees in the Midland Hotel, Manchester. I'm pretty certain it was 'A Night In'. We felt it was important to do one show entirely in the cell, since prison is, after all, about being locked in. We also felt it should touch on how tough it is, especially for a young prisoner. It ended up as one of our favourite episodes, a 'two-hander' between Ronnie Barker and Richard Beckinsale, who wonderfully captured all of Lennie's fear and vulnerability.

The last series was written in California, where we were already doing the American version of the show. The writing process for Network TV was totally different, quite horrible and we never ever wanted to do it again. However, we kept it on the air for an entire season – twenty-two shows – and had run out of the original scripts. So as a matter of record, the story of the judge who sent Fletcher down turning up in Slade was originally done in America and then 'translated' back into English. It was sometimes difficult to remember if a line had originated in the American version or had already been used.

We're often asked about the differences between American humour and the English variety. The truth is, a good joke is a good joke. The real difference is to do with sociology and class in particular. Think of Shaw's *Pygmalion* or anything by Alan Ayckbourn. But when you mine for the American equivalent you run into race, a subject on which people are far more sensitive.

The last thing to say about writing *Porridge* is how painless it was. From the outset we knew we were writing for Ronnie Barker, in our view a comic genius.

Syd Lotterby did us an enormous favour when he cast Fulton Mackay and Brian Wilde for the pilot – though at the time we had no idea that it would become a series. But all three performances were firmly in our mind's eye – and ear – when we sat down to begin the series.

True, the research set us back, when we went round Wormwood Scrubs and Brixton, because we were hit by the harsh reality of life inside and how very unfunny it is. Even more reassuring, then, to picture Ronnie as Fletcher. The key was his attitude, his ability to make the very best of a bad situation and find little victories that get him through each day. He is a survivor, in the tradition of Falstaff or the Good Soldier Schweik. What would he say to that?

'Oh yes?'

DICK CLEMENT 2002

# EPISODE GUIDE

## THE PILOT

### PRISONER AND ESCORT

**Original transmission:** Sunday 1 April 1973, BBC2, 8.15 p.m.

**First repeat:** Tuesday 7 August 1973, BBC1, 8.30 p.m.

**Cast: Norman Fletcher** Ronnie Barker **Mr Barrowclough** Brian Wilde **Mr Mackay** Fulton Mackay **Prison Constable** Hamish Roughead

## SERIES ONE

### 1. NEW FACES, OLD HANDS

**Original transmission:** Thursday 5 September 1974, BBC1, 8.30 p.m.

**First repeat:** Friday 21 February 1975, BBC1, 8.30 p.m.

**Cast: Norman Fletcher** Ronnie Barker **Mr Barrowclough** Brian Wilde **Mr Mackay** Fulton Mackay **Lennie Godber** Richard Beckinsale **Cyril Heslop** Brian Glover **Medical Officer** John Bennett **The Governor** Michael Barrington **Other prison officers** Ronald Musgrove, Edward Cogdale and Keith Norrish

### 2. THE HUSTLER

**Original transmission:** Thursday 12 September 1974, BBC1, 8.30 p.m.

**First repeat:** Friday 28 February 1975, BBC1, 8.30 p.m.

**Cast: Norman Fletcher** Ronnie Barker **Mr Barrowclough** Brian Wilde **Mr Mackay** Fulton Mackay **Lennie Godber** Richard Beckinsale **Heslop** Brian Glover **Ives** Ken Jones **Lukewarm** Christopher Biggins **Evans** Ray Dunbobbin **Mr Appleton** Graham Ashley **Prison Officer** John Quarmby

### 3. A NIGHT IN

**Original transmission:** Thursday 19 September 1974, BBC1, 8.30 p.m.

**First repeat:** Friday 7 March 1975, BBC1, 8.30 p.m.

**Cast: Norman Fletcher** Ronnie Barker **Lennie Godber** Richard Beckinsale **Prison Officer** Paul McDowell

## 4. A DAY OUT

**Original transmission**: Thursday 26 September 1974, BBC1, 8.30 p.m.

**First repeat:** Friday 14 March 1975, BBC1, 8.30 p.m.

**Cast: Norman Fletcher** Ronnie Barker **Mr Mackay** Fulton Mackay **Lennie Godber** Richard Beckinsale **Ives** Ken Jones **Navyrum** Paul Angelis **Dylan** Philip Jackson **Scrounger** Johnny Wade **Vicar** Robert Gillespie **Verger** John Rutland **Chief Prison Officer** Arnold Peters **Landlord** Ralph Watson **Nurse** Peggy Mason

## 5. WAYS AND MEANS

**Original transmission:** Thursday 3 October 1974, BBC1, 8.30 p.m.

**First repeat:** Friday 21 March 1975, BBC1, 8.30 p.m.

**Cast: Norman Fletcher** Ronnie Barker **Mr Barrowclough** Brian Wilde **Mr Mackay** Fulton Mackay **Ives** Ken Jones **The Governor** Michael Barrington **McLaren** Tony Osoba

## 6. MEN WITHOUT WOMEN

**Original transmission:** Thursday 10 October 1974, BBC1, 8.30 p.m.

**First repeat:** Friday 28 March 1975, BBC1, 9.05 p.m.

**Cast: Norman Fletcher** Ronnie Barker **Mr Barrowclough** Brian Wilde **Mr Mackay** Fulton Mackay **Warren** Sam Kelly **Cyril Heslop** Brian Glover **The Governor** Michael Barrington **Lukewarm** Christopher Biggins **Sergeant Norris** Royston Tickner **Tolly** Emlyn Price **Isobel** June Ellis **Ingrid Fletcher** Patricia Brake **Norma** Susan Littler **Iris** Andonia Katsaros **Elaine** Rosalind Elliot **Trevor** Donald Groves

# SERIES TWO

## 1. JUST DESSERTS

**Original transmission:** Friday 24 October 1975, BBC1, 8.30 p.m.

**First repeat:** Thursday 20 May 1976, BBC1, 8 p.m.

**Cast: Norman Fletcher** Ronnie Barker **Mr Barrowclough** Brian Wilde **Mr Mackay** Fulton Mackay **Lennie Godber** Richard Beckinsale **Ives** Ken Jones **Warren** Sam Kelly **McLaren** Tony Osoba **Lukewarm** Christopher Biggins **Banyard** Eric Dodson **Mr Appleton** Graham Ashley **Mr Birchwood** John Rudling **Gay Gordon** Felix Bowness

## 2. HEARTBREAK HOTEL

**Original transmission:** Friday 31 October 1975, BBC1, 8.30 p.m.

**First repeat:** Thursday 27 May 1976, BBC1, 8 p.m.

**Cast: Norman Fletcher** Ronnie Barker **Mr Barrowclough** Brian Wilde **Mr Mackay** Fulton Mackay **Lennie Godber** Richard Beckinsale **Ingrid** Patricia Brake **Mrs Godber** Maggie Flint **Jackdaw** Cyril Shaps

## 3. DISTURBING THE PEACE

**Original transmission**: Friday 7 November 1975, BBC1, 8.30 p.m.

**First repeat:** Thursday 3 June 1976, BBC1, 7.55 p.m.

**Cast: Norman Fletcher** Ronnie Barker **Mr Barrowclough** Brian Wilde **Mr Mackay** Fulton Mackay **Lennie Godber** Richard Beckinsale **Mr Wainwright** Peter Jeffrey **Williams** Philip Madoc **Warren** Sam Kelly **McLaren** Tony Osoba **The Governor** Michael Barrington **Secretary (Mrs Heskith)** Madge Hindle

## 4. NO PEACE FOR THE WICKED

**Original transmission:** Friday 14 November 1975, BBC1, 8.30 p.m.

**First repeat:** Thursday 17 June 1976, BBC1, 8 p.m.

**Cast: Norman Fletcher** Ronnie Barker **Mr Barrowclough** Brian Wilde **Mr Mackay** Fulton Mackay **Blanco** David Jason **Warren** Sam Kelly **McLaren** Tony Osoba **Banyard** Eric Dodson **The Governor** Michael Barrington **Mr Collinson** Paul McDowell **Chaplain** Tony Aitken **Prison Visitors** Ivor Roberts, Barbara New and Geoffrey Greenhill

## 5. HAPPY RELEASE

**Original transmission:** Friday 21 November 1975, BBC1, 8.30 p.m.
**First repeat:** Thursday 24 June 1976, BBC1, 8 p.m.
**Cast: Norman Fletcher** Ronnie Barker **Mr Barrowclough** Brian Wilde **Mr Mackay** Fulton Mackay **Lennie Godber** Richard Beckinsale **Blanco** David Jason **Norris** Colin Farrell **Mr Collinson** Paul McDowell **Medical Officer** Terence Soall

## 6. THE HARDER THEY FALL

**Original transmission:** Friday 28 November 1975, BBC1, 8.30 p.m.
**First repeat:** Thursday 1 July 1976, BBC1, 7.55 p.m.
**Cast: Norman Fletcher** Ronnie Barker **Mr Barrowclough** Brian Wilde **Mr Mackay** Fulton Mackay **Lennie Godber** Richard Beckinsale **Harry Grout** Peter Vaughan **Jackdaw** Cyril Shaps **P.T.I.** Roy Sampson

# SERIES THREE

## 1. A STORM IN A TEACUP

**Original transmission:** Friday 18 February 1977, BBC1, 8.30 p.m.
**First repeat:** Friday 27 January 1978, BBC1, 8.30 p.m.
**Cast: Norman Fletcher** Ronnie Barker **Mr Barrowclough** Brian Wilde **Mr Mackay** Fulton Mackay **Lennie Godber** Richard Beckinsale **Harry Grout** Peter Vaughan **Harris** Ronald Lacey **Warren** Sam Kelly **McLaren** Tony Osoba **Lukewarm** Christopher Biggins **Spider** John Moore **Crusher** John Dair

## 2. POETIC JUSTICE

**Original transmission:** Friday 25 February 1977, BBC1, 8.30 p.m.
**First repeat:** Friday 13 January 1978, BBC1, 8.30 p.m.
**Cast: Norman Fletcher** Ronnie Barker **Mr Barrowclough** Brian Wilde **Mr Mackay** Fulton Mackay **Lennie Godber** Richard Beckinsale **Rawley** Maurice Denham **Harris** Ronald Lacey **Warren** Sam Kelly **McLaren** Tony Osoba **The Governor** Michael Barrington **Mr Collinson** Paul McDowell

## 3. ROUGH JUSTICE

**Original transmission:** Friday 4 March 1977, BBC1, 8.30 p.m.
**First repeat:** Friday 20 January 1978, BBC1, 8.30 p.m.
**Cast: Norman Fletcher** Ronnie Barker **Mr Barrowclough** Brian Wilde **Mr Mackay** Fulton Mackay **Lennie Godber** Richard Beckinsale **Rawley** Maurice Denham **Harris** Ronald Lacey **Warren** Sam Kelly **McLaren** Tony Osoba

## 4. PARDON ME

**Original transmission:** Friday 11 March 1977, BBC1, 8.30 p.m.
**First repeat:** Friday 3 February 1978, BBC1, 8.30 p.m.
**Cast**: **Norman Fletcher** Ronnie Barker **Mr Barrowclough** Brian Wilde **Mr Mackay** Fulton Mackay **Lennie Godber** Richard Beckinsale **Blanco** David Jason **Warren** Sam Kelly **Lukewarm** Christopher Biggins **The Governor** Michael Barrington

## 5. A TEST OF CHARACTER

**Original transmission:** Friday 18 March 1977, BBC1, 8.30 p.m.
**First repeat:** Friday 10 February 1978, BBC1, 8.30 p.m.
**Cast: Norman Fletcher** Ronnie Barker **Mr Barrowclough** Brian Wilde **Mr Mackay** Fulton Mackay **Lennie Godber** Richard Beckinsale **Spraggon** Alun Armstrong **Warren** Sam Kelly **McLaren** Tony Osoba

## 6. FINAL STRETCH

**Original transmission:** Friday 25 March 1977, BBC1, 8.30 p.m.
**First repeat:** Friday 17 February 1978, BBC1, 8.30 p.m.
**Cast: Norman Fletcher** Ronnie Barker **Mr Barrowclough** Brian Wilde **Mr Mackay** Fulton Mackay **Lennie Godber** Richard Beckinsale **Jarvis** David Daker **Warren** Sam Kelly **Ingrid** Patricia Brake **Crusher** John Dair

# CHRISTMAS SPECIALS

## NO WAY OUT

**Original transmission:** Wednesday 24 December 1975, BBC1, 8.25 p.m. (40-minute episode)

**First repeat:** Thursday 8 July 1976, BBC1, 7.50 p.m.

**Cast: Norman Fletcher** Ronnie Barker **Mr Barrowclough** Brian Wilde **Mr Mackay** Fulton Mackay **Lennie Godber** Richard Beckinsale **Harry Grout** Peter Vaughan **Prison Doctor** Graham Crowden **Warren** Sam Kelly **Lukewarm** Christopher Biggins **Sandra** Carol Hawkins **Nurse** Elisabeth Day

## THE DESPERATE HOURS

**Original transmission:** Friday 24 December 1976, BBC1, 8 p.m.

**First repeat:** Friday 1 April 1977, BBC1, 8.15 p.m.

**Cast: Norman Fletcher** Ronnie Barker **Mr Barrowclough** Brian Wilde **Mr Mackay** Fulton Mackay **Lennie Godber** Richard Beckinsale **Reg Urwin** Dudley Sutton **Warren** Sam Kelly **McLaren** Tony Osoba **The Governor** Michael Barrington **Keegan** Ken Wynne **Tulip** Michael Redfern **Mrs Jamieson** Jane Wenham

# PRODUCTION TEAM

**All episodes written by Dick Clement and Ian La Frenais**
**Producer/Director:** Sydney Lotterby
**Executive Producer:** James Gilbert (Pilot)

**Music:** Max Harris
**Film Cameraman:** Alan Featherstone (Pilot); Len Newson (S1, episodes 1, 2, 3 and 6); Keith Taylor (S1, episodes 4 and 5); Ken Willicombe (S2, episodes 2, 3, 4 and 6); Kenneth MacMillan (S2, episode 5); John Tiley ('No Way Out'); John McGlashan (S3)
**Film Editor:** Geoffrey Botterill (S1, episodes 1 and 2); Ray Millichope (Pilot; S1, episodes 3, 4, 5 and 6; S2, episodes 2, 3, 4, 5 and 6; 'No Way Out'); John Dunstan (S3)
**Film Sound:** Ron Blight (credited on 'No Way Out')
**Make-up:** Penny Delamar (Pilot); Sylvia James (S1); Ann Ailes-Stevenson (S2; 'No Way Out'); Suzanne Broad ('The Desperate Hours'; S3)
**Costume:** Penny Lowe (Pilot); Mary Husband (S1 and S3); Betty Aldiss (S2); Susan Wheal ('No Way Out'); Robin Stubbs ('The Desperate Hours')
**Lighting:** Peter Smee (Pilot; S1, episodes 1, 2, 3, 4 and 6; S2, episodes 1, 2, 3 and 4; 'No Way Out'); Peter Wesson (S1, episode 5; S3); Brian Clemett (S2, episode 5); Sam Barclay ('The Desperate Hours')
**Sound:** Mike McCarthy (Pilot); Anthony Philpot (S1; S2; 'The Desperate Hours'); Jeff Booth ('No Way Out'); John Holmes (S3)
**Production Assistant:** Ray Butt (S1); Dave Perrottet (S2); Alan Bell ('No Way Out'); Mike Crisp ('The Desperate Hours' and S3)
**Technical Adviser:** Jonathan Marshall (credited on S1, episodes 1–4)
**Designer:** Tim Gleeson (Pilot; S1, episodes 1, 2, 5 and 6; S2, episode 1; 'No Way Out'; 'The Desperate Hours'; S3); David Chandler (S1, episodes 3 and 6); Gerry Scott (S1, episodes 4 and 5); John Pusey (S2, episodes 2, 3, 4, 5 and 6)

# PILOT

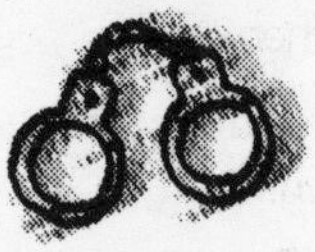

## PRISONER AND ESCORT

### 1. OPENING TITLES

### 2. STREET

***Fletcher, Mackay and a Police Constable walk towards a parked van. Barrowclough is sitting in the van reading a newspaper. He sees the men approaching and gets out. The others reach the back of the van.***

**POLICE CONSTABLE**

Right, he's all yours then. Happy New Year, Jock.

**MACKAY**

Aye, escort duty on New Year's Eve.

**POLICE CONSTABLE**

Happy New Year, Fletcher.

***Fletcher and Mackay get into the van.***

**FLETCHER**

Oh yes, very witty, very droll.

***Barrowclough gets in the van. The constable shuts the door, bangs on it and the van drives off. Zoom out as we see the van approach St Pancras station.***

**MAGISTRATE (*VOICEOVER*)**

(*Offscreen*) Norman Stanley Fletcher, you have pleaded guilty to the charges brought by this court, and it is now my duty to pass sentence. You are an habitual criminal, who accepts arrest as an occupational hazard, and presumably accepts imprisonment in the same casual manner. We therefore feel constrained to commit you to the maximum term allowed for these offences – we sentence you to five years' imprisonment. Do you wish to address the court?

### 3. RAILWAY CARRIAGE

***Mackay, Fletcher and Barrowclough are sitting in first-class compartment. The blinds into the corridor are drawn.***

**FLETCHER**

Cobblers.

**BARROWCLOUGH**

What?

**FLETCHER**

What Brian Clough says about London clubs.

**MACKAY**

(*Grabbing the paper*) That's my paper.

**FLETCHER**

Can I have a look at your *Penthouse* then?

**MACKAY**

Get your own.

**FLETCHER**

How can I get my own? We're in motion, aren't we?

**MACKAY**

Shoulda thought of that at the station.

**FLETCHER**

At the station I wasn't even permitted a Jimmy Riddle.

**MACKAY**

Shut your mouth.

***There is a pause.***

**BARROWCLOUGH**

You can have a look at my *Angling Times* if you like.

**MACKAY**

No, he can't. God Almighty, mollycoddling him already! People seem to forget what prison's for. He's paying a debt to society. Not having an all-expenses-paid holiday with privileges and magazines. You're going to prison to be punished.

***There is a pause. Then Fletcher leans across to Barrowclough.***

**FLETCHER**

I spy with my little eye something beginning with *(indicating Mackay with his head)* C.

**MACKAY**

You watch it, sonny.

**FLETCHER**

Constable?

**MACKAY**

Don't come it with me.

**FLETCHER**

I wouldn't, Mr Mackay, I wouldn't – otherwise you'd wait until the train picked up a fair bit of speed outside Hemel Hempstead and chuck me out of the window. Put it down as attempted escape.

**BARROWCLOUGH**

He wouldn't do that.

**FLETCHER**

No, I suppose not . . . he couldn't spell Hemel Hempstead, he'd wait till Rugby.

**MACKAY**

I'm a reasonable man. But one more allegation of brutality and I'll knock your block off . . .

**BARROWCLOUGH**

Look, it's a long journey ahead so . . . so let's not conduct it in an atmosphere of hostility and aggression. Why don't we all have a nice cup of tea?

***He starts to get to his feet.***

**BARROWCLOUGH**

Both take milk and sugar?

**MACKAY**

You sit still, I'll get them.

**BARROWCLOUGH**

(*Looking for money*) Well, let me pay. (*To Fletcher*) Anything you want?

**FLETCHER**
Thanks, mate. Tea with two sugars, and I'll have one of those individual fruit pies if they've got any . . .

***Mackay slams the door shut before Fletcher finishes.***

**FLETCHER**
He's a laugh, in' he?

**BARROWCLOUGH**
I suppose it's with bein' a Scotsman and being deprived of Hogmanay. I mean they do take it very seriously the Scots.

**FLETCHER**
Yeah, well they take any excuse for drinking seriously, don't they. Nothing social about their drinking, is there. With them it's not the case of a few friends mellowing over a glass of vino. No, no . . . they just drink to get drunk. (*Looking through a magazine*) Cor, look at 'er. Only one thing worse than a drunken Scot and that's a sober one.

**BARROWCLOUGH**
I'm Scots on my mother's side.

**FLETCHER**
Yeah, well second generation, in' it? Different fing.

**BARROWCLOUGH**
Anyhow, I'm a bit of all sorts. Scots, English, Irish . . . Polish –

**FLETCHER**
She got about a bit your mother.

**BARROWCLOUGH**
Oh no, I didn't mean . . .

**FLETCHER**
I'm pure London myself. In fact, pure North London. You go to the graveyard in Muswell Hill, it's full of Fletchers. Shall I tell you something? There's always been a Fletcher round my way, right back to . . . oh I should think Henry the Fourth Part One.

**BARROWCLOUGH**
Oh . . . I haven't got any heritage. I know me grandfather was an ironmonger in Accrington. But before that . . .

**FLETCHER**
My great-grandfather was William Wellington Fletcher. The last man in England to be hanged for horse-stealing. And Matthew Jarvis Fletcher – he was Newgate with Jack Sheppard, wun' he? That's well known.

**BARROWCLOUGH**
So it runs in the family, does it – crime, like?

**FLETCHER**
Possibly. I know there's a load of Fletchers in Australia.

**BARROWCLOUGH**
So you come from a rough neighbourhood?

**FLETCHER**
No, I told you – Muswell Hill. It's very suburban, Muswell Hill. Respectable.

**BARROWCLOUGH**
Broken home?

**FLETCHER**
Not at all. They've just celebrated their diamond wedding.

**BARROWCLOUGH**
Oh. I was just wondering why . . .
**FLETCHER**
Well, when I left school I went round the local Labour and appraised the professional opportunities open to me. Unfortunately my lack of scholastic achievement prevented me from doing the things I really fancied, such as stockbrokerin' or teaching tennis at a girls' school. And I didn't reckon working in a cardboard box factory. So I robbed this sub-post office off the North Circular.
**BARROWCLOUGH**
And you never looked back since, so to speak.
**FLETCHER**
No – nor have I ever been short of 3d. stamps.
**BARROWCLOUGH**
What have you gone down for this time?
**FLETCHER**
Aw, don't talk about it. Be a farce if it wasn't such a tragedy. Own fault, should have stuck to what I know best. Housebreaking. But I lifts this lorry. Impulse steal. You know what I mean, impulse steal. I think it's a doddle, don't I?
**BARROWCLOUGH**
I gather it wasn't.
**FLETCHER**
Yeah, you know why, though – flaming brakes failed. Criminal letting lorries on the road in that condition. And he was overloaded. So there I was, wiv five ton on me back roarin' down bloody Archway.
**BARROWCLOUGH**
Wonder you weren't killed.
**FLETCHER**
I nearly was. Went through three back gardens, went clean through a brick wall and finished up in somebody's tool shed.
**BARROWCLOUGH**
Did they get you for wilful destruction of property? I mean, knocking that wall down.
**FLETCHER**
Yeah. And I asked for six other fences to be taken into consideration.
***Barrowclough does not react to Fletcher's wit.***
**FLETCHER**
Get it, get it?
**BARROWCLOUGH**
Pardon?
**FLETCHER**
Oh never mind.
***There is a pause. He fumbles in his pocket and finds some chewing gum.***
**FLETCHER**
Here – tell you what. Have a bit of this.
**BARROWCLOUGH**
You've only two bits left.
**FLETCHER**
Yeah . . . what made you take up this lark then?
**BARROWCLOUGH**
Prison service?

**FLETCHER**
Yeah, what made you fancy it like?

**BARROWCLOUGH**
I always wanted a vocation which would satisfy my desire to perform useful public service . . . and get a free house and uniform.

**FLETCHER**
What's it like, this nick?

**BARROWCLOUGH**
Oh very good. Modern you see. Experimental. With a cricket pitch and a psychiatrist.

**FLETCHER**
Oh yeah. Bird's bird though, in' it?

**BARROWCLOUGH**
Not with this one. If you took advantage of our courses, of our many occupational and/or recreational activities . . . well, you put your mind to it, you could come out an intermediate welder or an accomplished oboe player.

**FLETCHER**
Oh yeah.

**BARROWCLOUGH**
Pity you're not in longer, you could have taken up civil engineering.

**FLETCHER**
Oh pity. That is a pity. Pity I didn't get a ten stretch. Then I could have took my welding finals, and be a doctor of philosophy.

**BARROWCLOUGH**
(*Tentatively*) I'm a bit of an amateur botanist myself. So sometimes I take some of the prisoners out on the fells to explore the natural phenomena of our countryside.

***At this Fletcher's eyes register interest.***

**FLETCHER**
Out on the fells, is it?

**BARROWCLOUGH**
Yes, lovely views.

**FLETCHER**
I might put down for that. That might interest me. Natural phenomena of our countryside – how far's the nearest railway station?

**BARROWCLOUGH**
Oh that's the beauty of it you see, we're miles from anywhere.

**FLETCHER**
(*Less enthusiastically*) Oh are we.

**BARROWCLOUGH**
We also have an arts and crafts section. Or you could learn woodwork.

**FLETCHER**
Listen, squire, I don't want no courses, no reconditioning, resettlement. All I want to do is mind me own business, do my porridge and count the days till I get out.

**BARROWCLOUGH**
You'll change you know.

**FLETCHER**
What?

**BARROWCLOUGH**
Even the most cynical and hardened criminals have changed at this place. They've responded you see to our approach which is based not on

correction and punishment, but sympathy and understanding.

***The door of the compartment slides open and an unsympathetic Mackay enters, carrying three cardboard cups.***

**MACKAY**

I forget if you took sugar or not but it makes no difference 'cos I spilt most of yours on the way back, but what you gonna do about it?

**FLETCHER**

Where's this sympathy and understanding? How's he working at your nick? Blimey, he'd bring back the birch at the drop of an helmet.

**MACKAY**

What's he on about?

**BARROWCLOUGH**

Mr Mackay runs several of our group activities.

**FLETCHER**

Yeah. Like rock-breaking and compulsory pot-holing.

**MACKAY**

I'll soon have you in shape, Fletcher. I'll soon have you a shadow of your former self.

**FLETCHER**

I bet he's secretary to the Lord Chief Justice Goddard Appreciation Society.

**MACKAY**

Just keep your nose clean, lad. Just show me some respect and keep your nose clean, you'll be all right. I'm hard but fair.

**FLETCHER**

Like Leeds United?

**MACKAY**

If you like. You play ball with me, and I'll play ball with you, and you'll find me a reasonable man.

**FLETCHER**

Good, good . . . could I have a look at your *Penthouse* now?

**MACKAY**

Can you hell!

**FLETCHER**

You've got to admire consistency . . .

***Barrowclough offers Fletcher his Angling Times.***

**FLETCHER**

Try page twenty-four.

## 4. RAILWAY STATION

***A train is leaving the station. As the last coach passes, Fletcher and Barrowclough are walking along the platform. They leave the station. Outside they walk to a waiting minibus.***

**FLETCHER**

How far we got to go then?

**MACKAY**

About an hour and a half. Across the fells.

**FLETCHER**

Can I have a Johnny Riddle then?

**MACKAY**

You should have thought of that earlier.

**FLETCHER**

I did think of it earlier. There's been

nothing else on my mind for ages. Why are you so reluctant to let me go to the lavatory?

***Mackay holds up handcuffs.***

**FLETCHER**

Oh I see.

***Barrowclough starts undoing the minibus doors.***

**BARROWCLOUGH**

You'd better let him go, we can't stop in transit.

***Mackay unlocks the handcuffs.***

**MACKAY**

All right then, behind the bus.

**FLETCHER**

Thank you, Mackay.

***He goes round behind the minibus. He looks at the petrol cap and his expression changes. Fletcher checks in the direction of Mackay and Barrowclough to make sure they are not watching and takes off the petrol cap. Then he unzips his flies.***

***In the distance the minibus can be seen driving along. Suddenly it stalls. Mackay gets out. He walks round to the front of the minibus and lifts the bonnet. Barrowclough and Fletcher join him.***

**BARROWCLOUGH**

What do you reckon it is?

**MACKAY**

How do I know? I'm no mechanic.

**FLETCHER**

Plugs, is it? Or ignition?

**MACKAY**

Put the bracelets on him.

***Barrowclough starts to comply.***

***Mackay moves back to try the starter.***

**MACKAY**

Don't you be thinking that fate's given you a last chance of freedom.

**FLETCHER**

Don't believe in fate.

***The starter makes unpromising noises.***

**BARROWCLOUGH**

Sounds like the carburettor.

**FLETCHER**

Have to get the bus then, won't we?

**MACKAY**

What bus?

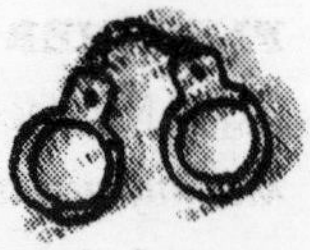

**FLETCHER**

Hitch a lift then.

**MACKAY**

Who drives round here on New Year's Eve?

**BARROWCLOUGH**

Who drives round here any time?

**FLETCHER**

Getting a bit parky, in' it?

**BARROWCLOUGH**

Be dark soon.

**MACKAY**

God Almighty!

**FLETCHER**

Don't you know how to fix it then? Hasn't one of your many instructional courses taught you how to cope with mechanical failure?

**BARROWCLOUGH**
It's survival we'll need out here. Be dark soon. And they forecast snow.

**MACKAY**
Pull yourself together Mr Barrowclough.

**FLETCHER**
No need to take it out on him.

**MACKAY**
Look, there's one thing for it. I'm going on. Going on to the prison. Now listen to me. You do not move. You do not move from here and you do not take the bracelets off him. Right?

**BARROWCLOUGH**
Right, Mr Mackay.

**MACKAY**
(*To Fletcher*) And you behave yourself.

**FLETCHER**
Right, Mr Mackay.

***Mackay walks off down the road. Fletcher and Barrowclough are shivering. To keep warm Fletcher flaps his arms across his chest, forgetting the handcuffs. He jerks Barrowclough.***

**FLETCHER**
Sorry, mate.

## 5. MINIBUS

***Outside the wind howls loudly. Barrowclough and Fletcher, still handcuffed, are sitting side by side in the minibus. Barrowclough blows on his hand, as Fletcher blows on his.***

**FLETCHER**
By the time they find us we'll be dead with exposure. Like Robert Taylor at the end of that picture.

**BARROWCLOUGH**
What picture?

**FLETCHER**
Western about buffalo hunting. In the deep frozen North. And he had to spend the night out in the open. Up a tree he was.

**BARROWCLOUGH**
Why was he up a tree?

**FLETCHER**
What? Well I 'spect he was avoiding marauding buffalo, driven half-crazy by the extreme cold.

**BARROWCLOUGH**
Oh yes, marauding buffalo . . .

**FLETCHER**
Driven half-crazy by the extreme cold. Much as we'll be in an hour or two. Ain't there no houses or farms near here?

**BARROWCLOUGH**
There's a cottage not far.

**FLETCHER**
Well, let's go there then.

**BARROWCLOUGH**
Mr Mackay says we're not to leave the van.

**FLETCHER**
All right – we'll die in the van.

**BARROWCLOUGH**
Anyway it will be all locked up, they only use it in the summer.

**FLETCHER**
So what?

**BARROWCLOUGH**
How will we get in?

**FLETCHER**
Mr Barrowclough . . .

**BARROWCLOUGH**
Yes.

**FLETCHER**
I'm only a flaming housebreaker, in' I?

## 6. COTTAGE: LIVING ROOM

***It is night time. Fletcher and Barrowclough come in from the kitchen. They walk to an old sofa and sit as near as possible to the glowing fire. They have mugs of black coffee in their outside hands, but their inside hands are still handcuffed together.***

**BARROWCLOUGH**
I wish we had a drop of milk.

**FLETCHER**
It's the hot drink that counts.

**BARROWCLOUGH**
And you'd think they'd've had some sugar somewhere.

**FLETCHER**
Tell you what – try a drop of this in it.
***He puts his hand in his pocket and produces a hip flask.***

**BARROWCLOUGH**
What is it?

**FLETCHER**
I'm not sure –
***With this he moves the two handcuffed hands together to unscrew the cap. Then he sniffs it.***

**FLETCHER**
Scotch.

**BARROWCLOUGH**
Oh no, anyway – I'm on duty.

**FLETCHER**
It's medicinal. Help to revive us. Take the chill out of our numbed bones.

**BARROWCLOUGH**
Where d'you get it?

**FLETCHER**
It must have accidentally fallen out the back of Mr Mackay's pocket, when he got off the van.

**BARROWCLOUGH**
You stole it!

**FLETCHER**
I didn't. I told you, it fell off the back of the van.
***He drinks.***

**BARROWCLOUGH**
Is whisky medicinal?

**FLETCHER**
Yeah. I always feel better after I've had a few.

**BARROWCLOUGH**
Oh all right then, if it's medicinal.
***Fletcher pours some whisky into Barrowclough's mug.***

**BARROWCLOUGH**
That's enough.
***Fletcher takes a quick swig out of the flask before pouring some whisky into his coffee. Then he looks at his watch.***

**FLETCHER**

Hey . . . it's New Year now, you know.

**BARROWCLOUGH**

Is it? Oh, all the best then.

**FLETCHER**

Yeah, and to you, mate.

***They sip their drinks.***

**FLETCHER**

Like *The Defiant Ones*.

**BARROWCLOUGH**

Beg your pardon?

**FLETCHER**

That was pictures an' all. *The Defiant Ones*. 'Bout these two convicts on the run, chained together like we are. Only one was black, one was white. Fact, if you had a bit of coloured blood in you, 'stead of all that Polish rubbish you've got, you could have been Sidney Poitier to my Tony Curtis.

**BARROWCLOUGH**

We have a Cinema Club at the prison. Only last Tuesday we showed *Irrigation in the Gobi Desert*. On the same bill with *Birds of the Farne Islands*.

**FLETCHER**

Standing room only, was it?

**BARROWCLOUGH**

No, we didn't have much of a turnout that night.

**FLETCHER**

I'm amazed.

**BARROWCLOUGH**

My wife likes the pictures. But we don't go much these days.

**FLETCHER**

No wonder – so bloomin' remote. Stuck in the middle of Cumberland where you going to find a cinema?

**BARROWCLOUGH**

That's the trouble. My wife, she feels very bad about being deprived of the excitement and amenities that a city can offer. She's always terribly unsettled every time we come back from our monthly day trip to Workington.

**FLETCHER**

Oh yes. I can see how the lights of Workington might turn a young girl's head.

**BARROWCLOUGH**

How d'you mean?

**FLETCHER**

Well, come on, mate. Amenities in Workington? Ain't got Christianity up here yet so you can't even go to a church social.

**BARROWCLOUGH**

Different for you – Londoners. My wife's always wanted to be cosmopolitan. Should have put in for a transfer to the Scrubs – or Brixton.

**FLETCHER**

No, if you was going to go to Brixton, mate, you'd have to be Sidney Poitier.

**BARROWCLOUGH**

(*Leaning back*) Too late now.

**FLETCHER**

So er, your old lady feels . . . deprived, does she?

**BARROWCLOUGH**
Well, she sees a future of frustrated ambitions stretching before her. She doesn't like what I do or where we live. So over the years she's grown bitter and unsettled, full of restless urges. Which have manifested themselves in various ways like bad temper, spots and sleeping with the postman. (*Drinks*) And there were liaisons with other men. We got to rowing all the time. Things went from bad to worse. Eventually we went to see this marriage guidance counsellor.

**FLETCHER**
That help, did it?

**BARROWCLOUGH**
It helped her! She ran off with him.

**FLETCHER**
Oh well, you're well out of it, aren't you, mate. You're well out of a slag like that.

**BARROWCLOUGH**
She's come back.

**FLETCHER**
Oh I see . . . well, people change.

***Barrowclough moves along the sofa and lies back.***

**BARROWCLOUGH**
I blame myself. I'm a failure. I'm only hanging on to this job by the skin of me teeth. I got so depressed I thought I'd take advantage of the prison psychiatric department. See them about my inferiority complex. Well, it's not a complex really – I am inferior.

**FLETCHER**
Aw come on, leave it off. Look, I don't know you very well. I can tell that you're a man of kindness, compassion and humanity. Now, you can't buy those, can you? Would you swap them for a colour telly and a penthouse in Workington? 'Course you wouldn't.

**BARROWCLOUGH**
I suppose not.

***Fletcher empties flask into Barrowclough's mug.***

**FLETCHER**
Here finish this. You can't go through life thinking that you should have been something else. You're doing the job you always wanted to do. You must think, this is what I am. I am what I am, and when it's all over I'll look God straight in the eye and say, I've done it my way.

**BARROWCLOUGH**
I've done it my way.

**FLETCHER**
Confidence in yourself.

**BARROWCLOUGH**
Confidence . . .

**FLETCHER**
Trust your own judgement and initiative.

**BARROWCLOUGH**
Initiative . . .

**FLETCHER**
Why don't you take these handcuffs off?

**BARROWCLOUGH**
(*Not hearing this*) D'you know, I've

never talked to anyone before – not really talked.

**FLETCHER**

Yeah – yeah . . . why don't you take these handcuffs off?

**BARROWCLOUGH**

Handcuffs?

**FLETCHER**

It's the circulation, in' it? Cuttin' off the supply to my head.

**BARROWCLOUGH**

We have rules . . .

**FLETCHER**

What about judgement – initiative. Are you going to do it their way, or are you going to do it your way? Confidence in yourself.

***Barrowclough thinks very hard for a minute, then comes to a decision.***

**BARROWCLOUGH**

I'm going to take them off. Yes. I am taking them off. I am taking them off because if I don't I'm betraying the principles of my prison and myself in approaching prisoners with sympathy and understanding.

***Fletcher watches anxiously as Barrowclough fishes for the key.***

**BARROWCLOUGH**

You are a criminal – habitual and hereditary. But until we show *you* trust, how are you going to *learn* trust?

**FLETCHER**

That is irrefutably true. What more can I say?

***The handcuffs come off, and both men rub their wrists with relief. Barrowclough yawns, lying back against the sofa.***

**BARROWCLOUGH**

Made me quite sleepy that whisky has. Quite drowsy.

**FLETCHER**

Another good reason for taking them off. We couldn't have kipped down there like Babes in the Wood, could we?

**BARROWCLOUGH**

I can hardly keep me eyes open.

**FLETCHER**

You get your feet up, my old son. Get a decent bit of shut-eye. I'll push these two chairs together.

***He does so, settling in the chairs, but in a position to watch Barrowclough.***

**BARROWCLOUGH**

You know, Fletcher, I hope you do decide to join my botany group.

**FLETCHER**

I'll give it serious consideration, squire.

**BARROWCLOUGH**

I feel a better man for tonight. More confident. I don't feel a failure. I feel that for once I've used my judgement, and I'm right.

**FLETCHER**

Right?

**BARROWCLOUGH**

Right about you, Fletcher.

***Fletcher watches Barrowclough who has fallen asleep.***

**FLETCHER**

Mr Barrowclough?

***There is no reply. Fletcher gets up.***

**FLETCHER**

Mr Barrowclough?

***Fletcher rushes out. Barrowclough continues sleeping.***

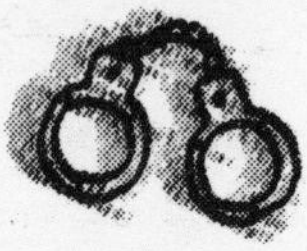

## 7. COUNTRYSIDE

***It is night time. Fletcher escapes. He is seen running and scrambling up and down hillsides. Eventually he reaches the edge of a farm but the fierce barking of a dog forces him to change direction. As dawn breaks he is still running. As he runs past a brick wall, he notices there is a gap in it. Through it can be seen a cottage. Fletcher comes back and looks at the cottage. He decides to check it out. He runs towards the cottage.***

## 8. COTTAGE: SCULLERY

***Morning. Fletcher opens a window and climbs into the scullery. He moves one of the doors. Suddenly he hears a cough (offscreen). He grasps a heavy bucket and moves behind the door. The door opens and Barrowclough walks in.***

**BARROWCLOUGH**

Fletcher, are you out here?

***Fletcher drops the bucket in surprise.***

**FLETCHER**

Mr Barrowclough.

**BARROWCLOUGH**

What a shock you gave me. What are you doing here?

**FLETCHER**

That's what I'd like to know.

**BARROWCLOUGH**

What are you doing with that saucepan?

**FLETCHER**

Milk – milk . . . I've just been out to get you some milk for your coffee – thought I might find a stray cow about.

**BARROWCLOUGH**

You look terrible, as if you've been up all night.

**FLETCHER**

Couldn't sleep, could I?

**BARROWCLOUGH**

It was a very nice thought but all the same you shouldn't have done it. You could have got lost. People are always getting lost on these fells. Wander around in circles they do.

**FLETCHER**

Do they?

## 9. FLETCHER'S CELL

*Fletcher is lying on his bunk. Mackay walks in.*

**MACKAY**

So – whose good behaviour last night made him the Governor's blue-eyed boy?

**FLETCHER**

I must be the first man to have earned remission before I even got here.

**MACKAY**

Don't give me any of your officious lip, Fletcher. I know you were trying to work one last night.

**FLETCHER**

On what do you base that supposition, Mr Mackay?

**MACKAY**

On the evidence of our motor mechanic's report on the van.

**FLETCHER**

Oh.

**MACKAY**

It appears that the petrol tank had more in it after our journey than before. Only what was in it certainly was not 5-star. Now I'm going to be watching you like a hawk, 'cos nobody goes over the wall at this prison.

**FLETCHER**

No, Mr Mackay, no one takes the petrol out of you.

*Mackay goes out, passing Barrowclough who walks into the cell.*

**BARROWCLOUGH**

What did you say to the Governor?

**FLETCHER**

What?

**BARROWCLOUGH**

What did you say to the Governor?

**FLETCHER**

Why – give you a rollicking, did he?

**BARROWCLOUGH**

Far from it. He congratulated me on my handling of the situation. He said I was a credit to the service, praised my judgement and initiative and my capacity to remain calm under crisis.

**FLETCHER**

That's all right then.

**BARROWCLOUGH**

But you must have said something.

**FLETCHER**

All I said was that any naughty thoughts I'd harboured of escape were quickly dispelled by the cool authority of my escort, Mr Barrowclough. A man to whom I later owed my life, owing to the fact that he forced me from the vehicle against my will, to take shelter against the elements, supporting or half-carrying my exhausted body across several miles of rough terrain. Just what anyone would say, really.

**BARROWCLOUGH**

Did you mean all that, Fletcher?

**FLETCHER**
No – p'raps I coloured the incidents of the night a little. But I see no reason why you and I shouldn't start the New Year on a good footing with the authorities.

**BARROWCLOUGH**
I've never been praised before.

**FLETCHER**
How's it feel?

**BARROWCLOUGH**
Wonderful. You know, Fletcher, you've done a lot for me the last twenty-four hours. You've given me strength, confidence and . . . friendship. Is there nothing I can do for you in return?

**FLETCHER**
Well, I expect a few things might occur to me during the ensuing months . . . in fact there is one little thing now.

**BARROWCLOUGH**
Yes?

**FLETCHER**
If you could see your way clear to bringing me some reading matter, nothing too heavy, the odd glossy nude.

**BARROWCLOUGH**
Certainly.

**FLETCHER**
And when you've got turned round p'raps you'd do something about this cell – like, shifting me to one that faces south-west 'cos I'm not going to get much sun in here, am I? Oh, and this botany club of yours, nature walks, is it? Outside the prison?

**BARROWCLOUGH**
That's right.

**FLETCHER**
Put me down for it will you, as soon as possible.

***He walks Barrowclough round the cell, discussing what he can do.***

1

# SERIES ONE

# 1 SERIES ONE

## EPISODE ONE: NEW FACES, OLD HANDS

### 1. PRISON LANDING

***A key is seen going into lock.***

***A door opens. Mackay, the chief Prison Officer and Barrowclough walk through. They lock the door and walk along the gantry, stopping outside a cell door.***

**MACKAY**

The three new arrivals, Mr Leach. Heslop, Cyril, forty-one. Three years, robbery third stretch. Thick as two short planks – no ulcers with that one. Godber, Leonard Arthur, twenty-three. First offender, two years breaking and entering. Seems somewhat naïve. Could be corrupted. Possibly by this one – Fletcher, Norman Stanley, forty-two. Five years. He's the one I brought up from Brixton. Knows the score, done a lot of bird, water off a duck's back. (*Stepping back from spyhole*) I'll be watching that one.

### 2. RECEPTION ROOM

***Weak sun is filtering through a barred window.***

**MACKAY**

(*Voiceover*) What a beautiful day.

***The camera reveals Mackay standing at the window looking out.***

**MACKAY**

For the time of year, quite astonishing. Beautiful day.

***The camera now shows Fletcher, Godber and Heslop standing in a line on the other side of the room.***

**FLETCHER**

Oh lovely. P'raps later on we can all go out for a cycle ride.

**MACKAY**

Know what they say about New Year's Day? "What you do on the First Day of the Year, you do all the year round." In the case of you three gentlemen that's perfectly true. (*Addressing Lennie*) You, laddy – you Mr Godber – first time, isn't it? You must be wondering what an average day in prison is like. Tell him, Fletcher.

**FLETCHER**

It's exactly like the day before, Mr Mackay.

**MACKAY**

The voice of experience. And tell him how the average day begins, Fletcher.

**FLETCHER**

Begins at 7.00 a.m. You'll be woken by a persistent and deafening bell. Then the screws will come round –

**MACKAY**

I beg your pardon.

**FLETCHER**

The prison officers will come round. Offering such encouragements as 'Wakey wakey, get your socks on, move you 'orrible creatures.' We shall respond to this badinage with such remarks as 'Good morning, sir, Good Lord is that the time,' or 'Who's been having your old lady while you've been on night duty?'

**MACKAY**

Very comical, Fletcher. Eight o'clock slop out, eight ten breakfast. Eight fifteen return to cell, nine o'clock – yes, Fletcher?

**FLETCHER**

Slop out again, Mr Mackay, followed by work till eleven fifteen when we –

**MACKAY**

Exercise. Walking in pairs, five to six yards apart, no conversing to pairs in front or behind. This is followed by the highlight of the day, quiet Fletcher I'm asking Heslop.

**FLETCHER**

Who?

**MACKAY**

You've been inside Heslop, what is, the highlight of the day?

**HESLOP**

Er . . . er . . . visiting hours?

**MACKAY**

We're in Cumberland, man. A barren windswept fell north of the Pennines. We are two weeks from Euston! When you see your loved ones it'll be the highlight of the *year*.

***Fletcher turns to an increasingly dismayed Lennie.***

**FLETCHER**

Glad you came?

**MACKAY**

Fletcher –

**FLETCHER**

Sir?

**MACKAY**

Highlight of the day.

**FLETCHER**

Highlight of the day – dinner, sir.

**MACKAY**

Which is –

**FLETCHER**

Nourishing.

**MACKAY**

Nourishing is it not.

**FLETCHER**

Can't wait, sir.

**MACKAY**

Midday, bang up.

***Lennie looks hopeful.***

**MACKAY**

Not what you think, laddy – back to your cells. Thirteen hundred, slop out, work, tea, evening association, which means in principle that you can follow a wide range of recreational activities; which in practice means television or ping pong.

**HESLOP**

Telly?

**FLETCHER**

Yeah, but only till seven. When there's only news and kids stuff. So if you're a fan of *Z Cars*, my son, forget it. You'll have to get your kicks from the Wombles of bleedin' Wimbledon.

**MACKAY**

Seven thirty, slop out, supper, seven forty-five, lights out, any questions?

**FLETCHER**

Any point?

**MACKAY**

None whatsoever. At ease.

***He starts to prepare for documentation.***

**LENNIE**

So this is Colditz.

**FLETCHER**

Colditz! You're joking. Compared to this place Colditz was a doddle. Load of public schoolboys playing leapfrog and making tunnels. This is nick this is. We spend our day slopping out and sewing mailbags. And by seven forty-five our lights are out. Colditz that time of night, they'd be brewing cocoa and having pillow fights.

***There is a knock on the door. Lennie takes out a cigarette.***

**MACKAY**

(*Crossing to Lennie*) Godber, who said you could smoke – did I say you could smoke?

**FLETCHER**

(*Taking the cigarette*) Don't think he wants you to smoke.

**LENNIE**

I was trying to give 'em up anyway.

**FLETCHER**

I'll help you.

***Barrowclough comes in with documents.***

**MACKAY**

I'm leaving you with Mr Barrowclough. Oh one more thing. Nice to have you with us.

***He leaves.***

**HESLOP**

My wife was coming next week.

**FLETCHER**

What? Who said that?

**HESLOP**

He says once a year. My wife was coming next week. Wrote to me. Staying overnight with her cousin in Barrow-in-Furness. Not fair. Not fair if she has to stay there indefinitely.

**FLETCHER**

Not fair on anyone to stay in Barrow-in-Furness.

**BARROWCLOUGH**

Heslop.

**FLETCHER**

Who?

**BARROWCLOUGH**

Will you step up here, please. Christian name?

**HESLOP**

Cyril.

**BARROWCLOUGH**

Date of birth?

**HESLOP**

1st April 1933.

***He hands over his personal effects to Barrowclough who puts them in box.***

**LENNIE**

What's happening now?

**FLETCHER**

We're about to be dehumanised. First they give us a number, take away our personal possessions. Then they give us a thorough medical check-up, and we have a bath in six inches of lukewarm water. Watch out for the bath-house cleaners.

**LENNIE**

Why?

**FLETCHER**

Lot of trustee poofs work the bath-house.

***He crosses the room and sits down.***

**LENNIE**

Know all the form, don't you?

***He sits down.***

Been here before?

**FLETCHER**

Not here – all the same though. Porridge is porridge, in' it?

**LENNIE**

First time for me. Don't know how I'll get through.

**FLETCHER**

Cheer up. Could be worse. State this country's in. Could be free. Out there with no work, and a crumbling economy. Think how 'orrible that would be. Nothing to do but go to bed early and increase the population.

**LENNIE**

Won't be doing that for a while.

**FLETCHER**

Oh no, course not. Shouldn't have said that, tasteless joke.

**LENNIE**

I'm going to feel ever so deprived. 'Cos I had this fiancée, Denise, who was ever so active in that direction.

**FLETCHER**

You'll have to drink a lot of tea.

**LENNIE**

What good's a cup of tea going to do?

**FLETCHER**

It's what they put in it.

**LENNIE**

What?

**FLETCHER**

Something which will moderate your memories of Denise.

**LENNIE**

I don't drink tea.

**FLETCHER**
You are in trouble.
***He pauses.***
**FLETCHER**
So's the bloke you share a cell with.
**LENNIE**
I'll have to throw myself into my mailbags – is that what you do here?
**FLETCHER**
Depends. Word of advice, son. What you tell 'em today can decide how tolerable your life here's going to be. I mean, if you want to work somewhere cushy and warm, like the kitchens or the library or the Governor's office, then you got to invent yourself a new career.
**LENNIE**
Oh.
***Heslop, now in his underclothes, moves off to wait.***
**BARROWCLOUGH**
All right. Let's have one of you.
***Fletcher and Lennie get up. Fletcher gestures to Lennie to sit down.***
**FLETCHER**
Me, Mr Barrowclough.
***He winks at Lennie.***
**BARROWCLOUGH**
It's Fletcher, of course, isn't it?
**FLETCHER**
Yes, Mr Barrowclough.

**BARROWCLOUGH**
Christian name?
**FLETCHER**
Norman Stanley.
**BARROWCLOUGH**
Date of birth?
**FLETCHER**
2–2–32.
**BARROWCLOUGH**
Next of kin?
**FLETCHER**
My beloved Isobel. The little woman. Well, she ain't so little. I said to her the other day, Isobel, I'll never get over you, I'll have to get up and go round.
***He laughs and turns to the others for their reaction. Heslop does not react.***
**BARROWCLOUGH**
Address?
**FLETCHER**
107 Alexandria Park Crescent, N.5.
**BARROWCLOUGH**
Occupation?
**FLETCHER**
Librarian during the day.
**BARROWCLOUGH**
During the day?
**FLETCHER**
Yeah. At night I was a chef. Library or the kitchen, I don't mind.

## 3. PRISON GOVERNOR'S OFFICE

***Inside the office there is a tropical fish tank. Venables, the Governor, is***

***sprinkling food on the surface of the water.***

***The office is furnished strictly to Home Office specifications in terms of furniture, filing cabinets and cream distemper. On one wall there is a professional diploma, and a photograph of a younger Venables as a policeman in Kuala Lumpur. On his desk is a photograph of his son, Guy, graduating at Keele University in Geography.***

***Venables takes the Daily Telegraph which is on his desk. His books are about the law, reform, rehabilitation and the diseases of tropical fish. Venables looks into the tank rather anxiously when there is a knock at the door, and Mackay enters, coming to attention.***

**MACKAY**

Good morning, Governor.

**VENABLES**

Not sure if it is, Mr Mackay, not sure if it is.

**MACKAY**

Oh, sir? What's wrong.

***Venables beckons him across to the tank. Mackay registers impatience.***

**VENABLES**

It's my four-eyed butterfly fish.

**MACKAY**

Would that be one with four eyes, sir?

**VENABLES**

No, no, it's just called that. *Chaetodon Capistratus*. (*Pointing him out*) There's the little fellow, this one.

**MACKAY**

(*Bending down with Venables to look at the fish*) Poorly is he, sir?

**VENABLES**

You noticed?

**MACKAY**

I assumed, from your concern.

**VENABLES**

Yes. I'm rather afraid, Mr Mackay that he may have developed fin rot.

**MACKAY**

Oh dear, sir.

***He stands up.***

**VENABLES**

Either that or lymphocystis.

**MACKAY**

Oh dear, sir.

**VENABLES**

(*Stands up*) Contagious, you see. Have to isolate the little fellow.

**MACKAY**

Much as I've had to do with Evans, sir.

***Venables turns away from his fish.***

**VENABLES**

Evans?

**MACKAY**

Had to isolate him again, sir.

**VENABLES**

What has he done now?

***He crosses to the desk.***

**MACKAY**

Been eating light bulbs, sir.

**VENABLES**
Light bulbs? Did he say why he was eating light bulbs?

**MACKAY**
Yes, sir. Said it was because he couldn't get hold of any razor blades.

***Venables sits down.***

**VENABLES**
What have you done with him?

**MACKAY**
Locked him in his cell, sir. Taking the precautions first of all of removing the light bulb.

**VENABLES**
Is the MO free?

**MACKAY**
He's with the new arrivals at the moment, sir. But I can hurry them through.

**VENABLES**
As quick as possible. This is a very urgent situation.

**MACKAY**
I'll get him to Evans right away, sir.

**VENABLES**
I don't mean Evans. I mean here.

**MACKAY**
Here?

**VENABLES**
Fin rot can be fatal, Mr Mackay.

## 4. MEDICAL ROOM

***Inside Fletcher, Lennie and Heslop are sitting on a bench waiting for the Medical Officer.***

**FLETCHER**
Oh, I meant to tell you – when you see the doc tell him you've got bad feet.

**LENNIE**
Why?

**FLETCHER**
'Cos then you might get your brothel creepers back. Otherwise you'll have to wear those prison-issue shoes. Guarantee you bad feet for the rest of your life, they will.

**LENNIE**
Oh, I see.

***Heslop starts to laugh. The others look at him.***

**FLETCHER**
It's not funny. Perfectly true.

**HESLOP**
No, I don't mean that. I mean that's funny about your wife being a big woman and you havin' to get up and go round.

**FLETCHER**
Oh. I see. Thank you. Anyhow, remember that about the feet. What religion are you?

**LENNIE**
C of E, I suppose.

**FLETCHER**
That's no good. Get no perks with C of E. Whereas if you was a Sikh you could grow your hair long. Or if you was a Muslim they'd have to send you in special grub from outside.

**LENNIE**
Don't like Chinese food.

**FLETCHER**
Muslim ain't Chinese.

**LENNIE**
What is Muslim food then?

**FLETCHER**
What? . . . Well it's . . . it's well, it's more exotic grub than the filth you'll eat here, otherwise the Muslims wouldn't eat it, would they? Or you could say you were Jewish. Yeah, say you're Jewish. Oh no, you couldn't get away with that, could you? Doctor's just going to examine you. He'd spot the evidence.

**LENNIE**
Evidence?

**FLETCHER**
With Jews it's only circumstantial. (*Explaining*) They been circumstanted.

***Medical Officer enters, coughing, and walks across to the table.***

**MEDICAL OFFICER**
Tropical fish.

**FLETCHER**
Pardon?

**MEDICAL OFFICER**
Nothing . . . I'm the (*Coughing*) Medical Officer.

**FLETCHER**
That's reassuring, in' it?

**MEDICAL OFFICER**
Now I have to give you men a stringent medical. It's important that we ascertain your medical history and state of health. (*Coughing again*) Right, Fletcher.

***Fletcher limps forward. During the questioning a cursory inspection takes place, with particular attention to the armpits.***

**MEDICAL OFFICER**
Have you ever had crabs?

**FLETCHER**
No – I don't eat fish.

***The Medical Officer winces.***

**MEDICAL OFFICER**
Lice?

**FLETCHER**
No.

**MEDICAL OFFICER**
VD?

**FLETCHER**
No.

**MEDICAL OFFICER**
(*Looking in Fletcher's ear*) Suffer from any illness?

**FLETCHER**
Bad feet.

**MEDICAL OFFICER**
Suffer from any illness?

**FLETCHER**
Bad feet.

**MEDICAL OFFICER**
Paid a recent visit to a doctor or hospital?

**FLETCHER**
Only for my bad feet.

**MEDICAL OFFICER**
Are you now or have you been at any time a practising homosexual?
**FLETCHER**
With these feet? Who'd want me?
**MEDICAL OFFICER**
Right – A1.
***He stamps Fletcher's form.***
**FLETCHER**
A1 – hang on, hang on. I can hardly walk.
**MEDICAL OFFICER**
Fletcher – everyone in this prison's trying to pull something, (*crossing to the scales*) lying about their feet or their teeth or their eyesight or their appendix. And on top of that I've got a Governor who's got fin rot.
**FLETCHER**
Got what rot?
**MEDICAL OFFICER**
Fish, tropical bloody fish.
***He puts Fletcher under the height measure.***
**FLETCHER**
Oh? Interest of his, is it?
**MEDICAL OFFICER**
Obsession. That and pigs.
**FLETCHER**
Pigs?
**MEDICAL OFFICER**
(*Crossing to desk*) He's started a prison farm to indulge his interest in livestock. Only it's the rest of us who have to look after it. His pigs and his fish and his favourite Jersey cow. I'm a man of medicine not a vet. Half the pills in here are for animals. Prisoner came in here yesterday with earache and I gave him pills to dry up his milk.
***He takes a spoon of medicine.***

**FLETCHER**
You must be rushed off your feet, doc.
**MEDICAL OFFICER**
I cannot cope, man.
**FLETCHER**
Good job they ain't bad feet like mine.
**MEDICAL OFFICER**
You're A1. I've told you. (*Pointing to some flasks on the table*) You see those flasks? I want you to fill one.
**FLETCHER**
From here?
**MEDICAL OFFICER**
Behind the screen. Now, where's Heslop?
***Heslop walks toward the Medical Officer as Fletcher takes the flask.***
**LENNIE**
Didn't pull that one did you, Fletch?
**FLETCHER**
What?
**LENNIE**
Prison shoes for you, eh.
**FLETCHER**
All right, sonny Jim. Lose a few, lose a

few. But my little chat was invaluable. Know something about the Governor, don't I? That's another priority for your first day.

**LENNIE**

Oh. I see, yes.

**FLETCHER**

Know your Governor.

**LENNIE**

Here, Fletcher.

**FLETCHER**

What?

**LENNIE**

What's he mean by practising homosexual?

**FLETCHER**

One who ain't quite got it right yet. Cheers.

***Goes behind the screen.***

## 5. PRISON MESS

***Barrowclough and other Prison Officers sit at a table playing cards. Fletcher, Lennie and Heslop move to another table with trays of food.***

**LENNIE**

Will we eat with everyone else tonight?

***They all sit down.***

**FLETCHER**

Don't be in no hurry to get thrown in with the others. Bunch of criminals, they are. And don't eat too much of that stuff. Otherwise you might dull your palate for tonight's piss de resistance.

**LENNIE**

What's it likely to be?

**FLETCHER**

Likely to be lumpy, lukewarm, grey and gritty. I told you to say you was a Muslim.

**HESLOP**

Sheep's eyes.

**FLETCHER**

Yeah – what?

**HESLOP**

What Muslims eat. Figs. Desert. Wadis and things.

**FLETCHER**

Oh I see. Yeah well . . . thank you, Lawrence of Arabia.

**LENNIE**

Why didn't you put down Muslim?

**FLETCHER**

I don't need to, do I? Going to be working in the kitchens.

**LENNIE**

But they haven't allocated us jobs yet.

***Fletcher indicates the card players.***

**FLETCHER**

Look, that screw. Barrowclough. Tall one. Looks like Arthur Askey on stilts. Well, I got him there, ain't I? Putty. He'll see me all right.

**LENNIE**

How come?

**FLETCHER**

He brought me up from Brixton. Handcuffed we was. Well, you establish a rapport with a man what you're handcuffed to on a long trip.

**LENNIE**

S'pose you must do. Specially when you go to the lavatory.

**FLETCHER**

(*Put out slightly*) Oh, you've got a sense of humour, I see. Come in handy during the grim nightmare of your next two years.

**LENNIE**

Will it be that bad?

**FLETCHER**

Listen – the important thing is to remember who you once was. And to keep a bit of that person intact up here.

***He taps his temple.***

**FLETCHER**

Don't get bitter, or militant, or try to screw the system, 'cos it'll only screw you. Just keep your nose clean, bide your time and do your porridge.

**LENNIE**

I'm only here due to tragic circumstances.

**FLETCHER**

Which were?

**LENNIE**

I got caught.

**FLETCHER**

Oh yes, I've had a few tragedies of that nature.

**LENNIE**

It was my fiancée, Denise. She has this nice flat in a tower block in Smethwick. Well, it's her mam's, like. Very nice. Overlooks the M6. So I thought I'd get her some nice things for it. So I didn't want to have far to cart 'em, like, so I did the flat next door, 'cos I knew he'd be away, like, 'cos he drives a juggernaut from West Bromwich to Brussels. Only he had a puncture outside Coventry and came home and found me and kicked me head in.

**HESLOP**

Ramsgate.

**FLETCHER**

Pardon?

**HESLOP**

Took the wife.

**FLETCHER**

Took the wife where Mr Heslop?

**HESLOP**

To see *Lawrence of Arabia*. It was raining see. Couldn't go on the beach at Ramsgate. Took her to the pictures.

**FLETCHER**

Rains a lot in Ramsgate.

**HESLOP**

Rained the next day.

**FLETCHER**

Told you it would.

**HESLOP**

But she'd seen the film on at the other cinema so we come home. Although we did stop for a cup of tea at her sister's in Sidcup.

**FLETCHER**

Why don't you put that on a postcard and send it to Tony Blackburn's magic moments.

**HESLOP**

What?

**FLETCHER**

One thing I shall miss about not sharing a cell with you two will be the cut and thrust of your intellectual conversation.

**LENNIE**

Won't we all be in together?

**FLETCHER**

No, I'm having a single cell. I like my privacy. I prefers to be alone see. Don't like sharing. Don't like dominoes or cribbage or other people's sweaty feet.

**LENNIE**

I'd prefer a single cell. 'Cos I want to study.

**FLETCHER**

Study?

**LENNIE**

Well, I've had an education. I've got an 'O' Level in geography.

**FLETCHER**

Oh, that'll come in handy that will. If there's an escape party from here you're bound to be included 'cos you'll know the way to Carlisle station.

**LENNIE**

Very interesting, geography. It's all part of education.

**FLETCHER**

Yeah, but it's not the sort of subject you can make a career out of. Only reason people learn geography is so they can teach other people geography. Ain't no use to anybody. No use knowing the capital of Siam or what an isthmus is.

**LENNIE**

Well, I don't have to use geography, I can learn a trade they said.

**FLETCHER**

In principle; you can come out with a diploma in some glamour occupation like house-decorating or shoe repairing. Or you can become a welder. There's a riveting profession – get it, get it.

***He looks at Heslop.***

**HESLOP**

What?

**FLETCHER**

Oh never mind.

**LENNIE**

Here, won't I be able to learn a trade then?

**FLETCHER**

Oh yes, there are certain things you can learn inside that you can become expert at. Like how to open a safe, steal a car, forge a banknote. Bloke I was in Maidstone with – Charlie Mossop, first offender he was, by the time he come out he was a brilliant forger. But brilliant. And he only went in for reckless driving.

**LENNIE**

I'm fed up with crime, I want to go straight.

**FLETCHER**

(*Looking appalled*) How old are you, son?

**LENNIE**

Twenty-three.

**FLETCHER**
Twenty-three and you want to go straight, what sort of attitude is that? Got your whole life before you.

**HESLOP**
What's an isthmus?

**FLETCHER**
What, what? What is it now, Dr Bronowski?

**HESLOP**
What you said – isthmus. What's an isthmus?

**FLETCHER**
Oh. Well it's a thing in' it . . . a thing in geography. A geographical expression –

**LENNIE**
It's a strip of land joining together two larger pieces of land.

**FLETCHER**
Yeah, strip of land, right.

**LENNIE**
See, education.

**FLETCHER**
I'm not saying don't put down for the educational classes. Current affairs, pottery, archaeology. I'll be putting down for that. What. Hour every night in a nice warm classroom. Bit of luck you get a woman teacher. See a bit of thigh when she drops her chalk. Oh yes, I've nothing against education.

***Lennie gets out a packet of cigarettes, which he offers to the others.***

**LENNIE**
Fag?

**FLETCHER**
Oh ta.

***Fletcher and Heslop both take one and put them straight into their pockets.***

**LENNIE**
Oh.

**FLETCHER**
We're not bein' impolite, Lennie, my son. It's just that him and me we've been inside before, and you see inside, snout is like gold. You was mad to give us those.

**LENNIE**
But you took them.

**FLETCHER**
Ah yes well, learn the hard way, isn't it? Learn not to be so lavish, you're not Paul Getty. Should have just lit one and shared it.

***Heslop takes Lennie's cigarette and has a puff at it, then passes it to Fletcher.***

***Barrowclough gets up from the card game and comes to them.***

**BARROWCLOUGH**
Right, drink up lads, shall we?

**FLETCHER**
What's next on the agenda, Mr Barrowclough?

**BARROWCLOUGH**
Got to see the Governor, haven't we? Right. Clear the stuff up. Put that fag out.

***Fletcher pinches out the cigarette and pockets it.***

**FLETCHER**

Waste not, want not.

**LENNIE**

Here –

**FLETCHER**

Learn the hard way, son. Now come on, clear up.

***Lennie and Heslop take their trays away. Fletcher takes Barrowclough aside.***

**FLETCHER**

Did you er – get what I asked you for, Mr Barrowclough?

**BARROWCLOUGH**

Well, there wasn't much in the library, just this booklet. (*Gets it from his pocket*) *Know your Tropical Fish*.

**FLETCHER**

Oh good – it's my hobby, you see.

**BARROWCLOUGH**

D'you know, by an extraordinary coincidence that's the Governor's hobby.

**FLETCHER**

Really? Would you believe it.

**BARROWCLOUGH**

Likes all animals. On the local committee of the RSPCA. Between ourselves I often think he'd have been better off in charge of a zoo than a prison.

**FLETCHER**

Caged animals – well, we're all the same, ain't we? Talking of cages, you will get me one facing south, won't you – on me own. I'm not a sharer you see. I mean the boy, he's all right, but he sniffs a lot. And Heslop, he's not on my intellectual level. Don't think he's on anybody's level really. If the Governor *did* open a zoo, Heslop'd be a big attraction.

**BARROWCLOUGH**

Fletcher, you must understand that I'm a Prison Officer and you are a prisoner. You must recognise that relationship. I am not here to be cajoled or coerced into doing what you want, when you want it.

**FLETCHER**

Mr Barrowclough, please, of course not. Would I ever?

***He turns and leaves. Barrowclough is left holding Fletcher's tray.***

**BARROWCLOUGH**

Well, as long as that's understood.

***Barrowclough realises he has got the tray and bangs it down on the table.***

## 6. EXERCISE YARD

***Camera shows the prisoners marching in the exercise yard. Fletcher is marching; Heslop is marching; Lennie is marching. Mackay watches Fletcher and Barrowclough march across the yard.***

## 7. GOVERNOR'S OFFICE

***Venables, Mackay and Barrowclough are in the Governor's office.***

**MACKAY**

Fetch them in, Mr Barrowclough.

***Barrowclough brings in Fletcher, Lennie and Heslop.***

**MACKAY**

Stand straight in front of the Governor. (*Pointing them out*) Heslop, Godber, Fletcher, sir.

**VENABLES**

Thank you, Mr Mackay. Now you men have been sent here for varying offences and varying terms of imprisonment. This is not a top-grade security prison, you are C class prisoners. However, if any of you abuses the less stringent security measures which we impose here, you will quickly find that we are on you like a ton of . . .

***He breaks off noticing that Fletcher is staring in another direction.***

**VENABLES**

Are you listening, Fletcher?

**MACKAY**

Face the front.

**FLETCHER**

I am sorry, Mr Venables, sir. I just couldn't help noticing your aquarium. Interest of mine, you see, indoor fish, tropical fish.

**VENABLES**

Oh really?

**MACKAY**

All right, Fletcher.

**FLETCHER**

Sorry, Mr Mackay. Sorry, sir. But something is bothering me.

**VENABLES**

What is bothering you, Fletcher?

**FLETCHER**

Well, sir, this is only a first impression but . . . I think your four-eyed butterfly fish has got a touch of fin rot.

## 8. FLETCHER'S CELL

***There are two bunks and a chair inside the cell. Heslop is lying on the top bunk rolling a cigarette. Lennie sits on the chair, while Fletcher lies on the bottom bunk reading a copy of* Farmers Weekly.**

**LENNIE**

Crafty old nurk, aren't you, Fletcher?

**FLETCHER**

Hang about, I'm just finishing this on Artificial Insemination what the Governor gave me.

**LENNIE**

Fell for it, didn't he? He really believed your interest in fish and livestock.

**FLETCHER**

Ain't been a bad day. I told you this is the day what conditions how tolerable your life'll become here.

**LENNIE**

I think he was impressed by my 'O' Level in geography.

*The cell door is unlocked and Mackay enters, carrying a pair of shoes.*

**MACKAY**

All right, lads, on your feet. Exam results. Been a full and exciting day. Firstly Godber – your shoes, courtesy of the M.O.

*He hands Lennie his shoes.*

**FLETCHER**

How d'you work that?

**LENNIE**

Told him about my flat feet, didn't I?

**MACKAY**

Which he believes, Fletcher. Young Godber's still got some credibility. Unlike yourself. I'm afraid we're having to split this lovely threesome up. One of you're going to a sing.

**FLETCHER**

Oh yes – only right.

*He starts to gather his things.*

**MACKAY**

Not so fast, Fletcher.

**FLETCHER**

You what?

**MACKAY**

Get your things together, Godber.

**FLETCHER**

Godber – him. A cell on his own.

**MACKAY**

Governor thought it would be more conducive to study.

**LENNIE**

Oh, that's lovely. I didn't fancy sharing – no offence.

**FLETCHER**

You didn't fancy sharing. What about me – you leaving me here with the Brain of Britain here?

**MACKAY**

There'll be three of you. We're moving Evans in here.

**FLETCHER**

Evans! That Welsh lunatic who eats light bulbs!

**MACKAY**

Only when he can't get razor blades.

**FLETCHER**

Oh marvellous. Can I have permission to grow a beard?

**MACKAY**

Jobs. Kitchen – Godber.

**LENNIE**

Oh that'll be nice – all warm and second helpings.

**MACKAY**

Library – Heslop.

**FLETCHER**

Library! Him! He's an illiterate.

**HESLOP**

I read a book once. It was green.

**FLETCHER**
And what's he got the kitchen for. First time in, God Almighty he should be breaking rocks or something – paying his dues. This is victimisation! I'm an old hand, I should have something befitting my seniority.

**MACKAY**
Special duties.

**FLETCHER**
What?

**MACKAY**
Special duties. Who's the Governor's blue-eyed boy?

**FLETCHER**
Well, we had a bit of a rapport yes. Cementated by our common interest in all things bright and beautiful, all creatures great and small.

**MACKAY**
Governor said you're just the man he's been waiting for.

**FLETCHER**
Oh. Oh I see. All right then. (*Turning to Lennie*) Kitchens – eat your heart out, Godber. Green it was.

## 9. PRISON FARM

***The prison Governor and Fletcher are outside in the prison farm.***

**GOVERNOR**
Good morning, Fletcher.

**FLETCHER**
Morning, sir.

**GOVERNOR**
It always gives me great pleasure to place a man in a job which gives him real fulfilment.

**FLETCHER**
Fulfilment, yes, thank you, sir.

***Fletcher is cleaning out the pigsty. He is surrounded by pigs.***

**GOVERNOR**
Oh, the article in *Farmers Weekly*, did you finish it?

**FLETCHER**
I'm afraid I didn't, sir. Oh, I would have done, only Evans ate it.

***Fletcher continues digging.***

# 1 SERIES ONE

## EPISODE TWO: THE HUSTLER

### 1. HEN HOUSE

***Chickens in a coop. Offstage the voices of Fletcher and Ives can be heard.***

**IVES**

Come on, come on. You can do it, my love.

**FLETCHER**

Come on gel, come on gel. Force it out. Effort! Effort!

**IVES**

Come on, my son.

**FLETCHER**

Hang about. It's a girl, you nurk. 'My son'.

**IVES**

How d'you know it's a girl?

**FLETCHER**

Hens is all girls, Ives.

**IVES**

Are they?

**FLETCHER**

Course they are. All hens are females. Your male is your cock.

**IVES**

Oh yes . . . here, listen, there's a hell of a lot more females than males.

**FLETCHER**

'Course there are. That's why your cock always looks so smug. Always knows it's there. Hence the expression, cock sure.

***They resume their encouragements.***

**FLETCHER**

Come on gel, force it out.

**IVES**

Mine's looking inament.

***Fletches takes a quick look at Ives's bird.***

**FLETCHER**

Nodded off, she has.

**IVES**

Here, listen, want to double the bet?

**FLETCHER**

Certainly.

**IVES**

Right. Done.

**FLETCHER**

You certainly have been.

**IVES**

Why?

**FLETCHER**

Jackpot.

***An egg rolls down its little channel.***

***Fletcher picks it up.***

**FLETCHER**

Thanks, gel. And thank you, Ives.

***Ives disgruntledly takes out two handed-rolled snouts from his breast pocket. He is about to hand them over when he has a thought.***

**IVES**

Listen, double or quits.

***He takes the egg from Fletcher and puts both hands behind his back.***

**IVES**

Which hand's it in? Go on, fair's fair. Double or quits.

**FLETCHER**

All right.

***Ives holds out his hands. Fletcher thinks, then taps one.***

**FLETCHER**

That one.

***Ives shouts with delight and opens an empty hand.***

**IVES**

Ha! We're even.

**FLETCHER**

Oh in that one, was it?

***He squeezes Ives's other hand breaking the egg within.***

**IVES**

(*Shaking off the sticky egg from his hand*) Oh Fletcher, not funny, not funny.

**FLETCHER**

Can't take a yolk some people.

**VOICE OFF**

(*Shouting*) Ives!

***Ives picks his bucket up and leaves.***

***Fletcher checks that he has gone and then moves to Ives's hen.***

**FLETCHER**

Poor old Ives, what a loser. If Elizabeth Taylor had triplets and he was one of them, he'd be the one in the middle on the bottle . . . You're not a loser are you, gel? You'd 'a won by rights, if I hadn't cut off your access.

***He removes a crumpled handkerchief from the channel beneath the chicken and an egg rolls down. He goes to the door and checks then puts some eggs in a bag of grain.***

**FLETCHER**

This, girls, is what you might call one of the perks of this job. Now with those eggs I can get myself a quarter ounce of shag, or two tubes of toothpaste, or three bars of fruit and nut, or I could take them along to E Wing and see Smutty Garland, King of the Porn. Trade 'em in for one of his dirty books. Filled with full frontal naked nubiles . . . No, I'd rather have the fruit and nut.

## 2. PRISON FARM

***Close up of a trough. Swill is being poured into it. Pigs come over to eat. Fletcher looks at them.***

**FLETCHER**

Gawd, you're messy. And you eat like pigs. Here, can you lot run? There's a thought, pig-racing. That would make a nice little flutter, wouldn't it? The Slade Prison Selling Plate for Pigs . . . the Royal Cheltenham Pork Cup . . . I could have a book. Become an owner, and have my own stable – sty . . . Yeah, thought appeals, thought appeals. The Bacon Handicap.

***He laughs and moves away.***

**FLETCHER**

The Bacon Handicap.

***A pig looks up at Fletcher.***

## 3. HEN HOUSE

***Fletcher walks into the hen house and looks at the chickens.***

**FLETCHER**

Hello, darlings, still trying, are you?

**BARROWCLOUGH**

(*Appearing*) 'Morning, Fletcher.

**FLETCHER**

Oh morning, Mr Barrowclough. How's things?

**BARROWCLOUGH**

That man Ives, what was he doing round here?

**FLETCHER**

What – oh he was just dropping in on his way to the silos.

**BARROWCLOUGH**

Wasn't taking bets, was he?

**FLETCHER**

Bets?

**BARROWCLOUGH**

It has been suspected that he's Harry Grout's runner.

**FLETCHER**

(*Innocently*) Runner? Mr Barrowclough. Runner?

**BARROWCLOUGH**

Taking bets.

**FLETCHER**

Oh yeah.

**BARROWCLOUGH**

Harry Grout's a long-term prisoner and he's not the pleasantest of men, and he seems to exert an unhealthy influence. We're fairly sure that he runs both gambling and tobacco in this prison. I – I'm telling you this Fletcher because . . . well you're a good chap and I wouldn't want you to get sucked into that circle.

**FLETCHER**

Don't worry. Oh Mr Barrowclough, have no fear on that score. Gambling appals me. Seen the consequences too often.

**BARROWCLOUGH**

It's like a plague in this prison.

**FLETCHER**

Not one of my vices – got too many other things to do – 'ere do you think pigs can run?

**BARROWCLOUGH**

Run?

**FLETCHER**

Could they be trained to run?

**BARROWCLOUGH**
Why?
**FLETCHER**
What! Oh I just thought it would make a change for them. The exercise.
**BARROWCLOUGH**
Well, it's good to see you're taking an interest in your fellow creatures.
***He goes to sit down but is stopped by Fletcher.***
**FLETCHER**
Don't sit there, Mr Barrowclough. You'll dirty your uniform. I'll get you a chair.
***He moves to get a chair and then back again.***
**BARROWCLOUGH**
I gather you're settling in, down on the farm.
**FLETCHER**
(*Goes to sit, realises*) Oh . . . it ain't too bad, tell the truth. When I was assigned to it, well I took offence at first, 'cos I've never been a rural man. Always had a deep mistrust of animals.
**BARROWCLOUGH**
I thought you told the Governor you had a keen interest in farming and livestock.
**FLETCHER**
(*Guiltily*) Oh, yes, that. Farming and livestock, yes. Just that I ain't so keen on the animal end of it.
**BARROWCLOUGH**
(*Obviously not seeing*) Oh, I see. You're very lucky to be here, you know. Normally a trusty gets a job like this. Privileged position.
**FLETCHER**
Don't think I don't appreciate it, Mr Barrowclough. I'm sure you had something to do with it, knowing your kind and generous nature.
**BARROWCLOUGH**
No, nothing to do with –
**FLETCHER**
(*Knowingly*) Say no more, say no more. When you going to get me a single cell then?
**BARROWCLOUGH**
It's not in my power, Fletcher.
**FLETCHER**
See, I'm not a sharer. And those two I'm in with, Heslop and Evans, well I mean there's no rapport . . . no intellectual stimulus. You know what I mean.
**BARROWCLOUGH**
Evans, yes, he's a strange fellow. Is he still eating light bulbs?
**FLETCHER**
No, he's got a taste for other things now. Ate my shaving mirror yesterday.
**BARROWCLOUGH**
I'm afraid there's little I can do. And it's wrong of you to ask me.
**FLETCHER**
What? Oh no. Wait. Please. You mustn't think – you must NOT think that I'm trying to influence you, to coerce you to . . . I can hardly bring myself to say the word . . . BRIBE you.

*Barrowclough reacts.*

**FLETCHER**

What – a prison officer what's been specially chosen by the Home Office for his integrity and honesty.

*He has a quick look round.*

**FLETCHER**

'Ere would a dozen eggs make a difference?

*Barrowclough looks shocked.*

**FLETCHER**

No, of course not.

## 4. PRISON FARM/PRISON

*Barrowclough is seen locking up. Fletcher is waiting for him. Barrowclough moves to Fletcher and they walk off together to the prison gates. There they knock. The door is opened by a Prison Officer and they go in.*

**FLETCHER**

Lovely day for it.

**PRISON OFFICER**

You won't be getting it for a long time.

**FLETCHER**

You obviously ain't had it for a long time.

*Prison Officer reacting.*

## 5. PRISON KITCHEN

*Lennie is washing down one of the big hotplates. Also in the kitchen is a trusty cook; he is called Lukewarm, after his cooking. Fletcher enters, putting down his boxes of eggs on the working surface. He has with him his plastic bag of grain with the concealed eggs. He's followed in by Prison Officer Appleton.*

**FLETCHER**

There y'are, Lukewarm. Three dozen and two.

**LUKEWARM**

What? What's wrong with those hens since you took over? Shell shock?

**APPLETON**

Thievin' are you, Fletcher?

**FLETCHER**

No need for that is there, Mr Appleton, no need for that sort of defamatory.

**APPLETON**

Always pilfering, the whole lot of you.

**FLETCHER**

(*Outraged*) Now listen, Mr Appleton, I resent that. I may have done some bad things in my life, wouldn't be here if I hadn't, but I ain't a petty sneak thief, that's not my style at all.

**APPLETON**

All right, all right.

*He turns away and Fletcher nimbly picks up a packet of margarine from the working surface and slips*

***it into his pocket, as he crosses to the table, gingerly putting down his bag of grain.***

**FLETCHER**

Er . . . Lennie . . . anyone er . . . left a message here for me?

**LENNIE**

Yeah. Bloke come in and said Harry Grout said permission granted.

**FLETCHER**

Did he? Oh, good.

**LENNIE**

Permission for what?

**FLETCHER**

Permission to hold a game.

**LENNIE**

What game?

**FLETCHER**

Keep your voice down.

**LENNIE**

(*Quieter*) What game?

**FLETCHER**

A game of chance, my son.

**LENNIE**

How d'you mean?

**FLETCHER**

Oh for gawd's sake, Godber. A gamble. A flutter.

**LENNIE**

But gambling ain't allowed.

**FLETCHER**

'Course it ain't allowed. That's precisely why we're doin' it.

**LENNIE**

Why d'you have to get permission off this Grout?

**FLETCHER**

(*Pained*) Godber, son, you've been here a week, ain't you learned nothing? Officially this hotel is run by a governor appointed by the Home Office, Mr Venables. But in practice of course we knows different. In practice General Harry Grout can bring this nick to a standstill if he so wishes.

**LENNIE**

What d'you play for – big stakes, is it?

**FLETCHER**

We will do if Lukewarm can nick some from the meat safe. We play for anything negotiable. Snout mostly. But it won't be for chicken feed . . . pity really 'cos I got plenty of that.

**LENNIE**

I've noticed people are always betting on something. I suppose it's their way of generating excitement to counter the misery of their monotonous existence.

**FLETCHER**

What? Oh yes – right. It ain't just the excitement of the game, what you win or what you lost. It's the pleasure what you get for doing it under their noses, surruptitious, like.

**LENNIE**

There's two blokes next door to me who've had a bet on how many bricks there are in their cell.

**FLETCHER**

Oh yes. Commonplace that.

**LENNIE**
I can't think or study. It's driving me mad, listening to 'em. Recount after recount. Three hundred and forty-one, three hundred and forty-two . . .

**FLETCHER**
Blokes doing stir'll bet on anything. Two flies going up a wall, hymn numbers in the chapel. Two flies going down a wall . . . I even laid an egg on a bet today – made a bet on egg laying. There was a big game last night in D Wing. Weren't you aware of the atmosphere in the air? It was electric – the tension.

**LENNIE**
Tension, I noticed that. But I thought that was because Tuesday's the day that female social worker comes round.

**FLETCHER**
What, gruesome Glenda? Her with the brogues and the bicycle. You'd be hard pushed to have an erotic fantasy about that one.

**LENNIE**
I dunno. Nifty Small's in love with her. He stole her bicycle saddle.

**FLETCHER**
Really? Gawd the ride back must have been painful for her. He won't have that long. They'll soon find it.

**LENNIE**
What, under his pillow! I bet they won't.

**FLETCHER**
(*Instantly*) All right, you're on. How much? Two fags?

**LENNIE**
'Ere, 'ere, I'm not gambling. My mother said gambling will get you into trouble.

**FLETCHER**
Son, it may have escaped your notice but you're in prison. Your mother was too late. You is in trouble.

**LENNIE**
Yeah, well nevertheless I'm not gambling. I'm not counting bricks or watching flies. Gambling's one thing I'm going to resist inside.

**FLETCHER**
Bet you can't.

**LENNIE**
Oh yes I can.

**FLETCHER**
Bet you a bar of soap you can't.

**LENNIE**
I bet I can.

**FLETCHER**
There you are. You bet me you wouldn't bet me. So you just lost your first bet. That's a bar of soap you owe me. Work that out.

***Ives walks in carrying a sack of potatoes.***

**APPLETON**
Where are you going, Ives?

**IVES**
Er just er . . . got the spuds, Mr Appleton . . .

**APPLETON**
Get on with it, Ives.

**FLETCHER**

(*Walking across*) Got the spuds, Ives?

**IVES**

'Ere listen, Fletcher. How much do they weigh then?

**FLETCHER**

You know already.

**IVES**

'Course I don't. No scales out there.

**FLETCHER**

What's the bet then?

**IVES**

All the eggs you've got in there.

**FLETCHER**

You crafty nurk.
Against what?

**IVES**

Ounce of snout.

**FLETCHER**

Fair enough.

**IVES**

Are you in, son?

**LENNIE**

No, I'm not.

***Fletcher appraises the bag expertly then picks it up, testingly.***

**FLETCHER**

Nearest one, eh!

**IVES**

Nearest one.

**FLETCHER**

Twenty-three pounds.

**IVES**

I'll say twenty-seven.

**FLETCHER**

Gave that a lot of thought, didn't you?

**IVES**

Just over twenty-seven.

***Ives lifts the potatoes on to the scales. They weigh just over twenty-seven pounds.***

**IVES**

Well I never, would you believe it?

**BOTH**

Just over twenty-seven.

**IVES**

Thank you . . . Sh-ting.

**FLETCHER**

You knew, didn't you?

**IVES**

Here listen. I ain't no cheat.

**FLETCHER**

What? You're in here for fraudulent conversion. It's your career that is, cheating.

**IVES**

Lose gracefully, come on, here listen.

**FLETCHER**

You're a crafty conniving gink, Ives.

**IVES**

Bad loser.

**FLETCHER**

Here you are then.

***He hands over the eggs.***

**IVES**

(*Putting them in his pockets*) Come in handy these. Owes Grout, don't I. Don't do to owe Grouty.

**FLETCHER**

Now naff off.

***Mackay enters.***

**MACKAY**
Morning, Mr Appleton.
***Everyone redoubles their illusion of activity, including Appleton.***
**APPLETON**
Morning, Mr Mackay.
**MACKAY**
Fletcher! What are you doing, Ives?
**IVES**
Oh – I just brought the spuds, Mr Mackay.
***Fletcher tries to leave with his bag of grain.***
**MACKAY**
Where are you going, Fletcher?
**FLETCHER**
Pig swill.
**MACKAY**
Pardon!!
**FLETCHER**
See about the pig swill, Mr Mackay. Little fellows need their swill this time of day.
***Fletcher starts to go.***
**MACKAY**
(*Gesturing*) Just a minute.
**FLETCHER**
I've swept all that Mr Ma . . .
**MACKAY**
Fletcher – come here.
***Fletcher goes across.***
**MACKAY**
I'm told your chickens are on short time. I'm told that since you arrived at the farm egg production has fallen drastically.
**FLETCHER**
Don't blame me, Mr Mackay. Perhaps they're in a foul mood . . .
**MACKAY**
Don't you come it with me, Fletcher. Now, what have we here?
**FLETCHER**
Crown jewels. Chicken meal, Mr Mackay.
**MACKAY**
Empty it. (*To Ives*) Ives, stands still.
**FLETCHER**
Empty it?
**MACKAY**
Empty it.
**FLETCHER**
Make ever such a mess.
***Godber walks over.***
**MACKAY**
Godber . . . Empty it.
***Fletcher tips bag of grain on to table. Mackay pokes about in it with his truncheon.***
**MACKAY**
All right, Fletcher. But if I catch you thieving . . .
**FLETCHER**
I won't.
**MACKAY**
Won't what?
**FLETCHER**
Let you catch me, Mr Mackay.
***Mackay sees Ives.***
**MACKAY**
Ives – where are you going, horrible Ives?

**IVES**

'Ere listen, I'm behindhand Mr Mackay. I've got them turnips –

**MACKAY**

Come here, Ives.

**IVES**

Yes, but –

**MACKAY**

Come here, Ives.

***Ives complies reluctantly.***

**MACKAY**

Bit of a jackdaw yourself, aren't you, Ives? Last time we caught you in the kitchens you were trying to steal a meat cleaver.

**IVES**

Only to sharpen my pencil, Mr Mackay.

**MACKAY**

No, it was not, Mr Ives. It was used to persuade your cell-mate to part with his Pirelli calendar.

***He raises Ives's hands and starts to pat his pockets.***

**MACKAY**

Now what have we picked up today – a meat skewer?

***He pats hands down Ives's body. The crunch of eggs is heard as he bangs on pockets. Ives reacts in discomfort.***

**MACKAY**

Follow me, Mr Ives.

***Mackay marches out. Ives follows walking awkwardly. He looks at Fletcher.***

**FLETCHER**

Yolk's on you again, son.

## 6. PRISON LANDING

***It is association hour. Ives walks past several prisoners and goes up stairs, along the gantry and towards Fletcher's cell.***

## 7. FLETCHER'S CELL

***It is a three-cell with a double-tiered bunk on one side and a single bed on the other. There is a chair beside the washbasin under the barred window, on which Fletcher is sitting cleaning his shoes. On the top bunk lies Heslop, thinking.***

***Evans is on the lower bunk, rolling snout.***

***The cell door is open. Fletcher looks under his feet as if having mislaid something.***

**FLETCHER**

Here, Evans, you haven't eaten my shoe polish, have you?

**EVANS**

No, course I haven't.

**FLETCHER**

You sure?

**EVANS**

'Course I'm sure. What would I eat shoe polish for?

**FLETCHER**

I don't know. Maybe it was to make my shaving mirror go down easier.

***Ives enters.***

**IVES**

'Ere listen.

**FLETCHER**

Don't we knock, don't we knock?

**IVES**

No, no, 'ere listen. Word is you've got a game going.

**FLETCHER**

Oh say it a bit louder. Few people in E Wing didn't catch that. Why don't you bellow it from the bleedin' rooftops.

**IVES**

It's all right, the screws are brewing up.

**FLETCHER**

(*Sitting*) Subtle as an air-raid you are, Ives.

**IVES**

No, listen, is that gen? You got a game put together?

**FLETCHER**

Yup.

**IVES**

Grouty give the OK, did he?

**FLETCHER**

At a price, yeah.

**IVES**

When is it?

**FLETCHER**

Saturday afternoon. When the world is watching *Grandstand*, and the screws are playing E Wing at football.

**IVES**

Can I be in?

**FLETCHER**

Sorry, old son. Full house.

**IVES**

Who's in then?

**FLETCHER**

Myself. Mr Heslop, here. Lukewarm from the kitchen. And Mr Evans – providing he don't eat the dice.

**IVES**

Oh it's dice, is it?

**FLETCHER**

(*Rising*) What? Oh well, possibly, possibly. Said enough, said enough.

**IVES**

You can make room for one more.

**FLETCHER**

Not your sort, Ives.

**IVES**

'Ere listen –

**FLETCHER**

It's all been arranged, it's all set up, right? So naff off.

**IVES**

You telling me you going to set a game up? In this place. What? You ain't got a snowball's. Gambling here?

**FLETCHER**

Same in any nick. Question of integrity. Where there's a will there's a way.

**IVES**

(*Sitting*) You're so lairy, aren't you, Fletcher? Well it might have been a doddle in your last nick. But they cut off privileges here for the toss of a coin.

**EVANS**

I've had my privileges cut off.

**FLETCHER**

Oh yes, did it hurt much?

**IVES**

They'll have your guts for garters if they see you gambling with anything. Draughts, dominoes. Even that whatsit, that game with the wooden spelling . . .

**FLETCHER**

Scribble?

**IVES**

Scribble, that an' all. Venables comes down like the clappers he did. Ever since the Earwig Derby.

**FLETCHER**

The what?

**IVES**

The Earwig Derby.

**EVANS**

Earwig Derby yes, tragic that.

**FLETCHER**

When was this?

**IVES**

Last Earwig season, wasn't it. Organised by Grouty, of course. Very much on the lines of the Jockey Club. There was handicaps, eliminators, and then in September, the Grand Final – well, the Derby. Over eight yards across the Laundry floor. Whole prison was on. Then Mackay finds out, doesn't he. How we never knew.

**FLETCHER**

What did he do?

**IVES**

Put his foot down.

***He starts stamping his foot down by way of illustration.***

**IVES**

Right on top of 'em.

**EVANS**

No need for that, there wasn't.

***Heslop belatedly joins in.***

**HESLOP**

It's dice, is it?

**FLETCHER**

Oh you're with us are you, Mr Heslop?

**HESLOP**

You never told me it was dice.

**FLETCHER**

I did, I told you Saturday, only it's obviously just permutated.

**IVES**

Listen Fletcher, you've got no chance, no chance at all.

**FLETCHER**

I don't agree, I find geraniums do very well in chalky soil providing you give them a drop of moisture and you don't let the cat near them.

***Barrowclough enters.***

**FLETCHER**

Oh, here's Mr Barrowclough, well, well, what a nice surprise.

**BARROWCLOUGH**

Evans . . . Oh yes, Ives, up to no good?

**IVES**

'Ere listen.

**BARROWCLOUGH**

Usually are, Ives, it has to be said.

**FLETCHER**

It transpired that Mr Ives and I have a common interest in geraniums.

**IVES**
Oh yes, geraniums. Nice little fellas. My cousin used to breed them.

**FLETCHER**
Grow them.

**IVES**
Grow them.

**BARROWCLOUGH**
Really? Now you know something, I'm a bit of a horticulturalist myself.

**FLETCHER**
Oh really . . . oh gawd.

**BARROWCLOUGH**
Anyhow no time to go into that now.

**FLETCHER**
Oh. More's the pity.

**BARROWCLOUGH**
Come along Evans – time for your visit to the psychiatrist.

**IVES**
'Ere listen – you still trying to work one by eating things?

**FLETCHER**
Yes, he is. Playing havoc with my personal possessions.

**EVANS**
Playing havoc with my digestion.

***He leaves the cell, rubbing his stomach.***

**IVES**
Listen, Fletcher. Where d'you get the dice then?

**FLETCHER**
Lukewarm made them in the kitchen. Out of pastry. He baked them.

**IVES**
Won't they break?

**FLETCHER**
Not his pastry.

**HESLOP**
I'm very fond of geraniums.

***Fletcher lies down. Ives sits down.***

**HESLOP**
Flowers, things like that. Not that we had a garden. My house just had a yard. A yard with a wringer and a bicycle in it. But the wife's sister's house in Sidcup, that has a riot of colour. What with his vegetables, she never had to want for anything.

**FLETCHER**
Is that it?

***Ives looks and nods.***

**FLETCHER**
Comes in bursts like that. Another of those poignant anecdotes from the rich pageant of Mr Heslop's past, the Patience Strong of Cell Block 11. You can see how lucky I am to be in here with him.

**IVES**
I can see why you dealt him in.

**FLETCHER**
First come, first served.

**IVES**
'Ere listen. You'll never pull it off.

**FLETCHER**
What you talking about?

**IVES**
Organise this game and get away with it.

**FLETCHER**
(*Rising*) It's already organised.

**IVES**
But I bet you can't get away with it.

**FLETCHER**
Put your money where your –

**IVES**
Mouth is, I will do.

**FLETCHER**
Go on then.

**IVES**
How much?

**FLETCHER**
Try me.

**IVES**
A biggy.

**FLETCHER**
Big as you like.

**IVES**
How big?

**FLETCHER**
Try me.

**IVES**
Snout.

**FLETCHER**
Obviously.

**IVES**
All right then. Half a pound.

***He says this as if expecting the reaction "Don't be ridiculous", but instead Fletcher agrees.***

**FLETCHER**
Fair enough.

***Fletcher's nonchalance unnerves Ives.***

**IVES**
Did you hear me, Fletcher? I said half a pound.

**FLETCHER**
I heard you.

**IVES**
That's eight ounces.

**FLETCHER**
Nice one, Einstein.

**IVES**
Now let's get this perfectly clear – and you're a witness.

***He indicates Heslop, then checks the door again.***

**IVES**
I'm betting you half a pound of snout that you won't see your game through. You'll get found out, or busted, or whatever.

**FLETCHER**
You're on.

***Ives looks visibly shaken at the size of the bet.***

**IVES**
All right then. That's done then. I'll be off then.

**FLETCHER**
I'd lay a little of that off if I was you, my son.

***Ives leaves.***

**HESLOP**
Got a lot of bottle, Fletcher, a lot of bottle.

**FLETCHER**
Where there's a will there's a way. Here's my shoe polish.

**HESLOP**

When I was doing bird in Shepton Mallet we used to bet on the number of bricks in a cell.

**FLETCHER**

Oh original yes. How did you get on?

***Fletcher walks to the table, then to the bed.***

**HESLOP**

All I know is there was over thirty-seven.

**FLETCHER**

Oh roomy, wasn't it? When I was in Maidstone, d'you know what we had going? We only had a roulette game going that's all. With a dartboard, see. People bet on it. You could be on red or black, evens or odds, sequences or individual numbers. And your croupier was a bloke what was blindfolded and threw the dart. We used to play in association and we bribed this screw to turn a blind eye. Big game it was, mammoth.

**HESLOP**

Oh crafty that, roulette.

**FLETCHER**

Yeah . . . pity it came to such a tragic end.

**HESLOP**

What happened?

**FLETCHER**

One night the croupier got a bit careless. Now the screw turns a blind eye to everything.

## 9. COKE STORE

***Inside the coke store Evans, Heslop, Lukewarm and Fletcher are sitting on boxes round a tea chest.***

**HESLOP**

You sure they won't find us in here?

**FLETCHER**

Lukewarm here assures me they won't – he being a trusty, happens to have access to the coke store key. Cosy, ain't it?

**LUKEWARM**

They'll never look down here today.

**FLETCHER**

No – officially, as you know, we're all watching E Wing play the screws at football, a game that will occupy a lot of attention.

**LUKEWARM**

And the attention of the hospital as well later on, the way they go at each other.

**FLETCHER**

Yeah – should be quite a bloodbath, with any luck.

***There are murmurs of approval and agreement.***

**FLETCHER**

I did try to persuade Tommy Macready to put forward his escape attempt to today. 'Cos knowing Tommy he'll cock it up and the diversion would have come in very handy. However, he couldn't be swayed as he pointed out, quite rightly, state this country's in you can't rely on trains at the weekend.

**HESLOP**
I didn't know Tommy was going over the wall.

**LUKEWARM**
Oh yes, common knowledge.

**EVANS**
Domestic problems.

**FLETCHER**
Wife's got nerves or something.

**LUKEWARM**
Things are getting on top of her, are they?

**FLETCHER**
Quite the reverse. She's sleeping with a limbo dancer.

**LUKEWARM**
A limbo dancer? Is he black?

**FLETCHER**
Black and blue, I should think, knowing her. What a raver! Now then . . .

**LUKEWARM**
Oh, before I forget – something to nibble at for later.

***He hands out packets of sandwiches.***

**EVANS**
Ooh, lovely – I haven't had a square meal for ages.

**FLETCHER**
Not since my shaving mirror. Thanks, Lukewarm – you spoil us. I wish I'd had a mother like you. I might have gone straight.

**LUKEWARM**
Or bent.

**HESLOP**
Can I eat mine now?

**FLETCHER**
No you can't – he's like a big kid, ain't he? Soon as you get outside the front door, you want to start the picnic. Wait! Now the rules, gentlemen. One: Stakes – minimum bet, one fag. You cannot raise more than half the kitty. Two: Losers – and some of us have to lose, don't we? Divvy up within twenty-four hours – if not Mr Heslop here will come round with a reminder – just like the Post Office.

**EVANS**
The Post Office?

**FLETCHER**
Yeah, he'll stick one on you. Now we're all set. Right?

**OTHERS**
Right.

**FLETCHER**
Right.

**LUKEWARM**
And the game.

**FLETCHER**
And the game gentlemen.

***He stands up and gets his shirt out from his trousers. There are snakes and ladders drawn on it.***

**FLETCHER**
The game is snakes and ladders.

## 10. FILM

***Mackay enters closely followed by Barrowclough.***

**MACKAY**
I knew something was up,

Mr Barrowclough. My antennae told me. I know when there's a Big Deal at Dodge City in this place.

*Mr Barrowclough shuts and locks the door.*

**BARROWCLOUGH**

I sometimes think it's a waste of our manpower – trying to crack down on gambling – I mean, men will gamble.

*Barrowclough and Mackay walk along the alley.*

**MACKAY**

Gambling leads to debts, Mr Barrowclough. And debts lead to ill-feeling, antagonism. Lack of discipline.

**BARROWCLOUGH**

Did your antennae tell you where this game is taking place?

**MACKAY**

No, that was Ives, horrible Ives.

**BARROWCLOUGH**

No honour among thieves.

**MACKAY**

Not where there's gambling at stake, that's why it has to be stamped out.

**BARROWCLOUGH**

Where are they?

**MACKEY**

We're getting warmer.

*They stop walking.*

**MACKAY**

They're down there.

**BARROWCLOUGH**

What – in the boiler house?

**MACKAY**

In the coke store.

**BARROWCLOUGH**

Well, should we –

**MACKAY**

No, wait a moment. I've arranged for a special delivery.

*He moves round the corner and gives the signal. Coal is seen going down the chute. Mackay and Barrowclough move to the doorway and wait. A door opens and Evans, Heslop, Fletcher and Lukewarm rush out covered in soot.*

**MACKAY**

Welcome to the Black and White Minstrel Show.

*They move up the alley.*

## 11. CELL

*Fletcher is collecting his things together inside the cell, when Ives puts his head round the door.*

**IVES**

Evening, Fletcher.

*Fletcher gives him no acknowledgement.*

**IVES**

I – I heard this time the coke was on you.

**FLETCHER**

What? Oh yes, you're a very witty man. Full of that irrepressible Liverpudlian wit we've all heard about.

**IVES**

What the Governor say then?

**FLETCHER**

Said I'd abused his trust. Said I'd lost my privileged position on the farm. Said I'd lose my privileges for the next four weeks. Also said I was an evil influence and not the sort of man who should be sharing a cell and corrupting the likes of Heslop and Evans. So he's shifting me to a single cell.

**IVES**

Oh dear, how tragic. I am sorry.

**FLETCHER**

All right, don't give me all that. I know you grassed, Ives. As does the entire prison. As you will find out when you take your first turn round the recreation yard. I'm not saying there'll be any unpleasantness, but if I were you I'd try and borrow some shin pads from the PTI.

**IVES**

'Ere listen, Fletcher.

**FLETCHER**

Not that I bears you any ill-feeling, you 'orrible contemptuous despicable git you. No, no, you was just a pawn in my grand strategy.

**IVES**

Never mind about that, there's still the bet, there's still the bet – you owes me, Fletcher.

**FLETCHER**

That is true, that is true. And that half pound of snout may provide some consolation to you in the nightmare days that lie ahead.

*Barrowclough comes in.*

**BARROWCLOUGH**

Ready, Fletcher?

**FLETCHER**

Just coming, Mr Barrowclough.

**IVES**

'Ere listen, you take the heat off me and we'll forget about the bet. We're even. I mean you're never going to raise half a pound of snout, are you?

**FLETCHER**

No, there's no problem. I'll take it out me winnings.

**IVES**

Winnings? What winnings?

**FLETCHER**

Lose a few, gain a few. I was betting the whole landing half a pound of snout I'd be in a single cell by Sunday. I'm going to be rolling in it.

## 12. PRISON LANDING

***Barrowclough and Fletcher come out of the cell and walk along the gantry. A prisoner passes Fletcher some tobacco.***

***They go down the stairs. Prisoners hand over tobacco to Fletcher. They go down more stairs. More prisoners give him tobacco.***

# 1 SERIES ONE

## EPISODE THREE: A NIGHT IN

### 1. PRISON

***It is association hour. Lennie goes down stairs.***

***He walks past other prisoners on his way to Fletcher's cell.***

### 2. FLETCHER'S CELL

***Lennie walks in. Fletcher is sitting on the lower bunk writing a letter. Lennie is a bit diffident.***

**LENNIE**

Oh er . . . hello, Fletch.

***He is met with silence.***

**LENNIE**

You er . . . you was expecting me? I mean they informed you?

**FLETCHER**

They informed me, yes.

**LENNIE**

Only temporary they said.

**FLETCHER**

You bet your life it's only temporary. Single cell this is, by rights.

**LENNIE**

Not my fault.

**FLETCHER**

I'm just saying.

**LENNIE**

Only temporary.

**FLETCHER**

Look, park your stuff, get out the light.

***Lennie pauses awkwardly, indicating the lower bunk.***

**LENNIE**

Er . . . is this where you want me to sleep?

**FLETCHER**

What?

**LENNIE**

Well, I presume I'm in the bottom bunk. I mean, top bunk's status in the nick.

**FLETCHER**

'Course it is. You're in the bottom bunk, yes.

**LENNIE**

Well, if you wouldn't mind shifting your stuff, I could –

**FLETCHER**

What? Oh, all right. God Almighty.

***He moves his stuff to the top bunk.***

***Lennie begins to unpack his stuff and make up his bunk.***

**LENNIE**

Not my fault.

**FLETCHER**

No no, so you keep telling me.

**LENNIE**

Not my fault if they have a riot on my landing. My cell mate, Banksy, he was one of the ringleaders, like. He set fire to his mattress. And mine.

**FLETCHER**

Head case, that Banks.

**LENNIE**

He's being transferred.

**FLETCHER**

Head case.

**LENNIE**

He wasn't a bad bloke to share a cell with. He was always very nice to me. He showed me the ropes and taught me cribbage. And he never displayed no violence. He was the gentlest of men.

**FLETCHER**

Oih . . .

***He nods to Lennie indicating that he should go to the other washstand.***

**LENNIE**

(*Crossing over*) Oh . . . He found this kitten and smuggled it into the cell and from the way he handled it you could see the gentle side of his nature.

**FLETCHER**

You what? Before he lit his mattress I heard he threw a screw off the top landing.

**LENNIE**

Well, he weren't hurt. He hit the safety net.

**FLETCHER**

That, Godber, is somewhat academic. The point is that a fifteen-stone prison officer was hurled from a top landing by your cell mate, mighty Joe Banks.

**LENNIE**

Only because he said he couldn't keep the kitten.

**FLETCHER**

Hardly an excuse, sonny Jim. Hardly an excuse. Can't see that cutting much ice with his parole board.

**LENNIE**

Where's the harm in keeping a kitten?

**FLETCHER**

It's not allowed, that's the point. It's against prison procedure. Caged birds, well yes, sometimes they'll let you keep caged birds. Insects in a matchbox. But you can't keep cats. And Banks knows that, the porridge he's done.

**LENNIE**

It was only a little kitten.

**FLETCHER**

A kitten differs from a cat only in scale. They share the same lavatorial tendencies, they pee on your blankets.

**LENNIE**

Just don't see the harm.

**FLETCHER**

There are rules. For example, I have

certain rules in this cell here. Well, not so much rules as standards. This is my cell, in which you're a temporary resident, and as such you will honour those standards.

**LENNIE**

Which are?

**FLETCHER**

You don't rabbit, you don't snore, and you don't pick your nose.

**LENNIE**

I don't think I do any of them.

**FLETCHER**

Good, good. Then we should get on passably well.

**LENNIE**

Banksy never complained anyhow.

**FLETCHER**

Well, he wouldn't, not an animal like Banksy.

**LENNIE**

But I don't.

***He sits down.***

**FLETCHER**

Good good, fine fine – you're sitting on my paper.

**LENNIE**

Oh, sorry.

***He gets up off a crumpled copy of the Sun and passes it over.***

**FLETCHER**

Oh another thing. Newspapers. You can read the paper, but when, and only when I've finished with it.

**LENNIE**

All right.

**FLETCHER**

Right – get out of the way.

***There is a pause while Fletcher climbs up into the top bunk and settles down with his paper. His shoes are off, and there is a big hole in one of his socks.***

***Lennie starts to set out a few personal possessions, including a photograph of his fiancée, only inscribed "Lennie – for always, Denise". He has also got some needle and thread, a tin of shag tobacco and some papers, a tin of throat lozenges, a box of liquorice all-sorts and shaving kit.***

**LENNIE**

I've got some grey darning thread.

**FLETCHER**

(*Irritably*) What?

**LENNIE**

I've got some grey darning thread if you want that hole darned up.

**FLETCHER**

(*Politer*) What? Oh yes, thanks – yes.

***He takes off his sock and hands it down to Lennie, who by his reaction registers that he had not expected to do the darning himself. He decides not to make a stand.***

**LENNIE**

Your standards don't include sweaty feet, I notice.

**FLETCHER**

Man who don't sweat ain't healthy. Like a dog with a dry nose.

**LENNIE**
(*Getting the darning kit*) Settling in OK, are you?

**FLETCHER**
I'm all right, keep me pecker up. Can't grind me down. Bide your time, that's what it's all down to, bide your time.

***Bells start to ring and doors start to slam, signalling lockup time. Voices are heard in the distance.***

**LENNIE**
Unnatural in't it, men in cages.

**FLETCHER**
Bide your time.

**LENNIE**
I don't mind work. And as I'm in the kitchens I always get plenty of grub. And the screws ain't too bad, by and large . . .

***A prison officer appears, gives a cursory check, then slams the door and locks it.***

**FLETCHER**
Goodnight, sunshine . . . Charmless nurk. Oh dear, I forgot to put me shoes out to be cleaned.

***Lennie walks across to the window.***

**LENNIE**
This is the bit I can't stand though.

**FLETCHER**
What?

**LENNIE**
Lockup. It's only quarter-to-eight. Barely dark. If I was at home now I'd just be going out for the evening.

**FLETCHER**
That's the point you see, son. We're here to be punished, ain't we? Deprived of all our creature comforts. And the little things you've been taking for granted all these years. Like a comfy shirt, decent smoke, a night out.

**LENNIE**
A night out . . .

***There is a pause.***

**FLETCHER**
Look, if you're so keen we'll go out. We could find a couple of girls – two of them darlings what dance on *Top of the Pops*. Yes, Pan's People. Beautiful Babs – don't know what her name is. Arrange to meet them in some dimly lit Italiano restaurant. Then we could go on somewhere if you like. Some night club . . . dance till dawn. Then back to their luxury penthouse, and wallop. But you see I done all that last night so I'm a bit knackered. Also we'd have to get all ponced up and you'd have to darn me socks. So why don't we just have a quiet night in? All right?

**LENNIE**
If you say so, Fletch.

**FLETCHER**
That's what you've got to tell yourself. You're just having a quiet night in.

***He goes back to the Sun. There is a pause.***

**LENNIE**
(*Gloomily*) Trouble is I've got six

hundred and ninety-eight quiet nights in to go.

**FLETCHER**

Less than some.

***Lennie looks at the picture of Denise.***

**LENNIE**

D'you think she'll wait?

**FLETCHER**

(*Abstractedly*) What?

**LENNIE**

D'you think she'll wait?

**FLETCHER**

Who?

**LENNIE**

Denise. My fiancée.

**FLETCHER**

Oh yes, Denise, fiancée.

**LENNIE**

Well, do you?

**FLETCHER**

I dunno. I shouldn't think she'll wait *in* for six hundred and ninety-eight nights.

**LENNIE**

She is my fiancée.

**FLETCHER**

Yes, I know, but when she said she'd love you for ever she didn't know you were going to get put away for two years, did she?

**LENNIE**

I miss her so much. I can't sleep for thinking about her.

**FLETCHER**

Doesn't do no good that. Don't do no good lying awake at night brooding and twitching about what you ain't going to get no more. Carnal thoughts – well, best to give them the Big E, the elbow. Less you think about women the better – cor, look at that. 'Beauty Queen shocks Council. Lovely Sharon Spenser, twenty-two, shocked members of her town Council when they learned that she played the title role in the new sex-sational film *The Virgin and the Vicar*.'

**LENNIE**

I wonder which she played?

**FLETCHER**

'"Had we known," said a Council spokesman, "We would never have crowned her floral Queen." "I don't know what all the fuss is about," said Sharon, a former convent girl, whose hobbies include water ski-ing and carpentry. "I am proud of my body and what I do with it in my spare time is none of the Council's business".' She'd never get planning permission for that.

***Both stare at the photograph for several seconds, their eyes glazing with obvious relish.***

**FLETCHER**

Yes . . . yes . . . got every right to be proud of a body like that. Oh yes. Ravishing little thing, isn't she? Mischievous little mouth. Look at that mouth. Full of mischief. I bet that's been up to some mischief. Yes . . . what was I saying?

**LENNIE**
You were saying the less you think about women the better.

**FLETCHER**
Oh yes, yes, carnal thoughts, yes, fatal.

**LENNIE**
She reminds me of Denise a bit.

**FLETCHER**
Which bit?

**LENNIE**
No – Denise. My fiancée.

**FLETCHER**
Oh yes, the lovely Denise, yes right.

**LENNIE**
Not that they're similar in appearance, but they're both . . . physical. Know what I mean?

**FLETCHER**
You're not telling me your Denise is a star of the silver screen, are you? Albeit a grubby one in a backroom.

**LENNIE**
Oh no, nothing like that.

**FLETCHER**
Not a model, then?

**LENNIE**
Oh no, though I once took some provocative Polaroids of her when we were caravanning in the Gower Peninsula. I don't mean mucky, like. But she was sort of expressing herself . . . Posing, like.

***He gives his impression of Denise posing provocatively on the Gower Peninsula. Fletcher looks disapproving.***

**FLETCHER**
Come on, son! Leave it off! What will the neighbours think?

***He is aware of the spyhole in the cell door.***

**LENNIE**
Oh sorry, Fletch.

**FLETCHER**
Ain't thinking of me, son. They know which side my bread's buttered . . . It's you. Harm can come to a growing lad. You're the one could drive the fairies round here into a frenzy.

**LENNIE**
But I'm engaged to Denise.

**FLETCHER**
Means naff all to them, my son. They're all engaged to each other. Denise is a thing of your past. A letter in your top pocket. A photograph under your pillow. A warm tingle in your loins.

**LENNIE**
In me what?

**FLETCHER**
Your loins.

**LENNIE**
What are loins?

**FLETCHER**
(*Exasperatedly*) Loins is . . . look, when you think of her, when you thinks of Denise in the still of the night, think of the times you once had, don't you ever get a warm tingle?

**LENNIE**

Oh – yes.

**FLETCHER**

Well, where you gets it, that's your loins.

***There is a pause.***

**LENNIE**

I thought they were my –

***He lies down on the bottom bunk.***

**FLETCHER**

Well there's lots of words for them.

**LENNIE**

She is a very physical girl, Denise. She was a Beauty Queen. Finalist at the Office Machinery Exhibition. Miss Duplicating, she was. And her picture was in the paper and she became a pin-up of two thousand sailors in an aircraft carrier in Gibraltar. They wrote to her and said she was the girl they'd most like to ink their rolls.

**FLETCHER**

That must have made you very proud, Lennie, knowing that your fiancée was the sexual fantasy of an entire aircraft carrier.

**LENNIE**

Oh, I didn't know her then. That was before she moved to Smethwick, before that never-to-be-forgotten day when I met her at a supermarket in the Bull Ring – oh that's in Birmingham. She was stamping 'Special Offer' on giant-sized jars of pickled onions. I came round the corner from condiments and sauces and my wire trolley went over her foot. It was a magic moment. We both knew. I said to her straight off 'Will you meet me outside?' I said. And she said, 'All right.'

**FLETCHER**

God preserve us, Godber. Romance.

***He gets down from his bunk.***

**LENNIE**

How d'you mean? I told you it was beautiful.

**FLETCHER**

I know, son, I know. But all I'm saying is if you had your time again, you might pick a more romantic setting to meet the love of your life. 'She was stamping "Special Offer" on giant-sized pickled onions,' I mean bloody hell, it's not Romeo and Juliet, is it.

***He sits down. There is a pause.***

**LENNIE**

Was your courtship any more romantic?

**FLETCHER**

Well no . . . in truth it wasn't really. I'm a city boy like you. And it was after the war. I had a bit more space than you, but that was mostly bomb sites. There was the pictures – the Muswell Hill Odeon. Or the back seat of a car – if I could open one. But somehow we had more chance to improvise. Today these great cold hostile concrete blocks. No hiding place. Can't make love in a launderette.

***There is a pause.***

**LENNIE**

We did.

**FLETCHER**
What? Oh . . .

**LENNIE**
It was very quiet at the time.

**FLETCHER**
That's a relief to us all.

**LENNIE**
We had three bagfuls to do . . . and it was bitter out.

**FLETCHER**
Hardly entitles you, I'd have thought. However I don't know Birmingham. Now, my eldest, Ingrid –

**LENNIE**
Ingrid?

**FLETCHER**
Yes, my old lady called her that after Ingrid Bergman what was a famous film star who was sweeping the country at the time, but I don't suppose you remember her, *For Whom the Bell Tolls, Casablanca, Spellbound*.

**LENNIE**
Oh I think I've seen that on the telly. Is that the one about the scientists in the secret laboratory in Arizona and this man drinks this substance by mistake and turns into a werewolf and carries off the mad doctor's niece and does things to her in the catacombs?

**FLETCHER**
No.

**LENNIE**
Oh.

**FLETCHER**
No, that weren't one of Ingrid's. No, I can say without fear of contradiction that Ingrid was never in no catacomb with no werewolf. My daughter Ingrid might have been, but certainly not the lovely Miss Bergman.

***He rises and crosses to stick up the photograph.***

**LENNIE**
What were you going to say about your daughter Ingrid?

**FLETCHER**
(*Sitting down*) What? Was I? Oh yes, my point was that my eldest, was – this is between ourselves, Godber – she was conceived in Highgate Cemetery. You see we weren't married at the time. Of course we got married when we realised young Ingrid was on the way. But at the time we wasn't. And we needed somewhere to consummate the passion we felt for each other.

**LENNIE**
But a cemetery!

**FLETCHER**
Oh yes, but a very famous and historic cemetery.

**LENNIE**
Still seems a bit indecent to me.

**FLETCHER**
(*Indignantly*) No more indecent than doing it in your local launderette three bags full. Anyhow it wasn't premeditated 'cos we'd gone there to see Karl Marx's tomb. I was politically minded at the time, and very randy. Mind you, my

political career never got beyond painting slogans on viaduct walls.

**LENNIE**

I've done that. Last thing I painted was Lennie Godber loves Denise Shorter on a warehouse wall.

**FLETCHER**

Denise Shorter?

**LENNIE**

My fiancée?

**FLETCHER**

Oh that Denise Shorter.

***He gets up and gets a chair.***

**LENNIE**

(*Hanging up photo*) I wrote to her in association hour. Helped to pass the time. I didn't have a class, you see.

**FLETCHER**

What class are you on?

**LENNIE**

Shoe repairing.

**FLETCHER**

Oh that's useful, yes. Very elevating, yes. You're not in the shoe repairing class are you? . . . Load of cobblers that.

**LENNIE**

Just helps kill the time. Anything to take me mind off the monotony of this place.

**FLETCHER**

Listen, this ain't so bad, this nick. Compared to Leicester, Parkhurst, high security places like that. Got closed circuit cameras there. Can't even go to the lavatory without it being on television. Not that that would worry an exhibitionist like yourself, of course. Someone who makes love in launderettes.

***The lights go out.***

**LENNIE**

Oh, I ain't got me things off yet.

**FLETCHER**

Move over, will you, son?

***He moves, then gives a yell of pain.***

**FLETCHER**

Owww!

**LENNIE**

What's the matter?

**FLETCHER**

Something stuck in me foot.

**LENNIE**

That must be me darning needle.

**FLETCHER**

Well, what's it doing there?

**LENNIE**

I was darning your sock.

**FLETCHER**

Well, do it in the morning.

***Lennie, trying to help, inadvertently steps on Fletcher's foot.***

**FLETCHER**

Now you're standing on me other foot.

**LENNIE**

Oh, I'm sorry.

***He moves.***

**FLETCHER**

You've just injured both my feet, Godber.

**LENNIE**

I didn't mean –

**FLETCHER**

Just go to bed, son.

**LENNIE**

I'm not undressed yet.

**FLETCHER**

Just go to bed till I get into bed, then you can get out again.

***Lennie complies. Fletcher climbs up on to the top bunk, muttering as he does.***

**FLETCHER**

Not enough room to share . . . no privacy . . . bet he snores . . . he certainly rabbits.

**LENNIE**

D'you want a liquorice all-sort?

**FLETCHER**

No, I don't want a . . . liquorice all-sort.

***There is a pause.***

**FLETCHER**

How d'you get liquorice all-sorts?

**LENNIE**

(*Taking his shoes off*) I swopped them for a pound of marge I whipped from the kitchen.

**FLETCHER**

Learning, aren't you?

**LENNIE**

(*Taking his trousers off*) Little victories, you told me that.

**FLETCHER**

Shall we get some kip?

***Lennie has been undressing and now gets into the lower bunk. There is a long pause.***

**LENNIE**

Fletcher . . .

**FLETCHER**

(*Wearily*) Wha-at?

**LENNIE**

D'you know what I've found useful since I've been inside?

**FLETCHER**

What have you found useful, Godber?

**LENNIE**

I've started to do something which I haven't done since I was a kiddy.

***Fletcher wonders whatever is coming next.***

**LENNIE**

I find it helps. D'you know what I do?

**FLETCHER**

I shudder to think, son.

***There is a pause.***

**LENNIE**

I pray.

**FLETCHER**

Pray?

**LENNIE**

Yes, I've started saying me prayers.

**FLETCHER**

God preserve us.

**LENNIE**

That's what I keep asking him. So if you don't mind –

**FLETCHER**

If you must.

***Lennie closes his eyes and starts praying.***

**LENNIE**

Dear God, thank you for getting me through another day. Thank you for the letter from Denise and the liquorice all-sorts. Please look after Denise in your infinite wisdom. And the same applies to me Mum, Dad – wherever he is – and me Aunty Vi and Uncle Donald, Uncle Les and Aunty Con, me Aunty Rita in Newport Pagnall, and Cousin Rita in Walsall. And Cissie, and Stu, and Vic, and all the lads in the darts team at the Bell and Dragon.

***He pauses.***

**LENNIE**

And Norma and her husband who emigrated to Melbourne.

**FLETCHER**

Is this a prayer? Or a dedication on the Jimmy Young show?

***There is a slight pause. We think Lennie has shut up but we are wrong.***

**LENNIE**

And please God, look after Fletcher and forgive him for being such a bad-tempered, evil-minded, cantankerous old git.

***Fletcher's face reflects his indignation.***

## 3. PRISON

***It is night. In the prison there is almost complete silence, save for a lone prison officer making his rounds on the landing and a few assorted snores.***

## 4. CELL

***Night time. A match flares as Fletcher lights up a smoke. Lennie speaks from below.***

**LENNIE**

You awake, Fletch?

**FLETCHER**

No.

**LENNIE**

Oh.

***There is a pause.***

**FLETCHER**

Why?

**LENNIE**

Nor me neither.

**FLETCHER**

Your God in his infinite wisdom isn't giving you a peaceful night then.

**LENNIE**

Wasn't one of the things I asked for.

**FLETCHER**

That's true. He won't be getting much kip either, the list you gave him.

**LENNIE**

Don't be irreverent.

**FLETCHER**

You've changed your spots, ain't you? Day we come in, when we went through reception you didn't even know if you was C of E, Pressed Beef or a flaming Buddhist.

**LENNIE**

Don't think it matters much. I just believe in God – doesn't matter which lot you support. I admit my belief's only been revived since I come in here. 'Cos I prayed when I was a kid, like. When I was up in Juvenile Court and when Villa looked like doing well in the Cup. But I became disillusioned with religion. I got probation and Villa got knocked out by Rotherham one-nothing.

**FLETCHER**

That's typical, in' it? Most people never give a second thought, do they? When things are going well, ticking along with scant regard for the ten commandments. Stealing, committing adultery, coveting each other's oxes. Then, wallop. In the face of adversity – (*In a cringing falsetto*) 'Please God, please help your loyal and trusted servant.' Huh!

**LENNIE**

You're right. But I am in the face of adversity. I hate prison, Fletch. It makes me depressed and it makes me afraid. I hate the air of defeat and the smell of disinfectant. I hate the shouting and the keys. And I hate not having a handle on the inside of that door.

***He nods towards the cell door. Fletcher is not unsympathetic.***

**FLETCHER**

(*Getting down from his bunk*) Kids like you shouldn't be in prison, son. It's the system, see. You ain't here to be reformed or rehabilitated. You're here because of public revenge. Now it's different for me. Occupational hazard being as my occupation's breaking the law. But my family ain't gone short, most years. Three kids and my old lady. Show you their picture when it's light. Now my youngest, he just got into Grammar School.

**LENNIE**

Has he?

**FLETCHER**

Yes, lovely school. Costs a bit, you know. Books, equipment. But when my son showed up first day he was short of nothing. Rugby boots, blazer, scarf, the lot. Now he wouldn't have had all that if his dad had been a struggling clerk or a – or a shoe repairer. No. The reason he had all that was that his dad robbed a school outfitters.

**LENNIE**

What would your son think if he knew the truth?

**FLETCHER**

He'd think 'Oh so that's why the blazer's a bit big.' But he'll grow into it.

**LENNIE**

So you only do it for your family then?

**FLETCHER**

And my old lady, yes.

***He gets up and goes across for some water.***

**FLETCHER**

Twenty-four years we been together. Married at nineteen see – too young, 'course it is, but that's Highgate Cemetery for you.

**LENNIE**

You must love her very much.

**FLETCHER**

Yeah, well . . .

**LENNIE**

'Cos when you were asleep like, you were saying things.

**FLETCHER**

Who me – what? Saying what?

**LENNIE**

Just saying her name over and over again. 'Gloria, my love – oh Glor, Glor, my love.'

**FLETCHER**

Was I?

**LENNIE**

Yes. I found that very moving – even though it woke me up.

***There is a long pause.***

**FLETCHER**

Thing is . . . my old lady's called Isobel.

**LENNIE**

Then who's Gloria?

**FLETCHER**

(*Puzzled*) You may well ask. You sure it was Gloria?

**LENNIE**

Positive.

**FLETCHER**

Gloria. Gloria? . . . (*Remembering*) Yes, there was a Gloria once – well, more than once in fact – many, many times.

**LENNIE**

Was that before you met your Isobel?

**FLETCHER**

(*Confidentially*) In truth er – it wasn't, Lennie. This was a little indiscretion round about 1955. I remember that 'cos at the time I was King of the Teds in Muswell Hill. And Gloria she was a machinist – clothing factory. So I used to go round to her place, get me evil way and get me trousers narrowed at the same time.

**LENNIE**

I could never be unfaithful to Denise.

**FLETCHER**

Ah now, listen, listen. Don't get no wrong impression. This was an indiscretion. You must imagine my position. You can't be King of the Teds and say at ten o'clock I've got to go home to the wife. Not after you've just smashed up an Amusement Arcade.

**LENNIE**

So you don't make a habit of indiscretions?

**FLETCHER**

'Course not. Look, Isobel's my old lady and she knows it.

***There is a pause.***

**LENNIE**

Then who's Sharon?

**FLETCHER**

Sharon!!

**LENNIE**
After Gloria you was moaning about a Sharon.

**FLETCHER**
I couldn't have been, I don't know no Sharons – here hang about! She was the girl in the *Sun*, weren't she? Beauty Queen shocks Council. Yes, yes, I was having this dream and she was in it, comes back to me now . . .

**LENNIE**
(*In censure*) Carnal thoughts.

**FLETCHER**
Listen, Godber. No one asked you to eavesdrop on my dreams. It's about the only place you have any privacy inside – your head. You want to remember that, son. Dreams is your escape. No locked doors in dreams. No boundaries, no frontiers. Dreams is freedom.

***This impresses Lennie.***

**LENNIE**
Freedom.

**FLETCHER**
No locked doors.

**LENNIE**
That's true, Fletch, that's really true.

**FLETCHER**
Well, I'm getting back to mine and I suggest you do the same.

**LENNIE**
I will do, I will. And thank you, Fletch.

**FLETCHER**
(*Quite grumpily*) All right. Goodnight.

***He turns over.***

**FLETCHER**
Now, where was I . . .

**LENNIE**
Beauty Queen shocks Council.

**FLETCHER**
Oh yes . . . the way she was performing in my dream, I can see why.

## 5. PRISON

***The prison is bathed in the light of dawn. Early morning sounds can be heard. On the prison landing officers walking along the building, banging their keys against the doors and shouting their wake-up calls.***

## 6. CELL

***Fletcher is waking up.***

**FLETCHER**
There's my alarm call.

***He swings himself into a sitting position and his feet hit Lennie's head.***

**FLETCHER**
Oops. Sorry, son.

**LENNIE**
No, no, Fletch. It's your cell. Sorry if my head hit your foot.

***He gets up.***

**FLETCHER**
How d'you sleep then?

**LENNIE**
Very well since our midnight chat.

**FLETCHER**
Did you dream? Did you find that

freedom I promised you, that land of exotic fantasy?

**LENNIE**

Oh yes. It was Denise and I. We were in the launderette and we got through five bagfuls without stopping. Trouble is this bloke came in and spoilt it.

**FLETCHER**

Oh what a pity.

**LENNIE**

It was you.

**FLETCHER**

Couldn't have been. I was with Sharon Spencer all night up at the Hylton.

**LENNIE**

Fletch . . .

**FLETCHER**

What?

**LENNIE**

In the rush, moving here I well, er – I like, mislaid something.

**FLETCHER**

What?

**LENNIE**

My toothpaste.

**FLETCHER**

Oh yes.

**LENNIE**

Well, er – could I possibly have a loan of yours?

**FLETCHER**

Have a loan of my toothpaste?

**LENNIE**

Just a squeeze, like.

**FLETCHER**

Have a loan of my toothpaste?

**LENNIE**

I'll give you a liquorice all-sort.

**FLETCHER**

Oh!

**LENNIE**

(*Getting them from under his pillow*) I've got some left.

**FLETCHER**

Got the round one with the pink coconut? There's only one, you know.

**LENNIE**

Yes.

**FLETCHER**

All right then.

***There's a slight pause.***

**LENNIE**

Fletch.

**FLETCHER**

Now what? Suppose you ain't got no shaving cream.

**LENNIE**

No. I just wanted to thank you.

**FLETCHER**

Oh?

**LENNIE**

For helping me out. With advice, like. You know, it's like that song – 'Help me make it through the night.'

**FLETCHER**

What song's that?

**LENNIE**

Don't suppose you'd know it. More contemporary than your era. Suppose as King of the Teds your tastes were more Eddie Cochran and Conway Twitty.

**FLETCHER**
No. No my tastes were a bit more mellow. What was it I used to like? Kay Starr. Rosemary Clooney. And what was that song . . . (*Sings*) 'See the Pyramids along the Nile' . . . Jo Stafford.

**LENNIE**
Don't know him.

**FLETCHER**
He was a girl you nurk. Jo's a girl's name. They don't write songs like that now. Had a bit of melody in them days.

**LENNIE**
You're a sentimentalist at heart.

**FLETCHER**
(*Suspiciously*) What?

**LENNIE**
I know that under that gruff unpleasant exterior there's a kind man with feelings.

**FLETCHER**
(*Gruffly*) Yes, well –

***He sits down to put his shoes on, then leaps up in pain, hitting his head on the top bunk.***

**FLETCHER**
Bloody hell, bloody hell.

**LENNIE**
Oh, was it the darning needle again?

***There is the sound of a door being unlocked.***

**FLETCHER**
I'll swing for you, Godber, I swear it.

***The cell door is opened by a dour Prison Officer.***

**PRISON OFFICER**
What's going on here then? Did you assault this man, Godber?

**LENNIE**
He sat on my darning needle.

**PRISON OFFICER**
Is that true, Fletcher?

**FLETCHER**
Oh naff off. Can't you see I'm in agony?

**PRISON OFFICER**
Why don't you get a move on?

**FLETCHER**
Why don't you go home and find out who's been sleeping with your old lady while you've been on night duty?

**PRISON OFFICER**
(*Re-entering*) Oh that's original, Fletcher. I've been having that for the last seven years.

***He leaves. Lennie and Fletcher sit down.***

**FLETCHER**
Yeah, and so has she.

***A Prison Officer can be heard unlocking another door.***

**PRISON OFFICER (*VOICEOVER*)**
(*Offscreen*) Come on, move it.

**VOICE (*VOICEOVER*)**

(*Offscreen*) Who's been sleeping with your old lady then?

***Fletcher gets his boots and sits down to put them on.***

**LENNIE**

Here you are, you can have these.

**FLETCHER**

What?

**LENNIE**

Go on – all of them. Present like.

**FLETCHER**

Oh, all right then. Not say no, son.

**LENNIE**

It's meant as a thank you. 'Cos when that door's locked I am depressed and I am afraid, and you – you know – just make it a bit more tolerable.

**FLETCHER**

You'll get used to it, Len. And the night's not so long, is it? It's your human spirit, see. They can't break that, those nurks. We'll be all right, you and me, son. Here, we'll go out tonight if you like.

**LENNIE**

With those dancers?

**FLETCHER**

If you like. Or I could ring Miss Sharon Spencer, eh? She'll have a big friend. Bound to. Soft lights, music, night club . . .

**LENNIE**

It's discos now.

***He stands up.***

**FLETCHER**

What? Oh well – as you say. Anyhow, think about it.

**LENNIE**

I will, I will. See how I feel. On the other hand, Fletch –

**FLETCHER**

Yeah.

**LENNIE**

If we don't feel like it, we might just have a quiet night in.

**FLETCHER**

Right. Right.

***Fletcher picks up the pot. Lennie picks up the bucket and they move to the cell door.***

***Prisoners are walking along the landing with buckets etc. for slop-up. Fletcher comes out of his cell, followed by Lennie and they join the line.***

# 1 SERIES ONE

## EPISODE FOUR: A DAY OUT

### 1. PRISON

*Prison Officers are seen knocking up prisoners.*

### 2. FLETCHER'S CELL

*Fletcher wakes up and sees that Lennie has almost finished dressing.*

**FLETCHER**
Oh yes, what's your rush? Getting released, are you?

**LENNIE**
Been looking forward to today.

**FLETCHER**
What's so special about today? Only one good thing about a new day in here, it replaces the old one. Crossed one off, haven't we?

**LENNIE**
But we're going out today. Aren't we? Breath of fresh air. Trees. Walking on grass. The sounds of birds in the branches.

**FLETCHER**
Don't get so flaming lyrical, Wordsworth. All we're going to do is dig drains for the council. Stooped six hours over a shovel. Doing a job they'd only give to prisoners, seeing as any civilised geezer would tell 'em to stuff it.

**LENNIE**
I don't care what they make us do. We're going outside that's all I care. A whole day out of here.

**FLETCHER**
You're like a kid on a school trip, aren't you?

**LENNIE**
You don't fool me, Fletch. You just mask your enthusiasm, you do. But if you were that indifferent, why would you have gone to the trouble of bribing yourself on to the party?

**FLETCHER**
Yuh, well . . .

**LENNIE**
Yeah, well.

**FLETCHER**
Well I can't deny the thought of fresh air appeals. Get the smell of disinfectant out me nostrils. Not to mention your festering feet.

**LENNIE**
I change my socks every day.

**FLETCHER**
Pity you can't change your feet.

**LENNIE**
If it ain't one thing it's another . . . I don't complain about your personal habits.

**FLETCHER**
What personal habits? I don't have any personal habits.

**LENNIE**
Yes, you do.

**FLETCHER**
I do not!

**LENNIE**
You do.

**FLETCHER**
Like what?

**LENNIE**
You talk with your mouth full, you whistle out of tune, you snore, you spit . . .

**FLETCHER**
How dare you? I do not whistle out of tune. You've got a cheek you have, you've got a flaming nerve. This is supposed to be a single cell, this is – by rights, mine. You've got a nerve talking about my personal habits. You was dragged up in some Birmingham backstreet.

**LENNIE**
I had a good upbringing, I did. We may not have had much money but my mother kept us spotless.

**FLETCHER**
Well you ain't spotless now, are you? Your clothes are covered in gravy stains. So don't give me no stick about personal table manners.

**LENNIE**
Look, everybody at our table is covered in gravy stains – it's your gravy! I told you, you talk with your mouth full.

***Fletcher starts cleaning his teeth.***

**FLETCHER**
You'd better watch it, Godber. I'm warning you. I do not talk with my mouth full.

**LENNIE**
Look, you're doing it now, I'm covered in toothpaste.

**FLETCHER**
Cheeky young nurk.

**LENNIE**
Don't let's fall out, Fletch. We don't want to spoil things this early. Today's the big day.

**FLETCHER**
It ain't that big a day, son. Ain't a coach trip to Southend. Not a day at the seaside, with a trip up the pier and a big nosh up and reduced rates at the local knocking shop. We're only going across a remote Cumberland moor, to a remote Cumberland village to dig drains. Sustained by the remote possibility that the district nurse might pass by on her bicycle and give us all an exciting glimpse of stocking top.

**LENNIE**
A woman . . . a woman on her bicycle.
**FLETCHER**
Maybe, maybe.
**LENNIE**
No, Fletch, I can see her. Clear as day. In her uniform, on her bicycle.
**FLETCHER**
District nurse, huh. Some old spinster with brogues and bike rider's buttocks.
**LENNIE**
No, she's young, Fletch, honest, young and nice looking. Well, more than that, beautiful really. And the prim uniform which she so proudly wears can barely conceal the voluptuous figure within.
**FLETCHER**
Oh. Voluptuous figure within, is it?
**LENNIE**
Yeah. Which her prim uniform cannot conceal.
**FLETCHER**
Barely.
**LENNIE**
Her face is at once innocent and knowing.
**FLETCHER**
I know them innocent faces.
**LENNIE**
Obviously primitive passions are stirring deep within her breast.
**FLETCHER**
Oh deep one, is it?
**LENNIE**
Oh definitely.
**FLETCHER**
Here hang on, what's this gorgeous deep-chested thigh-flashing bit of nooky doing up this neck of the woods?
**LENNIE**
(*Hesitates for only a second*) Well, you see, she comes home to nurse her dad what's been sick with a fatal, tropical disease.
**FLETCHER**
Fatal is it, that could kill you.
**LENNIE**
She turned her back on the bright lights like out of duty.
**FLETCHER**
Of course she did, didn't she? Could've been a model, girl like that, cover girl, chased by playboys and Arab princes.
**LENNIE**
Instead of which –
**FLETCHER**
Instead of which she returns to nurse her ailing dad, trying hard to subdue her primitive stirrings, until the day when fate decrees she has a puncture right next to the drain I'm digging.
**LENNIE**
Here, hang on, I saw her first.
**FLETCHER**
Naff off, Godber, age before beauty. I'm at her side, picking her up, dusting her down, and not failing to notice as I do her proud, firm body. She's sprained her perfectly formed ankle, and I carries her over several miles of

ploughed sludge, staggering at last, exhausted, into her lonely cottage miles from anywhere, leaving the two of us thrown together as night falls.

**LENNIE**

What about Dad, then?

**FLETCHER**

Oh he's dead. There's just us. Me and her. Together. Alone. And she pours me a drink, after slipping out of her wet uniform. Slip, slip. Then she gets me some grub. And I eat, and we talk.

**LENNIE**

There you go again, Fletch.

**FLETCHER**

What?

**LENNIE**

Talking with your mouth full.

***Fletcher throws a shoe at Lennie.***

## 3. ASSEMBLY ROOM

***Navyrum, Ives and Scrounger are waiting.***

**NAVYRUM**

Hey Ives, how did you work your way on this doddle? Bribed a lot of people in high places.

**IVES**

'Ere listen –

**NAVYRUM**

You're not a working man. Not a bird bones skiving little git like you.

**IVES**

'Ere listen –

**NAVYRUM**

I'm a working man. Always have been. Stoker. Paid my dues. Tankers. Persian Gulf. Big sweat I'll tell ye.

**IVES**

'Ere listen, Navyrum, I'll do my share, don't you worry.

**SCROUNGER**

I had a job once, worked on a road gang. Motorway. Naffing job that was. Had to live on a caravan site with the old woman and two nippers. Always mud. Work in mud, come home to mud.

**IVES**

Should feel at home today then.

***The door is unlocked and Barrowclough brings Fletcher and Lennie in then locks the door again.***

**OTHERS**

Hello, Fletch, Lennie.

**LENNIE**

Hello lads.

**FLETCHER**

Gentlemen . . . all right, Scrounger. Here, how did this little runt fiddle his way on this?

**IVES**

'Ere listen –

**FLETCHER**

Can't even shovel his peas he can't without getting tennis elbow.

**IVES**

Don't you worry, I'll do my share.

**NAVYRUM**

'E's a skivin' git.

**FLETCHER**

That's exactly what he is Navyrum,

you're not wrong there. And how are you? D'you know young Lennie Godber, my temporary cell mate?

**LENNIE**

(*Nods*) Hello.

**NAVYRUM**

Hello, son.

***Fletcher and Lennie sit down.***

**FLETCHER**

Me and Navyrum were in Maidstone together. When he gets to know you a bit better he might let you come round one night and read his tattoos.

**SCROUNGER**

Who are we waiting for?

**NAVYRUM**

Dylan.

**FLETCHER**

Dylan! That long-haired anarchist nurk. We've got a right lot here, ain't we, for a hard day's work. A twelve-stone weakling and the King of the Huddersfield Hippies.

***The door is unlocked and Barrowclough comes in with Dylan. Dylan acknowledges the others with a nod.***

**FLETCHER**

Well now, Dylan, speak of the devil.

**DYLAN**

Listen man, my name's Melvyn, what's all this Dylan scene?

**FLETCHER**

Not out of malice, son, we calls you that out of affection. We calls you that 'cos you reminds us of Dylan.

**DYLAN**

Bob Dylan?

**FLETCHER**

No, that hippy rabbit on *The Magic Roundabout*.

**DYLAN**

I'm not a hippy.

**FLETCHER**

You're the nearest thing we've got to one. You wear an earring and you got chucked out of art school for writing on the walls, and you're the only one here what's tidied their prison uniform.

**DYLAN**

Oh man . . .

**BARROWCLOUGH**

I didn't know you watched *The Magic Roundabout*, Fletcher.

**FLETCHER**

Yes, good ain't it?

**DYLAN**

*Magic Roundabout.*

**FLETCHER**

All right, all right. Gives a lot of innocent people a lot of pleasure. Even gives us guilty people a lot of pleasure. Simple pleasures are very precious to us, ain't they, Scrounger?

**SCROUNGER**

Like this day out.

**LENNIE**

Oh yeah, be great to see a bit of grass, smell the flowers.

**BARROWCLOUGH**

Oh you'll have to join our Botany Club, you'll enjoy that. I run it in the summer. We get out on the fells exploring the natural phenomena of our countryside.

**FLETCHER**

Oh do you? All young Lennie and I want to explore is that young nurse, eh, son?

**NAVYRUM**

Nurse? What's this then? Which nurse?

**LENNIE**

She's mine. He commandeered my fantasy.

**NAVYRUM**

What we waiting for then?

**BARROWCLOUGH**

We're waiting for Mr Mackay.

**FLETCHER**

Oh dear, Scotland the brave – is he coming?

**BARROWCLOUGH**

Mr Mackay's in charge, yes.

**NAVYRUM**

Git.

**DYLAN**

Pig.

**FLETCHER**

Charmless nurk.

***The door has been unlocked and Mackay enters.***

**MACKAY**

What's going on then?

**FLETCHER**

Oh morning, Mr Mackay. Just voted you man of the year.

**MACKAY**

On your feet all of you.

***They all stand.***

**MACKAY**

None of your facetious lip, Fletcher.

**FLETCHER**

You'll get none of it today, Mr Mackay.

**MACKAY**

Now as this work party is composed of such a spineless, delinquent obstreperous rabble, let's make a few things crystal clear. There will be no skiving, no fraternising with members of the public, no kipping in the long grass, and another thing there will not be is visits to the nearest pub masquerading as Irish labourers working on a mythical motorway extension. Any questions?

**FLETCHER**

Yeah, I've got a question.

**MACKAY**

What?

**FLETCHER**

Is the ball and chain worn outside the wellington boot or inside?

## 4. PRISON

***A bus approaches the prison gates. The warder opens the gate and the bus drives through and away.***

## 5. ROAD AND DITCH

***Camera shows a churchyard. Not far away a nurse is cycling up a hill. The prisoners' work party are at the roadside.***

***The nurse cycles past them. They come out of the ditch and react to her. She wobbles on her bicycle.***

**MACKAY**

Quiet the lot of you.

***He crosses to the ditch.***

**MACKAY**

Just get on with it. Ives, put some effort into it.

**IVES**

'Ere listen, everyone picks on me. I do my share.

**FLETCHER**

I think you'd have us in chains, wouldn't you, Mr Mackay – if you had your way.

**MACKAY**

With the greatest of pleasure.

***He turns to leave.***

**DYLAN**

Pig.

***Mackay turns back.***

**MACKAY**

Did you speak, Bottomley?

**DYLAN**

Dig. I was just telling Fletcher to dig.

**FLETCHER**

Who're you calling a pig?

**LENNIE**

Can we sing?

**MACKAY**

Sing?

**FLETCHER**

What we got to sing about?

**LENNIE**

No, but it would help like. Keep our spirits up. Like the Negro slaves on the plantations in the deep South. Work songs, things like that, kept their spirits up, didn't it? We're working in a gang, just like them.

**FLETCHER**

If you chuck much more mud about we'll all look like 'em an' all.

**NAVYRUM**

Used to sing in the Gulf. Stoking. Sing opera.

***He starts singing. The others join in.***

**FLETCHER**

Oh dear.

**MACKAY**

Thank God for that.

**FLETCHER**

Thank gawd for that.

**MACKAY**

I'm just popping down to the village to er . . . get some part for my lawnmower.

***He moves to the door of the van and addresses Barrowclough.***

**MACKAY**

So er . . . you take charge, all right?

**BARROWCLOUGH**

You'll not be long, will you?

**MACKAY**

(*Getting into van*) You're perfectly capable, man.

**BARROWCLOUGH**

Ah, but you see there's a lot of them and only one of me.

**MACKAY**

Pull yourself together, Mr Barrowclough.

***The van starts up.***

***In the ditch Fletcher notices the van's departure. The group cheers.***

**SCROUNGER**

Where's he going then?

**FLETCHER**

He's going after that district nurse, he ain't so fussy as us, is he?

**BARROWCLOUGH**

(*Moving to the ditch*) Now listen, you men. Let's knuckle down. My approach may not be as rigid as Mr Mackay's but there's work to be done and I'm here to see it gets done, so there'll be no shirking, no slacking and no taking advantage of my good nature. Right.

**ALL**

Right, Mr Barrowclough.

***They start chatting.***

## 6. CHURCH

***Inside the church the work party are having a smoke and taking it easy.***

**LENNIE**

Nice this, isn't it Fletch? Being out I mean.

**FLETCHER**

Oh yes, well, makes a change. Get a bit more exercise. Mind you I'd like today to be a bit more to write home about. Pub just down the road. Wouldn't half like to be in it. Pop in the village shop. Get some sweets, and a *Reveille*.

**LENNIE**

Ain't possible, is it?

**FLETCHER**

It's been done.

***Barrowclough comes in.***

**BARROWCLOUGH**

Oh no – now come along men, you've had a good long smoke break, it's high time we got back to it. We shouldn't be smoking in here at all.

**FLETCHER**

We had to have somewhere to sit, couldn't sit on the damp grass, could we? 'Cos it's bad for you, very bad for you.

**BARROWCLOUGH**

It's usual to sit on the earth you dig out – form little piles.

**FLETCHER**

Exactly, that's what I'm worried about, forming little piles.

**BARROWCLOUGH**

That's enough, Fletcher. Now we really must knuckle down. (*Counting*) One, two, three . . . Now, where's Ives?

**FLETCHER**

He's outside desecrating holy ground, isn't he?

**BARROWCLOUGH**

How do you mean?

**FLETCHER**

Gone for a slash in the churchyard.

***At that moment there is a terrible scream and Ives comes in clutching his trousers.***

**IVES**
'Ere listen, help, I've been stung.

**FLETCHER**
Obviously the Lord's retribution, you vulgar nurk. Bee, was it?

**IVES**
I don't know what it was, I ain't a flaming zoologist.

**LENNIE**
Maybe it was a wasp. Or a hornet.

**IVES**
What difference does it make?

**FLETCHER**
Makes a lot of difference. Different degree of pain and poison.

**IVES**
It was a great big thing.

**FLETCHER**
Oh hornet, fatal.

**IVES**
What you mean, fatal?

**FLETCHER**
Listen lads, if one of us don't suck the poison out of Ives's system he's going to die.

*There is a silence.*

**FLETCHER**
You're going to die, old son.

**IVES**
'Ere, listen, that's not funny.

**BARROWCLOUGH**
Don't joke, Fletcher, the man is in some distress – it's all right, Ives, it's almost certainly just a wasp sting.

**IVES**
I'm dying.

**FLETCHER**
(*Knocks Ives*) Yes, come on again. (*Moving to Barrowclough*) Permission to make a suggestion, Mr Barrowclough.

**BARROWCLOUGH**
What?

**FLETCHER**
Why don't someone go down the village get some ointment or TCP. Then the only problem's getting a volunteer to rub it on. I'd be willing to go and get some.

*The others cough.*

**BARROWCLOUGH**
Go to the village?

**FLETCHER**
I'd be willing to take that long walk on this mission of mercy.

**BARROWCLOUGH**
Well, I suppose . . . if you went straight there and back.

**FLETCHER**
What else, Mr Barrowclough? Man's life at stake. Need money, of course. Expensive those antibiotics.

**BARROWCLOUGH**
All right, well here, I've only got a pound.

**FLETCHER**
That should cover it.

**BARROWCLOUGH**
Now look, Fletcher –

**FLETCHER**
Mr Barrowclough please, every second counts.

*He goes.*

## 7. PUB

***In the pub Fletcher hands over a pound note to the landlord and takes a pint of beer.***

**LANDLORD**

Thank you, sir. You look as if you need that one.

**FLETCHER**

Thanks. I do, don't I? First one I've had for ages. Well, I'm not allowed, am I? Doctor says I'm not to drink – ulcer, you see. Can't take it any more. But just occasionally I have a little sip.

***He sinks back the pint in about three seconds flat and bangs the glass on the counter.***

**FLETCHER**

Fill it up, then.

***The landlord takes the glass.***

**FLETCHER**

Oh and six packets of crisps.

**LANDLORD**

With an ulcer?

**FLETCHER**

No – cheese and onion. Not for me, for the lads.

**LANDLORD**

Lads?

**FLETCHER**

What lads? Oh yes, what lads – oh well, we're working on the motorway, aren't we?

**LANDLORD**

What motorway?

**FLETCHER**

The . . . the *new* by-pass.

**LANDLORD**

But we've never heard of the new by-pass.

**FLETCHER**

No, it's that new, that's why you ain't heard of it. I've only just heard of it myself.

**LANDLORD**

But this is outrageous. This whole area's National Trust. What's the use in having a by-pass through here?

**FLETCHER**

Now look, mate, it's none of my doing, is it? I see your point of view, despoiling England's green and pleasant land, it worried me – that's how I got the ulcer, isn't it?

***The vicar and his verger walk into the pub.***

**VICAR**

Good morning all.

**VERGER**

Did you hear the thunder? It's going to p-pelt down in a minute.

**LANDLORD**

Vicar, have you heard?

**VICAR**

Heard what?

**LANDLORD**

They're building a new by-pass.

**VICAR**

Where?

**FLETCHER**

Where? Ah well. Over there, isn't it?

***He points vaguely in the direction of the Gents.***

**VICAR**
But what's the point of a by-pass? There's nothing to bypass, except for the prison, of course.

**FLETCHER**
What prison, eh?

**LANDLORD**
Six hundred bloody criminals on our doorstep.

**VICAR**
Now now, Frank, you mustn't pre-judge these men. They're serving their penance.

**FLETCHER**
Quite right, Rev. Public revenge, isn't it? Eye for an eye. Tooth for a nail.

**VICAR**
No, we must treat them with tolerance and compassion. I don't mean to sound pious but people must keep an open mind. My mind, like the doors of my church, is always open.

**FLETCHER**
Well spoken, Rev. Greater joy in heaven over a sinner what repenteth.

**VICAR**
Repenteth, yes indeed. I was wondering – would you like to –

**FLETCHER**
I would, yes. Pint, please.

**VICAR**
Oh fine, yes . . . would you do the honours Frank . . . in fact I was going to ask if you'd like to bring your chums over to evensong on Sunday.

**FLETCHER**
Oh? What? Well . . . much as we'd like to we may not be able to get out, er across. Tell you what, we'll come if we're free – all right? Cheers.

**OTHERS**
Cheers.

***Mackay walks in.***

**VICAR**
Ah here's a man with a different point of view. Morning, Mr Mackay.

**MACKAY**
Morning Padre, sir.

**LANDLORD/VERGER**
Morning, Mr Mackay.

**MACKAY**
Morning, gentlemen. Different point of view to what?

**VICAR**
To our friend here.

***They turn to Fletcher but he has gone.***

**LANDLORD**
Oh, where's he vanished to?

**VICAR**
Oh.

**MACKAY**
I'll have a whisky with a pint chaser.

**LANDLORD**
On duty?

**MACKAY**
I'm only half on duty. Got a works party down the road.

**VICAR**

Works party?

**MACKAY**

They're digging ditches down Felton Bank.

**VICAR**

Prisoners?

**MACKAY**

Oh yes.

**VICAR**

Verger, why don't you pop down to the church?

**VERGER**

But it's going to pour again any minute.

**VICAR**

You've got your bike, pop down and lock the church door.

**VERGER**

But why?

**VICAR**

You heard what he said – there's a bunch of criminals loose in the area.

## 8. PUB

***Verger walks out of the pub. He puts on his bicycle clips, then turns to bike but there's an empty space where his bicycle should have been.***

## 9. ROAD

***Fletcher is cycling along the road. He puts his hand in his jacket and gets out a beer mug. He drinks from it, then chucks the mug over a fence. Sheep bleat in the background. Fletcher cycles on down the road.***

## 10. CHURCH

***Inside Navyrum is showing Lennie his tattoos. The other members of the work party and Barrowclough are also present.***

**NAVYRUM**

This one was done in Valparaiso. That's in South America. Chile. Very Catholic country, Chile. Hence the religious overtones.

**LENNIE**

What's her name – Doris? Doesn't sound very Chilean.

**NAVYRUM**

No, she weren't. She were from Bootle. Stranded there with a juggling act. What with me being from the Pool that's how we got on so well, hence the affectionate overtones.

**LENNIE**

'I'll always . . .'

**NAVYRUM**

Don't read it out loud, son – not in here.

***Fletcher walks in.***

**FLETCHER**

What you all doing in here? You was just going out when I left.

**BARROWCLOUGH**

We heard the thunder and Navyrum assured me we were due for a heavy storm, him having been in the Navy he knows the signs. Well, have you got the ointment?

**FLETCHER**

Ointment?

**IVES**
I'm dying – 'ere listen.

**FLETCHER**
Oh, about the ointment, oh yes, thing is see the village shop it was closed, wasn't it? Closed for lunch hour.

**BARROWCLOUGH**
But it's only half-past eleven.

**FLETCHER**
Yeah well, it's not my fault, is it? They close for lunch earlier in the country, don't they, 'cos they get up earlier and they get hungry.

**IVES**
Oh come on, I'm in agony. I'm ablaze.

**FLETCHER**
Stick it in the font, then.

**IVES**
I might die.

**FLETCHER**
Anyone know the burial service?

**NAVYRUM**
I buried a bloke at sea once.

**FLETCHER**
Oh you're all right, Ives, then, there's a reservoir up the road.

**BARROWCLOUGH**
Oh dear, this day's turning into a disaster. Come on, there's not going to be any storm. It's passed over. We should be getting that ditch dug.

***He goes to the door.***

**LENNIE**
You crafty nurk, Fletch, you've been down the pub, ain't you?

**SCROUNGER**
You have, haven't you?

**FLETCHER**
Don't think I'd forget the lads, do you?

***He hands out packets of crisps.***

**FLETCHER**
Here you are, then. That'll put hair on your legs.

**BARROWCLOUGH**
Is all this out of my pound, Fletcher?

**FLETCHER**
It was, and me and the lads are more than grateful, aren't we?

**LENNIE**
Yes, Mr Barrowclough.

**SCROUNGER**
Thank you, Mr Barrowclough.

**NAVYRUM**
You're a toff, Mr Barrowclough.

**FLETCHER**
Eat up, lads. Now we've got all that protein inside us we can get on with the digging.

**BARROWCLOUGH**
Digging, yes, there's been precious little done so far. Come on, lads.

**SCROUNGER**
Come on, Ives, you're not dead yet.

**LENNIE**
That's funny, this door's stuck.

**FLETCHER**
Let's have a look. It's not stuck, it's locked.

## 11. ROAD AND DITCH

***The verger is walking along the***

*road. A van drives up to him and stops. Mackay gets out.*

**VERGER**

Someone's stolen my bike, I bet it's one of your lot.

**MACKAY**

Nonsense, my lot are hard at it. Without my say-so they wouldn't dare move.

*He moves to the ditch.*

**MACKAY**

All right, you lot.

*He looks down and sees an empty ditch.*

**MACKAY**

Oh my God, they've scarpered.

## 12. CHURCH

*The prisoners are locked in the church. Barrowclough has failed to find a way out and joins the others.*

**BARROWCLOUGH**

The vestry's locked as well – there's no other way out.

**IVES**

'Ere listen, we could break a window.

**FLETCHER**

That window's four hundred years old. This is a church, you nurk. Have you got no sense of reverence? You're a Palestine, that's what you are, a Palestine.

**BARROWCLOUGH**

Philistine, I think you mean.

**FLETCHER**

Yeah well, depends on your religion, don't it?

**DYLAN**

Let's ring the bell, some cat might hear that.

**BARROWCLOUGH**

They never use this bell. It's ancient, you see, like the tower. Last time it was heard in these parts was to warn the villagers of marauding Scots.

**FLETCHER**

Marauding Scots, was it?

**BARROWCLOUGH**

In the sixteenth century, yes. They came over the border, pillaging crops and, well, ravishing the womenfolk and all that.

**FLETCHER**

Oh well, that bell'll put the wind up a few vests, won't it? Probably all flee south with their possessions strapped to the back of their Vauxhall Vivas. Mind you, I reckon a few of the womenfolk might stay. Eh? I mean, it's been four hundred years since they had a good ravishin'.

**BARROWCLOUGH**

Can't you do something? You've been convicted for breaking and entering.

**FLETCHER**

Breaking and entering, yes. Entering, is the operative word. I ain't never been convicted for breaking out of nowhere.

**LENNIE**
Flippin' hell. We get one day out from nick and what happens. We get locked in.

## 13. FILM

***Camera shows a telephone dial. A finger is dialling.***

**MACKAY**
Chief Officer Barrett, Mackay here, sir . . . Mackay. Something has occurred, sir, to which I feel I ought to draw your attention.

***Camera shows a van. Mackay and Barrett are inside talking.***

**BARRETT**
Just down this road, are they?

**MACKAY**
Not any more, sir. I still say you should put out a full scale alarm, Mr Barrett.

**BARRETT**
And I still say your judgement is impaired, Mr Mackay. And I am not making a fool out of Slade Prison or burdening the taxpayer with a full scale alert until I have personally verified the facts.

***The van pulls up at the ditch and both men get out.***

**MACKAY**
What did I tell you, there, what did I tell you?

***The ditch is empty. The work party comes up and greets the officers.***

**BARROWCLOUGH**
(*Standing up*) Afternoon, Mr Barrett, sir. Mr Mackay. All present and correct, sir.

**BARRETT**
Pull yourself together, Mr Mackay.

***Fletcher winks at Barrowclough who is looking at him.***

## 14. CELL

***Fletcher, Lennie and Mackay are in Fletcher's cell.***

**MACKAY**
I have been dropped in it, have I not, Fletcher? I have been put upon from a great height.

**FLETCHER**
Oh dear, Mr Mackay. I'm sorry to hear that, Mr Mackay. Anything we can do to alleviate it, as it were?

**MACKAY**
When I am in it, Fletcher, I absorb it with a stiff upper lip.

**FLETCHER**
No choice have you, if you're up to (*Gesturing*) here in it.

**MACKAY**
Stand still. I absorb it with cool Celtic calm, like a man. And then I relieve my frustrations by making sure that everyone down the line below me suffers.

**FLETCHER**
What?

**MACKAY**
Suffers.

**LENNIE**
Hey, that's not fair.

**MACKAY**
Fair?
**LENNIE**
Why take it out on us? Nobody's fault we got locked in the church.
**FLETCHER**
Yeah, we might still be there now if it hadn't been for that funeral.
**MACKAY**
Why were you in the church to begin with if you weren't skiving? Abusing our trust. Taking advantage of Barrowclough's laxity.
**FLETCHER**
I didn't know Mr Barrowclough had laxity, did you, Lennie?
**LENNIE**
No, poor fellow. 'Cos we were miles from anywhere.
**MACKAY**
Godber.
**LENNIE**
Sir.
**MACKAY**
Do not imagine that you will be excluded from my spiteful resentment. Over the next few weeks you'll both suffer some terrible indignities. Your feet Fletcher, your dinky little size sevens, will not touch the floor. I harbour grudges.
***He goes out.***
**LENNIE**
He means it.
**FLETCHER**
Yeah well.
**LENNIE**
It was worth it though, weren't it, Fletch?
**FLETCHER**
'Course it was, my son. A day out. Pint of beer, bag of crisps. Ives in agony. All that and him being dropped in, wallop! We did all right, son.
**LENNIE**
You did better than most, Fletch.
**FLETCHER**
Yeah well, naturally.
**LENNIE**
I got something out the day meself.
**FLETCHER**
Oh yes. What?
**LENNIE**
Something I nicked from the church.
***He produces a crumpled surplice.***
**LENNIE**
A surplice.
**FLETCHER**
You stole? From the church?
**LENNIE**
It's the only place you can get 'em.
**FLETCHER**
What do you want it for anyway?
**LENNIE**
It'll satisfy a need I've had for some time, this will.
**FLETCHER**
What you talking about?
**LENNIE**
It's to cover me from the gravy when you talk with your mouth full.

# 1 SERIES ONE

## EPISODE FIVE: WAYS AND MEANS

### 1. PRISON WORKROOM

*Fletcher, Ives, McLaren and other prisoners are making fishing nets. Barrowclough is supervising them.*

**FLETCHER**

Oh shame on it.

**BARROWCLOUGH**

What's the matter?

**FLETCHER**

I've just dropped a stitch. (*Sewing*) Oh f . . .

**BARROWCLOUGH**

Is something wrong, Fletcher?

**FLETCHER**

'Course something's wrong. It's the job that's wrong, in' it? Grown men spending eight hours a day sewing fishing nets. Can you think of anything more demeaning or indignified?

**BARROWCLOUGH**

Mailbags. It's a step up from mailbags.

**MCLAREN**

This isn't a job, it's a punishment. Everyone in this room's being punished, 'cos we haven't been good little boys.

**IVES**

Pity you lost that cushy job on the farm, eh? Fresh air – free eggs every day.

**FLETCHER**

Free – more like half a dozen.

**BARROWCLOUGH**

I knew you were pilfering eggs.

*He walks across to Fletcher.*

**FLETCHER**

Yeah, well it's like young McLaren says. I'm being punished, in' I? What chance has a man got? When all the establishment forces are aligned against him.

**BARROWCLOUGH**

Now, Fletcher, you've been in prison long enough to know the score. You've broken the rules. You've upset Mr Mackay and you must accept the consequences.

**FLETCHER**

I thought you was going to appeal to the Governor on my behalf, Mr Barrowclough.

**BARROWCLOUGH**

The Governor has no time for you, Fletcher. He's very disappointed in you, just as I am.

**FLETCHER**

All right, Mr Barrowclough, all right. We knows society's extracting its revenge on those what never had a chance to begin with. Look at McLaren here. Never had a chance, have you, son?

**MCLAREN**

Cowing used to it, ain't I?

**BARROWCLOUGH**

Yes, he's being punished just like you.

**FLETCHER**

Why? What did he do?

**MCLAREN**

I spoilt the stinking soup.

**FLETCHER**

He spoilt the soup! And for that he has to pay the penance – well, what chance has any of us got?

**BARROWCLOUGH**

McLaren, that's not the whole truth as you well know. You spoilt the soup because you held a prison officer's head under it for two minutes.

**MCLAREN**

Yeah, well . . .

**BARROWCLOUGH**

You tried to drown that prison officer, McLaren. It was a vicious and unprovoked attack.

**FLETCHER**

(*Amused*) Tried to drown him!

**MCLAREN**

He cowing asked for it.

**BARROWCLOUGH**

You could have severely scalded him.

**FLETCHER**

Not in this nick you couldn't. Not with the lukewarm soup we get. Poisoned him possibly, yeah, could have poisoned him.

**IVES**

What sort of soup, was it?

**MCLAREN**

Mixed vegetable.

**FLETCHER**

Mixed vegetable. Stone me. I bet he was furious. All those bits of barley and carrot up his nose.

**BARROWCLOUGH**

It's not funny, Fletcher. It was a vicious attack, and that's why McLaren's here. And your attitude makes it quite clear why you're here.

**FLETCHER**

Oh I see, yes, well. Yes, well, I see, yes, well.

**MCLAREN**

I was provoked.

**FLETCHER**

I bet you were, my son.

**MCLAREN**

He called me a black bastard.

**BARROWCLOUGH**

Now if that were true if he really did say that, you could have gone straight to the Governor, McLaren.

**FLETCHER**

Oh yeah, fat chance. I mean technically he ain't got a leg to stand on. Technically the facts as stated by the prison officer are not wholly inaccurate. Being as how he is 'a' negroid, and 'b' illegitimate.

**MCLAREN**

It was the way he said it.

**FLETCHER**

I know that. You know that. He'll probably tell the Governor that in the course of conversation he simply observed that you were non-caucasian and born out of wedlock.

**BARROWCLOUGH**

Now that's enough talking, all of you. Work to be done.

**FLETCHER**

Work! Knitting string vests for hippopotamuses. This probably won't fit me anyway. They're cunning, ain't they? 'Cos giving you a job like this, they knows that we won't cock it up. They knows we wouldn't do nothing slipshod, 'cos we'd be screwing up those brave fishermen of England, wouldn't we? Leave a few holes in here and they'd be coming back half a ton of cod short. And the price of fish fingers would rocker. Not to mention cod pieces. Whereas of course mailbags, well – don't care if we do a sloppy job there, do we? It makes it easier for our mates that rob mail trains.

**BARROWCLOUGH**

Fletcher, one just has to listen to you for a matter of minutes to know your type. When you first came here I had high hopes for you, I won't pretend I didn't. It has to be said, you're surly and hostile.

**FLETCHER**

Yeah, well, years of prison hardens you, doesn't it? Well-known fact.

**BARROWCLOUGH**

But you've only been here six weeks.

**FLETCHER**

I'm not really hostile, I'm just resentful. Well, when I first come in here I thought between the two of us there was some sort of rapport there, you know?

**BARROWCLOUGH**

(*Sitting down next to Fletcher*) You mean you thought I was 'in your pocket' – is that the term for it?

**FLETCHER**

Terrible thing to say. What a terrible thing to say. Just 'cos I asked you one or two little favours. What a terrible thing to say! In themselves they was meaningless but they would just have made life that little bit more tolerable.

**BARROWCLOUGH**

Your little favours were supposed to include getting you a new cell, with a window facing south-west, not to mention the extra blankets and the bit of carpet, the special soap, extra tobacco, carpet slippers, a set of darts, a roll of soft toilet paper and some Kendal mint cake.

**FLETCHER**

All right, don't exaggerate. I said you needn't bother with the darts if you were pushed.

**BARROWCLOUGH**

Now, I haven't forgotten that you've given me very helpful advice on . . . domestic matters. Don't think Mrs Barrowclough and I don't appreciate that 'cos we do. But I'll be damned if I'll let you treat me like some glorified batman.

**FLETCHER**

I ain't just referring to your . . . marital problems. Though one can't help reflect that there's been some change in your old lady's attitude . . .

**BARROWCLOUGH**

How can you tell that?

**FLETCHER**

Oh just little things. In the morning your general demeanour. A spring in your step. That certain smile that plays around your lips when you comes round in the morning ordering us to slop out.

**BARROWCLOUGH**

What certain smile?

**FLETCHER**

The smile of a man who's getting his oats.

**BARROWCLOUGH**

(*Embarrassed*) Fletcher!

**FLETCHER**

Are you denying it?

**BARROWCLOUGH**

Look, I've said I'm grateful.

**FLETCHER**

Oh yes. Well, yes. I don't want your gratitude, Mr Barrowclough. I've learnt my lesson. It's them and us.

**BARROWCLOUGH**

Look, Fletcher –

**FLETCHER**

Now, if you'll excuse me, I must get back to my knitting. Talking to you I'm getting all behind like a cow's tail. I might not get my full sixty pee this week. Sixty pee a week . . . Still it's just enough money to cover the cost of a jar of Wintergreen Ointment. 'Cos all my money goes on medicaments. 'Cos I've never been a well man. Always been suspect to lumbago and rheumatics . . . all those illnesses what are caused by not having enough blankets, having a cold draughty cell facing north-east, and walking around on concrete floors without carpet slippers.

**BARROWCLOUGH**

I'll see about the extra blanket.

**FLETCHER**

No. No, no, no, no. I want nothing from you or no one. Nothing, nothing, nothing . . .

***Barrowclough moves.***

**FLETCHER**
Well, there is one thing, since you insist. One very minor thing.

**BARROWCLOUGH**
What thing?

**FLETCHER**
I want a job in the library.

## 2A. FLETCHER'S CELL

***He is washing his blistered hands. Fletcher's cell door is open as it is association hour.***

**FLETCHER**
Gawd Almighty. I hope the fishermen of England flaming appreciate me. I won't never play the harpsichord again. I doubt if I'll even be able to wipe me own nose.

***Fletcher picks up a towel and bar of soap and leaves his cell.***

## 2B. PRISON LANDING

***As he goes out he collides with McLaren, causing him to drop a newspaper, a couple of oranges and his metal comb.***

**MCLAREN**
Cowing hell.

**FLETCHER**
Sorry, son, sorry.

**MCLAREN**
(*Threateningly*) Can't you watch where you're cowing going, Fletcher?

**FLETCHER**
(*Backing off*) I've said I'm sorry, son. My fault, my fault. Won't happen again. Promise you.

**MCLAREN**
Watch it.

**FLETCHER**
I will, son. I promise. No borra, eh? I'm not a well man.

***McLaren gives him another evil glance, then bends down to pick up his oranges.***

***As he does so his head is facing inside Fletcher's cell.***

**FLETCHER**
I don't want no trouble with you, McLaren.

***He kicks him up the backside causing him to fall on his face inside Fletcher's cell.***

## 2C. CELL

***Before McLaren can recover, Fletcher has grabbed the kid by the collar and hauled him to his feet, pushed him over the table, their faces a couple of inches apart. Fletcher speaks to him, disguising his genuine threat with a gentle, reasonable voice.***

**FLETCHER**
Now I know you're an 'ard case, son.

We all do. We know you're full of nasty militant feelings. But if you ever speaks to me like that again, I shall twist your head round like a cork in a bottle of Beaujolais. Pull it off and give it to that poof Roland in B Block to keep his wigs on.

**MCLAREN**

(*Choking*) Yes, Fletch.

**FLETCHER**

And are we sorry?

**MCLAREN**

Yes we are, Fletch.

**FLETCHER**

Right. Don't lie about there. Got any snout?

**MCLAREN**

No.

**FLETCHER**

There's some under that pillow. Help yourself.

**MCLAREN**

Oh ta.

***As he does so Fletcher picks up the oranges, the paper and the comb.***

**FLETCHER**

Here you are – here's your things. Your own worst enemy, ain't you, son?

***He sits down.***

**MCLAREN**

Oh yes?

**FLETCHER**

Sit down, sit down. I know things ain't easy for you. Being black with a Scottish father. I mean, it's an unfortunate mixture. It's the Scottish side what brings out all that aggression in you.

**MCLAREN**

Is it?

**FLETCHER**

Yeah, course it is. I mean, it subdues your basic West Indian personality. Which is one of exuberant high spirits. All them steel bands, and carnivals, like. Lordy Lordy bit. Someone just has to score a boundary in a test match and they have a firework display.

**MCLAREN**

I've never set foot in the West Indies. I was born in Greenock. Or at least found. Some copper found me up an alley wrapped in a *Glasgow Herald*.

**FLETCHER**

Yeah, well, I did admit, didn't I, you ain't had it easy.

**MCLAREN**

I never knew my father. Mam who didn't want me. Flaming orphanage, and I'm black with a Scottish accent. What you want me to be, Fletcher, happy-go-bloody-lucky?

**FLETCHER**

It could be worse, son, couldn't it?

**MCLAREN**

Could it?

**FLETCHER**
(*Thinks hard*) . . . No, I don't suppose it could, in all honesty. But you don't want to let that illegitimate tag worry you. Lots of famous people was illegitimate. Royalty like. And William the Conqueror . . . Lawrence of Arabia . . . Leonardo da Vinci . . . Napper Wainwright.

**MCLAREN**
Who's Napper Wainwright?

**FLETCHER**
He was a screw in Brixton . . . mind you, he was a right bastard.

**MCLAREN**
Never let you forget.

**FLETCHER**
It ain't a stigma no more. Not these days, in these liberated times. Out of fashion, marriage is. All these glamour people, these trendsetters, your pop stars and television personalities, well all their offspring's outta wedlock, isn't it? Frankly, in a few years time, illegitimates is going to be fashionable figures. Like homosexuals are at the moment. In fact, being an illegitimate black poof's about as chic as you could get.

**MCLAREN**
(*Rising*) I'm not a –

**FLETCHER**
Oh come on, I know that –

**MCLAREN**
If anyone suggests –

**FLETCHER**
'Course no one won't. See the way you fly off the handle? Own worst enemy. Come the hard man, where's it get you?

**MCLAREN**
Got me pride.

***Sits back on the bunk.***

**FLETCHER**
Oh yes, pride is it? Listen, we ain't even got privacy in here, and where's a man's pride when he ain't got no privacy! You have to learn to turn the other cheek. Yes sir, no sir, three bags full, sir.

**MCLAREN**
Makes me sick to my guts.

**FLETCHER**
(*Rising and sitting at the bottom of the bunk*) Look sonny Jim, sonny Jock. You're nipping along the by-pass in a restricted area, right? And the police stop you. Then you think – what have I done, what's their game? So you leaps out the car and really has a go at them. 'Cos you're not going to take no stick from some jumped-up copper who's been watching too many *Z Cars*. In other words, you come on strong. So what happens? A night in the cooler – fifty-pound fine, lose your licence for six months. And they'd only stopped you to point out your rear light was wonky.

**MCLAREN**
Don't see the point.

**FLETCHER**
The point is if you'd leapt out, all smarmy and subservient, 'What, constable, my off-side rear? My word, constable – what a blessing you boys in blue are so diligent.' And it's cost you nothing has it? Except your pride and two tickets to the Police Ball.

**MCLAREN**
You obviously had no reason to hate the law like me. I hate 'em all. They even open letters from my girlfriend.

**FLETCHER**
Oh yeah. Passionate, are they?

**MCLAREN**
I can't enjoy them if I feel that lot's read 'em already. It's not right.

**FLETCHER**
'Course it ain't right, son, but they still do it, don't they? We've all had that. I was on remand once in Brixton. I done this job – a jeweller's in Southwark. Only they got me, but they didn't get the stuff, see. I hadn't . . . you know what I mean. (*Indicating stashing it*) I'd . . . So I'm in Brixton. And I writes to my old lady, Isobel, and says how sorry I was that I got done. Then I says, 'As you may well be a bit short this winter without me providing why don't you plant your own vegetables? I suggest you dig over the back garden as soon as possible.' 'Course next morning there's twelve police round there with shovels, the devious nurks.

**MCLAREN**
Typical. Did they find the stuff?

**FLETCHER**
'Course they didn't, it was in the bottom drawer of the wardrobe. Just my way of getting the garden turned over, see. Why let Isobel do it when you've got twelve great big nosey coppers with spades – if you'll pardon the expression.

**MCLAREN**
You crafty nurk.

**FLETCHER**
We had some beautiful broccoli with Christmas dinner. I wrote to her next and suggested she swept the chimney, but they wouldn't buy that one.

**MCLAREN**
I get your point. You beat them at their own game.

**FLETCHER**
Subtle. Certainly more subtle than immersing a screw in the soup of the day.

**MCLAREN**
Wait till it's pea soup next time. Drown quicker in pea soup, it's thicker. Or maybe semolina pudding.

**FLETCHER**
How long you in for, son?

**MCLAREN**
Three years.

**FLETCHER**
You ain't going to be out for ten, the way you're going. Remission's all that counts. Gettin' out of here. I used to be like you once. Not 'ard but lairy, you know. Knew it all. But I wants out. And your time would come that bit sooner if you learned to turn the other cheek.

**MCLAREN**
I'm not as bad as people make out, you know. I ain't hit a screw for three months.

**FLETCHER**
No, you ain't actually hit one. But apart from the soup incident, you've tripped one down a flight of stairs, locked one in the deep freeze, caught one in the goolies with a football and put an overdose of cascara in the Padre's cocoa.

**MCLAREN**
Got a lot of pleasure out of that.

**FLETCHER**
Yeah, and a lot of solitary. Not as much as the Padre got. He was shut in the bog all week.

**MCLAREN**
Welfare Officer wants me to see a psychiatrist. Observation like. Thinks I need psychiatric help,

**FLETCHER**
Would you mind that?

**MCLAREN**
'Course not. I'd be crazy to turn it down. Cushy, hospital. Better grub, soft bed.

**FLETCHER**
So when you going to see him then?

**MCLAREN**
I'm not. Governor wouldn't wear it, would he? Said he knew my sort, I was trying it on.

**FLETCHER**
Yeah, he's shrewder than we credit him for, that Venables. It's my problem, see. Trying to ingratiate myself back in his good books. I've lost a lot of ground in the credibility stakes.

**MCLAREN**
Well thanks, Fletch, like. It's been more use than talking to the Welfare Officer.

**FLETCHER**
Turn the other cheek, son.

**MCLAREN**
I'll try. I know you're right in principle, like.

**FLETCHER**
For your own good.

**MCLAREN**
You're straight you are, Fletcher. Bloke can trust you.

**FLETCHER**
Don't forget your things.

**MCLAREN**
Oh, thanks. Where's me orange?

**FLETCHER**
Dunno son – in't it outside on the floor?

**MCLAREN**
(*Looking*) No, it's not there.

**FLETCHER**
Someone's had it – bunch of criminals in here, aren't they?

**MCLAREN**
Oh cowing heck. All right, tata Fletch.

**FLETCHER**
Mind how you go.

***McLaren leaves. Fletcher gets the orange out of his pocket and starts to peel it.***

## 3. FOOTBALL PITCH

***Mackay blows his whistle and leaves the shot. A fight ensues among the players.***
***Mackay moves to the players to separate them.***
***Barrowclough and Fletcher are watching.***
***Mackay and the players argue. He sends McLaren off.***

**BARROWCLOUGH**
He's got a natural talent that lad, but that's the third sending off in four games – it'll mean suspension.

**FLETCHER**
Own worst enemy.

**BARROWCLOUGH**
You know that lad needs help.

**FLETCHER**
Yeah . . . maybe I'm the one who could help him.

***Camera shows the players and Mackay again. He blows his whistle and drops the ball.***
***An alarm bell sounds.***

## 4. CELL

***It is association hour and the cell door is open. Fletcher is sitting on the bottom bunk reading. The alarm bell is still ringing.***
***Barrowclough enters and walks across to the window.***

**FLETCHER**
If that's for me tell them I'll ring back.

**BARROWCLOUGH**
It's McLaren.

**FLETCHER**
Oh he's gone over the wall, has he?

**BARROWCLOUGH**
He's on the roof and he won't come down. Threatening to chuck himself over, unless we answer his demands.

**FLETCHER**
Oh yes.

***He gets up and walks to the table.***

**BARROWCLOUGH**

Get the prison a bad name this sort of thing. If we don't get him down it'll be on *News at Ten*.

**FLETCHER**

(*Sitting on the chair*) Oh yes. Then *Panorama*. *World in Action*. Then the six-part serial in the *Sunday Times*, taking the lid off the penal system.

**BARROWCLOUGH**

It upsets the men this sort of thing.

**FLETCHER**

They'll be banging their mugs playing the *Anvil Chorus* on the radiators. You could have a full-scale riot on your hands by tea-time – hang about. What day is it?

**BARROWCLOUGH**

Thursday.

**FLETCHER**

Oh no, they won't riot this afternoon. Good tea on a Thursday, in' it? Cauliflower cheese.

**BARROWCLOUGH**

Fletcher, you take nothing seriously. There's a man's life in danger, to say nothing of the reputation of Slade Prison.

**FLETCHER**

Oh dear, we don't want to lose our goodwill do we? Or we won't get any bookings for next season.

**BARROWCLOUGH**

Your flippancy is in very bad taste at a time like this.

**FLETCHER**

How are they trying to get him down?

**BARROWCLOUGH**

At the moment the Padre's trying to talk him down through a megaphone.

**FLETCHER**

The Padre? Is he sober? I mean, the village pub's just closed, isn't it?

**BARROWCLOUGH**

He's not alone. He's with the Welfare Officer, Mr Gillespie.

**FLETCHER**

What's he know – the lad's just out of university. Got no experience of the practical. He's probably thumbing through his textbooks now. Trying to find the chapter on Negro nutters and how to deal with them.

**BARROWCLOUGH**

I think you're being a bit hard on Mr Gillespie.

**FLETCHER**

Mr Barrowclough! Permission to see the Governor.

***He is putting on his jacket.***

**BARROWCLOUGH**

What! Not now, Fletcher. Perhaps when it's all over.

**FLETCHER**

It's about now that I want to talk.

About the lad. I think I might be able to help.

**BARROWCLOUGH**

Help the lad?

**FLETCHER**

Come on then, are you going to take me or not?

**BARROWCLOUGH**

Well, I will if you think it might help – but Mr Mackay's in charge.

**FLETCHER**

There you are then. Anything's better than leaving it to Mr Mackay. He'd probably just let the lad jump . . .

***Barrowclough goes.***

**FLETCHER**

. . . and then jump on him.

## 5. PRISON GOVERNOR'S OFFICE

***Fletcher and Barrowclough are standing in front of the Governor's desk. Mackay walks across and to the left of Fletcher.***

**VENABLES**

In the circumstances I'm willing to listen to anybody. But what makes you think you can achieve what we can't, Fletcher? Do you know something we don't?

**FLETCHER**

I know something about what makes the lad tick. I'm not saying you're not an experienced man in these matters, Mr Venables. As is Mr Mackay here and Mr Gillespie and the Padre. But in his mind you all represent the establishment which only inflames his feelings of hostility and persecution. I mean the Padre's been out there rabbiting for two hours, and all he's had for his trouble's a brick up his megaphone.

**VENABLES**

(*To Mackay*) How is the Padre?

**MACKAY**

He's very upset, sir. Very upset that he couldn't get through to the man. Very upset also about losing two of his front teeth.

**BARROWCLOUGH**

There'll be no sermon on Sunday.

**VENABLES**

Thank heaven for small mercies.

**FLETCHER**

You see, it's a question of attitude, isn't it, sir? Last thing the lad wanted was all that preaching and sermonising. Same with our well-meaning intrepid Mr Gillespie. Asked for trouble, didn't he, going up that ladder.

**VENABLES**

How is Mr Gillespie?

**MACKAY**

As comfortable as could be expected, sir.

**BARROWCLOUGH**

We must do something. We can't leave McLaren where he is, sir.

**MACKAY**
Why not? Let him sweat it out. Then tonight when that cold wind comes whistling over the Pennines, let him freeze it out. If we give way to him by just one inch, we'll establish a regrettable precedent. We'll have prisoners crawling on every inch of rooftop, clamouring for extra blankets, cleaner sheets, bigger helpings.

**FLETCHER**
On the other hand –

**VENABLES**
Yes?

**FLETCHER**
On the other hand, I could go up and talk to the lad. He don't trust you lot, right? And you can't send for friends or family 'cos the lad ain't got none. But maybe – and I say maybe – he may respond to the overtures of one of his fellow inmates.

**MACKAY**
Poppycock!

**VENABLES**
Quiet, Mr Mackay. There is a point here, a very good point. It could be quite dangerous, Fletcher.

**FLETCHER**
Yes, yes. I know. I'm aware that I'm putting life and limb in some jeopardy. But you try not to think about things like that. Try to ignore the tight knot of fear in the stomach, which I ain't had since Kuala Lumpur.

**VENABLES**
Kuala Lumpur?

**FLETCHER**
Yes, I was there National Service. Fighting those Malayan bandits for Queen and Country. Jungle warfare. Wading through swamps up to here, rifle above your head to keep the barrel dry. (*To Mackay*) You know what I mean. You'd had some of that, sir. Suddenly you're in a clearing, there'd be nothing but the sound of the night creatures in the undergrowth, and Taffy Williams's stomach rumbling. Anyway –

**VENABLES**
Has this any relevance to McLaren's predicament?

**FLETCHER**
Oh. Only to show that I'm no stranger to danger.

**BARROWCLOUGH**
Do you know I was in Singapore for my National Service. RAF Equipment.

**FLETCHER**
Oh, Singapore. Doddle, Singapore. We'd have given our eyeteeth for Singapore. All them historical temples and hysterical brothels.

**VENABLES**
Gentlemen, there's a man on the roof.

**MACKAY**
Sir, we cannot let a prisoner go up. We have to deal with our own problems, we can't leave them in the hands of a prisoner.

**FLETCHER**

Oh, in that case, sir, then we might as well accept the alternative.

**VENABLES**

What alternative?

**FLETCHER**

You'll have to go up.

## 6. PRISON BUILDINGS

*McLaren is on the rooftop waving. Camera shows emergency vehicles and people watching, among them a fireman, a medical orderly, a warder. Fletcher walks into shot, looks up at the roof and then at the fire engine. Camera zooms to the ladder. Fletcher looks at it.*

**MACKAY**

Cold feet, eh?

**FLETCHER**

What me? No never. Let's get on with it.

*He leaves the shot.*

**MACKAY**

Kuala Lumpur!

*Fletcher starts climbing up the ladder.*

*Mackay is watching him.*

*The fireman is working the levers on the engine as Fletcher goes up the ladder. It extends.*

*Fletcher looks down at the scene below and looks horrified.*

*The fireman is watching him.*

*Fletcher reaches the roof gutter and starts to get off.*

**MCLAREN**

Hi, Fletch. Lovely view up here.

*Fletcher is panting on the edge of the roof.*

**MCLAREN**

Hey watch out for them slates, they're a bit dodgy.

**FLETCHER**

Yeah, yeah.

*He scrambles up on the roof.*

**FLETCHER**

High enough, in' it?

**MCLAREN**

It was your idea. You said climb a roof.

**FLETCHER**

Did you have to pick such a high one? I'm not a bleedin' steeplejack if you are.

**MCLAREN**

Makes you look more of a hero. Got more dramatic impact.

**FLETCHER**

Don't use words like impact, will you? Not at this height.

**MCLAREN**

Want a bit of chewing gum?

**FLETCHER**

'Course I don't. Let's get down off of here.

**MCLAREN**

We can't go yet. You're supposed to talk me out of it. I'm a nutter, remember. We'll be up here at least an hour before I succumb to your eloquent persuasion.

**FLETCHER**

An hour? I've got vertigo. I'm sick. I'm dizzy.

**MCLAREN**

We'll go down in time for tea. It's cauliflower cheese today, isn't it?

***Fletcher falls out of shot. Slates rushing past. Barrowclough reacts to Fletcher's falling.***

***Mackay reacts. The camera reveals Fletcher is astride the chimney pot.***

**MCLAREN**

Hey, Fletch, where you going – it's not teatime yet.

***Fletcher is perched on the edge of the roof.***

## 7. PRISON HOSPITAL

***It is a small ward with seven beds in it. Only one is occupied, by Ives. A breezy-looking Fletcher enters, pushing a trolley with books on it.***

**FLETCHER**

Ding-dong, Fletcher calling. Your friendly mobile library!

**IVES**

'Ere listen –

**FLETCHER**

Oh, it's you Ives – how'd you work this number?

**IVES**

What d'you mean, I'm ill – gastro-enteritis.

**FLETCHER**

Oh, they're not difficult symptoms to fake. Keep running to the bog every five minutes clutching your stomach and screaming in agony.

**IVES**

I didn't fake nothing. I really got it.

**FLETCHER**

(*Looking at chart*) Oh, that's unusual. Must be some sort of record, a genuine illness in this hospital.

**IVES**

What about you? I heard you was in here last week.

**FLETCHER**

I had a few bruises, but they say I can still have children.

**IVES**

I heard it was shock. They told me you couldn't stop shaking for two days.

**FLETCHER**

All right, Ives – wouldn't you be shaking after an heroic ascent like that?

**IVES**

Your descent weren't so heroic. The kid had to bring you down on his back.

**FLETCHER**

Look, don't needle me, Ives. Otherwise you won't be getting anything worth reading off here at all. I shall be palming you off with *Lamb's Tales from Shakespeare* without benefit of mint sauce.

**IVES**

'Ere listen –

**FLETCHER**

No, you listen to me, Ives. That little rooftop caper was all set up, it was all arranged between McLaren and me. He went up there so I could rescue him.

**IVES**

Oh yeah.

**FLETCHER**

All right, I didn't expect to get a dizzy turn like I did. But at least I goes up a hero and he comes down one. As a result of which I have leapfrogged my way back into the Governor's good books. My slate is clean and all my misdemeanours is writ off. And here I am – assistant librarian. And the kid McLaren, who they've decided to treat with sympathy and understanding . . .

**IVES**

Yeah, I've seen him – hospital orderly – cushy number. 'Ere listen, what about a decent book – know what I mean.

**FLETCHER**

You mean something a bit risqué.

**IVES**

Won't be risky, I won't tell anyone.

**FLETCHER**

Risqué means dirty, you nurk.

**IVES**

Oh dirty, yes. That's what I mean, yes.

**FLETCHER**

Well, I could offer you this one – it's all about the sex-starved lady pygmies of the Malaysian jungle.

**IVES**

What's it called?

**FLETCHER**

*Little Women.*

**IVES**

*Little Women.*

**FLETCHER**

It's an erotic classic. Don't you remember that trial at the Old Bailey?

**IVES**

Er, vaguely like. 'Ere, what's it doing in the prison library?

**FLETCHER**

Library? What? I nicked that from the Governor's private bookshelf. It was concealed next to the tropical fish year book for 1973. Here listen to this . . .

*He opens the book and starts reading.*

**FLETCHER**

'She come out of the clearing her flimsy shift soaked by the sudden monsoon. Through it Gilbert could discern the firm contours of her proud young Malaysian body. She stood there unashamed staring him straight in the kneecap. She was everything that he had imagined on that long train ride from Kuala

Lumpur. He gazed in awe at her half-naked uptilted perfectly formed –'

*He shuts the book.*

**IVES**

'Ere listen, perfectly formed what, perfectly formed what?

**FLETCHER**

I'll give you a clue. There was two of them, and they went up and down when she ran, and I don't mean her eyebrows. Now if you was to borrow this torrid saga of Malaysian love rites, well it could be yours for only two snouts, couldn't it?

**IVES**

Done.

**FLETCHER**

In advance.

**IVES**

Done.

**FLETCHER**

You certainly have been.

***He wheels the trolley off. As he does so, McLaren comes up with another trolley and they bump into each other.***

**MCLAREN**

Just watch it, you clumsy nurk.

**FLETCHER**

Hey, hey, hey. Have we learnt nothing? Where did that ever get us?

**MCLAREN**

Oh . . . sorry, Mr Fletcher.

**FLETCHER**

That's all right, Mr McLaren. And how's things in the medical world?

**MCLAREN**

Cushy, Mr Fletcher. And the library?

**FLETCHER**

A doddle, Mr McLaren.

**MCLAREN**

Did you get me *The Godfather*?

**FLETCHER**

Did you get me the Wintergreen Ointment?

***McLaren hands Fletcher the ointment and Fletcher hands McLaren the book.***

# 1 SERIES ONE

## EPISODE SIX: MEN WITHOUT WOMEN

### 1. PRISON

***Camera shows the prison warder. Then zooms to Warren who is sweeping. He looks and sees Fletcher planting flowers.***

***Warren glances at the warder, then moves towards Fletcher.***

**WARREN**

'Ere, Fletch . . .

**FLETCHER**

Naff off. I'm thinking.

**WARREN**

Thinking?

**FLETCHER**

Yes – thinking. I realise, Warren, that to you and the rest of that lot, thinking is an alien pastime. But some of us – more endowed with a bit of grey matter where it matters, namely up here, preserve our identity and sanity in this place by thinking.

**WARREN**

But what are you thinking?

**FLETCHER**

At the moment I'm thinking 'Why won't this bloke Warren naff off and leave me alone?'

**WARREN**

Look, Fletch, I realise you're a man of . . .

**FLETCHER**

Intellect.

**WARREN**

Intellect, yes –

**FLETCHER**

And erudition.

**WARREN**

That an' all, Fletch, if you say so. But that was why I wanted to have a word, see. I got this letter . . .

***He produces a letter.***

**FLETCHER**

(*Taking letter*) Oh yes. Yes. From a woman, I would assess.

**WARREN**

That's right. How can you tell?

**FLETCHER**

It's in the handwriting, isn't it?

***The warder is approaching. Fletcher drops the letter and starts to dig.***

*The warder walks past.*
*Warren reacts to letter being buried.*
*Fletcher stops digging after warder has passed and bends down to pick up the letter. He sniffs at it.*

**FLETCHER**
Female handwriting, in' it? And judging by the stationery and the perfume, a woman of little sophistication or class.
*He hands the letter back to Warren.*

**WARREN**
That's right, it's from the wife.

**FLETCHER**
Oh, I don't mean to infer –

**WARREN**
No, you're a clever bloke, Fletch. That's why I wanted your help, really.

**FLETCHER**
Oh, I see another one. My counsel is it? Advice to the lovelorn. Now you want me to assess the situation and compose an appropriate response.

**WARREN**
No, it's simpler than that . . . Just want you to read it to me . . .

## 2. ASSOCIATION ROOM

*Fletcher is sitting at a table with Warren, Heslop, Lukewarm and Tolly. He has Warren's letter in front of him.*

**FLETCHER**
Now, this letter of Warren's – it's very, very typical. It's your classic wives' letter after you've done eight months to a year – that sort of period. I mean wives make all those marital vows, but you have to be around to make sure they do love, honour and obey, don't you?

**TOLLY**
Yuh.

**WARREN**
Right.

**HESLOP**
Yes.

**LUKEWARM**
How true.

**FLETCHER**
You see, after a while a wife gets restless urges. So having got restless, chances are they weaken and gets naughty.
*Warren thumps his fist against the table.*

**WARREN**
I'll kill her. I'll throttle her.

**FLETCHER**
Yes . . . that is one solution, but what we're looking for here is something a little more constructive. Besides, you're in here and she's in Bolton.

**WARREN**
It's visiting day next week.

**FLETCHER**
Yes, yes, we know. But if you was to strangle your wife on visiting day there's a good chance you'd lose half your remission.

**WARREN**

I'm just saying.

**LUKEWARM**

Ooh, he's so impulsive.

**WARREN**

I'm just saying.

**TOLLY**

Leave it off, Warren. Leave it to Fletch, he knows, doesn't he?

**FLETCHER**

Thank you, Tolly, for the vote of confidence. Now, where was I?

**LUKEWARM**

Just getting to the naughty bit.

**FLETCHER**

Oh yes. Now having got naughty she gets guilty. So in my reply that I've written out here I have sought to achieve subtlety with strength. An obvious display of affection but carrying beneath it a hint of menace.

***The others murmur. Fletcher starts reading.***

**FLETCHER**

'My darling – I realise these are difficult times for you. Here we are, men without women – and you are women without men with all your attendant frustrations' – nice phrase that, isn't it?

***They murmur assent.***

**LUKEWARM**

Well chosen.

**FLETCHER**

Got it out of the *Reader's Digest*. 'I realise my love, that it is a lot to ask, to ask you to wait for me. But I will be upset, dearest one, if I hear about you having a nibble of something you shouldn't. In other words, dear heart, I have friends on the outside, who have friends who have friends. And any word of hanky panky will be followed by swift and merciless retribution. I hope the weather is nice and you are feeling well in yourself. Yours etc.' – blah, blah, blah.

**LUKEWARM**

Subtlety with strength, oh yes.

**TOLLY**

Very good, Fletch. I told you, Warren, Fletch knows.

**HESLOP**

My wife's sister lives in Sidcup. And sometimes we stay there, or drop in for a cuppa when we bin to the coast.

***The others exchange looks.***

**HESLOP**

(*Leaning forward*) Anyhow, once we was there, and while my wife was upstairs powdering her nose prior to going to see *Paint Your Wagon* by the Sidcup Operatic, her sister touched me.

***There is an expectant pause, but Heslop fails to go on.***

**FLETCHER**

Where, where?

**HESLOP**

In the kitchen. She got very . . . heated. Had me pressed up against the Aga.

**FLETCHER**

'Spect you got fairly heated then didn't you, up against the Aga?

**HESLOP**
She was saying how she'd always fancied me, she knew it was wrong, being as she was the wife's sister, but she couldn't control her true feelings no longer. I had to say 'Now listen Gwendolyn' – that was her name, see – I said, 'Listen, Gwendolyn, this is no way to behave. It's not right, it isn't decent and what happened must never happen again.'

**WARREN**
But nothing did happen.

**FLETCHER**
All you did was give her a lecture.

**HESLOP**
That was an hour later when we were getting out of bed.

**FLETCHER**
Look, look, what point is it you're making, Einstein? You're on a different time scale to all the rest of us. His head's about twenty minutes slow. Now then, I'd done copies of this letter . . . (*Starts distributing them*) . . . there's one for each of you. You just have to write 'em out in your own handwriting. I'll do yours Warren for a small fee, as you can't write. And of course you must fill in the names of your loved ones. (*To Heslop*) My beloved Iris . . . (*To Tolly*) My darling Norma . . . (*To Lukewarm*) My dearest Trevor. Now post these sharp 'cos we want them to read these before they comes up visiting day. So that they can be duly humble and apprehensive.

**HESLOP**
There's no evidence that my Iris has strayed from the straight and narrow.

**FLETCHER**
What? Oh well, post it in any case. A stitch in time saves a hole in the trousers.

**HESLOP**
Oh right, I'll post it then.

**FLETCHER**
No sense leaving these things to the last minute.

***A bell sounds.***

**FLETCHER**
Now gentlemen, haven't we forgotten something?

**WARREN**
Oh yes, fair's fair. Cough up, lads.

***They all produce little tins of tobacco and hand over a hand-rolled cigarette.***

**TOLLY**
You got no problem on this score then, Fletch? Marriage, like?

**FLETCHER**
No, no. I been married a bit longer than you lad, ain't I? And she knows her place.

**LUKEWARM**
Doesn't she get upset that you keep going inside all the time?

**FLETCHER**
I don't keep going inside all the time.

**LUKEWARM**
You are fairly consistent. And she's got a home and three kids to run – I don't know how she does it, I don't know how she does it.

**FLETCHER**
Oh, I'm not saying it ain't hard, obviously. A few weeks ago she had to build a new coal bunker. That's a terrible job for a woman, isn't it?

**LUKEWARM**
You mean she had to mix all the cement and all that?

**FLETCHER**
Oh no, no, no, that was all right. Her mother came over and did that.

**BARROWCLOUGH**
Come on now, lads . . . Well, Fletcher, have you employed yourself usefully this evening?

**FLETCHER**
Just giving the lads the benefit of my experience, Mr Barrowclough.

**BARROWCLOUGH**
I've heard that your opinion is sought in this prison. Mr Gillespie, the Welfare Officer, he was saying he's running out of customers.

**FLETCHER**
Yeah, well, Welfare Officers – like the Padre, they're not to be trusted.

**BARROWCLOUGH**
I think you're being a bit harsh on a very well-meaning body of men and women.

**FLETCHER**
I ain't saying they ain't well-intentioned. But the lads, you know, they bring me their problems, they know I speak their language.

***He sits down.***

**FLETCHER**
By the way, how's things with your old lady?

**BARROWCLOUGH**
What? Oh well . . . difficult, you know, Fletcher, she's been a bit better since you and I had that chat, but well, things could be easier. She's not an easy woman to live with, my wife.

**FLETCHER**
No, no . . . not still the postman, is it?

**BARROWCLOUGH**
Oh no – heaven forbid. He's in the sorting office in Carlisle now.

**FLETCHER**
Sorted him out, did they?

**BARROWCLOUGH**
Pardon?

**FLETCHER**
Nothing, nothing. Shouldn't joke at your expense.

**BARROWCLOUGH**
No, no. Well, I'm afraid I'll have to ask you to . . .

***Fletcher picks up chair.***

**FLETCHER**

Yeah, I know. Time I turned in.

**BARROWCLOUGH**

I hate this part of the job you know, Fletcher. Shutting men up, caging them in.

**FLETCHER**

Yes – it is a shame. Just when the good telly's starting an' all. All we ever see's the flaming news. And *Town and Around*. Fat lot of interest to us that is. Locked in here.

**BARROWCLOUGH**

No. I've never got used to bolting those doors. I think of you in that little cell . . . and I think of me going out of here, and going home, to my house. To my wife, who's waiting for me.

***He stops as if something's occurred to him.***

**FLETCHER**

(*Rising*) What's wrong, Mr Barrowclough?

**BARROWCLOUGH**

I sometimes wish I was in here with you lot . . .

## 3. PRISON LANDING

***The cell doors are open, leaving the prisoners free to fraternise within their own landing. Prisoners with towels and slop buckets are moving among themselves. Camera follows Warren as he walks along the corridor and enters a cell.***

## 4. FLETCHER'S CELL

***Fletcher is on his bunk reading when Warren enters with a slop bucket.***

**WARREN**

Fletch . . . Would you do the honours?

***He produces another letter and hands it over.***

**FLETCHER**

What read this you mean? All right . . . (*Sniffing the letter*) . . . the wife?

**WARREN**

(*Sitting*) Yeah, knows her perfume anywhere.

**FLETCHER**

Not surprised, Warren. It's very distinctive. Should think it kills ninety-nine per cent of all known germs.

**WARREN**

Don't you like it – should I tell her to change it?

**FLETCHER**

No, no, my son. You're safe from other men as long as she wears this.

***He starts to read.***

**FLETCHER**

'My dear Bunny'. Bunny?

**WARREN**

Yes, Bunny Warren.

**FLETCHER**

Oh – Bunny Warren. 'I got your letter, for which many thanks. It's wonderful that already prison has taught you to write and spell proper. Who knows what you may come out . . .' – what's this word? Oh . . . 'qualified as'. It was the k-w that fooled me . . . 'Now

Bunny, about this other thing. I don't know where you've got these doubts from. I spend my nights watching the box on which is placed your picture which I cut out the *Manchester Evening News*. It is the one of you resisting arrest, but I have cut off the two policemen. I've left the Alsatian on as I know how fond you are of animals. I did go out Sunday I admit, but only to see your mother who has had to go into Salford again with her feet.' How she usually go in then – on her hands and knees?

**WARREN**

No, no, what she means is er – she's had to go back to chiropodist like. She's always had these feet, you see.

**FLETCHER**

Has she? The same ones? Oh. Anyhow . . . 'Never mind the expense, I am coming up visiting day, to put your mind at rest.'

***Warren gives a thumbs up sign.***

**FLETCHER**

'I will get Saturday morning off at the laundry. I miss you and I think of us when you were at home and you used to take my . . .'

***He breaks off.***

**WARREN**

What – used to what?

**FLETCHER**

Oh well, this last bit's a bit intimate, Warren, I don't think I should read it aloud in front of me. Personal, isn't it?

**WARREN**

What is it? What's she say?

**FLETCHER**

Er . . . well, how can I say it? Well, the gist of it is . . . she missed your er – no. Put it another way . . . which you obviously did. No, it's just that . . . well, she regrets that you're not home providing for her.

**WARREN**

Oh. Oh good. Anything else?

**FLETCHER**

Anything else would be a bit of an anti-climax. It just says 'I wish you were here. Oh well, I must stop and get on my lover . . . Oh, must stop and get on, my lover . . . See you Sat. Elaine.'

**WARREN**

Oh. Yes, she's a good girl Elaine. No problems there – what you think, Fletch?

**FLETCHER**

It's a nice letter, Warren. Heartfelt. You can tell. And coming up Saturday, isn't she?

**WARREN**

Aye. And so is Heslop's missus. All the way from Kent. And Tolly's wife. You're a clever lad, Fletch.

**FLETCHER**

Yeah, well.

**WARREN**

Your ole lady coming, is she?

**FLETCHER**

She'll be here.

**WARREN**
You had a letter like?

**FLETCHER**
No, I ain't actually but . . . she'll be here.

**WARREN**
I think Lukewarm's fella's coming up as well.

**FLETCHER**
Is he now? 'Course Lukewarm's got a different sort of problem from the rest of you. His Trevor's the insecure one there, isn't he? I mean there's six hundred men in here. So whereas you're all worried what your wives are up to on the outside, Trevor's worried what Lukewarm's up to on the inside.

***Mackay walks in.***

**WARREN**
Morning, Mr Mackay. See you, Fletch. And thanks again, mate.

***He leaves.***

**MACKAY**
Thanks? What was all that about?

**FLETCHER**
Bit of advice . . . Matter of the heart, Mr Mackay. Between him and me.

**MACKAY**
Tell me, Fletcher, is it true that this is the office of Slade Prison's Miss Lonelyhearts?

***He laughs.***

**FLETCHER**
That why you're here then, is it? Problems of that nature.

**MACKAY**
I do not have problems of that nature.

**FLETCHER**
Oh come on, Mr Mackay, all screws, beg your pardon, all prison officers have problems in that area. I mean matrimonially you and me are very similar. 'Cos while we're in here we can't be too sure what our old ladies are getting up to, can we? No difference.

**MACKAY**
There is a major difference, Fletcher. Your wives are criminals' wives. They belong to the criminal classes with all their inherent traits of slovenliness and promiscuity. Our wives are the wives of uniformed men, used to a life of service and duty, decency and moral fibre. My house reflects my wife.

**FLETCHER**
Big, is it?

**MACKAY**
It's spotless. And when I get home of an evening my uniform for the next day has been cleaned and pressed, the jacket with its buttons gleaming, the trousers with razor sharp creases and the shirt crisply laundered.

**FLETCHER**
Oh yes? So what's that prove? Your old lady's having it away with the bloke from the dry cleaners.

**MACKAY**

I refuse to rise to your bait. It's obvious that your cynicism derives from some bitter personal experience of your own.

**FLETCHER**

No, no, no, no. Nothing wrong with my marriage. No doubts about my Isobel. My wife and I have always got on very well.

**MACKAY**

You've spent half your married life in prison, man.

**FLETCHER**

Absence makes the heart grow fonder in our case. Bet your old lady wouldn't mind a break from all that ironing and cleaning.

***He sits on the bed.***

**MACKAY**

My wife has never had any desire other than to be by my side. Before Prison Service you know, Fletcher, I was in the Army. I was a drill sergeant in the Argyll and Sutherland Highlanders.

**FLETCHER**

I'd never have guessed that!

**MACKAY**

And even though I was posted to some far-flung places, Marie would always be with me.

**FLETCHER**

I bet she was. Brassing up, polishing, blancoing. Female batman. I can just see you coming in of an evening off the parade ground – 'Marie, Stand by your ironing board!!!'

**MACKAY**

Seventeen years of domestic contentment.

***He starts to go.***

**FLETCHER**

Er – Mr Mackay – drill sergeant, was it?

**MACKAY**

That's right, Fletcher, drill sergeant.

**FLETCHER**

Do everything by numbers, did you?

***Mackay returns.***

**MACKAY**

I am not rising to your bait, Fletcher, and it's naïve of you to assume that I would.

***Finally he leaves.***

**FLETCHER**

Even with your old lady. Numbers is it. 'Marie, I am about to make passionate love to you – stand by your bed. Wait for it! Wait for it! Knickers down – two three!'

***An enraged Mackay re-enters, pointing his truncheon at Fletcher threateningly.***

**MACKAY**

I'll have you, Fletcher!

**FLETCHER**

Don't you hit me!

## 5. COUNTRY ROAD/COACH

***A coach is seen travelling along a country road. Inside are Elaine, Iris, Norma and Ingrid talking.***

**NORMA**

Couldn't be much farther this place, could it?

**INGRID**

I've had to come from London. Had to be at Euston by eight. And there was no buffet on the train.

**NORMA**

Never is, is there? Or if there is, it's only yesterday's sausage rolls.

**ELAINE**

I've only come from Bolton. But it's taken me all morning to get here. Change at Manchester. Change at Carlisle. Least when he was in Strangeways I only had a bus ride.

**NORMA**

It's us that suffers chuck. Us that has to cope with no money and a family to run, and no man around the house.

**IRIS**

They thinks you've got a man about the house. I've come all the way from Kent because of his suspicious mind. I had this letter.

**ELAINE**

Me an' all.

**NORMA**

Me too.

**IRIS**

Yeah but what a nerve – listen to this.

*She gets her letter out and starts reading.*

**IRIS**

'I realise my luv that it is a lot to ask, to ask you to wait for me. But I will be upset dearest one, if I hear about you having a nibble of something you shouldn't.'

*The other wives get their letters out. Trevor also produces his letter. The bus arrives at the prison gates, they open and the bus drives in.*

## 6. VISITING ROOM

*Heslop, Warren, Lukewarm and Tolly are jostling at a window to catch a glimpse of the arriving visitors.*

**HESLOP**

There's my girl, there she is.

**WARREN**

Can see my Elaine.

**HESLOP**

Look at the little darlings. Don't you want to have a look, Fletch?

**FLETCHER**

See her soon enough, won't I? I know what she looks like.

**BARROWCLOUGH**

Come on now, sit down, let's have some order.

*The prisoners move away from the window and take up their seats.*

**TOLLY**

Did the trick then, Fletch?

**FLETCHER**

Yeah, well.

**HESLOP**

Kent's a long way, you know.

**LUKEWARM**

Trevor's come all the way from Southport. He'll have had to close the shop. He's a watch repairer.

**WARREN**

I did a watch repairer's once.

**FLETCHER**

Yeah and now you're doing time for it. Did you get that, Mr Barrowclough?

**BARROWCLOUGH**

Oh yes, very funny, Fletcher, very funny. Nice to see you all in such good spirits.

**WARREN**

I'm sure I can smell Elaine's perfume.

**FLETCHER**

No, that's the sheep dip from the prison farm, that is.

***There is a knock on the door. Barrowclough unlocks it. The wives walk in and join their husbands. Ingrid moves to Fletcher.***

**FLETCHER**

Ingrid!

**INGRID**

Hello, Dad.

**FLETCHER**

Where's your mother?

***Others are immediately captivated by this.***

**FLETCHER**

I said, where's your mother?

**INGRID**

She couldn't come, Dad.

**FLETCHER**

Not ill, is she?

**INGRID**

No, she –

**FLETCHER**

She, what?

**INGRID**

She's found another man, Dad.

## 7. GOVERNOR'S OFFICE

**VENABLES**

(*Crossing to his desk and sitting down*) Morose you say, Mr Barrowclough.

**BARROWCLOUGH**

I have the Welfare Officer's report here, sir. Mr Gillespie feels that psychologically Fletcher is overcompensating for the traumatic shock of –

**VENABLES**

Oh, don't spout that university clap trap at me. Young Gillespie – what does he know? These lads come in here with no experience of life. How can they have? Not two minutes ago they were in rag parades, blowing clarinets and throwing flour bags at old ladies.

**BARROWCLOUGH**

I think you're being a bit harsh on a very well-meaning body of men, sir. Mr Gillespie has done work in the field, sir.

**VENABLES**

In Welwyn Garden City! Hardly a walk on the wild side. What is it? Compassionate parole?

**BARROWCLOUGH**

Just forty-eight hours to help him sort out his problems. They have been married twenty-four years.

**VENABLES**

Alright – wheel him in then.

***Barrowclough walks across to the door and opens it to admit a melancholy Fletcher who stands in front of the Governor's desk.***

**VENABLES**
Now, Fletcher, as we all know . . . you've had this domestic . . . well, I suppose, crisis isn't too strong a word, is it?

**FLETCHER**
My wife's scarpered. Yes, I think crisis is a very good word.

**BARROWCLOUGH**
She hasn't actually left you yet, Fletcher.

**FLETCHER**
She's about to.

**VENABLES**
What do we know about the other man?

**FLETCHER**
Well apparently, from what I 'licited from my eldest, he's a heating engineer – see we was getting new central heating installed. So obviously he was round there quite a while . . . younger man, bit of patter, from what I heard, new Capri in mustard yellow with wing mirrors.

**VENABLES**
Younger man, was it?

**FLETCHER**
Yeah, with wing mirrors, bound to turn a woman's head.

**VENABLES**
It couldn't just be an infatuation?

**FLETCHER**
Not according to my eldest, Ingrid. She knows the score, my girl. She says they're planning a new life together in Hemel Hempstead.

**BARROWCLOUGH**
Oh I know Hemel Hempstead. Pass through it on the train – it looks nice there.

***Venables and Fletcher look at him.***

**VENABLES**
Yes, yes . . . well now the Welfare Officer seems to think it would help if we gave compassionate parole.

**FLETCHER**
Parole – what get out, like?

**VENABLES**
Not so much get out as go out. For forty-eight hours only. You could go on Friday. Report to the local police on arrival, but otherwise the weekend would be your own.

**FLETCHER**
I see . . . well, no harm in trying, get a decent Sunday dinner I suppose.

**VENABLES**
Now, Fletcher, if that's your attitude –

**FLETCHER**
No, no, Governor, I'm sorry. My flippancy was only masking my deep wounds. If you see fit, sir. I shall go. For the sake of my marriage and your trust in me I'll go. I wonder if Spurs are playing at home?

## 8. POLICE STATION

***Camera shows sign outside the police station. Then Fletcher and Sergeant Norris come out. They***

*walk round a corner and carry on up the street.*

**FLETCHER**

Look I've checked in – you know where I live, you don't have to walk me home.

**SGT NORRIS**

I don't mind, Fletch. Breath of fresh air.

**FLETCHER**

I'm going home to see my old lady. It's personal, matters of a personal nature. That's the reason for my parole.

**SGT NORRIS**

It's the personal nature that concerns me Fletch. Want you to greet your wife with sympathy and understanding. Don't want you to force her head through the mangle.

## 9. FLETCHER'S HOUSE: HALLWAY AND STUDIO

*Ingrid opens the front door to see Fletcher and the Sergeant.*

**INGRID**

Hello, Dad.

**FLETCHER**

Hello, love. Your mother in, is she?

**INGRID**

In there.

**FLETCHER**

You know Sergeant Norris, don't you?

**INGRID**

Met him in court.

**SGT NORRIS**

Only stopping a minute, love.

*They file through into the living room. Isobel is waiting, standing in front of the fireplace, composed and assured. She is an attractive woman in her forties, dressed neatly.*

**FLETCHER**

Isobel . . .

**ISOBEL**

Norman . . .

**FLETCHER**

I got this compassionate parole.

**ISOBEL**

So they told us.

**FLETCHER**

Yeah well . . .

**ISOBEL**

There's no need for you to stay Sergeant Norris. Thank you.

**SGT NORRIS**

I just thought that –

**ISOBEL**

Yes, well, there's no need for worries on that score is there, so if you'll excuse us?

*Fletcher and Isobel greet each other with warmth and affection. They hug each other.*

**ISOBEL**

Hello, Norman!

**FLETCHER**

Hello, my love.

**ISOBEL**

It worked then?

**FLETCHER**

Like a flaming charm.

**ISOBEL**

I knew it would. It worked in Maidstone. Knew it would again.

**FLETCHER**

Like a flaming charm. 'She's found another man . . .'

**ISOBEL**

Ingrid, go and get your dad's slippers and put the kettle on.

**FLETCHER**

And don't be in too much of an hurry to come back, neither. Your mother and I have got a lot to make up.

**INGRID**

It's just like when I was a kid – if you give me some money I'll go to the pictures.

**FLETCHER**

It's worth it. (*Goes to get money then stops*) Hang on – that's how her brother was born. Puddle off.

### 10. STREET

***On the street is parked a car. A man is washing his car.***

### 11. LIVING ROOM

***Fletcher, shoes off, feet up, is reading a Sunday paper. Isobel comes in with grip and carrier bag.***

**ISOBEL**

You'll have to move I'm afraid, love.

**FLETCHER**

Won't take long to get to Euston on a Sunday.

**ISOBEL**

Did Sergeant Norris say he'd drive you there? I've given you some apples. And a banana. And some tangerines – what a price they are. But you need the fruit, it's good for your complexion. You should get shaved, love. Norris'll be here soon.

***Fletcher gets to his feet and turns off the TV set.***

**FLETCHER**

Yeah, I suppose so.

**ISOBEL**

It's been lovely having you, Norman.

**FLETCHER**

Done me a power of good, Isobel. See you and the kids. Colour telly, home cooking . . . Spurs winning at home, and soft lavatory paper.

**ISOBEL**

It's all here when you come out. Just bide your time, love.

**FLETCHER**

Tell you one thing, gel. I ain't going back in again after this stretch.

**ISOBEL**

You've said that before.

**FLETCHER**

I mean it. I've had me fill of porridge. It's full of kids these days. Talk about a generation gap. Father figure, I am. No, it's been a mug's game my life. And seein' and seein' the kids, and realising I'm missing them growing up . . . and all the things this weekend gave me. I tell you . . . the best things in life ain't free . . . but the best thing in life is bein' free.

**ISOBEL**

Oh Norman, you say lovely things, what made you think of that?

**FLETCHER**

I didn't . . . Randolph Scott said it just before you came in.

## 12. OUTSIDE PRISON

***The minibus carrying Fletcher approaches the prison gates and drives through.***

## 13. ASSOCIATION ROOM

***Prisoners are carrying on with their activities. Fletcher and Barrowclough enter the area. Lukewarm sees Fletcher and nudges Heslop. They all see Fletcher.***

**WARREN**

Er . . . you all right, Fletch?

**FLETCHER**

What?

**WARREN**

No, Fletch, listen – me and the lads just wanted to say – we're sorry. I mean I know we laughed about it last week but, you know – well, look, the fact that you're not so clever after all, just makes you more human like the rest of us.

**FLETCHER**

Oh yeah. Let me ask you something Warren – what you done – this weekend?

**WARREN**

What? Well –

**FLETCHER**

I'll tell you. Same as you did last weekend. Had a freezing shower, cleaned your shoes, washed your vest, had your dinner, had another freezing shower, spent the evening lying on your bunk picking your nose. Some of us was in the pub, some of us was eating roast beef, or watching Spurs play at home, or having a sing-song with their friends and relatives. (*Crossing to behind Heslop*) Or lying in a big crisp bed with their crisp old lady. (*To Heslop*) Have a banana.

***He crosses to his cell.***

***Mackay and Barrowclough are walking along.***

**MACKAY**

All right, let's have you – come on.

**BARROWCLOUGH**

You can see the difference in Fletcher. I think Mr Venables sending him home has made him realise what he's missing. It's suddenly dawned on him that he's been on a mug's game all these years.

**MACKAY**

Oh yes. He's had the cockiness knocked out of him. We've seen the last of his lairy insolence. You can't beat the system, Mr Barrowclough.

***They reach Fletcher's cell door and Mackay flicks open the eyepiece. Fletcher is sitting on the lower bunk, looking depressed. He looks up: gives an evil grin and thrusts up two fingers in a vulgar gesture.***

# 1 MEMORIES

**Sydney Lotterby** (Producer/Director)

'As soon as I saw the pilot script, "Prisoner and Escort", I knew I wanted to direct it. It was such a good script and just pleading to be done. It revealed the essence of Dick and Ian's writing: they don't write jokes, they write situations and explore the personalities of the characters, which is why they're such good writers. The humour in their scripts comes from the situations they put their characters into. With *Porridge*, their work was very accurate and seemed to reveal how a prisoner felt – it was almost as if they'd experienced prison life themselves!

'Despite the quality of the pilot script, however, I doubted whether the idea for a prison-based sitcom gave enough scope for an entire series, it was too confined – that is until I received the scripts for the first series.

'A director's job is easy when you have quality scripts; there are no problems with the dialogue or the situations, all you have to do is make sure that both you and the actors interpret the script accurately and without ostentation, and the end result will be perfect.'

**Philip Jackson** (Dylan in 'A Day Out')

'*Porridge* was one of my first TV jobs. Syd Lotterby had seen me in a *Play for Today* called *Blooming Youth*, an improvised film about students. He obviously thought I was the man to play Dylan, the Huddersfield hippie; mainly, I suspect, because of my extraordinary hairstyle! It was the first time I was ever offered a job with no interview or audition.

'Rehearsals in London were hilarious, then much bonding was made in the hotel bar when we filmed the outside scenes in South Wales. During frequent stoppages for the bad weather, Ronnie played poker with the crew, taking care not to win! The studio was my first experience of recording in front of a live audience, and I found it incredibly nerve-wracking. Just before we began, I saw Ronnie in the wings and even he looked petrified, but as soon as he went on, the panic disappeared from his face and you never for a second could have believed he was nervous.

'The initial scene with Richard and Ronnie was a bit edgy at first, and Ronnie did a deliberate cock-up halfway through, which relaxed the audience and actors alike. He was brilliant at gauging the atmosphere at any one time and constantly came up with ideas to relieve any tension. If an actor (me, for example) had a good line that didn't get a laugh, he was always able in some way to do something funny and make it look as if it wasn't you who'd messed it up. This was a total comedic instinct on display and I learned a great deal from watching him. Several of his lines came from larking about, ad-libbing in rehearsal, and the best ones stayed in. I remember the line about cheese and onion crisps in the pub came from such a moment.

'Looking back after nearly thirty years, I think there was a great sense that we were involved in something special. The show has lived on and my amazing hairstyle is still on regular display!'

**Tony Osoba** (McLaren in the series)

'Although transmitted fifth out of the six episodes of series one, "Ways and Means" was actually the last to be recorded and I recall joining a team which had been together for several weeks and who had all got to know each other well. However, I was made very welcome and soon felt at ease, thus dispelling the natural nervousness that I had been experiencing in the lead up to rehearsals.

'A week or two before, I had been invited to attend a casting to meet Ronnie Barker and Sydney Lotterby at the BBC rehearsal block in west London. I later discovered that a television director I'd recently worked with had recommended me and I shall be eternally grateful to Mike Vardy for that. When I learned that I had been offered the part, I was consumed with excitement and nerves in equal measure and couldn't wait to start work.

'As I say, I was quickly made to feel at home by the cast and crew and filming at the various locations passed all too quickly as I revelled in playing the rather hotheaded prisoner, McLaren, wonderfully written by Dick Clement and Ian La Frenais. Among the many kindnesses, I recall the reassurance and humour shown to me by Ray Butt, the PA, who later received great acclaim as a comedy producer/director in his own right.

'The scene on the roof which ends with Fletcher sliding down the tiles and straddling a drainpipe is one that always brings tears to people's eyes: tears of sympathy as well as laughter. Two roofs were used during the shooting of the scene: a school roof in Ealing for the close-ups and the roof of a psychiatric hospital near Watford for the longer shots. As we filmed in the hospital there would be many people milling around the grounds – crew and technicians, cast, patients and hospital staff; it was difficult telling who was who at times! I remember standing talking to a female member of the crew and a hospital doctor. We chatted for several minutes and then the doctor suddenly pulled the woman's skirt up before running off. It turned out, of course, that the "doctor" was actually a patient.

'In the studio, I was new to the tricky technique of playing television comedy in front of a live audience, but adapted fairly well under the sure but gentle guidance of Ronnie and Syd. However, I was mortified at one point when, during a break in recording, a voice from the audience called out: "Where's my orange?" It was a tag line from a part of the show that we hadn't arrived at yet. Ronnie looked startled and whispered under his breath: "How do they know that?" I didn't have the nerve to tell him that I had recognised the voice as that of my sister Trish. She and my mother were in the audience that evening and a few days earlier I had proudly been showing them the script and discussing my role, including that tag line. Fortunately, as ever in the studio, time was pressing and we could no longer dwell on the possible identity of the mystery caller!

'The evening was a success and I was delighted when the character of McLaren was incorporated into the subsequent series. I owe a great deal to *Porridge* and this episode in particular.'

**Patricia Brake** (Ingrid in the series)

'In September 1972 I starred in a *Play for Today* purely because I happened to be in the right late stage of pregnancy with my daughter Hannah. My part in *The Bouncing Boy* was arduous and when I had a really early call the make-up artist Ann Ailes, as she was then, came to my home. We became good friends and it was a great piece of luck that she then went on to work on *Porridge* and recommended me to Syd Lotterby. Luckily, I had already appeared in a sit-com called *Second Time Around*, playing the young wife, so I had a little experience of recording with an audience.

'In my first episode, *Men Without Women*, I had to say, "Hullo, Dad" several times which seemed to make Ian and Dick laugh, and thankfully they wrote me into more episodes where I had a great deal more to do. Ronnie was a delight to work with and I learnt a great deal from him. Always generous, he often made sure that the camera was on me for a particular moment during a scene together, very unusual in this business, and the way he could develop and add to an already very funny script was simply pure genius. In *Heartbreak Hotel* I appeared not wearing a bra, very risqué in 1975, and hanging on my bathroom wall now is a certificate made by the props department commemorating this momentous occasion. Later on I was cast several times in *The Two Ronnies*. Ronnie B said it was simply because my surname began with a B, and when he'd been through *Spotlight*, the actors directory, several times and got back to me he said, "She'll do." Now, many years later, I'm so proud to have been a part of *Porridge* and watch the repeats with delight, and I'm still rather secretly pleased that Clive James fancied me.'

# 2 SERIES TWO

- EPISODE ONE: JUST DESSERTS
- EPISODE TWO: HEARTBREAK HOTEL
- EPISODE THREE: DISTURBING THE PEACE
- EPISODE FOUR: NO PEACE FOR THE WICKED
- EPISODE FIVE: HAPPY RELEASE
- EPISODE SIX: THE HARDER THEY FALL

## MEMORIES

**Sam Kelly** (Warren in the series)
**Tony Osoba** (McLaren in the series)
**Philip Madoc** (Williams in 'Disturbing the Peace')

# 2 SERIES TWO

## EPISODE ONE: JUST DESSERTS

### 1. FLETCHER'S CELL

*Fletcher is searching anxiously among his meagre possessions. He is obviously angry at losing whatever it is he cannot find. He goes to Lennie's bed and looks under the pillow.*

*He looks at the picture of Denise and replaces it.*

*An air of resolution comes over his face. And he goes out of the cell.*

*Fletcher walks along the catwalk and down the stairs into the association area.*

*He goes up to the table where Lukewarm, Banyard and Warren are sitting.*

*Ives is next to them at a table alone reading the paper.*

*They all greet him with 'Good mornings, etc.'*

**FLETCHER**

Never mind the good mornings.

**WARREN**

What's up, Fletch?

**FLETCHER**

What's up, I'll tell you what's up. Are you listening, Ives?

*Ives looks up from his reading.*

**IVES**

(*Putting the paper down*) Oh sorry – yes.

**FLETCHER**

I don't know how to tell you this, gentlemen, but . . . there is a thief among us.

*The others look at each other.*

**WARREN**

There's nigh on six hundred people in this prison and I should think two-thirds of them are in for stealing something.

**FLETCHER**

That was stealing on the outside, Warren. Against civilians. That's work, that is. Making a living. Skullduggery. But the theft to which I'm referring has been perpetrated within these walls. Which is despicable. A crime which offends the dignity of any normal law-abiding criminal.

**BANYARD**

What is the nature of this alleged offence?

**FLETCHER**

There's nothing alleged about it,

Mr Banyard. Someone has crept into my cell and lifted a two-pound tin of pineapple chunks.

**IVES**

(*Impressed*) Pineapple chunks?

**FLETCHER**

Keep your voice down. We are discussing contraband after all.

**IVES**

(*Quieter*) Pineapple chunks?

**FLETCHER**

Correct. One tin of chunks, pineapple. Thickly cut chunks of delicious pineapple, soaked in a heavy syrup, from the sunkissed shores of Honolulu.

**LUKEWARM**

Mmmm, lovely.

**FLETCHER**

(*Sharply*) I trust the look on your face doesn't convey a pleasant memory, Lukewarm?

**LUKEWARM**

'Course not, Fletch. I haven't had your chunks.

**BANYARD**

Have you any idea who took them?

**FLETCHER**

I was hoping that our little chat might throw some light on the matter. 'Cos I can tell you, I'm extremely dischuffed about this. Luxuries are few and far between in this neck of the woods. I'd been looking forward to that, I had. Particularly partial to tinned pineapple. Very fond of all tinned fruits but particularly tinned pineapple. In the absence of tinned pears, that is. Bad enough if I'd had some snout nicked, or a new razor blade. Or even money, God forbid. But never my tin of pineapple chunks.

**WARREN**

When did you discover they was missing, Fletch?

**FLETCHER**

Just now, you nurk! I was going to have some of them after my Sunday lunch. For dessert. To supplement your wretched cuisine, Lukewarm.

**LUKEWARM**

I do the best I can with the materials provided.

**IVES**

'Ere listen, I had something whipped last week.

***The others laugh.***

**IVES**

No, honest, listen. You remember visiting day when Ronnie Arkwright's old lady said she weren't coming back no more, 'cos she was going to live with a Maltese ponce in Morecambe. And Ronnie went berserk and attempted to strangle her until restrained by that Scottish screw with the harelip.

**FLETCHER**

You paint a pretty picture, Ives, go on. They could use you on *Jackanory*.

**IVES**

Well, during the commotion my missis slipped me a jar of her mother's homemade gooseberry preserve. Now, 'ere listen . . . on the Tuesday, I'd had most of it, and d'you know I was only out the cell for half an hour, but in that time some scroat whipped the rest. While I was in the Hobby Shop making me Bugs Bunny Money Bank.

**FLETCHER**

(*Sarcastically*) Oh yes. Well, now we're getting somewhere, aren't we? We've narrowed the trail down. The net is closing in. We know the thief has a sweet tooth.

***Banyard seems bored with the proceedings and gets up as if to go.***

**BANYARD**

Look, any speculation you have about who took your pineapple chunks, I hardly think applies to me.

**FLETCHER**

Oh yes, Mr Banyard. Would you mind reseating yourself and elaborating on that if you would.

**BANYARD**

Well, unlike the rest of you, I'm not a common criminal.

**FLETCHER**

Has it escaped your attention that you're doing porridge and have been for eighteen months now?

**BANYARD**

You know what I mean. I'm a professional man, a dentist, and consequently –

**FLETCHER**

Just let's get the record straight. You *was* a dentist. It's been some time now since they struck you off their list. Following those regrettable incidents with the laughing gas. You may not consider yourself a criminal but to the ladies in question it certainly weren't no laughing matter.

**LUKEWARM**

He is a good dentist though. He did a lovely job on my bridge when the old one fell in the soup.

**FLETCHER**

I'm not questioning his dental ability. Just making the point that he can't set himself above the rest of us.

***The others react with indignation.***

**IVES**

'Ere listen.

**FLETCHER**

No, you 'ere listen. Pass the word round, right? I'm going for me shower now to stretch me legs, an' wash 'em an' all. Then I'm going to chapel to contemplate the errors of my ways and make peace with my bookmaker. If, when I come back my tin of pineapple has not been returned, we'll have to open a full scale enquiry. A thing like this can spread. If we can't live 'ere together and trust one another then where are we?

***There is a murmur of reluctant agreement and Fletcher leaves.***

**WARREN**

Quite right.

***He goes to get some Polos.***

**WARREN**

Here – who's pinched my Polos?

***Fletcher enters his cell, and gestures for the others to follow.***

***The prisoners troop in. They include Banyard, Ives, Lukewarm and Warren, and about five others. The cumulative effect is a bit like the cabin scene in Night at the Opera. As they walk in Fletcher is saying:***

**FLETCHER**

Come on in, make yourselves as comfortable as possible . . .

**WARREN**

(*Enjoying himself*) Pass right down the cell, please.

**FLETCHER**

This is not a laughing matter, Bunny.

**WARREN**

Sorry, Fletch.

**FLETCHER**

Who's keeping an eye open?

**IVES**

Gay Gordon. He's at the end of the landing.

**FLETCHER**

Bit conspicuous, isn't she? She's got her hair in curlers.

**LUKEWARM**

Nifty's at the other end.

**BANYARD**

I take it that the pineapple chunks have not been returned?

**FLETCHER**

No, they haven't. Now I've established when the crime was committed, and each of you lot had the MMO. Means, motives and opportunity.

**BANYARD**

(*Very Agatha Christie*) Are you saying that the thief is one of us . . . here in this very room?

**FLETCHER**

That's exactly what I am saying, Monsieur Poirot, yes.

***They all look at each other uneasily.***

**FLETCHER**

You lot were all on this landing before bang-up last night.

**WARREN**

Weren't you?

**FLETCHER**

Not all the time. At one stage I went over to see genial Harry Grout, didn't I, to negotiate the tobacco concession.

***McLaren enters with difficulty.***

**MCLAREN**

Kangaroo court aye, heard about it.

**FLETCHER**

Ah, McLaren, can we make room for McLaren, budge up.

***It is difficult, but they manage it.***

**MCLAREN**

No reason to exclude me you know, Fletch. All in this together. Finger of suspicion points at everyone. Just like to mention, of course, that if anyone points it at me, I'll clobber 'em.

**FLETCHER**

Good of you to be so reasonable, McLaren. Now just to recap, I've established that the crime was perpetrated during the fifteen minutes before bang-up last night.

**MCLAREN**

I was in the gym, working on me weights.

**LUKEWARM**

I was playing ping pong. With these two and Gay Gordon. Mixed doubles.

**BANYARD**

I was teaching Atlas chess.

**WARREN**

I was watching telly – (*To another*) Well you were as well, weren't you? And Crabs.

**FLETCHER**

Oh hello, Crabs, I didn't see you there. We don't need sworn statements from everybody.

**BANYARD**

Nevertheless, we should adhere to the fundamental principles on which our legal system was founded.

**FLETCHER**

You mean that every man is innocent until proven guilty.

**BANYARD**

Quite.

**FLETCHER**

True, true. On the other hand it's nearly lunch and there is amongst us one who is notorious for this kind of petty two-faced gittery, so I suggests we grab hold of Ives now and extract a swift confession.

*All eyes turn to Ives.*

**IVES**

'Ere listen . . .

**MCLAREN**

I'll extract the confession.

*He gets Ives in a headlock.*

**IVES**

'Ere listen, it wasn't me, straight up. I was in the Hobby Room. Making me toys, honest.

**MCLAREN**

Oh wait. That's true, that is. Saw him meself. On the way back from the gym. Making a big fluffy panda he was. He's good. Have you seen his Bugs Bunny Money Bank?

**FLETCHER**

No, is he doing it now?

**MCLAREN**

I think you're barking up the wrong tree, Fletch.

**IVES**

(*Hoarsely*) Could you let me go?

**MCLAREN**

Fletch?

**FLETCHER**

Yeah. Let him go, let him go.

*McLaren does so.*

**FLETCHER**

So we still live with the knowledge that there's a thief among us.

**BANYARD**

Where d'you get the pineapple in the first place?

**FLETCHER**

Stole it from the kitchen, didn't I?

*A head peeps round the door. It is Gay Gordon.*

**GORDON**

Mackay . . .

*He disappears.*

**FLETCHER**

(*Quietly*) All right, lads – we all know what we're here for. The initial gathering of the newly formed Slade Prison Cowboy Club. All together now . . .

*He conducts them and they sing.*

**ALL**

Home, home on the range . . .
Where the deer and the antelope play,
Where seldom is heard –

**MACKAY**

Quiet the lot of you, you horrible rabble!

*Mackay arrives.*

**FLETCHER**

(*Speaking*) A discouraging word?

**MACKAY**

What is going on here?

**FLETCHER**

Oh Mr Mackay. It's Mr Mackay, pardners.

**ALL**

Howdy, Mr Mackay.

**MCLAREN**

How.

**MACKAY**

I said, what is going on here?

**FLETCHER**

Cowboy Club, sir.

**MACKAY**

The what?

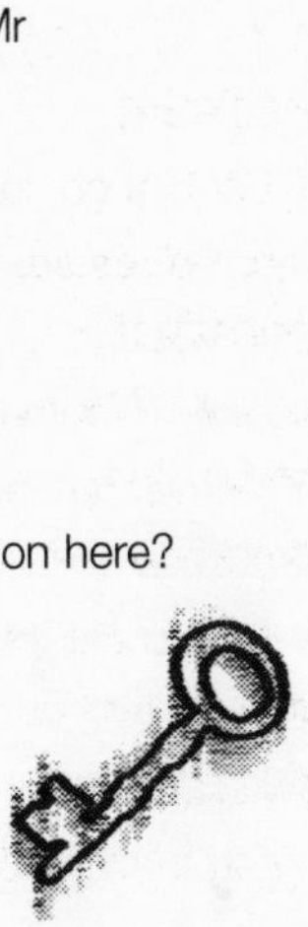

**FLETCHER**

Friends of the West. Kindred spirits, brought together by a mutual love and interest in those far-off days of the new frontier. We plan to meet, sing the songs –

**MACKAY**

Poppycock! This is an unlawful assembly, Fletcher. Prison regulations clearly state that no more than three prisoners will at any time congregate in a cell.

**FLETCHER**

Ah there, Mr Mackay, you have the advantage over me. Try as I might I have been unable to obtain a copy of the current Home Office Regulations.

**MACKAY**

Get on your feet the lot of you. There are only two rules in this prison. One: you do not write on the walls. Two: you will obey all rules. Back to your cells, the lot of you.

**FLETCHER**

All right lads, you'd better mosey along.

*They start to troop out.*

**WARREN**

See you later, Fletch. I'll bring round me Gene Autry songbook.

**LUKEWARM**

Adios, amigos . . .

*Fletcher and Mackay are left alone.*

**FLETCHER**

Well . . . highlight of the week coming up, Sunday lunch – can I offer you a sherry?

**MACKAY**
There is a growing current of insubordination and laxity in this prison. A definite rise in insolence. And pilfering.

**FLETCHER**
Pilfering, yes. Me and some of the lads have noticed that.

**MACKAY**
I'm not referring to petty sneak thieving amongst yourselves. That's to be expected amongst incorrigible criminals. I'm referring to thefts of prison property. Mark my words, Fletcher – it will not be tolerated.

***Lennie enters in his kitchen whites and small chef's hat and spots Mackay.***

**LENNIE**
Oh.

**MACKAY**
Ah yes, Godber. What are you up to?

**LENNIE**
Off work, sir. Been up since six this morning.

**FLETCHER**
Yes the lad's tired, sir. So if you'll excuse us –

**MACKAY**
This is a very unfortunate combination.

**FLETCHER**
Oh yes, how's that?

**MACKAY**
Godber with his opportunities to steal from the kitchen. And you with your distribution network.

**LENNIE**
Here, I don't steal, I resent that!

**MACKAY**
Oh you resent that, do you, Godber? Butter wouldn't melt in your mouth.

**FLETCHER**
That's a good idea, how much could you get in your mouth?

**LENNIE**
Don't make waves, Fletch.

***Mackay starts to search Lennie.***

**LENNIE**
No, I want to say. This is not on, Mr Mackay. (*As Mackay searches him*) All right, I'm inside, I have done wrong, and I've got that stigma to bear. But I'm paying my penance, I'm paying my dues.

**MACKAY**
What makes you think you're any different from anyone else?

**LENNIE**
Certain circumstances brought me here. Environment. Lack of parental guidance. Times were tough, I did go off the rails but I did have a few decent qualities underneath and I've learnt my lesson. Now I won't grass and I won't cheat and I will not steal.

**MACKAY**
Hmmm. All right, sonny Jim, we'll say no more . . . for the present.

***Mackay goes.***

**FLETCHER**
Well said, son. You even impressed

Mackay with your eloquence and obvious sincerity.

**LENNIE**
Should think so. Suspicious old scroat.

**FLETCHER**
Good thing you were clean though.

**LENNIE**
Good job he didn't look under me hat.

***He takes it off, revealing half a pound of marge perched on the top of his head.***

**3. PRISON**

***Camera shows the prison in the early evening, after lock-up but before lights out.***

**3A. CELL**

***It is night time. Fletcher is cleaning his teeth in his underclothes, Lennie is looking for something under his bed.***

**LENNIE**
Fletch?

**FLETCHER**
Whah?

**LENNIE**
Can I have a loan of your black boot polish?

**FLETCHER**
(*Spitting*) Why?

**LENNIE**
Why? Why do you think? Me mascara's run out.

**FLETCHER**
Don't be cheeky, young Godber.

**LENNIE**
I just want to clean me shoes.

**FLETCHER**
Borrow someone else's.

**LENNIE**
It's after lock-up.

**FLETCHER**
Then you should have thought of that earlier.

**LENNIE**
Aren't you going to give me a measly bit of shoe polish?

**FLETCHER**
No. I think that in the light of certain events, it would be better if in the future what one has one keeps.

**LENNIE**
I notice you didn't say this till after I shared my margarine with you.

**FLETCHER**
I've done enough for you, Godber. Boot polish, snout, toothpaste – the first night you moved in here I give you my toothpaste.

**LENNIE**
You give me one squeeze.

**FLETCHER**
On three successive nights! That adds up to a lot of toothpaste.

**LENNIE**
Your squeezes don't.

**FLETCHER**
That weren't no ordinary toothpaste, neither. That had hexochloroform in

the stripes. I got that special to match my pyjamas.

***Lennie starts to darn his socks.***

**LENNIE**

I gave you liquorice all-sorts for that toothpaste. Fair exchange is no robbery.

**FLETCHER**

When you were at death's door last month with your inflamed bronchs, who gave you a TCP throat lozenge?

**LENNIE**

Yeah. Lozenge. Singular.

**FLETCHER**

Who saved you all those matchsticks when you wanted to make a model of the *Cutty Sark*?

**LENNIE**

And who sat on it?

**FLETCHER**

Well, it was a pointless exercise. You need a ten stretch to finish the *Cutty Sark* in matchsticks. You should have used chair legs like I told you.

**LENNIE**

Who stole nails for you from carpentry classes so you could stick your pin-ups on the wall? And who gave you half his mother's home-made shortbread?

**FLETCHER**

Home-made shortbread, yeah. I used that to hammer the nails in with.

**LENNIE**

You ungrateful nurk.

**FLETCHER**

Who loaned you their darning wool then?

**LENNIE**

You did. And who's darning whose socks then?

**FLETCHER**

Oh. Oh are they my socks?

**LENNIE**

'Course they are. I don't go through my socks.

**FLETCHER**

Oh I didn't realise . . .

**LENNIE**

Apparently.

**FLETCHER**

Yeah well. Ta very much then.

**LENNIE**

(*Sulkily*) My pleasure.

**FLETCHER**

Go on then, here's me shoe polish. Don't take too much.

***Lennie takes a small smear on his brush.***

**LENNIE**

You told me when I moved in here that our best protection against those nurks out there was mutual interest. Team spirit.

**FLETCHER**

Yes, but my trust has been misplaced, hasn't it, as that missing tin of pineapple has proved. I was careless enough to forget that this is a jungle in here. You can't trust no one.

**LENNIE**

Here! Are you including me in that remark?

**FLETCHER**
What remark was that?

**LENNIE**
About not trusting anybody.

**FLETCHER**
Look after number one, that's what it's all about.

**LENNIE**
That's not answering my question.

**FLETCHER**
What question's that then?

**LENNIE**
Do you think I nicked your chunks?

***Fletcher is deliberately vague and evasive.***

**FLETCHER**
Who knows who took them?

**LENNIE**
Fletcher, don't evade me. This is a very critical point in our relationship.

**FLETCHER**
Never mind that. You just darn your socks . . . my socks.

**LENNIE**
No. No. I want an answer. I respect you, Fletch. I owe you a lot, and I'm not talking about stripey toothpaste. I've never pretend to be cool or off-hand about doing stir. It bleeding petrified me. But you made it tolerable. You taught me the right approach. In me head. I get by now. Just, but I get by. I'm grateful, very grateful. And do you think I'd repay that by stealing your tin of naffing pineapple chunks . . . not even me favourite fruit.

**FLETCHER**
(*Pacifying him*) Here, here, here . . . it never entered my head, Lennie. If there's one person I know didn't take them it's you.

**LENNIE**
Yeah well.

**FLETCHER**
Of course. You and me. Oppoes, ain't we?

**LENNIE**
I dunno.

**FLETCHER**
You know we are. Living like this, like caged animals we're bound to get the needle sometimes. But I trust you. Implicit. I know you didn't take my pineapple.

**LENNIE**
How can you be sure?

**FLETCHER**
'Cos I know you. I know the type of person you are.

***There is a pause while Lennie digests this.***

**FLETCHER**
'Sides, when you were in the shower I went through all your gear!

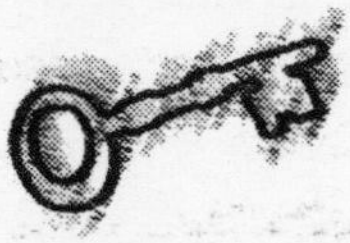

**4A. CORRIDOR**

***Camera shows Barrowclough walking along a corridor towards library door.***

## 4B. LIBRARY

*To describe this as a library is an overstatement. It is a small dusty room, full of old books with broken spines and grubby paperbacks. There is a locked door with a meshed grille at the back of the room. A chipped table has an old filing cabinet on it. There is also a very ancient typewriter behind which sits Fletcher, tapping out index cards as he catalogues new books. Barrowclough unlocks the door and walks in. Fletcher looks up.*

**FLETCHER**

Ah, morning, Mr Barrowclough.

**BARROWCLOUGH**

Fletcher . . .

**FLETCHER**

Have a nice weekend then, did you?

**BARROWCLOUGH**

Not especially.

**FLETCHER**

Least the weather kept nice.

**BARROWCLOUGH**

Did it? The sun rarely shines in my household.

**FLETCHER**

You should put another window in.

**BARROWCLOUGH**

I wasn't referring to the architecture.

**FLETCHER**

Oh dear.

**BARROWCLOUGH**

But I haven't come to discuss my domestic situation . . .

**FLETCHER**

Your problems are my problems.

**BARROWCLOUGH**

I'm aware of that. I'm aware that's true at times. And that's why I've been lenient with you, Fletcher.

**FLETCHER**

Lenient?

**BARROWCLOUGH**

I haven't had a chance to talk to you since I went off duty for the weekend, but on Saturday afternoon when you were all out watching the football match, Mr Malone and I were detailed by Mr Mackay to do an RSC.

**FLETCHER**

A what?

**BARROWCLOUGH**

A random security check.

**FLETCHER**

Oh yes. The vocabulary varies from nick to nick. In practice it's the same thing though, isn't it? Burgling, a despicable infringement of civil liberties.

**BARROWCLOUGH**

The practice is justified though, Fletcher, when one finds stolen tins of pineapple chunks.

*There is a long pause. Then Fletcher makes a game try.*

**FLETCHER**

Where?

**BARROWCLOUGH**

Don't play games with me, Fletcher.

It was in your cell as you well know, and by rights I should have reported it.

**FLETCHER**

(*With a glimmer of hope*) You didn't then?

**BARROWCLOUGH**

No. As it happened, Mr Malone's attention was distracted. He was in the showers at the time, taking up the tiles looking for a missing hatchet. Fletcher, if I had reported that find you would have lost this job, had loss of privileges and probably solitary confinement.

**FLETCHER**

(*Contritely*) Well, what can I say, Mr Barrowclough?

**BARROWCLOUGH**

You can promise me to keep your nose clean. I reckoned I possibly owed you a favour, and the consequences would have been a bit severe. But that's wiped the slate clean. Now we're all square, right?

**FLETCHER**

Right, sir.

**BARROWCLOUGH**

You know this is a very cushy number here. This is a better job than most *trusties* have got.

**FLETCHER**

It's not all that easy. I've got a very complicated index to complete.

**BARROWCLOUGH**

Yes and you've been doing it for five weeks.

**FLETCHER**

I want to avoid mistakes, don't I?

**BARROWCLOUGH**

You want to avoid finishing it. 'Cos then you've got to decorate the room, which is why you were put in here in the first place.

**FLETCHER**

Waiting for the paint, sir.

**BARROWCLOUGH**

Where is it?

**FLETCHER**

Stolen, sir.

**BARROWCLOUGH**

What is happening to this prison?

**FLETCHER**

Strong criminal element in here, sir.

**BARROWCLOUGH**

There's just too much petty pilfering going on. Mr Mackay is on my back to stamp it out. I've let you off the hook, Fletcher. And in return I expect to see a sharp decrease on your block.

**FLETCHER**

Rest assured, sir.

***Barrowclough seems satisfied with this.***

**FLETCHER**

By the way . . . the tin of pineapple, did you manage to return it to the food store?

***Barrowclough now looks slightly uncomfortable.***

**BARROWCLOUGH**

Not exactly. I took it home and the wife did gammon steak Hawaii.

**FLETCHER**
Oh very nice, very nice. Gammon steak Hawaii. So the pineapple has been consumed!

**BARROWCLOUGH**
I hadn't intended to. But the wife found it and . . . insisted that we ate it. I could do very little about it.

**FLETCHER**
Only eat it.

**BARROWCLOUGH**
Under protest.

**FLETCHER**
On top of gammon. Well now we have quite a different situation here, don't we? I mean, if I did commit the alleged offence – which in the absence of evidence is somewhat difficult to prove – you are unquestionably an accessory before, after and during the facts. You're a felon same as me.

**BARROWCLOUGH**
I am aware of the situation. I would suggest that we purchase another tin of pineapple, and replace it in the food store.

**FLETCHER**
What do you mean we? I can't just troll down the village store at will.

**BARROWCLOUGH**
Oh no. I realise that, Fletcher. I shall get it. You shall pay for it.

## 5. KITCHEN

***It is mid-morning, before lunch. There is a bustle of activity. Huge cauldrons of soup are bubbling. Several prisoners are going about their various tasks under the watchful eye of a Prison Officer.***

***Lennie brings over a tray of Cornish pasties to a hotplate by which Lukewarm is standing. He talks to him quietly.***

**LENNIE**
Hey, Lukewarm. Make a bit of a commotion in a minute, will you?

**LUKEWARM**
What for? You're not going to escape, are you? It's a good lunch today. We've got jelly.

***Lennie looks around to make sure no one's in earshot.***

**LENNIE**
I'm going to whip Fletch a tin of pineapple.

**LUKEWARM**
What for?

**LENNIE**
Surprise, like.

**LUKEWARM**
Bit dodgy. There's only one tin left.

**LENNIE**
Well . . .

***He moves across the kitchen towards the store cupboard. Then turns and nods at Lukewarm. Lukewarm looks sadly at the tray of pastries.***

**LUKEWARM**

(*To self*) They came out lovely an' all.

***He drops them on the floor. The Prison Officer comes over to Lukewarm.***

**PO**

What's all this, Lewis? Get all this mess cleared up at once!

***While the hubbub is going on Lennie goes into the store cupboard. Warren goes past the cupboard with a laundry basket. A hand drops a tin into it. Lennie comes out and reacts with pleasure, but then reacts again in alarm. Mr Birchwood, the civilian catering administrator, walks across to the cupboard and goes in.***

**BIRCHWOOD**

Good morning, Mr Appleton.

**APPLETON**

Morning, Mr Birchwood.

***Warren and Lennie exchange anxious glances as he goes into the cupboard. Birchwood comes out of the cupboard and confronts Appleton.***

**BIRCHWOOD**

Mr Appleton – there's a tin of pineapple chunks missing.

**APPLETON**

All right . . . (*Turns to a prisoner*) You – fetch Mr Mackay from the Mess Hall.

***The prisoner goes.***

**APPLETON**

Everyone stay just where they are. (*To Lennie*) You, where you are off to?

**LENNIE**

I've forgotten where I was.

***He moves back. Appleton starts to search them.***

**APPLETON**

Come on, arms up.

**LUKEWARM**

Come on, Mr Appleton, we haven't got time for all this – I've got a whole trayful of pasties to get ready.

**APPLETON**

They'll have to wait, won't they?

**LUKEWARM**

They can't wait, they have to do twenty-five minutes on Regulo 6.

***They continue talking as Barrowclough enters and crosses over to the store cupboard. He looks very shifty and nervous. He opens the door and puts the tin back on the shelf. He comes out of the cupboard and moves away. Mackay comes into the kitchen.***

**MACKAY**

All right, what's going on here?

**APPLETON**

Pilfering we think, sir.

**BIRCHWOOD**

Tin of pineapple chunks, sir. There was a tin in that cupboard half an hour ago. I'm sure of that.

**MACKAY**

Who was last seen in that vicinity?

**APPLETON**

(*Indicating Lennie*) Godber was there a minute ago.

**MACKAY**

Oh, was he? Well, that makes sense. Your come-uppance is well overdue, Godber.

***As Mackay speaks, he approaches Lennie.***

**MACKAY**

Why is your hat standing to attention, Godber?

***He prods it with his stick.***

**LENNIE**

Ow, Mr Mackay.

***Mackay removes the hat. Naturally there is nothing underneath it. Mackay is disappointed.***

**MACKAY**

All right. Now just stand there. All of you. Very well, Mr Birchwood. Where was the crime perpetrated?

**BIRCHWOOD**

From this cupboard, Mr Mackay.

***He leads Mackay to it.***

**BIRCHWOOD**

I saw straight off, 'cos there was only the one tin there.

***He opens the cupboard door. Mackay goes in and comes out with a tin of pineapple. He hands it to Birchwood.***

**MACKAY**

Is this the one that's missing?

**BIRCHWOOD**

(*Looking at it*) That's the one, yes, sir.

**MACKAY**

Pull yourself together, Mr Birchwood.

***Lennie reacts with relief. Warren is on his knees praying.***

## 6. CELL

***Lennie is alone in the cell finishing a shave.***

**WARREN**

Here . . .

***Warren produces the tin of pineapple chunks from under his jacket, and hands it to Lennie who quickly hides it under his pillow.***

**WARREN**

(*Wanting reassuring*) Now, listen. Tell me. There *were* two tins there, weren't there?

**LENNIE**

Just the one.

**WARREN**

Then I was right. It were a miracle.

**LENNIE**

Apparently. No other explanation.

**WARREN**

Scares you a bit though, doesn't it?

**LENNIE**

I don't pretend to understand.

**WARREN**

'The Miracle of Slade Prison'. I tell you something, Len, I was brought up a Catholic – not a very good one. But after this – well. Makes you think, doesn't it?

**LENNIE**

God moves in a mysterious way. His wonders to perform.

**WARREN**

See you in church.

*He goes. Lennie takes the tin from under his pillow. He gets a label with 'surprise, surprise!' written on it in large letters and ties it round the tin. He looks at Fletcher's bunk. There is a towel on it. With a grin he places it under Fletcher's towel.*

*He moves away quickly on hearing Fletcher enter. Fletcher is not in the best of moods.*

**LENNIE**

'Lo, Fletch.

**FLETCHER**

Oh yes . . .

**LENNIE**

What's the matter?

**FLETCHER**

What's the matter, some new paint's arrived.

**LENNIE**

So?

**FLETCHER**

So, it means I've got to decorate that library, doesn't it?

**LENNIE**

Can't you get rid of it, like all the other consignments?

**FLETCHER**

No – not a chance. There's not a screw left who hasn't got a gleaming front fence.

**LENNIE**

(*Happily*) Well never mind, life could be worse.

**FLETCHER**

Oh yes?

*Fletcher picks up his towel, but still looking at Lennie, not noticing the tin.*

*Lennie starts to snigger. In pleasurable anticipation of Fletcher's discovery.*

**FLETCHER**

What's got into you, Godber?

*He throws his towel on the tin again.*

**LENNIE**

You'll find out soon enough.

*Mackay enters.*

**FLETCHER**

Oh that's all we need, isn't it?

**MACKAY**

Haven't come to see you, Fletcher.

**FLETCHER**

What a shame, sir.

**MACKAY**

Came to see Godber. Now laddie, don't want you developing a chip. Don't want you to think I'm picking on you. I have a job to do. And whatever else I am, I'm firm but fair. I want you to know that I treat you all with equal contempt.

**LENNIE**

I appreciate that, Mr Mackay.

**FLETCHER**

What's all this about?

**LENNIE**

He thought I'd been pilfering again.

**FLETCHER**

Oh, did he? Well that should come as no surprise to you, son. They think we're all at it, don't they? Think we're all thieves in here. We're under continual harassment. Suspicion. Sneaking around, poking through our belongings, with any justification whatsoever. Now if you'll excuse me I'm going for a shower.

**LENNIE**

No.

**FLETCHER**

You what?

**LENNIE**

You don't need to, Fletch. You're so . . . clean.

**FLETCHER**

What's got into you, Godber? (*To Mackay*) You lot are warping this lad's mind.

***Fletcher picks up towel and moves towards the door. The tin of pineapple is left uncovered. Mackay sees it.***

**MACKAY**

Fletcher . . .

***Lennie winces. Fletcher comes back.***

**FLETCHER**

What?

**MACKAY**

What is that?

**FLETCHER**

What's what?

***He looks to where Mackay is pointing.***

**FLETCHER**

Bloody hell!

**MACKAY**

Come along with me, Fletcher.

**FLETCHER**

Now, listen.

**MACKAY**

You won't need your towel.

**FLETCHER**

It's a plant.

**MACKAY**

Oh no, it's not, it's a tin of pineapple. Come along with me.

**FLETCHER**

I've been framed.

***Mackay leaves. Fletcher follows, picking up his shirt.***

***Lennie moves across to get the tin. Takes off the label and makes for the door. Camera shows Mackay, followed by Fletcher, walking along the catwalk.***

***Lennie comes out of the cell with the tin.***

**LENNIE**

Anyone got a tin opener?

***Fletcher reacts then moves on.***

# 2 SERIES TWO

## EPISODE TWO: HEARTBREAK HOTEL

### 1. FLETCHER'S CELL

***A small transistor radio is on in the cell.***

***From it comes the voice of a DJ with romantic mood music playing in the background. Lennie is sitting on his bed, darning his socks and listening intently.***

**DJ**

Here's a request from Brigit in Dundee for a boy, she only knows him as Ricky but he has blue eyes, dark curly hair and looks a bit like David Essex. Brigit is sixteen and works in product control in a cake factory and her job is to spot flawed almonds.

***Fletcher comes into the cell as the DJ gives the last fascinating piece of irrelevant detail.***

**DJ**

Brigit was on a coach trip to the Ayrshire coast last summer and met Ricky briefly at a dance. All she knows is that he's from Glasgow.

***Fletcher turns off the radio and takes over from the DJ.***

**FLETCHER**

She knows he's from Glasgow and his hobbies include getting drunk and beating up lavatory attendants.

**LENNIE**

Here, I was listening to that.

**FLETCHER**

Yeah, well, I'm not. Teenage sentimental slush.

**LENNIE**

I have to sit through your *Gardeners' Question Time* and *Friday Night is Music Night*.

**FLETCHER**

All right, all right. And I sit through *Rosko's Round Table* but I draw the line at David 'Diddy' Hamilton. The wireless is never off in this nick.

**LENNIE**

Well, the screws think it makes us work harder. They're piping Tony Blackburn through to the kitchens now.

**FLETCHER**

They're doing that 'cos they believe we're in prison to be punished.

**LENNIE**

I wanted to hear that bit. 'Cos that was their special request slot. That was their 'Hello Young Lovers' corner.

**FLETCHER**
Oh yes?
**LENNIE**
And I'd written in, like. For a record. For Denise.
**FLETCHER**
Denise?
**LENNIE**
My fiancée.
**FLETCHER**
Oh yes, that Denise, of course, yes.
**LENNIE**
Just wanted to convey my undying feelings of affection and devotion. 'Everlasting Love' that was the record I asked for.
**FLETCHER**
You should have asked for 'My Ding-a-Ling'.
**LENNIE**
I been listening all week, but it ain't been on yet. Not fair. You'd think my needs were greater than an almond sorter's from Dundee.
**FLETCHER**
Hang about. Did you write this on prison notepaper?
**LENNIE**
Yes. If you remember I gave you me last sheet of Basildon Bond.
**FLETCHER**
That's it then.
**LENNIE**
Why? Are they biased against prisoners?
**FLETCHER**
P'raps not officially. But I don't recall ever having heard a prisoner's request on the air. Forces yes. Aircraft carriers or ack-ack batteries, but never heard nothing from no one from the *nick*.
**LENNIE**
It's a disgrace. We have a rotten enough life in here without having our requests refused. That's discrimination that is. And five five and a halfpenny stamps up the spout.
**FLETCHER**
You can see it from their point of view. The public what pay their radio licence faithful every year. Take offence, wouldn't they? Sitting down to Sunday lunch with their beloved *Family Favourites*. Suddenly they read out a card with a Parkhurst postmark. Says could Tommy 'Mad Dog' Hollister please have 'Clair de Lune'.
***Mackay enters.***
**MACKAY**
'Clair de Lune'?
**FLETCHER**
Oh. Yeah, it's French, Mr Mackay. French for 'By the light of the silvery moon'.
**MACKAY**
I thought for a moment, Fletcher, you were having a cultural conversation.
**LENNIE**
P'raps you could tell us the ruling, Mr Mackay.

**MACKAY**

The ruling, Godber?

**FLETCHER**

Miss Lonelyloins here, lovelorn Lennie, he wants to know whether the BBC plays prisoners' requests?

**MACKAY**

No. The answer to that is no, on the grounds that it caused embarrassment.

**LENNIE**

Embarrassment?

**MACKAY**

To the prisoners' families. The family might have excused his absence by telling the neighbours that the felon in question was abroad, or working on a North Sea oil rig.

**LENNIE**

Oh I see.

**MACKAY**

No doubt your wife, Fletcher, has told your friends that you're on a five-year safari.

***He laughs.***

**FLETCHER**

(*Reading paper*) No, no. She tells them I'm doing missionary work in Scotland.

**MACKAY**

No, Godber. The practice was also open to abuse. There was nothing to stop prisoners sending messages in code across our airways.

**FLETCHER**

Ah, that's a point – yeah, that's a point. Listen to some heartwarming Christmas message from some poor lag. To his beloved wife and family and little Tiny Tim. Could he please hear Harry Secombe with 'The Impossible Dream'. Translated what he really meant was 'Nobby, have the ladder round the back of E Wing, Boxing Day – and bring me a mince pie.'

**LENNIE**

Oh it's a good idea, that.

**MACKAY**

It's an abuse of privilege, Godber. Which is why I'm here.

**FLETCHER**

Oh, I thought it was a social call.

**MACKAY**

Six rolls of soft toilet paper have disappeared from the Governor's closet – the Governor's own personal water closet.

**FLETCHER**

Oh dear. Would you Adam and Eve it? What next?

**MACKAY**

Knowing you, Fletcher, probably the seat.

***Lennie laughs.***

**FLETCHER**

Don't look at me.

**LENNIE**

Nor me. It's writing paper I'm short of.

**MACKAY**

It's not right. We've had to give the Governor standard prison issue tissue.

**LENNIE**

That's rough.

**FLETCHER**
Not half, it ain't. That'll wipe the smile off his face.
***They both laugh.***
**MACKAY**
Fortune has given you two privileged positions in this prison. You would be foolish to jeopardise them by any infraction of the rules . . . I'll say no more.
***He leaves. They call after him.***
**FLETCHER**
Thank you, Mr Mackay.
**LENNIE**
Yes, thanks for the advice.
**FLETCHER**
To which we'll pay great heed . . . now naff off.
**LENNIE**
Always picking on us, isn't he?
**FLETCHER**
Well, that's his devious suspicious mind, the nosy nurk. Care for a glass of toilet roll?
***He tips up the jug, revealing a pink roll of soft toilet tissue.***
**LENNIE**
Eh, you've got one!
**FLETCHER**
Yeah. I had six.
**LENNIE**
Where's the other five?
**FLETCHER**
I traded them, didn't I?
**LENNIE**
Who to?
**FLETCHER**
There are a few inmates with some refinement in this nick. Bottom landing, call at the end, there's some embezzlers in there. Mr Banyard, the unfrocked dentist. Well those middle-class white-collar felons . . . leapt at 'em, didn't they?
**LENNIE**
What d'you get?
**FLETCHER**
Well, they owe me, don't they? Lot of nice middle-class merchandise. I'm promised a cricket sweater, a pair of Hush Puppies and a box of after-dinner mints.
***Fletcher sits down, retrieves his socks and bundles them up.***
**LENNIE**
Hey.
**FLETCHER**
What?
**LENNIE**
Share and share alike.
**FLETCHER**
Yes. What!!
**LENNIE**
Rule of the house, isn't it?
**FLETCHER**
Share my toilet roll?
**LENNIE**
Only fair.
**FLETCHER**
Share my toilet roll!!! Godber.
**LENNIE**
Only fair.

***He sits glowering.***

**LENNIE**

Look at all them darned socks.

**FLETCHER**

All right then.

***He picks up the toilet roll and tears off one piece, handing it to Lennie.***

**FLETCHER**

Mind how you go.

## 2. VISITING

***A door is unlocked and wives, sweethearts, mothers, a few dads and brothers are ushered in under the watching eye of Mackay.***

***The camera picks out Ingrid, Fletcher's daughter, and an older woman soon to be revealed as Mrs Godber, Lennie's mother.***

***They move to their respective prisoners, who greet them at their individual tables. Fletcher and Lennie are sitting at adjacent tables.***

**INGRID**

Hello, Dad.

**FLETCHER**

Hello, Ingrid, love.

**LENNIE**

Hello, Mum.

**MRS GODBER**

Hello, son.

***Fletcher registers Lennie's visitor and Lennie makes the introductions.***

**LENNIE**

Oh er – this is me mum, Fletch.

**MRS GODBER**

Hello, Mr Fletcher.

**FLETCHER**

Oh, pleasure's mine, Mrs Godber. Got a fine lad there. This is my eldest, Ingrid.

**INGRID**

Hello.

**MACKAY**

(*Calling out*) Sit down, Fletcher! And you, Godber! This is not a royal garden party.

***He laughs. They sit down, muttering at Mackay.***

***Ingrid and Fletcher lean in closely towards each other and speak intimately.***

**INGRID**

Who's he then?

**FLETCHER**

That's Mr Mackay. Charmless Celtic nurk.

**INGRID**

And who's the boy?

**FLETCHER**

Oh that's Lennie. Lennie Godber, my temporary cell-mate. He's from Birmingham but he's got an 'O' Level in geography.

**INGRID**

Oh.

**FLETCHER**

Well, you have to find your way round Birmingham. Well, how's your mother then?

**INGRID**

Oh fine, Dad. Sends her love and everything.

**FLETCHER**
How's your sister?

**INGRID**
Oh, Marion's fine. Got a new job.

**FLETCHER**
Gawd, does she never keep a job for more than three weeks?

**INGRID**
It's the bosses she has trouble with. They molest her, she alleges.

**FLETCHER**
Well, that's her. Skirt right up to her expectations. Where is she now?

**INGRID**
Timothy White's.

**FLETCHER**
Oh. Oh, that's better. Shouldn't get molested there. All qualified pharmacists, aren't they?

**INGRID**
Her flat fell through.

**FLETCHER**
What flat's this?

**INGRID**
The one behind Olympia that she shared with six other people.

**FLETCHER**
Six? Fell through to the flat below I should think.

**INGRID**
No, the rent went up so she's home again, pro tem.

**FLETCHER**
And how's young Raymond?

**INGRID**
Oh, Raymond won the mile in the school sports.

**FLETCHER**
Oh, did he? Wish I had, I might not be in here now.

**INGRID**
And he came in second in the high jump. And he's swimming for the school. And he's stage manager in the play.

**FLETCHER**
Why isn't he in it? Last year he was Yum Yum in the *Mikado*.

**INGRID**
His voice has gone.

**FLETCHER**
Oh.

**INGRID**
Well, he's on thirty a day.

**FLETCHER**
Thirty a day, that's shocking. At fourteen! What a waste of money.

**INGRID**
He does save the coupons, Dad. He wants to buy himself an aqualung.

**FLETCHER**
He'll need one if he sticks to thirty a day.

**INGRID**
Wants to go skin diving in St Ives.

**FLETCHER**
I notice all his achievements are extra-curricular. Isn't there anything he fancies inside the classroom?

**INGRID**
Mostly the girls, Dad.

**FLETCHER**

(*Speaking as a parent*) Here, here! Tell him to watch that, to curb his appetites. Don't want him getting no girl into trouble.

**INGRID**

If you hadn't I wouldn't be here.

**FLETCHER**

Ingrid, there's no need for coarse remarks of that nature. I can't believe my ears when I talk to kids today.

**INGRID**

There's nothing wrong, Dad. You and Mum have proved that your love wasn't just a passing infatuation. Silver wedding.

**FLETCHER**

Nevertheless, I don't want my adolescent love life held up as a yardstick to young Raymond. He's only fourteen. When what happened happened to your mother and me we was mature responsible sixteen-year-olds. We had something behind us. We was in Highgate Cemetery – it was the tomb of Karl Marx. Your mother had a steady job in Gamages hardware department. And I had my plastering diploma from Borstal.

**INGRID**

Yes, Dad.

**FLETCHER**

Speaking of Highgate Cemetery, how's your love life? Not still that Eddie Risley, is it?

***Her look shows that it is.***

**FLETCHER**

I warned you enough about him, gel. He's a crook is Eddie Risley.

**INGRID**

Oh he's straight, Dad. Just he's a tough businessman. It's not fair what people keep saying about him. They tell you he'd sell his own mother.

**FLETCHER**

I heard that on very good authority.

**INGRID**

Who from?

**FLETCHER**

The two blokes who bought his mother.

**INGRID**

It's no use talking to you about Eddie. You got a blind spot about him.

**FLETCHER**

So have you, my gel. He's giving you a bad time. Isn't he?

**INGRID**

I just don't know where I am with him.

**FLETCHER**

You do pick them, Ingrid. You're a bonny girl with a lovely nature. You could have anyone, you could. And you're not getting any younger, you know. You're twenty-four, girl. Has to be said.

**INGRID**

That's not old.

**FLETCHER**

It is for a teenager, and a spinster.

**INGRID**

Oh Dad . . . things have changed since your day. Girls want to be . . .

well, lots of girls don't want to be tied down so quick. They feel there's alternatives to marriage.

**FLETCHER**

Not in Muswell Hill, they don't. Nothing's changed there.

**INGRID**

They've twinned the Odeon.

**FLETCHER**

I'm talking about standards. Moral standards. All these social commentators – they don't know Britain. They all live within a stone's throw of each other in NW1. They ain't never been north of Hampstead or south of Sloane Square. But in the real world – Birmingham, Bristol, Muswell Hill – the fundamentals haven't changed – here, are you wearing a bra?

**INGRID**

I don't need to, Dad.

**FLETCHER**

You what?

**INGRID**

I haven't done for years. My breasts are firm and pliant.

**FLETCHER**

(*Whispering*) Ingrid, please. This ain't San Tropay you know, this is Slade bleedin' Prison. There's six hundred men in here would go berserk at a glimpse of shin, never mind unfettered knockers.

***It's Ingrid's turn to be embarrassed.***

**INGRID**

Dad!

**FLETCHER**

I'm sorry, gel, but it has to be said. You're very naïve in certain ways. Very naïve about the effect your body has on the shackled male.

**INGRID**

Dad, you're naïve in certain ways. I shouldn't think anyone's even noticed.

***They look round. The camera reveals that all the male heads, Lennie's included, are focused firmly on Ingrid's unfettered womanhood.***

**3. LANDING**

***It is night time. There is the sound of snores and coughs.***

**3A. CELL**

***Lennie is asleep. Suddenly his bunk is shaken.***

**FLETCHER**

Godber . . . Godber! . . . GODBER!!

***Lennie opens his eyes, trying to emerge from a deep sleep.***

**LENNIE**

What, what, what???!!!

**FLETCHER**

Are you awake?

**LENNIE**

I am now . . . what's the matter?

**FLETCHER**

Got any snout?

**LENNIE**

No. Would you believe it?

**FLETCHER**

(*Grumpily*) I'd believe it, you inconsiderate nurk.

**LENNIE**

I thought you'd given it up.

**FLETCHER**

I feel like starting again.

***There is a pause. Fletcher gets out off the bunk and lowers himself to the floor. He looks uncharacteristically worried and preoccupied.***

**FLETCHER**

Mind your head.

**LENNIE**

Me mum brought me some Maltesers.

**FLETCHER**

No, thanks.

**LENNIE**

And some of her Parkin cake.

**FLETCHER**

No, thanks. If you ain't got no snout, naff off back to sleep.

**LENNIE**

Oh thanks very much, you bad-tempered old scroat. What's wrong with you anyway?

**FLETCHER**

Things on my mind, ain't there?

**LENNIE**

Like what?

**FLETCHER**

My business.

**LENNIE**

Oh come on, Fletch. Might as well talk it out. I mean, you woke me up.

**FLETCHER**

Get depressed at times that's all. Stinking stir.

***He kicks the table.***

**LENNIE**

That's not like you, Fletch.

**FLETCHER**

A father's place is at home, with his kids – giving them affection, parental guidance. I got three of 'em, you know.

**LENNIE**

Yes, I know.

**FLETCHER**

Fourteen, nineteen and twenty-four.

**LENNIE**

Quite a gap between each.

**FLETCHER**

Circumstances dictated that.

**LENNIE**

How?

**FLETCHER**

Kept going in prison for five years, didn't I?

**LENNIE**

Oh.

**FLETCHER**

The two youngest – well, that's a terrible age the teens, in' it? You expect trouble. But Ingrid, my eldest, you'd think she'd have learnt some lessons by now.

**LENNIE**

She looked a nice girl to me. She had lovely –

**FLETCHER**

(*Quickly*) I know what she's got lovely,

Godber. It's her father you're talking to, be very careful!

**LENNIE**

(*Calming him*) Eyes, I was going to say. Eyes. Big and blue.

**FLETCHER**

(*Mollified*) Oh.

**LENNIE**

Nice smile too which seemed to indicate a nice disposition and a warm and generous nature.

**FLETCHER**

Yes, yes. True, true. That's all right then.

**LENNIE**

(*Carefully*) Fletch, I hope you don't mind but I couldn't help overhearing a bit of what you was saying – well, most of us did.

**FLETCHER**

Oh yes?

**LENNIE**

Doesn't sound good enough for her, that Eddie Risley, if you ask me.

**FLETCHER**

He ain't. He used to say he was in the motor trade – know what he did? Forged car log books. Not that she'd believe it.

**LENNIE**

How could you be sure?

**FLETCHER**

'Cos I bought two off him.

***There is a pause.***

**FLETCHER**

They weren't much cop. He'd spelt Citroën with an S . . .

**LENNIE**

Well, with a bit of luck he'll get rumbled sooner or later and sent away. Give her a chance to find someone new. I should think your Marion awakening to the possibilities of her sex, she'll settle down at Timothy White's. And I wouldn't worry too much about your Raymond either. I was on thirty a day when I was fourteen. Oh, and by the way, congratulations on your silver wedding.

**FLETCHER**

Godber, did you earwig all my conversation? Couldn't you have talked to your poor old mum? It's a long shlep from Birmingham.

**LENNIE**

She doesn't have much to say for herself does Mum. She's a canny old soul but she only gives me a catalogue of family ailments.

**FLETCHER**

What about news of the lovely Denise?

**LENNIE**

She don't talk about Denise 'cos she don't approve of her.

**FLETCHER**

Why?

**LENNIE**

'Cos she uses green nail varnish and doesn't wear a bra.

**FLETCHER**

Sounds as if she and my Ingrid have got a lot in common.

***There is a pause.***

**LENNIE**
Your Ingrid's got nicer knockers.

## 4. ASSOCIATION AREA

***Fletcher is playing draughts. As he makes a move, Barrowclough shouts from the landing above.***

**BARROWCLOUGH**
Fletcher . . . could I have a word.

***Fletcher calls out from the table.***

**FLETCHER**
I'm playing draughts, ain't I?

**BARROWCLOUGH**
It is rather important. Wouldn't ask otherwise.

**FLETCHER**
So's this important . . .

***He makes a move. The other player makes a move and takes four of Fletcher's men.***

**FLETCHER**
Still, if duty calls, better abandon this game, Cecil. Call it a draw. Half each.

***He gets up and takes half the board with him. He walks to the stairs.***

## 4A. CELL

***Barrowclough walks in, followed by Fletcher.***

**BARROWCLOUGH**
I'm sorry to interrupt you in association hour.

**FLETCHER**
'S all right. Only draughts.

**BARROWCLOUGH**
Not your game as a rule, is it?

**FLETCHER**
What else is left? Only news on the telly and someone's trod on the ping pong ball.

**BARROWCLOUGH**
Oh, I am sorry. Anyhow I wanted a quiet word.

**FLETCHER**
I'm all ears.

**BARROWCLOUGH**
Do you know where Godber is?

**FLETCHER**
He'll be at one of his poxy evening classes. What is it today, Tuesday? Tuesday – woodwork.

**BARROWCLOUGH**
He's up in front of the Governor.

**FLETCHER**
What? The kid? What's he done?

**BARROWCLOUGH**
He attacked another prisoner. At work, in the kitchens. He attacked Jackdaw with a soup ladle.

**FLETCHER**
I don't believe it.

**BARROWCLOUGH**
It's true. A severe and unprovoked attack the officer said.

**FLETCHER**
I don't believe it. I know Jackdaw gets on your wick, he gets on all our wicks but young Lennie's a passive lad, he wouldn't hurt a fly.

**BARROWCLOUGH**
That's why I came to you. I thought

you might be able to shed some light on the matter.

**FLETCHER**

I dunno. He was his usual self this morning. And at lunch he was quite cheerful. Mind you, one of your colleagues, Mr Pringle, did slip on some orange peel and fall down some stairs hurting his back – so we were all quite cheerful.

**BARROWCLOUGH**

Fletcher, you must be serious. Godber's in trouble. It's so irrational. I mean I like that lad, I think he's got a lot of promise.

**FLETCHER**

Well, that's prison, isn't it? The system. Already turning a nice quiet lad into a violent criminal. You're sitting on a volcano which at any time might erupt in an explosion of desperate violence and mayhem.

**BARROWCLOUGH**

Fletcher – you've got your finger on the pulse. What can we do to avert it?

**FLETCHER**

There's only one thing which might help to postpone the inevitable holocaust.

**BARROWCLOUGH**

What? What?

**FLETCHER**

You'll have to indent for some new ping pong balls.

## 4B. FILM

***A warder unlocks the gate. Lennie enters and walks along the catwalk and past Barrowclough into Fletcher's cell.***

## 4C. CELL

***Lennie goes to the bed and takes off his jacket. Fletcher watches him for a moment.***

**FLETCHER**

Well then . . .?

**LENNIE**

Well then what?

**FLETCHER**

I heard.

**LENNIE**

Heard what?

**FLETCHER**

I heard you hit Jackdaw with a ladle.

**LENNIE**

Heard right then, didn't you?

**FLETCHER**

(*Fishing*) I'm sure you had your reasons.

**LENNIE**

Yes, I did.

***Fletcher waits but nothing else is forthcoming.***

**FLETCHER**

Ain't you going to the cooler then?

**LENNIE**

No. I'm not.

**FLETCHER**

Well, you're a lucky lad then, aren't you?

**LENNIE**

Lucky, am I?

**FLETCHER**

Assault! Ladling a fellow prisoner. Automatic cooler offence, ladling.

**LENNIE**

(*Staccato*) Governor gave me a severe reprimand and loss of privileges. Would have got cooler. But accepted my mitigating circumstances.

**FLETCHER**

Oh . . . mitigating circumstances. Well, you must have had . . .

***There is a pause.***

**FLETCHER**

Don't have to tell me.

***He gets off his bunk.***

**FLETCHER**

Don't have to tell me what drove a normal affable lad like yourself to the pitch where he suddenly launches himself on another prisoner with a deadly weapon, to wit a ladle.

**LENNIE**

I won't then. Rather not.

**FLETCHER**

I see.

***There is a pause.***

**FLETCHER**

Doesn't occur to you that your hitherto blameless record is due in no small part to yours truly. I'm just the bloke who showed you the ropes, helped you get by, kept you on the rails, loaned you his soft toilet paper.

**LENNIE**

I'm not ungrateful, Fletch, honest. Every time I go to the bog, I'm not ungrateful.

**FLETCHER**

Godber, having eavesdropped into every aspect of my private life, don't you think I'm entitled to know a bit of yours!

***Lennie sighs then says reluctantly.***

**LENNIE**

I had some news. Which upset me. Jackdaw thought it was a joke. Kept taking the mick. Wouldn't leave it off. So I hit him. While the balance of my mind was disturbed.

**FLETCHER**

News?

**LENNIE**

Yeah.

***There is a pause.***

**FLETCHER**

(*Sitting by Lennie*) What news?

***Lennie takes a letter out of his pocket and hands it to Fletcher, who opens it.***

**FLETCHER**

Oh, I see, it's a 'Dear John' letter, ain't it?

**LENNIE**

Yeah – Dear Lennie, in my case.

**FLETCHER**

Naturally, yours, no longer for ever, Denise, eh?

**LENNIE**

'S right.

**FLETCHER**

Dear, dear. So it's the demise of Denise then?

**LENNIE**

Not funny, Fletch.

**FLETCHER**

Was I making a joke?

**LENNIE**
Not what I call a joke, no.

**FLETCHER**
Don't you think I haven't seen this happen many, many times? Only natural. You could say inevitable. Least your Denise has been honest enough to write a letter. 'Cos they're all at it like knives while we're in here.

**LENNIE**
Came out of the blue though this, Fletch. No hint of it a fortnight ago in her last letter. Her only concern then was whether we should have a canary or a budgerigar.

**FLETCHER**
In your future life together?

**LENNIE**
Yes.

**FLETCHER**
Well, that's one decision you don't have to make.

**LENNIE**
No.

***There is a pause.***

**FLETCHER**
I know it's now academic, but speaking personally, from personal experience, I would say I would always without doubt plump for the budgerigar.

**LENNIE**
Oh, why?

**FLETCHER**
Budgies is friendlier. And they're very prone to draughts, canaries – it's the angle of the tail.

**LENNIE**
Oh.

**FLETCHER**
I speak from experience as I say. We had a canary once . . . surly little bleeder he was.

**LENNIE**
Yes, well as you say, it's a bit academic now, Fletch.

**FLETCHER**
So your Denise . . . has . . . er . . . she er . . . I mean er, there's another man is there, presumably?

***Lennie nods.***

**FLETCHER**
D'you know him?

**LENNIE**
His name's Kenneth – he's in the Merchant Navy. Third engineer, qualified. No contest, is there?

***He gets up, walks across the cell and sits down again.***

**FLETCHER**
Oh well, Jack the lad, isn't he? The blue-eyed boy with his navy blue uniform and the gold braid. Oh well, the sun shines out of his pot-hole. It's all temporary, son, all temporary. When he goes back to sea – sailor beware then. You'll be out with Denise, he'll be in the Persian Gulf. That's when you resume your rightful position, in her affections that is. I tell you, this is only a temporary setback.

**LENNIE**
I don't think so, Fletch.

**FLETCHER**
No sweat.

**LENNIE**
She's married him.

**FLETCHER**
She done what!

**LENNIE**
Last Saturday, Smethwick Registry Office. She thought it was my right to know.

**FLETCHER**
Married!

**LENNIE**
Apparently it kept fine for them and the Cross Keys did them proud. Pâté and ham salad.

**FLETCHER**
(*Rising and walking across*) Pâté and ham salad. Well, I'm appalled. Words fail me. I'm speechless. Nothing will surprise me any more.

***Jackdaw comes in with his arm in a sling and his head bandaged.***

**FLETCHER**
Jackdaw!

**JACKDAW**
Now look 'ere . . .

**FLETCHER**
God preserve us, Jackdaw, what do you look like?

**JACKDAW**
All right, all right.

**FLETCHER**
You been driving golf balls in your cell again.

**JACKDAW**
Ask him!

**LENNIE**
(*Walking over to Jackdaw*) I'm sorry, Jackdaw, straight up. There was no call for that.

**JACKDAW**
What d'you get?

**LENNIE**
Didn't get the cooler. Deserved it.

**JACKDAW**
'Ere listen, no hard feelings.

**LENNIE**
That's good of you, Jackdaw. 'Cos you're entitled.

**FLETCHER**
Yes, very commendable, Jackdaw. Why don't you shake on it?

**JACKDAW**
I'd sooner not.

***He indicates his bandaged right arm.***

**JACKDAW**
I just come in to say that I realise that you er . . . you er . . . that there were –

**FLETCHER**
The circumstances was mitigating.

**JACKDAW**
That's it. As you say, Fletch. That I bear no grudges, 'cos obviously you've suffered a great emotional upheaval. And it'll take some time to get over. Thing like this does, doesn't it, like? But as soon as you're back to normal and my wrist is better I'll er –

***He points to his head.***

**JACKDAW**

I'll get you for this!!

**5. VISITING ROOM**

***Ingrid is sitting in the same seat as before, facing Fletcher.***

**INGRID**

Mum's definitely coming up next month. She would have come today only the doctor expressly forbade it. Said she'd be a fool to herself.

**FLETCHER**

It's nothing serious though?

**INGRID**

Just something going round he says.

***There is a pause. Then comes the news.***

**INGRID**

Marion ain't with Timothy White's no longer.

**FLETCHER**

(*With heavy sarcasm*) Dispensed with her services, did they?

**INGRID**

It wasn't molestation this time. But she got a job selling shirts. She shows them round the offices.

**FLETCHER**

Well, make a change from showing her knickers round the office.

**INGRID**

And she's found a flat in Maida Vale, which she's sharing with some nurses. And what you'll be most glad to hear is that Eddie and me have split up.

**FLETCHER**

Not before time, gel. That's a relief to us all.

***A voice can be heard from their right. The camera reveals Lennie, sitting opposite his mum again.***

**LENNIE**

Yes, we was worried about that liaison.

**FLETCHER**

(*Indignantly*) Do you mind, Godber! I'm sorry Mrs Godber, no offence, but I've warned the lad about this before. Ain't you got any news from your home front?

**MRS GODBER**

I'm sorry, it's my fault. I can never think of what to say to him. It's like visiting people in hospital.

**FLETCHER**

Force yourself.

***Mackay bears down on them.***

**MACKAY**

Here, here, here, here! You all know the procedure. Conversations will be confined to the relative or friend opposite the prisoner in question. There will be no fractricide.

**FLETCHER**

That's what I was telling him, Mr Mackay. (*Then pointedly to Lennie*) So if you'll excuse us, Godber.

**LENNIE**

Sorry, Fletch. Sorry miss.

***He smiles at Ingrid, who smiles back.***

**INGRID**

That's all right.

**FLETCHER**
So anyhow, you give Eddie the elbow then? Good for you, girl. Just listen to your old dad in future.

**INGRID**
I do, Dad. Ain't you noticed how much more discreet I am today?

**FLETCHER**
How d'you mean?

**INGRID**
Well, last time I was here I obviously embarrassed you in front of your friends. Well, this time, I ain't given you no cause, have I?

**FLETCHER**
Ain't you? I don't get you, girl.

**INGRID**
Oh Dad . . . look – I'm wearing a bra.
*She pulls up her sweater to reveal a black bra. The entire room is goggle-eyed and sick with lust.*

**6. CELL**

***Lennie is folding a letter into an envelope and then licks and seals it. Fletcher enters, taking something furtively from his pocket.***

**FLETCHER**
Look at that.
***It is a ping pong ball.***

**LENNIE**
What?

**FLETCHER**
New ping pong ball. Two star.

**LENNIE**
But you don't play.

**FLETCHER**
(*With an expression that says, will he never learn*) *I* don't play. But all you other nurks do, don't you? There's a severe scarcity of ping pong balls in this nick. I'll get a quarter-pound of snout for this.

**LENNIE**
Oh. (*Seriously*) Fletch – can I ask you something?

**FLETCHER**
(*Looking for a hiding place*) Feel free.

**LENNIE**
You know when I was very down the other day. After Denise's letter.

**FLETCHER**
Yes.

**LENNIE**
When I was worried about the stigma of being an ex-con . . .

**FLETCHER**
Yes . . .

**LENNIE**
Well, will it be a problem for me? I mean, will I be able to work me way back into society?

**FLETCHER**
That depends, son. Depends on the breaks.

**LENNIE**
Have there been any problems for you? When you get out?

**FLETCHER**
Not for me, no. I've never had to worry about no references, no testimonials. 'Cos I've always gone straight, straight back into crime. It's different with you,

Lennie – you're young, you're healthy, you've got an honest face.

**LENNIE**

Is that enough?

**FLETCHER**

Yes, yes. Character. That's what I can read. And you've got it, son. You're a good lad.

**LENNIE**

So you think, if someone really cared for me, a girl, like . . . she'd overlook my past misdemeanours?

**FLETCHER**

Certainly. If she's any sort of human being of course she would. Like anybody would. Lennie, my son, you have to learn to believe in yourself. I believe in you.

**LENNIE**

Do you, Fletch?

**FLETCHER**

'Course I do.

***Lennie is cheered by this.***

**LENNIE**

Oh good. I'm going to send this then.

***He holds up the letter.***

**LENNIE**

Would you give it to your mucker Barrowclough? To post in the village.

**FLETCHER**

(*Reading the address*) BBC . . .?

**LENNIE**

It's on plain notepaper, so they won't know it's from a prisoner.

**FLETCHER**

'Hello Young Lovers Corner.' Oh gawd. Is all this soul-searching for the benefit of that slag Denise?

**LENNIE**

No, not her.

**FLETCHER**

Well who?

**LENNIE**

Ingrid.

**FLETCHER**

(*Quietly*) My Ingrid . . .

**LENNIE**

(*Quoting his letter*) Yeah . . . 'Our eyes met across a crowded room . . .'

**FLETCHER**

My daughter Ingrid!

**LENNIE**

'And though we didn't know each other, we both knew . . .'

**FLETCHER**

(*Exploding*) You think I'd let my beloved Ingrid take up with the likes of you! A bleeding juvenile delinquent from the backstreets of Birmingham!

***He raises his fist, about to bring it down on Lennie.***

**LENNIE**

(*Urgently*) Fletch, be careful, be careful.

**FLETCHER**

(*Checked*) What?

***Lennie unclenches Fletcher's fist.***

**LENNIE**

You've crushed your ping-pong ball!

# 2 SERIES TWO

## EPISODE THREE: DISTURBING THE PEACE

### 1. LIBRARY

***Fletcher is stacking the old books on to a trolley when the door is unlocked and Barrowclough enters.***

**BARROWCLOUGH**

Right, Fletcher, you'd better get on your rounds, hospital and Governor.

**FLETCHER**

Just picking something out special for the Governor, Mr Barrowclough. Got a good one for his wife an' all. 'A Perilous Odyssey of Love and Anguish Set in Turbulent Tuscany'. Very torrid according to the write-up.

**BARROWCLOUGH**

Not too torrid, is it?

**FLETCHER**

Have no fear. It's done in very good taste. They always put the lights out.

**BARROWCLOUGH**

Come on then, let's get along.

***He is trying to rush Fletcher. Fletcher produces a paper.***

**FLETCHER**

Oh, just before we go, could you sign this, Mr Barrowclough? Requisition for new books. I know how busy you are so don't trouble to read it, just sign at the bottom where I've indicated.

***Fletcher has placed the paper in front of him, but Barrowclough hesitates.***

**BARROWCLOUGH**

Just have a quick glance through . . .

**FLETCHER**

(*Disapprovingly*) Well, we are a bit behindhand, I mean, chop chop.

***Barrowclough, however, insists on checking the list, then frowns.***

**BARROWCLOUGH**

There's several here quite unsuitable, not suitable at all. Look at this . . .

**FLETCHER**

What?

**BARROWCLOUGH**

(*Shocked*) *The Great Escape* . . . *Nudes of the Naughty Nineties* . . . *A History of Erotica*.

**FLETCHER**

I couldn't find it on the map.

**BARROWCLOUGH**

I can't let these through, Fletcher. They're mostly sexual or subversive.

***He scratches them out.***

**FLETCHER**

Oh, leave *Voodoo Woman*. It's a classic, that.

**BARROWCLOUGH**

You've got a very privileged job in this library, Fletcher. Take care you don't lose it.

***He gives the list back to Fletcher, who, disgruntled, looks at what has survived the censor's pen.***

**FLETCHER**

I see you've allowed the Enid Blyton Omnibus. The lads'll be chuffed about that.

**BARROWCLOUGH**

There is a limit.

**FLETCHER**

Yes, yes, I can appreciate your point of view. There's always two sides, isn't there? Sort of thing I want to bring out in my forthcoming book.

**BARROWCLOUGH**

Book!

**FLETCHER**

Well, working in the library has rekindled my literary aspirations. So I'm working on this book, see. On prison life. From the man within, like.

**BARROWCLOUGH**

(*Not keen*) Prison life.

**FLETCHER**

Ah, but don't worry, I'm very objective. I haven't overlooked the difficult task which confronts you brave boys in blue and I've sought to shed light on your problems as much as the ones faced by my fellow felons.

**BARROWCLOUGH**

(*Reassured*) Oh good, good. What are you going to call your book, Fletcher?

**FLETCHER**

Don't Let the Bastards Grind You Down.

***Fletcher exits, pushing his trolley.***

## 2. GOVERNOR'S OFFICE

***Mr Venables is sitting at his desk going through the mail with his secretary, Mrs Heskith. She is in her latish thirties, a local lady wearing sensible shoes.***

**VENABLES**

Is this all the mail then, Mrs Heskith?

**MRS HESKITH**

Yes, Mr Venables. The Home Office have confirmed the dates of Mr Mackay's promotion course.

***Venables picks up the relevant letter, studying it doubtfully for a moment.***

**VENABLES**

What? Yes, yes . . . it's difficult enough running a prison without losing someone of Mr Mackay's calibre.

**MRS HESKITH**

Don't forget Tuesday is the magistrates' inspection.

**VENABLES**

Oh is it? We'd better put on a bit of a

show for them. We'll have a roast, and get out the tinned pears . . . with cream.

**MRS HESKITH**

Cream?

**VENABLES**

Well, you know . . . Carnation milk or whatever it is.

**MRS HESKITH**

Right, I'll get along then.

***She goes to the door and bumps into Fletcher who enters, pushing his little trolleyload of books.***

**FLETCHER**

Oh good morning, Mrs Heskith, what a rare treat.

***She gives him a coy smile and tries to edge round his trolley, a little flustered.***

**MRS HESKITH**

Oh yes, good morning, Fletcher.

**FLETCHER**

What a lovely cardigan. Goes with your eyes, two of your best features if I may say so, tho' I expect you've been told many times before –

**VENABLES**

Fletcher, what is it?

**FLETCHER**

Oh. Morning, sir.

**VENABLES**

Thank you, Mrs Heskith. You'd better go and get me that release form to sign.

***She leaves. Fletcher gives her a quick appraisal as she goes.***

**FLETCHER**

(*Sotto voce*) Well I would, if you wouldn't.

**VENABLES**

What is it, Fletcher?

**FLETCHER**

Books, sir. New consignment, sir. You always like to have first pick of a new consignment.

**VENABLES**

It's not a question of first pick. I like to look them over to ensure there's nothing unsuitable for the men.

**FLETCHER**

I found one book you wanted, sir.

***He gives him a book.***

**VENABLES**

(*Puzzled*) *Tom Brown's Schooldays.*

**FLETCHER**

The title's irrelevant, sir. Point is it's exactly three-quarters of an inch thick, which is just what you said you wanted to prop up your wobbly bookcase.

**VENABLES**

Oh splendid, Fletcher. Thank you.

***Venables bends down to prop up the desk with the book, withdrawing a telephone directory. Fletcher automatically takes the opportunity to pocket what he can: a rubber, a pencil sharpener, a felt pen, two cigarettes from an open packet and a paper clip. He also cranes his head to read the letter about Mackay, showing more than a passing interest in it. Then he straightens himself up, just as Venables is also doing so.***

**VENABLES**
Yes, that's much better. Much better. Well, Fletcher, cut along.
***Mrs Heskith re-enters with a release form for signature. Fletcher again watches her, as he makes to go.***
**MRS HESKITH**
The release form, sir.
**VENABLES**
Oh good . . . where's my pen?
***Not surprisingly, he cannot find it on the desk.***
**FLETCHER**
Oh . . . borrow mine, sir.
***He produces Venables's pen.***
**VENABLES**
Oh, thank you, Fletcher.
***He takes it and signs the form, handing it back to Mrs Heskith and pocketing the pen.***
***Meanwhile Fletcher is looking at her, causing her some slight embarrassment.***
**VENABLES**
Go on then, Fletcher.
**FLETCHER**
Yes sir, it's just –

**VENABLES**
What, what?
**FLETCHER**
My pen, sir.
**VENABLES**
Oh I'm terribly sorry.
***He hands it back.***
**FLETCHER**
They all look alike, don't they, sir?

## 3. ASSOCIATION AREA

***It is evening, association time. Mackay walks around the men.***

## 3A. CELL

***Fletcher is emptying his pockets and putting the items on the table.***
**LENNIE**
Is that it, then?
**FLETCHER**
Yes – apart from a very interesting bit of information. I always learn something when I go in the Governor's office.
**LENNIE**
Like what?
**FLETCHER**
Well . . . apart from the fact that there's something simmering between him and Mrs Heskith – which we'll bear in mind for future reference, won't we – I also saw a memo on Venables's desk. Upside down of course, but years of being in the nick have taught me to read memos upside down.
**LENNIE**
What did it say?
**FLETCHER**
'Eciffo emoh, laitnedifnoc'.
**LENNIE**
What the hell's that mean?

**FLETCHER**
'Home Office, Confidential', backwards.

**LENNIE**
What was it about then?

**FLETCHER**
Something to do with Mackay's going on a course.

**LENNIE**
When, where, what course?

**FLETCHER**
Naff off, you nurk, I only had four seconds. But I reckon it must be something to do with promotion or transfer.

**LENNIE**
He ain't let on, like.

**FLETCHER**
He don't know yet, only me and the Governor knows so far.

**MACKAY**
(*Offscreen*) Come on, you men!

**LENNIE**
Aren't those his dulcet tones now, on the landing? Shall we ask him?

**FLETCHER**
No, no, no. We've got a situation here which I can turn to my advantage.

**MACKAY**
(*Offscreen*) Get your hair cut.

**FLETCHER**
(*Getting paper*) No time like the present – pretend you're listening.

***Fletcher reads the paper. Lennie gets on his bunk.***

**FLETCHER**
I see here, Godber, that with Saturn passing through your opposite sign of Cancer, this may be an exhausting and turbulent month for you. Must be moving you out the kitchens on to dustbins.

**MACKAY**
Seeking solace in the stars now, are we?

**FLETCHER**
Oh evening, Mr Mackay. If you'll excuse me – 'As Uranus is one of the most powerful and unpredictable planets – future events will be likewise unpredictable.'

**MACKAY**
I should have thought all your futures were somewhat predictable – hm, hm, hm . . . Now if your stars were true they would say, 'Little change for the next four years. No opportunities for travel, and absolutely no prospect of romance on the horizon.'

**FLETCHER**
Only a question of scale. When you're deprived of romance as what we are, a chance brush with the Governor's secretary is like a naughty weekend in Boulogne with a teenage nymphomaniac, see it's only a question of scale.

**LENNIE**
When's your birthday, Mr Mackay?

**MACKAY**
April the twenty-fifth.

**FLETCHER**
(*Looking in the paper*) Oh yes, Taurus.

Not the subtlest of signs. The bull. Here we are. 'Endeavours you have been hoping for come to fruition.' Oh look at this . . . 'A favourable time for a move and seeking opportunities elsewhere.'

**MACKAY**

Poppycock.

**FLETCHER**

No, they're rarely wrong. You must be moving on, Mr Mackay.

**LENNIE**

Holiday?

**MACKAY**

Not till August.

**LENNIE**

Your retirement's not due just yet, is it?

**MACKAY**

Don't be insolent, Godber.

**FLETCHER**

Well, it's very clear in the stars, very clear. A move is clearly indicated.

**MACKAY**

Out of the question.

**FLETCHER**

Want a bet?

**MACKAY**

You'd wager on this nonsense?

**FLETCHER**

When it's as clear as this I would. Doesn't do to deride what you don't know. The paranormal, the psychic. Take my Uncle Godfrey. Walked under a ladder one day. Laughed about it he did. Walked under it. Purposely, like. And d'you know, over the next forty-three years he lost all his teeth.

**MACKAY**

You'd lose your shirt betting on this astronomical nonsense.

**FLETCHER**

It's not nonsense. I'll bet you anything that within a few days you'll be leaving your familiar surroundings.

**MACKAY**

Step outside, Fletcher.

**FLETCHER**

What have I said now?

**MACKAY**

Step outside.

***Fletcher gets up, passes Mackay and goes out. Mackay follows him out of the cell.***

**MACKAY**

You have the nerve to offer to bet with a prison officer? In front of young Godber.

**FLETCHER**

Oh, I never thought, Mr Mackay.

**MACKAY**

What are you trying to do, disillusion the boy?

**FLETCHER**

Sorry, Mr Mackay.

**MACKAY**

How much then?

**FLETCHER**

A quid?

**MACKAY**

You're on.

### 4. PRISON GATES

***Camera shows a minibus. Mackay approaches it, shakes hands with Venables and gets in. Cheering is heard from prisoners on work detail.***

### 5. ASSOCIATION AREA

***It is night time. Fletcher is at a table with McLaren, Warren and Williams, who are playing draughts. Fletcher himself is reading the Sun.***
***The mood is relaxed.***

**WARREN**
Eh, did he pay up, Fletch?

**FLETCHER**
Certainly. With all the ill-grace you'd expect from that charmless Celtic nurk.

***They grin in satisfaction.***

**MCLAREN**
Twos up with that paper, eh?

**FLETCHER**
When I've finished.

**WARREN**
You've had it long enough. Are there some nice birds in it?

**FLETCHER**
I ain't looking at birds, am I? I'm reading the editorial. I'm not like you lot. All you want out a paper is horses and nudes. Some of us is a bit curious about what's going on in the world. I like to keep abreast.

***Lennie joins them at the table, wearing his kitchen whites.***

**LENNIE**
Yes, he does. Got breasts pasted all over our cell.

***Fletcher looks at him.***

**FLETCHER**
What!

***The others chuckle.***

**WILLIAMS**
I'm not a breast man myself.

**FLETCHER**
I beg your pardon, Mr Williams?

**WILLIAMS**
My initial interest is always awakened by the leg.

**FLETCHER**
Just one of them?

**MCLAREN**
I hear you're a bit of a ladies' man on the outside, Williams.

**WILLIAMS**
I've had my moments. I have a large sexual appetite, see. Probably compensating for those years of deprivation in the Bridge End Choral School. Consequentially I suffer more than most in prison.

***Fletcher finishes reading the paper, which is grabbed by McLaren.***

**FLETCHER**
Well listen, from what I just been reading I think we're better off in here. This country's on the verge of economic

ruin. This once great nation is hovering on the brink of the abyss.

**MCLAREN**

That's the bosses' fault.

**FLETCHER**

It's not the bosses, Vanessa, it's the average man. The people who'd rather draw National Assistance than take a job. People who won't do a decent day's work for a decent day's wages . . . people much like ourselves.

**WARREN**

My Elaine says she doesn't know where it's going to stop.

**FLETCHER**

What?

**WARREN**

Prices, like. No one's got any money.

**LENNIE**

By the time you lot get out of here, there'll be no one worth robbing.

**FLETCHER**

By then Britain should be reaping the benefits of North Sea oil. Can tell the A-rabs to stuff it and can we please buy London back.

**MCLAREN**

Scottish oil. Don't forget that. Scottish oil.

**FLETCHER**

Oh, listen to the Scottish Nationalist, all of a sudden. Well, well, would you believe it. A dusky Rob Roy. What tartan do you wear, the Black Watch?

**MCLAREN**

Naff off, Fletcher.

**FLETCHER**

All right so it's Scottish oil. It's English expertise what'll get it out.

**LENNIE**

Texan.

**FLETCHER**

(*Exasperated*) I don't know why I get drawn into these pointless arguments with you nurks. The only point I was trying so painstakingly to make is that we're better off inside.

**WARREN**

He's not wrong, I've known worse stir.

**WILLIAMS**

Me an' all.

**FLETCHER**

Right. And with Mackay gone . . . happy days are here again. Chance to work a few things, in't there?

**WILLIAMS**

True. Old Barrowclough don't exactly rule with a rod of iron, does he?

**FLETCHER**

We can start having a flutter again. What about frog racing? We could revive that. Get them from the farm.

**WILLIAMS**

Should I tell you something about frogs? Which is a fact. Like me, the frog has an exceptional sexual appetite. When the frog and his mate, mate, he's at it for twenty-eight days non-stop.

**LENNIE**

Twenty-eight days.

**WILLIAMS**

Non-stop.

**FLETCHER**
No wonder his eyes bulge out.

***Barrowclough enters through the gates with Wainwright.***

**FLETCHER**
Oh gawd.

**WARREN**
What's up, Fletch?

**FLETCHER**
Happy days. Life of Riley. I think they're over.

**LENNIE**
What you talking about?

**FLETCHER**
You heard me mention a screw in Brixton, Napper Wainwright. Right bastard.

**LENNIE**
Yeah, why?

**FLETCHER**
He's just walked in the door, that's why.

***They all turn to see Wainwright and Barrowclough walking behind one of the other tables to the guarded curiosity of the prisoners sitting at it.***

**WARREN**
He looks a right one.

**MCLAREN**
You don't suppose he's Mackay's replacement?

**FLETCHER**
That's exactly what I am supposing.

**LENNIE**
Living legend, isn't he, in the Prison Service?

**FLETCHER**
Not only that, he's got promotion. Stripes, isn't it? Well, lads . . . let's hope success has mellowed him.

***As if for an answer, we hear Wainwright bawl out an unfortunate prisoner, in a voice which reveals him as a Londoner.***

**WAINWRIGHT**
(*Rapidly*) Something to say to me, have you? Have you? Well my name's Wainwright. You address me as 'Mr Wainwright' or 'Sir'. Now button your lip!

**FLETCHER**
It has!

**WARREN**
He's coming over.

***Wainwright approaches them.***

**WAINWRIGHT**
Norman Stanley Fletcher, on your feet. I knew our paths would cross again, my son. The day you left Brixton I said to you, 'This is not goodbye, Fletcher, this is merely au-revoyer.'

**FLETCHER**
I have to admit you did, Mr Wainwright, and I said to you, 'Why don't you . . .' That is, I gave you certain advice regarding the Warders' Comfort Offertory Box.

**WAINWRIGHT**
I haven't forgotten what you said!

**FLETCHER**
And did you manage it?

***Wainwright's narrowed eyes promise future retribution.***

**WAINWRIGHT**

It doesn't pay to come it with me, Fletcher. You remember me.

***He widens his audience to include the rest of the group at the table.***

**WAINWRIGHT**

I have this mean streak, see. I know it's despicable but I'm prejudiced.

**MCLAREN**

That'll make a nice change.

**WAINWRIGHT**

Sonny Jim, I'm not just prejudiced against you lot . . . *I'm* prejudiced against – (*Rapid-fire*) liberals, longhairs, pill-heads, winos, queens, slags, squealers, pikeys and grease-balls. Are you in there, sonny?

***He has suddenly switched his attention to Lennie.***

**FLETCHER**

Isn't everybody?

**WAINWRIGHT**

Quiet, Fletcher, I was talking to the boy. I said, are you in there?

***Lennie thinks seriously about it, then speaks with some relief.***

**LENNIE**

I don't think so, I'm Church of England.

***Wainwright's look once more promises further retribution. The others snigger.***

**WAINWRIGHT**

We've only just met, and already he's given me a grudge to bear.

***Barrowclough comes over to join Wainwright.***

**BARROWCLOUGH**

Oh, I see you men have been getting acquainted with Mr Wainwright.

**CHORUS**

(*Not thrilled*) Yes, yes . . .

**FLETCHER**

Some of us have had that dubious privilege earlier in our careers.

**BARROWCLOUGH**

Oh really?

**WAINWRIGHT**

(*Indicating Fletcher*) This one passed through Brixton on a couple of brief but memorable occasions.

**BARROWCLOUGH**

Oh well, it's nice to bump into old faces, old . . .

**FLETCHER**

Adversaries.

**BARROWCLOUGH**

No no, that's not the word, Fletcher. I keep telling these men, Mr Wainwright, that our role is to help them . . . to encourage them in a programme of self-improvement and rehabilitation. To prepare them for going back into society.

**WAINWRIGHT**

Our role, Mr Barrowclough, is to keep them away from society. Our role is to keep these scheming bastards locked in.

***He strides away.***

**BARROWCLOUGH**

Yes, well I . . . I expect he's a bit tired after the long journey.

*He goes after Wainwright.*

**MCLAREN**

Spoke too soon, Fletch.

**WILLIAMS**

(*Singing*) Happy days are here again . . .

*They all join in.*

**WAINWRIGHT**

(*Offscreen*) Quiet!

*The singing stops abruptly.*

## 6. CANTEEN

*Wainwright comes in, surveys the scene, then walks along behind the line of men being served. Lennie is dishing out potatoes. As Wainwright gets level with Lennie some potato drops on Wainwright's shoe.*

*He indicates for Lennie to come to him.*

*Lennie does so. He wipes the potato off Wainwright's shoe, then goes back to serving again.*

## 6A. ASSOCIATION

*A group of prisoners is watching a boxing match on television. Camera shows a hand which switches the set off. It is Wainwright, who says:*

**WAINWRIGHT**

Beddy byes . . .

## 6B. CORRIDOR

*Fletcher and other prisoners are washing the floor. Camera shows feet as they walk over floor leaving marks.*

**FLETCHER**

Oh Mr Wainwright, now look what you've done.

*Wainwright walks back to Fletcher.*

**FLETCHER**

Have to do it all again now.

*He gets a cloth from the bucket and throws it on the floor. It splashes Wainwright's boot. Fletcher washes the floor. Wainwright moves and steps on his hand.*

## 7. CELL

*Fletcher is unbandaging his hand. Lennie is building a model.*

**LENNIE**

What a swine, stepping on your hand like that.

**FLETCHER**

Be fair. Complete accident. His foot slipped. He was aiming for my head.

**LENNIE**

What are we going to do about it, Fletch?

**FLETCHER**

I'll have a word with Warren and McLaren, they're dab hands at sabotage.

**LENNIE**
Your stars didn't predict this, did they?
**FLETCHER**
Yes, well, that's all a load of cobblers isn't it? . . .
***Barrowclough appears at the cell door.***
**BARROWCLOUGH**
Mind if I come in?
**FLETCHER**
All right, wipe your feet.
***Barrowclough enters.***
**LENNIE**
You look a bit bushed, Mr Barrowclough.
**BARROWCLOUGH**
Well, I am. It's that Mr Wainwright. He's been through this prison like a dose of salts. He's reorganised the entire duty roster.
**FLETCHER**
Oh, tough titty. Any idea how many curtailments we've suffered? No fraternising in the exercise yard. Shorter telly hours. And he's only commandeered our ping-pong table for your bleeding mess.
**BARROWCLOUGH**
Only until our billiard table's been recovered.
**FLETCHER**
Oh yes, well . . .
**BARROWCLOUGH**
Well, it's your fault it needed recovering.
**FLETCHER**
Our fault?
**BARROWCLOUGH**
Some prisoner certainly tampered with it.
**FLETCHER**
Can you prove that?
**BARROWCLOUGH**
We can at least surmise it. When Nosher Garrett went over the wall he was picked up in Blackpool wearing a green baize suit.
**FLETCHER**
Look, I'm not being drawn into any more pointless arguments.
**BARROWCLOUGH**
No . . . well, I really came to say cheerio, 'cos you won't be seeing so much of me in the future. He's got me down for a transfer to the farm.
**LENNIE**
What?
**BARROWCLOUGH**
Says I should just be in charge of trusties. Says I'm not really suited to a cell block. Where I'm at the mercy of infractious and recalcitrant prisoners like yourself, Fletcher – no offence you understand, these are his words, not mine.
**FLETCHER**
Look, Mr Barrowclough, we've got to prevent this.
***He gets up and goes across to Barrowclough.***
**FLETCHER**
Trouble is you see, if truth be told,

your humanity is mistaken by them nurks as mollycoddling.

**BARROWCLOUGH**

I've only tried to be fair and encourage them –

**FLETCHER**

'Course you have. I knows that, and you know that. But you'll have to change your ways. If you don't want to spend the rest of your life down the farm, knee deep in cow dung in charge of trusty udder-pullers.

**BARROWCLOUGH**

Change my ways?

**FLETCHER**

Yeah. Don't let people take advantage. Come on strong. Wield the big stick.

**LENNIE**

Put on a bit of a show, like. You know . . . Mean, moody and magnificent.

***There is a pause.***

**BARROWCLOUGH**

Oh, I don't know.

## 8. CANTEEN

***Camera shows food, trays, men being served. A Prison Officer is walking up the line of prisoners. Lennie, who is serving, looks at McLaren. McLaren looks at Fletcher. Fletcher gets up and goes. He looks at the clock. Fletcher nods. Warren receives nod and nods the other way. McLaren receives nod and turns to Lennie.***

**MCLAREN**

Hey you. I'm talking to you.

**LENNIE**

Me?

***Heads turn.***

**MCLAREN**

Yes you, Fanny Craddock . . . there's a caterpillar on my plate.

**LENNIE**

Well a caterpillar don't eat much.

**MCLAREN**

You what?

***He leans across the counter and grabs Lennie.***

**LENNIE**

Ease up, Mac, it's only a make-believe riot.

**MCLAREN**

I know kid, but I have to make it look authentic.

**LENNIE**

But you're strangling me.

**MCLAREN**

I know, but nothing personal, you understand. This food's no fit for swine. We've had enough, lads.

***Warren gets up.***

**WARREN**

We want a riot.

***Camera shows tables being turned up, food being upset, plates dropped, Lennie with peas over his head thrown by McLaren. A Prison Officer blows his whistle and is showered with potatoes. Alarm bells start ringing.***

*Prison warders come running. There is the noise of cell doors being slammed. The warders run along the catwalk.*

*Camera shows Wainwright's head as he comes into view. The door is unlocked and he goes into the canteen.*

*The prisoners stop.*

*Wainwright starts to speak but food is thrown at him and he finally backs out.*

**9. GOVERNOR'S OFFICE**

*Camera shows a tray with a glass of water and two pink pills. Mrs Heskith gives it to Venables.*

**VENABLES**

Thank you, Mrs Heskith.

*He gulps the pills down.*

**MRS HESKITH**

You're only supposed to take two before retiring.

**VENABLES**

If we don't put a stop to this riot, that may be tomorrow.

*Mrs Heskith leans over the desk. Fletcher comes in at that moment, pulling his trolley load of books.*

**FLETCHER**

Oops! Oopsadaisy! Sorry.

**VENABLES**

What on earth do you want, Fletcher?

**FLETCHER**

Another load of new books, sir.

**VENABLES**

At a time like this!

**FLETCHER**

Oh yes, well I wasn't to know, was I . . .

**VENABLES**

I'm referring to the riot!

**FLETCHER**

Oh, the riot, yes. Another nasty situation, sir.

**VENABLES**

It is indeed. At the moment there's a systematic and wilful destruction of furniture and crockery. They're knee deep in plates in there.

**FLETCHER**

Like a Greek restaurant on New Year's Eve.

**VENABLES**

Don't be flippant, Fletcher. I'd've thought Mr Wainwright would have been the ideal man for this situation, but he seemed to make matters worse.

**FLETCHER**

If truth were told, sir, it's Mr Wainwright what aggravated the situation now in the first place. Now that's just between me, you, Mrs Heskith and the bedpost.

**MRS HESKITH**

I'll just get this typed up then.

**VENABLES**

I suppose I'll have to go down there myself.

**FLETCHER**

No offence, sir, but there's only one man in this prison who could quell that riot. Only one man who could confront that ugly vicious mob and defuse the powder keg of emotion.

**VENABLES**

Who? Who?

### 10. FARM

***Barrowclough is supervising the prisoners working on the pig farm. He turns.***

**BARROWCLOUGH**

Me, what do you mean me?

### 11. CANTEEN

***Riot is still going on.***

***McLaren is shouting 'Load, aim, fire!' Food is being thrown. The firing party throws potatoes.***

***Barrowclough goes to the canteen door. A PO unlocks it and Barrowclough walks in. The door is shut behind him. Barrowclough walks into the canteen. The prisoners stop.***

**BARROWCLOUGH**

Now we . . . why don't we all put those things down?

***The prisoners do so.***

**BARROWCLOUGH**

This mess will all have to be cleared up, you know.

***They start to clear up.***

**BARROWCLOUGH**

Not yet though . . . In the meantime, why don't we all file back to our cells in an orderly fashion.

***The prisoners start to file out of the canteen. As Lennie passes Barrowclough he stops.***

**LENNIE**

Mean, moody, magnificent!

### 11A. YARD/LANDING

***Camera shows Warren and McLaren being marched across the yard. They enter through the gate on to the prison landing and walk along the catwalk. The prisoners congratulate them.***

### 12. CELL

***Fletcher and Lennie are in their cell.***

**FLETCHER**

(*Speaking through the door*) Well done, lads.

**LENNIE**

Congratulations.

***Warren and McLaren walk in.***

**MCLAREN**

Worth it, wasn't it?

**FLETCHER**
Well worth it, my son.
**MCLAREN**
Barrowclough's back on the landing, then?
**FLETCHER**
Yes and Wainwright's back in Brixton, where he belongs. Loss of face, wasn't it? Had to leave, bloke like that.
**MCLAREN**
So happy days are here again, eh?
**FLETCHER**
Normal service has been resumed.
***They all laugh.***
***Meanwhile Mackay has entered the association area and is looking around, when he hears laughter from Fletcher's cell. He walks to it and goes in. Fletcher catches his eye at last.***
***Mackay looks.***
**FLETCHER**
Oh . . . Mr Mackay, what a nice surprise. Nice surprise, isn't it, lads?
***McLaren and Warren leave.***
**MACKAY**
I thought it might be, Fletcher. I think some of you wrongly assumed that I had left, gone for good, but as you see nothing could be further from the truth. Only I'm somewhat disturbed to hear what's been happening in my absence. So now, we're going to have a new regime here. Based not on leniency and laxity but discipline, hard work, and blind unquestioning obedience. Feet will not touch the ground, and lives will be made a misery – I'm BACK and I'M IN CHARGE HERE.
***Mackay leaves.***
***Fletcher and Lennie look at each other.***
***Mackay is walking along the catwalk when suddenly he hears Fletcher and Lennie singing 'For he's a jolly good fellow'. The camera shows Fletcher and Lennie singing in their cell. Gradually other prisoners are heard joining in the singing.***

# 2 SERIES TWO

## EPISODE FOUR: NO PEACE FOR THE WICKED

### 1. ASSOCIATION AREA

***Fletcher walks along the catwalk with a mug of tea and a magazine towards his cell. McLaren is fixing his boots. Then he moves off upstairs towards Fletcher's cell.***

### 1A. FLETCHER'S CELL

***Fletcher comes into his cell with the mug of tea and magazine. He is singing to himself.***

**FLETCHER**

Born free . . .
Till somebody shopped me
Now I'm doing solitree.

***McLaren walks in.***

**MCLAREN**

Got any chewing gum, Fletch?

**FLETCHER**

(*Chewing*) No, never use it.

**MCLAREN**

Aw come on, you mean old scroat.

***Fletcher reluctantly scoops a piece of gum out of his pocket, tears it in half and hands it over.***

**FLETCHER**

Here you are – don't eat it all at once.

**MCLAREN**

Ta. Going to watch the game?

**FLETCHER**

Naff off.

**MCLAREN**

Be a guid game.

**FLETCHER**

What, A and B Wing, that bloodbath.

**MCLAREN**

If we win we win the trophy.

**FLETCHER**

What trophy?

**MCLAREN**

It's a silver cup.

**FLETCHER**

Correction. It was a silver cup. It disappeared from the Governor's office on Tuesday night.

**MCLAREN**

Who'd have done that?

**FLETCHER**

I can't be sure but I've narrowed it down to six hundred suspects.

**MCLAREN**

Never see that again. Be melted down by now.

**FLETCHER**
Just have to play for the honour of the wing, won't you?

**MCLAREN**
You should cheer us on, Fletch. It's your wing.

**FLETCHER**
It's not my wing. I just happen to be incarcerated in this wing. At Her Majesty's pleasure. It's not your wing neither, is it? I'm surprised at you coming the Tom Brown's schooldays bit. Tom Black's schooldays, yes.

**MCLAREN**
I'm not. When I'm out there I'm playing for Morton. Against Celtic at Hampden. And we stuff them.

**FLETCHER**
I've got better things to do than watch people being stuffed at football.

**MCLAREN**
Got visitors?

**FLETCHER**
No.

**MCLAREN**
Got a card game going?

**FLETCHER**
No.

**MCLAREN**
Just watching the box, are you?

**FLETCHER**
No. Three times wrong in a row.

**MCLAREN**
What you doing then?

**FLETCHER**
I'm going fox-hunting, aren't I?

**MCLAREN**
No, seriously – you ought to do something. You've got five years, Fletch. If you don't do anything your stretch will be endless.

**FLETCHER**
Here listen to me, sonny Jock. Don't tell me how to survive in here. I was doing time when you was running around stealing mangoes on the plantation.

**MCLAREN**
What do you mean, plantation? I was brought up in a Greenock housing estate!

**FLETCHER**
All right, when you were stealing mangoes on a Greenock housing estate.

***He gets up on his bunk.***

**MCLAREN**
It's a beautiful day out there as well.

**FLETCHER**
It's a beautiful day in here as well – d'you know why? 'Cos all you lot are out there. That's what I like about the weekend. You're playing football, others are gambling away their hard-earned money, some of them are indulging in their pathetic hobbies. And I ends up with some peace and quiet. Go on then – enjoy your game. Take no prisoners.

***McLaren goes. Fletcher gets off his bunk and walks across the cell, humming to himself.***

**FLETCHER**
'I believe for every drop of rain that falls . . .'

***Warren walks in.***

***Fletcher notices him.***

**FLETCHER**
Oh – what do you want?

**WARREN**
Me and Mini Cooper want to go and play ping-pong.

**FLETCHER**
Don't let me stop yer.

**WARREN**
Er well . . . there aren't any balls, like. And Lugless Douglas said you had one.

**FLETCHER**
Who told Lugless?

**WARREN**
He just heard.

**FLETCHER**
He just what?

**WARREN**
Is it true?

**FLETCHER**
I've got one hidden – yes.

**WARREN**
Would you lend us it then?

**FLETCHER**
Lease. Let us discuss the possibility of leasing you the ball, Bunny. Then we might have some basis for negotiation.

**WARREN**
How much is it then?

**FLETCHER**
One snout . . .

***Warren starts to get one.***

**FLETCHER**
Ah, ah, ah . . . per hour. Minimum three hours.

**WARREN**
You're a hard man, Fletch.

**FLETCHER**
No. I'm not hard – I'm just taking advantage of something which happened to bounce my way. If you was dealing with Harry Grout's syndicate you'd have to leave your wristwatch as a deposit against the ball being trod on. And if you didn't return the ball your wristwatch would get trod on . . . ad infinitum.

**WARREN**
All right, Fletch, you're on.

***He hands over the snout.***

**FLETCHER**
What's this then?

**WARREN**
It's good shag, honest.

**FLETCHER**
All right . . .

***He puts it away.***

**WARREN**
Where's the ball then?

**FLETCHER**
Oh yes.

***He gets the ball.***

**WARREN**
It's a funny colour.

**FLETCHER**
I got it off McLaren.

**WARREN**
D'you want a game yourself later?

**FLETCHER**
Certainly not. Don't do you no good exercise.

**WARREN**
Helps to pass the time.

**FLETCHER**
I don't need any help to pass the time, thank you.

***Warren leaves.***

**FLETCHER**
Next?

***Banyard puts his head round the door.***

**BANYARD**
Erm, Fletcher . . .

**FLETCHER**
(*With a look saying what is it now!*) Yes?

**BANYARD**
Erm . . . a few of us have formed a drama group.

**FLETCHER**
(*Unenthusiastically*) Oh yes.

**BANYARD**
Well, I was wondering – do you have any theatrical inclinations?

**FLETCHER**
No.

**BANYARD**
You don't necessarily have to act. You could be prompter or work the lights or operate the wind machine.

**FLETCHER**
(*Getting on to bunk*) The wind machine, what you want one of those for, just enlist Ives, he's a walking wind machine he is.

**BANYARD**
We want to do some contemporary plays, we thought we'd start with a thriller, *Wait Until Dark*, d'you remember that one? They made a film of it with Audrey Hepburn.

**FLETCHER**
I don't think I could slim down in time.

**BANYARD**
Oh there's no shortage of Audrey Hepburns, it's prompters and lighting men we need.

**FLETCHER**
I don't really go for the theatre much. Now if you was getting up a concert party, well . . . could maybe help you out there. Singing. 'Cos in the old days I was always round the pubs in North London you know, like the Angel, Walthamstow, Friday nights. 'Ladzangenelmen . . . let's have a big hand for Frankie Fletcher.' 'Course it's Norman really, but Frankie sounded better, was more showbiz, know what I mean? What was the one we used to do? I say 'we' 'cos I was backed by Ted Prendergast and the Organaires. You remember Ted Prendergast?

**BANYARD**
I don't think so.

**FLETCHER**
You should do. He was on *Workers' Playtime* once. A cardboard factory in Letchworth.

**BANYARD**
No, I would have remembered.
**FLETCHER**
Yes – I suppose you would. We used to do – (*Singing*) See the pyramids along the Nile
Watch the sunrise on a tropic isle . . .
**BANYARD**
No, we're not doing a concert party.
**FLETCHER**
Oh well then, naff off Sir Lawrence, leave me be, eh.
**BANYARD**
I just thought it might relieve the boredom.
**FLETCHER**
The boredom will be relieved as soon as you leave this room.
**BANYARD**
Oh charming . . .
***He starts to go.***
**FLETCHER**
Give my love to Miss Hepburn.
***Fletcher settles back on his bunk and opens Penthouse.***
**FLETCHER**
(*Singing*) Time on my hands . . .
***He opens the centrefold and looks at the girl.***
**FLETCHER**
You in my arms . . .
***He glances towards the door where a large wooden mule can be seen peering round. Fletcher looks away, then looks back again.***
**FLETCHER**
What are you looking at?
***The mule is still there.***
**FLETCHER**
All right then, I give up.
***Blanco comes in through the doorway.***
**FLETCHER**
Hello, Blanco.
**BLANCO**
Hello, Fletch.
**FLETCHER**
Would you mind explaining?
**BLANCO**
(*Wheeling mule in*) It's my Muffin. It's Muffin the Mule. You know him what's on television.
**FLETCHER**
Muffin the Mule on television. When was the last time you watched television?
**BLANCO**
Some time back. I've been too busy making him.
**FLETCHER**
Well, he's very lovely. Is there any particular reason why you bring him round here though?
**BLANCO**
Just finished him. I wanted you to be the first one to see him. Taken me nigh on fifteen year.
**FLETCHER**
Fifteen years – has it? Still worth it though, isn't it?

**BLANCO**
D'you know now it's done . . . I'm at a bit of a loose end.

**FLETCHER**
Yes, well I expect you are, Blanco. You could always study – improve your mind.

**BLANCO**
I tried that once – I got a book out of the library, on memory training. Studied it for months. Then I had to pack it in.

**FLETCHER**
Why?

**BLANCO**
I forgot where I left the book.

**FLETCHER**
Oh dear. Here, try smoking yourself to death instead.

**BLANCO**
Bless you, Fletcher. I was making it for my three-year-old niece. She's grown up a bit, works as an air hostess. Never thought it would take this long.

**FLETCHER**
Time flies when you're having fun.

**BLANCO**
Oh. Aye. Can I borrow your magazine?

**FLETCHER**
No, you can't.

**BLANCO**
After you've finished with it.

**FLETCHER**
No, you can't.

**BLANCO**
See, now that I've finished Muffin I want to catch up on me reading.

**FLETCHER**
You should start with something a little less controversial, you know what your blood pressure's like. Try the *Radio Times*. Tell you what, will you settle for a Jaffa cake?

**BLANCO**
Have you got some?

**FLETCHER**
No. But let's see what providence will provide. Just get me boots on. (*To the mule*) Come on, Muffin, walkies . . .

## 2. ASSOCIATION AREA

***Fletcher goes out of the cell followed by Blanco with the mule. They walk along the catwalk and arrive at a cubby-hole door. Fletcher knocks.***

**COLLINSON**
(*Offscreen*) Come in.

***Fletcher goes in.***

## 3. CUBBY-HOLE (OFFICER'S ROOM)

***Inside the cubby-hole is a desk with papers on it.***

*On the wall is a 'switchboard' referring to each cell on the landing with lights that illuminate when a bell is rung from the cell. There are keys on the wall, some faded regulations, a single-bar electric fire. A youngish Prison Officer, Collinson, sits at the desk. He has a mug of tea, and on the desk a packet of Jaffa cakes. He is not the friendliest of men.*

**COLLINSON**

What is it?

**FLETCHER**

(*Quietly*) Mr Collinson, sorry to disturb you – I can see you're busy – not take a minute . . . It's just old Blanco. He's finished his wooden mule, and er, he'd like you to see it, know what I mean. Not take a minute.

**COLLINSON**

Oh. Oh, all right . . .

*He gets up, squeezes past Fletcher, who eyes the Jaffa cakes on the desk.*

## 4. ASSOCIATION AREA

*Collinson comes out of his cubby-hole. Blanco is waiting there.*

**COLLINSON**

Oh yes . . . this is the mule is it, Blanco?

**BLANCO**

Yes, sir, fifteen years.

**COLLINSON**

Oh well, it's worth it, you don't often see craftsmanship of that quality.

**BLANCO**

Thank you, sir, nice of you to say so.

**COLLINSON**

All right then, off you go, Blanco, then.

**BLANCO**

Yes, sir.

**FLETCHER**

Very kind of you, Mr Collinson. I mean a word from someone like yourself – you don't know how we appreciate that.

**COLLINSON**

All right then.

*He returns to the cubby-hole. Outside Fletcher gives Blanco a biscuit.*

**BLANCO**

You're a lad, Fletch.

**FLETCHER**

Yeah, well, say no more.

**BLANCO**

Sorry if I disturbed you.

**FLETCHER**

Any time for you.

**BLANCO**

I think I'll nip down and watch *Grandstand*.

*He picks up the mule.*

**FLETCHER**

Oh yeah, while you're down there put the word round, I'm incommunicado.

**BLANCO**

You're in the where?

**FLETCHER**

I don't want to be disturbed.

**BLANCO**
We'll tell 'em.
***He moves off down the stairs.***

**5. CELL**

***Fletcher enters his cell and walks to the bed. He climbs on to the top bunk and settles down with his magazine. He has an 'Alone at last' expression. After a moment we hear someone clearing his throat.***

**FLETCHER**
Yes?
***Barrowclough is in the doorway.***

**BARROWCLOUGH**
Oh Fletcher . . .

**FLETCHER**
Mr Barrowclough – on your way out would you lock me in so's I can get some privacy?

**BARROWCLOUGH**
On a lovely afternoon like this? I thought you'd be out in the yard, or in the hobby shop. Seems such a waste to be stuck in here.

**FLETCHER**
It's not a waste to me. I like to spend my Saturday afternoons in my cell. With my feet up and a bit of reading matter. I don't want to play games, or do exercises. Nor do I want to carve toys, take saxophone lessons, form an amateur dramatic group, or watch *The Blue Lamp* on BBC2, a film glamourising that despicable bunch what put me here in the first place.

**BARROWCLOUGH**
It's a damn sight better than lying on your bunk reading that lewd lascivious rubbish. If a man puts his mind to it a man can better himself in here. There's a lot more opportunities now than when I first joined the service. Spraggon, you know him in E Block, Spraggon has made a six-foot space rocket out of milk bottle tops.

**FLETCHER**
Really.

**BARROWCLOUGH**
It's a work of art. Belongs to a museum. He used three colours. The nose cone's in red, homogenised, the bulk of it's made out of ordinary silver top, and the Governor's gold tops provided a nice motif round the centre.

**FLETCHER**
Well, he'll never get it off the ground.

**BARROWCLOUGH**
There's Rafferty having his watercolours exhibited in a Carlisle art gallery. Not to mention all the professional qualifications that vocational training has given people in this prison. Brickies, plasterers. Even the Tooley brothers left here with a diploma in welding.

**FLETCHER**
Yes and what did they do with it, soon

as they got out? Welded their way into Barclays Bank in Blackburn High Street.

**BARROWCLOUGH**

Yes – well – the point I'm trying to make is that we at least gave them the opportunity to do something legitimate with their lives.

**FLETCHER**

And the point I'm trying to make is that they'll just abuse the opportunity. They're felons, Mr Barrowclough. You get a bloke in here. Teach him how to use a printing press. What's he do when he goes out? Does he join the *Northern Echo*, does he fairycakes. He stays at home and forges premium bonds – only sensible.

**BARROWCLOUGH**

I won't accept your cynicism. I just don't like seeing a fully grown man with a good brain – 'cos you're not stupid, Fletcher – wasting his time. You should do something whatever it is.

**FLETCHER**

Oh – is that the lecture over? Is that what you come in to say, Mr Barrowclough?

**BARROWCLOUGH**

I didn't come in to lecture you.

**FLETCHER**

No, well, we never did discover the purpose of your visit, you never said.

**BARROWCLOUGH**

Didn't I . . . I don't know – (*Thinks*) Oh well, I just dropped by 'cos I had nothing better to do.

**FLETCHER**

Would you believe it, would you Adam and Eve it? Your lives are emptier than ours.

**BARROWCLOUGH**

They are not! I have my allotment.

**FLETCHER**

Your allotment – listen, Mr Barrowclough, if the system wants to do something really constructive for us chaps, give us more freedom, better grub. Give us conjugal visits.

**BARROWCLOUGH**

Give you what?

**FLETCHER**

Conjugals. From the Latin, *conjugo*, meaning to have it off.

**BARROWCLOUGH**

We can't do that –

**FLETCHER**

With our old ladies! All above board, Bristol fashion. It's what some prisons do, have special quarters. Where wives come up, and we spend the whole weekend . . . manifesting our long-felt wants.

**BARROWCLOUGH**

I don't know of any prisons where they -

**FLETCHER**

Maybe not here. But certainly abroad. Certainly Holland, and America, where they have more enlightened penal systems.

**BARROWCLOUGH**

They just allow the wives to visit, and they spend the whole weekend . . .

**FLETCHER**

Conjugating, yeah.

**BARROWCLOUGH**

That's more than I'm allowed at home.

***Barrowclough moves off, shaking his head.***

**FLETCHER**

Mr Barrowclough.

***Barrowclough stops in the doorway.***

**FLETCHER**

Here you are, Mr Barrowclough, your needs are greater than mine.

***He offers Barrowclough the magazine.***

**BARROWCLOUGH**

Certainly not, Fletcher.

***He leaves.***

**FLETCHER**

(*Spreading out the centrefold*) Well, my little treasure. Alone at last.

## 6. ASSOCIATION AREA

***Mackay unlocks the door and three visitors enter the association area. Mackay closes it again.***

**MACKAY**

This is a typical cell block.

**WOMAN**

Why do you have the nets?

**MACKAY**

Suicide, ma'am. The prevention of.

**WOMAN**

Do you have many instances of that?

**MACKAY**

Certainly not, ma'am. It's against the rules.

**OLDER MAN**

I suppose it's also useful if any of these chaps get violent and take it into their heads to throw each other over the edge.

**MACKAY**

If they get violent, sir, they generally throw us over the edge.

**YOUNGER MAN**

Do you have a bad record of violence in this prison?

**MACKAY**

Oh no, sir. That's because we at Slade Prison encourage a wide range of activities. This helps the men express themselves in various ways, releasing much of the pent-up aggression endemic to the incarcerated male.

**WOMAN**

Is that what most of them are doing now?

**MACKAY**

Absolutely. You will notice how at the weekend every prisoner has seized the opportunity to enjoy the extensive facilities which we provide.

***Mackay looks into Fletcher's cell and then looks back again.***

**MACKAY**

There are always some exceptions, of course.

**WOMAN**

Could we have a look in a cell?

**MACKAY**

Certainly, ma'am . . .

***He ushers them into Fletcher's cell.***

## 7. CELL

***The three visitors and Mackay enter Fletcher's cell. He is still lying on his bunk reading.***

**OLDER MAN**

Is this man sick?

**MACKAY**

Are you sick, Fletcher?

**FLETCHER**

I'm sick of interruptions.

**WOMAN**

Oh please, this fellow's probably trying to relax.

**FLETCHER**

Oh be my guest.

**OLDER MAN**

Please don't get up.

**MACKAY**

This is a typical cell.

**WOMAN**

Single or double?

**MACKAY**

Double, ma'am, as indicated by the presence of the two bunks. Prisoners are, of course, allowed to personalise their cells. You notice the radio, the matches. And, of course, they're allowed to decorate their lockers with mementoes of family and home.

***He opens the cupboard door and is faced by several photographs of nudes.***

**FLETCHER**

Those two are the wife, and that's the wife's sister.

**MACKAY**

Perhaps you would like to see the recreation room.

**OLDER MAN**

Yes, we are rather disturbing this man's privacy.

**FLETCHER**

Privacy! Precious little of that in here.

**MACKAY**

Fletcher!

**YOUNGER MAN**

No, no, please, let the man speak.

**FLETCHER**

Well, have you noticed any signs of privacy on your rounds? Seen a door without a peephole? Seen a shower curtain or a cubicle door in the latrines? Very hard, you know, to retain a vestige of human dignity when you're sitting on the bog and a whole football team clatters past on their way to the showers.

**WOMAN**

Yes – well –

**FLETCHER**

Yes well – notice the way Mr Mackay

barged in here. Never so much of a by my leave or kiss my foot. Paid no more regard to me than he did the washbasin – in fact less.

**MACKAY**

Privacy is one of the privileges you forfeit when you transgress the law. This is not a hotel. They do forget that they're in here to be punished.

**FLETCHER**

Oh yes. Eye for an eye. Tooth for a nail.

**OLDER MAN**

You sound as if you're a Londoner.

**FLETCHER**

I am, sir, yes. It's the accent.

**OLDER MAN**

Long way from home up here. What's a Londoner doing in this neck of the woods?

**FLETCHER**

This particular Londoner is doing five years. What are you doing?

**MACKAY**

Fletcher!

**OLDER MAN**

No, no, fair question. Well, Fletcher, we're all attached to the Home Office in one capacity or another. And it's through these visits that we learn more about our penal system. And only by seeing things for ourselves and talking to people like yourself are we able to make recommendation for change and reform.

**FLETCHER**

Change yes . . . well, if you can supply a new coat of paint, give us an improved supply of ping-pong balls. But reform, save yourselves the bother.

**MACKAY**

I don't think this particular prisoner's opinion is particularly instructive.

**FLETCHER**

Oh, isn't it? Let me tell you I've been in more nicks than he has. So whose opinion is more instructive?

**WOMAN**

I would value it.

**FLETCHER**

I bet you would – oh, I see. Well, obviously we can't have total amnesty. Got to keep a few hard cases locked away so we can walk the streets at night. But you should do with the rest of us what they do in Scandinavia. Make us work off our debt to society. On farms, building sites, factories, hospitals.

**WOMAN**

That's one school of thought, of course.

**OLDER MAN**

You know despite what this man says about rehabilitation, I think his attitude proves the contrary.

**MACKAY**

You what?

**OLDER MAN**

Now this system of working off your sentence, I can see it working with men like you.

**YOUNGER MAN**

If you had a choice, what area would you choose to work in?

**FLETCHER**
Well, if I had the choice I'd probably choose the building site.

**WOMAN**
The fresh air?

**FLETCHER**
Yes . . . but mostly 'cos I could nick meself a fortune.

***He goes back to reading the magazine.***

**FLETCHER**
(*Reading*) Cor look at her!

**OLDER MAN**
The recreation room next is it, Mr Mackay?

***Mackay ushers the visitors out.***

**MACKAY**
Hopeless case, sir. Classic recidivist.

**YOUNGER MAN**
Bit of a surly character.

**OLDER MAN**
Yes, but articulate.

**MACKAY**
Like a lorry.

***They leave.***

**FLETCHER**
(*Getting off his bunk*) Is there anybody else?

## 8. ASSOCIATION AREA

***Fletcher comes out of his cell and stands on the catwalk. He looks around for any more interruptions, then goes back inside the cell.***

## 9. CELL

***Fletcher enters his cell. He swings straight up on top of his bunk and settles himself down, bashing his pillows and lying on his side. There is a pause. Then Warren's voice can be heard.***

**WARREN**
'Scuse me, Fletch –

**FLETCHER**
What!!

***He leaps straight up in the air, falls off his bunk and lands face to face with Warren.***

**WARREN**
Were you asleep?

**FLETCHER**
Sleep, what chance have I had to sleep?!! More chance of having a sleep at Waterloo in the rush hour! What's wrong with you nurks in here? Can't you see when a man wants to be left alone?

**WARREN**
I'm sorry, it's just . . . your ball's got a crack in it.

***Fletcher has to think about this for a moment.***

**FLETCHER**
Pardon?

***Warren holds up the ball.***

**WARREN**
Cracked.

**FLETCHER**
(*Menacingly*) Better than having no balls at all.

**WARREN**
Spoilt the game though –

**FLETCHER**
I'll have it back then.

**WARREN**
I'll have the fag back then.

**FLETCHER**
You will not. You should have examined the merchandise when the transaction was transacted.

**WARREN**
That's not fair, Fletch.

**FLETCHER**
Fair? Since when was life ever fair? Is it fair that I should suffer this continual bombardment of people who don't know how to occupy their own time and minds? Saturday afternoon provides a few sacred hours when one can enjoy one's own company. It's not much to ask. It don't last long. Only till teatime when we traipse across to have that hideous mixture masquerading as cottage pie. When will you blokes learn that surviving in stir is a state of mind? It's an attitude. It's learning to live with yourself.

**WARREN**
(*Sniffing*) Sorry, Fletch.

***Fletcher turns away, then softens his attitude to another approach.***

**FLETCHER**
I like you, Warren. Believe me there are many times when I crave your company. I love those action-packed anecdotes of yours of the days when you worked in your father-in-law's ironmonger's in Bury.

**WARREN**
Bolton.

**FLETCHER**
Bolton, yes, even better. I was only too eager to look at your snaps the other day. Of your wife's day trip to Lake Windermere.

***Warren reaches towards his top pocket.***

**WARREN**
Oh, I've got some more.

***Fletcher turns away and grasps the edge of the top bunk to prevent himself from grasping Warren's neck.***

**FLETCHER**
God, give me strength.

**WARREN**
They didn't come out too well, I expect it was the rain.

**FLETCHER**
(*Controlling himself*) Just . . . just put them on the table, Warren, and they'll help to while away my evening.

**WARREN**
Oh, fine, right.

***He does so.***

**WARREN**
I'll be off then, Fletch, I'll not disturb you no more.

**FLETCHER**
Promise?

**WARREN**
Yeah.

**FLETCHER**

Here – d'you promise?

**WARREN**

I promise.

***Warren goes. Fletcher laughs. Puts the photos down but drops them. Goes down on his knees to pick them up.***

**FLETCHER**

Dear God, you might think it's a bit of a liberty me asking you favours, but on the other hand there is more joy in heaven when a sinner repenteth. Isn't that right, sir? It's only a small thing I ask . . . keep these nurks off my back, can't you? 'Cos if anyone else walks through that door I might not be answerable for the consequences. Know what I mean, God?

***The Chaplain appears at the doorway.***

**CHAPLAIN**

Ah, Fletcher . . . I'd been meaning to have a bit of a chat for some time.

***Fletcher rises and moves towards the Chaplain.***

## 10. GOVERNOR'S OFFICE

***The office is empty. Then camera shows the door opening and Mackay's voice can be heard.***

**MACKAY**

Left, right, left, right, left, right . . .

***Fletcher is marched in by Mackay.***

**MACKAY**

Halt. Face the front. Stand still. For the chop, you know that. No exit. If ever I have any doubts about the system it's people like you that reassure me. Because in the final analysis, in the final analysis, your criminal character will always show through like ink on blotting paper.

**VENABLES**

(*Offscreen*) They're in there already, are they?

***Venables enters. He is wearing a football scarf, which he removes.***

**VENABLES**

Mr Mackay.

**MACKAY**

Yes sir, Fletcher, sir. Sorry to fetch you from the game.

**VENABLES**

Not at all. This is a serious matter, a desperately serious matter. These Home Office visitors, they weren't around when the incident took place?

**MACKAY**

No, sir. Fortunately I had them in the woodwork room at the time.

**VENABLES**

Thank heavens for that, 'cos we must hush up a thing like this.

**MACKAY**

Face the front.

**VENABLES**

Did anyone witness it?

**MACKAY**
Only old Blanco Webb, sir. And Mr Collinson heard the scream.

**VENABLES**
Fletcher, what got into you?

***Fletcher shrugs.***

**MACKAY**
Face the front.

**VENABLES**
I'm talking to you, Fletcher.

**FLETCHER**
Everyone's talking to me, sir. End of my tether, see. Think I'm losing my mind, sir. Possibly I should have psychiatric observation in the hospital, sir.

**VENABLES**
Psychiatric observation . . . well, I don't know . . .

**MACKAY**
No, you don't. Sir – an unprovoked attack. And even Slade Prison, which has had its share of violence, has never known a chaplain thrown off a balcony.

**FLETCHER**
I knew the safety net was there, sir.

**VENABLES**
That's hardly the point. The chaplain was shattered.

**FLETCHER**
He'll bounce back, sir. He did a bit.

**VENABLES**
Don't be insolent, Fletcher. I have no alternative but to give you the maximum period of solitary confinement. Then we'll have to discuss the matter further.

**FLETCHER**
Yes, sir.

**VENABLES**
You've only yourself to blame. You have a very regrettable attitude, Fletcher. Perhaps you'll dwell on that over the next three days in isolation.

**FLETCHER**
Three days is it, sir?

**VENABLES**
Yes, it certainly is. All right, wheel him out.

**FLETCHER**
Could I just ask one thing, sir?

**VENABLES**
What?

**FLETCHER**
Couldn't make it a fortnight, could you?

***Mackay marches him off.***

# 2 SERIES TWO

## EPISODE FIVE: HAPPY RELEASE

### 1. MEDICAL OFFICER'S ROOM

***The Medical Officer is examining a prisoner. Mackay enters.***

**MACKAY**

Is it true about Fletcher, sir?

**MO**

What? Oh morning, Mr Mackay.

**MACKAY**

Is it true about Fletcher, Doctor?

**MO**

Oh yes, I'm afraid it is.

**MACKAY**

Oh – definite?

**MO**

Yes, we had him down at Carlisle General, they verified it.

**MACKAY**

Where is he now?

**MO**

He's back here. We've just got him to bed.

**MACKAY**

No possibility of a mistake?

**MO**

No, no. The X-rays are positive.

**MACKAY**

In other words there's nothing we can do about it?

**MO**

Nothing.

**MACKAY**

Fletcher of all people.

**MO**

That's the way it is.

**MACKAY**

How long would you say?

**MO**

Three weeks. Maybe a month.

**MACKAY**

I had him down for the drainage detail you know . . . and now he gets three cushy weeks on his back with a broken ankle, there's no justice.

***Mackay starts to go.***

**MO**

I said it could even be a month.

## 2. HOSPITAL WARD

***Fletcher is in bed with his plastered leg in traction. Screens surround his bed.***

***Next to him is the old lag, Blanco, who is asleep. Opposite is Norris, another prisoner.***

***A prison orderly removes the screens from around Fletcher.***

**FLETCHER**

Thank you, Charlie. I'll do the same for you one day.

***Mackay enters.***

**FLETCHER**

Oh, Mr Mackay, how kind. I don't think it's official visiting hours, you know.

**MACKAY**

You're a lucky man, Fletcher.

**FLETCHER**

No grapes then?

**MACKAY**

I just wanted to verify with my own eyes that you weren't malingering.

**FLETCHER**

No, no. My foot is broken. You can see the plaster. The evidence is irrefootable.

***Fletcher laughs at his own joke.***

**FLETCHER**

Did you hear that Blanco, oh you're asleep.

**MACKAY**

I won't pretend your indisposition isn't very frustrating, Fletcher.

**FLETCHER**

Not to me, it isn't. Better grub in here. Better beds an' all. Got me own cushion here.

**MACKAY**

Since you lost your soft number in the library I was all ready to make your life a misery.

**FLETCHER**

I gathered that when you sent me up that twenty-foot ladder to clean pigeon droppings out the guttering.

**MACKAY**

Wouldn't surprise me if you fell intentionally.

**FLETCHER**

No, no, it's just poetic justice. You was out to victimise me, and all you've done is give me a passport to comfort and seclusion. Mind you, I do have to put up with that scroat Norris for the next few days.

**NORRIS**

Oh yeah, well it cuts two ways, don't it?

**FLETCHER**

Shut your face, Norris, or I'll hit you with me frying pan.

**NORRIS**

Violence now, eh?

**MACKAY**

Quiet, both of you.

**BLANCO**

(*Waking up*) What is it?

**FLETCHER**

Ssh, it's all right.

**MACKAY**

And you.

**NORRIS**
He started it. He's been at me all afternoon, Mr Mackay.

**MACKAY**
That's one thing I can't blame Fletcher for, Norris. You're not the pleasantest of men. In fact you're a horrible creature.

**NORRIS**
Here! I done my bird! I'm being released in two days.

**MACKAY**
Yes, and you're skiving to the last.

**NORRIS**
I've had surgery. Ingrown toenail.

**MACKAY**
I know the kind of surgery I would give you had I my way.

**FLETCHER**
Couldn't have waited till you got out, could you? Had to burden our overworked prison medical service.

**MACKAY**
Which is exactly what you're doing, Fletcher.

**FLETCHER**
Yeah, well we know whose fault that is, don't we?

**MACKAY**
Four weeks. Maximum. I can bide my time. I'll soon have you up on your foot.

**FLETCHER**
Not before it's mended.

**MACKAY**
You're in discomfort, are you?

**FLETCHER**
Well, nothing to speak of.

**MACKAY**
Oh come on, Fletcher, it's giving you hell, admit it.

***He pulls the traction.***

**FLETCHER**
No.

**MACKAY**
Not even the odd twinge?

**FLETCHER**
No, no. Not now the plaster is on.

**MACKAY**
There's no justice. (*Lets traction go*)

***He lets traction go, shakes his head and leaves.***

**FLETCHER**
And the next object is, a thwarted screw, a thwarted screw . . .

**NORRIS**
I'm in pain.

**FLETCHER**
Pardon?

**NORRIS**
I'm in pain.

**FLETCHER**
Good.

**NORRIS**
I've had surgery.

**FLETCHER**
I've had X-rays.

**NORRIS**
X-rays isn't surgery.

**FLETCHER**
Surgery. Ingrown toenail.

**NORRIS**
I haven't slept for days with the pain. Shadow of my former self I am.

**FLETCHER**
Well, your former self wasn't much to begin with, Norris.

**NORRIS**
Naff off.

**FLETCHER**
Soon as my broken foot's better I'm going to use it to stand on your ingrowing toenail.

**NORRIS**
Have to hurry, won't you? I'm out of here Thursday!

***The door is unlocked by a Prison officer.***

***Lennie is admitted, wearing kitchen whites and pushing a food trolley.***

**LENNIE**
Meals on wheels.

**FLETCHER**
Oh, look at this. Look at this, Blanco. What's on the menu then, Lennie? Apart from yesterday's gravy stains.

**LENNIE**
Braised steak and carrots, mashed potatoes, bananas and custard.

***Starts to serve.***

**FLETCHER**
Oh good – what's for afters?

**LENNIE**
Tomato soup.

**FLETCHER**
Hear that Blanco? Bananas and custard.

**BLANCO**
I've got no appetite.

**FLETCHER**
You've got to eat, Blanco. Keep your strength up. If you don't eat you will be ill – oh you are ill, aren't you?

**NORRIS**
If he won't have it, I'll have it.

**FLETCHER**
You will not! You leave it by his bedside, Lennie. Anything he don't fancy now he can have later . . . or I'll have it.

**LENNIE**
How are you then, Fletch?

**FLETCHER**
All right – surviving. How's yourself?

**LENNIE**
Not as comfy as you are. Look at those crisp, clean sheets.

**FLETCHER**
Yeah well – give us some more carrots.

**NORRIS**
Don't leave me short.

**LENNIE**
Shut up, Norris. Here you are, Blanco. I'll just put this here then. He don't look too chipper, does he?

**FLETCHER**
He's all right. Just a bit depressed that's all.

**LENNIE**
Looks at death's door to me.

**FLETCHER**
Shut up – gawd, you youngsters. Don't have much tact, do you? You don't make remarks about death's

door to people. Not in hospital. Specially when they're at death's door.

**BLANCO**

*(Laughing weakly)* Ha ha . . . that's a good one, Fletch.

**FLETCHER**

Well, you've got to laugh, ain't you?

**LENNIE**

(*Serving Norris but addressing Fletcher*) You're cheery enough.

**FLETCHER**

Can't complain. Life of Riley, in' it? And I had a nice day out, Lennie. Went down to Carlisle General and got plastered.

***Lennie laughs.***

**FLETCHER**

And there was some lovely nurses there – kept popping their heads round the door. Giggling like. 'Cos there I was, a convict. Mister Menace – handcuffed to a wheelchair.

**LENNIE**

Sort of like Ironside – only bent.

**FLETCHER**

Well yeah . . . it was my air of villainy what titillated them. 'Course some have bigger titillations than others. (*Lowering voice*) I was in this cubicle with this ravishing West Indian sister . . .

***A Prison Officer appears at the doorway.***

**PRISON OFFICER**

Come on lad, you've had long enough fiddling around with that.

**FLETCHER**

That's what she said.

**LENNIE**

Oh can I just hear the end of this . . .

**PRISON OFFICER**

No you can't, come along.

**LENNIE**

Tell me tomorrow then, Fletch.

**FLETCHER**

It'll keep.

***Lennie starts to wheel trolley away.***

**LENNIE**

Sleep well.

**FLETCHER**

And you. Look after yourself.

**LENNIE**

I will. Nice change having a cell to meself. It don't half smell fresh in there without your feet.

**NORRIS**

How do you think we feel?

**LENNIE**

Shut up, Norris.

***He leaves.***

**FLETCHER**

I should think you'll be glad to get out of here on Thursday, Norris, it'll give you a better opportunity to be more revolting to a larger number of people.

**BLANCO**

I'll certainly be glad to see the back of him. You know I never had much. Possessions like. But in the last three days before you came in here he's had 'em all.

**FLETCHER**

How d'you mean?

**BLANCO**
He's had me wireless. And me silver snuff holder. Real silver, Fletch. Antique. I kept me snout in it. He had all the snout an' all.

**FLETCHER**
(*To Norris*) Is this true?

**NORRIS**
Fair and square.

**BLANCO**
And me musical box which plays 'Waltzing Matilda' when you open the lid.

**FLETCHER**
What'd he do, he just took 'em? Well, he's going to put 'em right back I tell you that, Blanco.

**NORRIS**
Fair and square. Cards, wasn't it?

**FLETCHER**
Oh dear, oh dear, Blanco. You don't play cards with him.

**BLANCO**
Brag, nine-card brag.

**NORRIS**
Fair and square.

**FLETCHER**
You'll give those back, Norris.

**NORRIS**
Will I . . . heck.

***He goes.***

**FLETCHER**
Don't worry, Blanco, me old son, I'll get them back for you.

**BLANCO**
It doesn't matter, Fletch. What do I need with a 'Waltzing Matilda' music box where I'm going?

**FLETCHER**
You ain't going nowhere, mate, you've got another two years to do.

**BLANCO**
I'm going out of here sooner than that.

**FLETCHER**
You're too old to escape, Blanco. You'll never get over the wall. You been watching too much of that *Colditz*, you have.

**BLANCO**
I'm going out of here in a wooden overcoat.

**FLETCHER**
Oh come on, Blanco – dear me, what kind of talk's that?

**BLANCO**
No, me time's about up, Fletch. I'm not going to last the distance. Tired heart the doctor says. Tired everything more like. I come in here to die.

**FLETCHER**
No, you didn't. You come in here yester-die. Get it, get it?

**BLANCO**
(*With a wan smile*) Oh Fletch, they were cracking that when even I was at school.

**FLETCHER**
Well, that raised a smile.

**BLANCO**
You don't have to gee me up, lad. I'm not afraid. It's time I went to that great cell block in the sky.

**FLETCHER**
Rubbish. Bloke like you ain't ready for celestial porridge yet awhile. You're not old. You look old but that's prison. Prison puts years on a man's physical appearance. Got to remember you're only twenty-nine.

**BLANCO**
(*Smiling*) Sixty-three.

**FLETCHER**
Sixty-three, you're not past it at sixty-three. Most of the government's older than that.

**BLANCO**
And look at the state this country's in. Mind you it weren't much better when I were a lad. Depression. Hard times. No work. Took to stealing. Such a waste. Spent nigh on half me life in one nick or another. Lost all me family. Mostly through neglect. Mine. That's why I'm resigned to passing on. Well, more than that, relieved.

**FLETCHER**
Come off it, there's years of wear left in you yet. Charlie Chaplin become a father nigh on eighty. Winston Churchill was at least your age when he had his finest hour. As was my Uncle Wilfred.

**BLANCO**
What did he do?

**FLETCHER**
When he was seventy he married this gorgeous young dental assistant. 'Course it killed him. But you should have seen the smirk on his face in the coffin.

**BLANCO**
Died with his boots off, did he?

**FLETCHER**
Yeah – and his teeth out. Couldn't get the coffin lid down for three days. State of mind, age. You're as young as you feel. For instance, this old boy goes to the doctor, see. The doctor says, 'What's wrong then?' And the old boy says, 'Well it's the wife and I – we ain't getting any pleasure out of sex any more.' The doc like, he's a bit taken aback. He says, 'How old are you?' 'Eighty.' 'And the wife?' 'Seventy-nine.' He says, 'Well, when d'you first notice this?' And the old boy says, 'Last night . . . then again this morning.'

***They laugh.***

**BLANCO**
I heard that at school an' all.

## 3. HOSPITAL WING
***The camera shows the exterior of the hospital wing at night.***

## 3A. HOSPITAL WARD
***It is night time. The room is lit by a dim hospital night light and some moonlight through the barred window. Blanco is coughing, unable***

***to sleep. Norris is sound asleep, snoring lightly.***

***Fletcher is asleep but moves restlessly in his bed. Blanco coughs again.***

**BLANCO**

(*Quietly*) Fletch . . . Fletch!

**FLETCHER**

Mmmmh?

**BLANCO**

Want to talk to you.

**FLETCHER**

Whassamatter?

**BLANCO**

Wanted to tell you something – important, like . . . while he's asleep.

***He indicates Norris.***

**BLANCO**

He is asleep, isn't he?

***There is an answering snore from Norris.***

**FLETCHER**

Unless he snores when he's awake, yes.

**BLANCO**

Well, you see, I've got something of value.

**FLETCHER**

How do you mean?

**BLANCO**

Well, you see, I've got no family – I told you that. And the few things I've got – well, Norris has got them now, since the nine-card brag. But I still got one thing of value. And I'd like to bequeath it.

**FLETCHER**

You're getting morbid again.

**BLANCO**

I'm not. I'm being practical. 'Cos if owt happened to me, no one would know about my legacy.

**FLETCHER**

Listen, if you want to make a will, it's no good talking to me, Blanco. You want a solicitor, we got one on our landing. He'll see you right. Straight as a die, he is.

**BLANCO**

What's his name?

**FLETCHER**

Corkscrew Carter. Nice bloke.

**BLANCO**

My legacy is not the sort I can legalise.

**FLETCHER**

Why not?

**BLANCO**

It's ill-gotten gains. Buried somewhere in Leeds.

**FLETCHER**

Oh, ill-gotten gains, is it? Oh, I see.

**BLANCO**

Shall I tell you about it?

**FLETCHER**

Not now.

**BLANCO**

Well it was like this. There were three of us. And we done this wages van on the way to a fridge factory near Otley. Don't you remember reading about it?

**FLETCHER**

I don't Blanco, no.

**BLANCO**

It were in *Yorkshire Post*.

**FLETCHER**

If it didn't make the *Muswell Hill Examiner* or *Titbits* I wouldn't have seen it.

**BLANCO**

I s'pose not. Anyway it were an untidy job. Lot of things went wrong.

**FLETCHER**

You wouldn't be here if they hadn't.

**BLANCO**

The other two lads were brothers, Jack Brackett and Harry erm . . .

**FLETCHER**

Brackett, was it?

**BLANCO**

That's right. Did you know him?

**FLETCHER**

No, no. Only through his brother.

**BLANCO**

Oh, 'cos their escape were in *Yorkshire Post*. They got away in a fishing boat from Bridlington –

**FLETCHER**

Will this take long, Blanco – only my foot's gone to sleep, and I'd like to catch it up.

**BLANCO**

Not that the Bracketts knew where I'd put loot in any case.

**FLETCHER**

Blanco – fascinating as it is to stroll down felony lane with you –

**BLANCO**

I'm the one who's got the map. I'm the one who knows where it's buried.

**FLETCHER**

Oh gawd, it's bleeding Treasure Island now, is it?

**BLANCO**

Eight thousand quid.

**FLETCHER**

(*Eyes widen*) How much?

***Norris's eyes open but he remains still.***

**BLANCO**

Eight thousand quid.

**FLETCHER**

Eight big ones?

**BLANCO**

Maybe nine. Used notes. Didn't have time to count 'em. According to *Yorkshire Post* it were fifteen, but that were the thieving company, trying to diddle Lloyds.

**FLETCHER**

Now listen, me old son. I obviously never realised the magnitude of your legacy.

**BLANCO**

The map's yours, Fletch.

***He gives him the map.***

**FLETCHER**

I don't know what to say. Words fail me. I shall use the money wisely, Blanco, rest assured. Let me ask you one question. If you don't snuff it – which we all hope and pray for, that you won't that is – then on your release you'll presumably want your map back.

**BLANCO**

Oh . . . oh well, if I did last the distance I suppose so, yes.

**FLETCHER**

And you'd trust me to give it to you?

**BLANCO**

Of course I would, Fletch.

**FLETCHER**

D'you know, Blanco, in all my life I don't think anyone's ever shown me trust like that . . . probation officers, Borstal principals, judges. And yet here you are – a man who ain't known me long, or in great intimacy, entrusting me with everything he's got in the world.

**BLANCO**

I am that, Fletch.

***There's a pause.***

**FLETCHER**

You must be bleeding barmy.

## 4. HOSPITAL WARD

***Later that night, on his rounds, Barrowclough looks through the glass panel on the ward door, which adjoins the medical room. He moves off. Fletcher is fast asleep, as is Blanco in the next bed. Norris appears at Fletcher's bed. He is searching Fletcher's possessions. He checks the pockets of Fletcher's hospital issue robe. Nothing.***

***Norris freezes as Fletcher rolls over, but he now has his back to Norris, who pushes a cautions hand under the pillows. Fletcher moves again restlessly, rolling on to his back, thus trapping Norris's hand. Norris hesitates a moment, looking down at the sleeping Fletcher. Then he carefully slips his hand into the breast pocket of his pyjamas. Again nothing.***

***More gingerly than ever, Norris now starts to search under the sheets. His hand moves lower in the bed. Fletcher opens an eye, at first unsure what is going on. Then:***

**FLETCHER**

Help!!

***Norris, as if stung, leaps back and scurries across the room.***

**FLETCHER**

Help – what the hell's going on here? Who was that? Was that you, Norris?

***Norris slides back in bed and starts snoring before his head has even hit the pillow.***

**FLETCHER**

Norris, was that you?

**BLANCO**

(*Waking*) What's going on – what's happening?

**FLETCHER**

I'm not sure, Blanco. I think I've just been molested.

*The door is unlocked and the lights go on. Barrowclough enters, wearing his most anxious expression.*

**BARROWCLOUGH**

What is it? What was all that noise, what is it?

**FLETCHER**

Oh, Mr Barrowclough, thank God it's you!

**BARROWCLOUGH**

Why, Fletcher? Whatever's happening – what's going on?

**NORRIS**

(*Feigning waking*) What's happening? What going on?

**FLETCHER**

Don't give me that parrot fashion, Norris, you despicable nurk!

**BARROWCLOUGH**

Will you answer my question, Fletcher?

**FLETCHER**

I was awoken, Mr Barrowclough. Woken by a foreign hand.

**BARROWCLOUGH**

A foreign hand?

**FLETCHER**

Well, you know what I mean, Norris was over here, sir.

**BARROWCLOUGH**

What were you up to – stealing?

**NORRIS**

I haven't been up to anything.

**FLETCHER**

Don't give me that, you were over here rummaging in my pyjamas.

**BARROWCLOUGH**

Have you got any valuables here, Fletcher?

**FLETCHER**

Only what I always keep in my pyjamas.

**BLANCO**

He could have been after your lemon barley water.

**FLETCHER**

What – in my pyjamas? Funny shaped bottle.

**BARROWCLOUGH**

What have you got to say for yourself, Norris?

**NORRIS**

What's he got that I'd want to nick? One orange and a pair of smelly slippers.

**FLETCHER**

You've just put yourself right in it there. I got those slippers off Mr Barrowclough. Present they were. My first week in here.

**BARROWCLOUGH**

Yes well, we don't need to go into that now. They were second hand, and I happened to be finished with them.

**FLETCHER**

Nevertheless I appreciated and grew to love those, Mr Barrowclough. And I wouldn't like to see them falling into the wrong hands – or in this case, feet.

**NORRIS**

I don't want your tatty old slippers.

**BARROWCLOUGH**
They are not tatty. They cost thirty-two and six in the old currency.

***He looks at Norris's table.***

**BARROWCLOUGH**
You go out of this prison in two days' time, Norris. You must be ruddy mad to risk losing remission by going back to your nasty little habits.

**NORRIS**
Why d'you take his word for it?

**BARROWCLOUGH**
Fletcher's not the sort of person who's likely to scream out in the middle of the night over nothing. Though for the life of me I can't think what there is to steal. You're not hiding anything are you, Fletcher?

**FLETCHER**
Hiding?

***He looks at Blanco.***

**BARROWCLOUGH**
You're not hiding a bottle of surgical alcohol?

**FLETCHER**
Hide? No, sir.

***Barrowclough tugs at Fletcher's blankets.***

**FLETCHER**
Gerroff.

**BARROWCLOUGH**
Fletcher!

***Fletcher reluctantly releases his grip on the blankets. Blanco reacts anxiously. Barrowclough pulls back the blankets. While he makes a cursory inspection of the pillows and sheets, Fletcher is moaning bitterly.***

**FLETCHER**
Isn't it marvellous? Eh, Blanco? Marvellous, isn't it? The suspicion, the mistrust. Even in our sick beds, racked with pain we're still subject to these indignities.

**BARROWCLOUGH**
This won't take a moment, Fletcher, I just want to get to the bottom of this.

**FLETCHER**
Yes, you're well on your way an' all!

***He pulls the blankets back and examines underneath the bed, looking inside the slippers.***

**BARROWCLOUGH**
I thought for once I'd have some peace and quiet on this shift. But there's never a moment when one of you isn't up to something.

***He picks up the slippers.***

**BARROWCLOUGH**
Oh, you've broken the pom-poms.

***Sudden thought strikes him.***

**BARROWCLOUGH**
My God.

**FLETCHER**
Where are you going now?

**BARROWCLOUGH**
It just occurred to me that this whole farce has all the classic elements of a diversionary tactic. When I get back I'll probably find that the rest of the wing has tunnelled their way to freedom.

*He starts to go.*

**FLETCHER**

'Ere.

**BARROWCLOUGH**

What?

**FLETCHER**

Lights out.

*Barrowclough leaves.*

**FLETCHER**

He's left that door unlocked. It's not good enough is it – a burglar could walk straight in here.

## 5. PRISON

*Camera shows the prison in the morning.*

## 5A. HOSPITAL WARD

*Lennie is serving breakfast.*

**LENNIE**

Here you are, Blanco. Nice bit of marmalade here.

**FLETCHER**

What's the news from the outside world?

**LENNIE**

Mackay's in an ever so rotten mood. Villa drew. At home. Weather forecast said winds moderate to light. (*Giving food to Fletcher*) The hot water's working again. If you're quick. And it's cauliflower cheese for your supper tonight.

**FLETCHER**

Dear, oh dear. That's the trouble with being cooped up in hospital. You miss it all – don't you?

**LENNIE**

I only give the highlights. I missed out the boring bits.

**FLETCHER**

Well, when you come back later, can you bring me a newspaper – the *Sun*. And something to read. I've finished these two books . . . Oh er . . .

***He looks to see if Norris is watching but he is eating his breakfast.***

**FLETCHER**

Would you make sure these books go back to my cell?

***He gets the map from his plastered leg and puts it inside a book. He hands it to Lennie, winking at him.***

**FLETCHER**

I don't want those thieving nurks on the landing getting at them.

**PRISON OFFICER**

Come on, Godber.

**LENNIE**

Oh naffing hell. See you then, Fletch.

**FLETCHER**

Yes, drive carefully.

*Lennie wheels the trolley away.*

**FLETCHER**

(*To Blanco*) How's your tomato then, Blanco?

**BLANCO**

Had worse. But not much.

**NORRIS**
I'll have his.
**FLETCHER**
You'll have it all down your front if you're not careful.
**NORRIS**
Listen you two, I'd like a word. I'll come straight to the point. I was awake last night. I heard.
**FLETCHER**
Heard – heard what?
**NORRIS**
About the map.
**FLETCHER**
Don't know what he's talking about, do you Blanco? What map's this then?
**NORRIS**
Come on, Fletch, don't pee around. Listen, you could cut me in.
**FLETCHER**
I don't know what you're talking about.
**NORRIS**
You know what I'm talking about. The map, the gelt – the buried gelt, in Leeds.
**BLANCO**
Why should we cut you in?
**NORRIS**
Ah see – there is a map, isn't there?
**FLETCHER**
All right, then, all right, there is a map. But why should we cut you in?
**NORRIS**
I'm going out tomorrow.
**FLETCHER**
So.
**NORRIS**
Well, Blanco ain't out for two years, and you're not for three. Anything could happen. They could find it . . . or, or build a multi-storey car park on top of it. So I could keep it safe, couldn't I? Put it in a building society. Invest it, like.
**FLETCHER**
I know what you'd invest it in, Norris. You'd invest it in a brighter future for your despicable self. By the time we come out there wouldn't be a penny left. You'd squander it in a vulgar orgy of wining and dining northern tarts in northern night clubs.
**BLANCO**
Yeah. That's what I'd planned to do with it.
**FLETCHER**
You're entitled, Blanco. It's your money.
**NORRIS**
It won't be if he snuffs it, will it? You're going to cop it.
**FLETCHER**
I happens to be his chosen benefactor. And you happen to be someone he can't bear the sight of. You're only the bloke what cheated him out of his most treasured possessions. His snuff box and his radio, and his little Matilda what goes round. Tell you what though, Norris, if you can find the map you're welcome to a share.
**BLANCO**
Here, Fletch.

**FLETCHER**

Go on then, straight up. I mean I ain't been able to leave this room, have I? Not with this plaster.

**NORRIS**

That's a deal, is it?

**FLETCHER**

Have to find it first.

**NORRIS**

I know where you hid it.

**FLETCHER**

You ain't that clever, Norris.

***Norris lunges at Fletcher's plaster and tries to pull it off. Fletcher yells in agony.***

## 6. LANDING

***Norris, now fully dressed, makes his way up the steps towards the upper landing through the bustle of association hour.***

## 6A. CELL

***It is night time. Lennie is lying on the upper bunk, reading a paper, when Norris enters.***

**NORRIS**

'Ere, Godber.

**LENNIE**

Oh hello, Norris. Come to say your goodbyes, have you?

**NORRIS**

No, it's just that er – Fletch said when he give you those books, did he leave a bit of paper in it? By mistake, like.

**LENNIE**

Why?

**NORRIS**

He just wanted it. I said I'd take it over to him.

**LENNIE**

(*Suspiciously*) Bit of paper, like?

**NORRIS**

Yeah, quite meaningless.

**LENNIE**

Why's he want it then?

**NORRIS**

I dunno, it's meaningless –

***He sees the two books on a chair and grabs them. There is nothing in them.***

**LENNIE**

Meaningless, is it?

**NORRIS**

Was there a bit of paper in here?

**LENNIE**

Could be.

***Norris tries another tack.***

**NORRIS**

Look, Godber – I mean, Lennie – how d'you like to make some money? I mean real money. On the outside.

**LENNIE**

Not much use to me as I'm on the inside, is it?

**NORRIS**

All right. I've got gear on the inside. And my back wages.

**LENNIE**

What for – a meaningless bit of paper?

**NORRIS**

Ask no questions, son.

***Lennie swings down from his bunk.***

**LENNIE**

No questions about the fact that this is behind my mate's back. This, obviously, whatever it is, belongs to Fletch.

**NORRIS**

Never mind about Fletch. He only worries about number one. Look I'm offering you all my back pay. And my snout.

**LENNIE**

Fletch's my cellie. My mate.

**NORRIS**

(*Producing goods one by one*) I've got a silver snuff holder. Antique. Worth a lot of money.

**LENNIE**

He's been good to me, Fletch.

**NORRIS**

And a music box. Plays 'Waltzing Matilda'.

**LENNIE**

Contrary to popular belief in here, we're not all without scruples. Fletcher's shown me friendship. You can't buy that. Without him I'd've gone under in here.

**NORRIS**

There's a radio as well. Japanese.

**LENNIE**

All right, then, done.

***Norris grins in satisfaction.***

## 7. PRISON GATES

***Camera shows the prison gates. Norris walks out with a carrier bag and parcel and to a waiting minibus. He gets in and the minibus drives off.***

## 8. HOSPITAL WARD

***Lennie wheels the lunch trolley into the ward.***

**FLETCHER**

(*Indignantly*) Oh here he comes! The Judas Iscariot of Slade Prison.

**BLANCO**

Don't know how he dares show his face.

**FLETCHER**

Judas. You betrayed us, didn't you, Godber – you betrayed us to that evil Norris.

**LENNIE**

(*Unfazed*) Yes, I did.

**FLETCHER**

Thank God for that – how did it go?

**LENNIE**

Like a charm.

**FLETCHER**

(*To Blanco*) Like a charm – D'you hear that – like a charm.

***They all laugh.***

***Lennie picks up the cover on one of the trays.***

**LENNIE**

What have we here? One radio.

One snuff holder. And one Australian music box.

***He puts them on Blanco's bedside table.***

**FLETCHER**

There you are, Blanco, with all thy worldly goods we thee endow.

**BLANCO**

(*Chuffed*) Oh lads, lads.

**FLETCHER**

(*To Lennie*) What did you do with Norris's snout?

**LENNIE**

There was so much there wasn't room for it! And I've stashed the back pay.

**FLETCHER**

Split it three ways, fair enough?

**LENNIE**

When d'you cook this up, Fletch?

**FLETCHER**

That first afternoon when Norris was having his bath.

**LENNIE**

Lovely idea. He really thought you *had* some money buried.

**FLETCHER**

It's him. Lovely bit of acting. He had me going, he did in the small hours. 'Course we knew Norris would be earwigging. Person like that always does.

**BLANCO**

D'you think he'll go straight there?

**FLETCHER**

Oh gawd yes, the best is yet to come.

**LENNIE**

Should think he'll be in Leeds by midday.

**FLETCHER**

Yes. Then he'll go to an ironmonger's and buy a shovel – 'course he'll lie low this afternoon. Won't go there till everyone's gone home. (*To Blanco*) Here we'll listen to your wireless tonight. Might hear something on the nine o'clock news.

***They all laugh.***

## 9. FIELD

***A man is walking along. He stops, looks at a map, turns and walks on. Further along he stops walking, puts the map away and starts to dig. Lights start coming on. The sign 'Leeds United' can be seen. It is a floodlit football ground. A guard with a dog is walking towards Norris.***

## 10. HOSPITAL WARD

***Fletcher and Blanco are listening to the radio.***

**ANNOUNCER**

(*Voiceover*) Later a man was detained at Leeds Police headquarters, charged with trespass and causing wilful damage to the property of Leeds United Football Club. He is being remanded . . .

# 2 SERIES TWO

## EPISODE SIX: THE HARDER THEY FALL

### 1. ASSOCIATION AREA 1.

*Lennie is seen walking through the association area and going upstairs. A prisoner at a table speaks to him.*

**PRISONER**

Hey, Len, heard you made the team.

**LENNIE**

Yeah, well . . .

*He carries on up the stairs. At the top he meets Barrowclough.*

**BARROWCLOUGH**

The champ, is it?

**LENNIE**

Not yet.

**BARROWCLOUGH**

Double rations then.

**LENNIE**

If I want 'em.

**BARROWCLOUGH**

I thought that was the whole point in boxing. Getting a double ration chit.

**LENNIE**

Well, you see, if I have double rations of Slade Prison's food I won't be a middle-weight, I'll be an overweight.

**BARROWCLOUGH**

I trust you're not complaining about the food, Godber?

**LENNIE**

No complaints, sir.

**BARROWCLOUGH**

It's a jolly sight better than a lot of people get in their own homes. And I speak from experience. Of prison food, that is.

**LENNIE**

Yes, sir. I mean it's not much to look at, but then neither is ready-mixed concrete, and that doesn't taste very nice either.

**BARROWCLOUGH**

Well, that's all right then . . . I'm glad to hear you're taking a sensible . . .

*Lennie has gone.*

**BARROWCLOUGH**

Pardon?

## 2. CELL

***It is evening. Fletcher has just finished a game of draughts with another prisoner. They pack up.***

**FLETCHER**

Cheerio – thanks for the game.

***The prisoner goes, passing Lennie on his way in. Lennie is wearing a tracksuit.***

**LENNIE**

'Lo, Fletch.

**FLETCHER**

Oh gawd, the athlete.

**LENNIE**

Nothing wrong with that. Keep in shape. Better than draughts. You could do with losing a few pounds, Fletch.

**FLETCHER**

Thanks to draughts, I just won two pounds, ain't I?

**LENNIE**

You cheat at draughts.

**FLETCHER**

Here, you watch your tongue, or I'll knock your block off.

**LENNIE**

Oh no, you won't, Fletch . . .

***He starts to shadow box at Fletcher.***

**LENNIE**

Made the boxing team, didn't I . . .

***He starts slapping Fletcher's face in an irritating manner.***

**LENNIE**

Didn't I, didn't I . . . Come on, Fletch, where's your guard?

**FLETCHER**

He's outside, want me to call him in? Naff off, sit down, will you? Boxing now, is it?

***Lennie nods.***

**FLETCHER**

Gawd, Godber, you've taken every miffing course in this prison. Arts and Crafts, 'O' Levels, Pottery, Spanish. What are you going to do with Spanish, become an interpreter, are you?

**LENNIE**

Si, si, Señor.

**FLETCHER**

That's it, is it? Six weeks of concentrated study and what have we got – 'Si, si, Señor!'

**LENNIE**

No, listen . . . No tiene vaca, pero tiene uno burro.

**FLETCHER**

Go on then, I'll buy it.

**LENNIE**

I haven't got a cow, but I have got a donkey.

**FLETCHER**

Oh that'll come in handy, that's extremely useful, that is. On your first Spanish holiday, pick up a shy little señorita, she starts whispering sweet nothings up your nose and what do you say? 'Well, I haven't got a cow, darling, but I have got a donkey.'

**LENNIE**

Vaya con Dios – that's Spanish.

**FLETCHER**

People like you from Birmingham would be better off learning English. I hope this boxing lark won't last long. 'Cos you do bring a terrible smell of sweat and liniment into my room.

**LENNIE**

Takes away the smell of your aftershave. Seriously though, Fletch, I'm dead chuffed at making the boxing squad. Big match next week.

**FLETCHER**

You're only boxing for our wing.

**LENNIE**

I know but . . .

**FLETCHER**

Against another wing.

**LENNIE**

Even so.

**FLETCHER**

Hardly Madison Square Garden, is it?

**LENNIE**

It's a start, Fletch. I'm going to work at this. It's the great working-class escape, sport. That and rock and roll.

**FLETCHER**

No doubt you'll get round to that sooner or later.

**LENNIE**

I've got all the credentials to be a fighter. Deprived childhood, terrible background. Mr Hopkins, the PTI, says I've got natural ability.

**FLETCHER**

If you show all the flair in the ring that you show for Spanish, my son, you ain't half due a clobbering.

**LENNIE**

Que sera, sera . . .

**FLETCHER**

Kiss her what?

*Jackdaw comes in.*

**JACKDAW**

Hey, Fletch, Grouty wants to see you.

**FLETCHER**

Pardon?

**JACKDAW**

Grouty. Wants a word.

**FLETCHER**

Are you running for Harry Grout, now, Jackdaw?

**JACKDAW**

I'm one of his firm.

**FLETCHER**

He must be scraping the barrel.

**JACKDAW**

Watch it.

**FLETCHER**

Oh hark at him. Now that he's under the protective wing of genial Harry Grout he's full of bravado, isn't he?

**JACKDAW**

Well are you coming then?

**FLETCHER**

I might stroll across in due course, yeah.

**JACKDAW**

I'm supposed to take you with me.

**FLETCHER**

I'm a bit heavy to lift, Jackdaw. Tell you what, you scurry back,

I know the way. Tell Harry I want to change me socks and cut me toenails, all right?

**JACKDAW**

On your head be it.

***He leaves.***

**LENNIE**

Was that wise?

**FLETCHER**

Yeah – he's all right Harry. I know he has a long past of mayhem and violence, but this is the last year of a long, long stretch. He ain't going to come the heavy and cock up his release at this stage, is he?

**LENNIE**

S'pose not.

**FLETCHER**

He's happy being the tobacco baron, and running all the rackets.

**LENNIE**

Wonder what he wants to see you for?

**FLETCHER**

Maybe he wants a slice of my draughts action.

***They laugh.***

**FLETCHER**

Now where's me clippers?

**LENNIE**

Oh Fletch, you're not going to cut your toenails in here.

**FLETCHER**

Well I ain't going to grow them indefinitely, and I'm not tall enough to get me feet out the window.

**LENNIE**

All right, but you always cut 'em on my bunk.

***He walks over to the table and sits down.***

**FLETCHER**

Oh I'm sorry if it offends your sense of Birmingham propriety. I hope you're going to take a shower to wash that liniment off. Smells like a Turkish wrestler's jock strap in here.

**LENNIE**

Yes well, you've travelled Fletch, you know these things.

***Mackay comes in and walks across to Lennie.***

**MACKAY**

Hello, Godber. No, sit down. I'm told congratulations are in order.

**LENNIE**

Oh, the boxing. Thank you, Mr Mackay, yes.

**MACKAY**

Fine outlet, boxing. The noble art. Teaches you discipline, dedication and team spirit. Oh yes. I was no slouch myself at your age. I once boxed for Midlothian Boys.

**FLETCHER**

Who against, Lanarkshire Girls?

**MACKAY**

In the Army I boxed for the battalion.

**LENNIE**

Did you, Mr Mackay?

**MACKAY**

First Battalion. Argyle and Sutherland

Highlanders. Great regiment, great tradition. A regiment I was proud to serve.

**FLETCHER**

A regiment which is now defunct. Despite all those nurks who put stickers in their car windows.

**MACKAY**

I expect you were in the Ordnance Corps, Fletcher. Something which kept you well out of the line of fire. Probably served your time embezzling stores in some cushy posting like Shoeburyness.

***He laughs.***

**FLETCHER**

Well, you're wrong there. I did active service. Malaya. Kuala Lumpur. That's where I did my embezzling. And I wasn't in no Ordnance Corps. I was in the RASC.

**LENNIE**

What's that stand for?

**FLETCHER**

Run Away Someone's Coming.

***He laughs.***

**MACKAY**

National Service would have done you good, Godber. The Army's good to its boxers.

**FLETCHER**

I don't reckon boxing's such a noble art at all.

**MACKAY**

No?

**FLETCHER**

I had a friend once – haven't told you this before, have I? He was a light-heavy. Good strong, boy. Won a few fights. Suddenly thought he was the bee's knees. Fast cars, easy women. Classic story of too much, too soon. He just blew up. He got into debt and ended up in one of those travelling booths. Four fights a night, seven night a week. Well the body can't take that punishment. His brain went soft, his reflexes went. You know – punchy. Just became like a vegetable – an incoherent non-thinking zombie.

**MACKAY**

What became of him?

**FLETCHER**

He joined the prison service as a Warder. Doing very well.

***Mackay knows he's been had.***

***He goes.***

## 3. LANDING

***It is evening. Fletcher moves up on to the landing. He passes a Prison Officer on the stairs and gives a polite nod.***

## 3A. GROUT'S CELL

***It is evening. Grout's cell is extremely well furnished. It is a single cell with a quilted counterpane on the bed; an expensive radio and record player; a lamp made from an old***

***Chianti bottle; and several framed pictures of friends and well-known sporting personalities. He also has chintzy curtains, a rug, a magazine rack and a budgie in a cage. Harry Grout himself is a heavy-set man; an affable East London villain though one should be aware of a sense of power when he chooses to switch off the charm. He is listening to the radio on stereo headphones when Fletcher enters. Harry looks up and sees him, indicating that he should wait a moment till he has finished listening.***

***Fletcher enters the cell, looks around, touches the birdcage and waits.***

**GROUTY**

*Archers*. Never miss.

**FLETCHER**

They still on, are they?

**GROUT**

Doris is in a bit of a state. She's got Dutch Elm disease.

**FLETCHER**

Oh dear, poor Doris.

**GROUT**

Don't you follow *The Archers*?

**FLETCHER**

I don't, Grouty. Not for some years. Not since Grace copped it when I was in Shepton Mallet. That's nice.

***Grout is putting on a dressing gown.***

**FLETCHER**

I like the radio, mind. *Gardeners' Question Time* and *Desert Island Discs*.

**GROUT**

I like a good play meself. And a *Book at Bedtime*, never miss that.

**FLETCHER**

I like that. But of course they don't allow us the wireless that late.

**GROUT**

Don't they? No one's ever told me.

**FLETCHER**

Don't suppose anyone's ever dared. Nice place you got here.

**GROUT**

Do you like it?

**FLETCHER**

All the creature comforts. Like the lamp.

**GROUT**

Memento. Of Alassio. That's in Italy that is.

**FLETCHER**

Wasn't it Alassio that they extradited you from?

**GROUT**

That's right. I came back handcuffed to Scotcher of the Yard on Alitalia. I paid the extra and moved us both up into first class. Bit of a perk for him, he's never been south of Worthing before. Bought the Chianti for me, duty free, and got him a bottle of Sambuca.

**FLETCHER**

In the light of your subsequent sentence, it might have been better if you'd given the judge the Sambuca.

**GROUT**

I offered him five hundred quid, what more could I do?

**FLETCHER**
Oh I suppose not . . .

***Jackdaw enters with a tray of cocoa.***

**GROUT**
Yes, come in, Jackdaw. Cocoa, Fletch?

**FLETCHER**
Oh, don't mind if I do.

**GROUT**
Sugar?

***Hands Fletcher a two-pound bag.***

**FLETCHER**
Thank you.

**JACKDAW**
(*Holding up a packet of bird seed*) Should I feed Seymour, Harry?

**GROUT**
Yeah, go on.

***Fletcher looks round.***

**FLETCHER**
Seymour? Oh your feathered friend. Very nice.

**GROUT**
He's company of an evening. When I was in Parkhurst I had a pigeon.

**FLETCHER**
Oh like the Birdman of Alcatraz.

**GROUT**
Not really, no.

**FLETCHER**
No, not really I suppose. Took a bit more room though, didn't he? A pigeon.

**GROUT**
Just a bit, yeah. On the other hand how else could I keep in touch with the bookmakers?

**FLETCHER**
Oh I see – yeah.

***He pauses.***

**GROUT**
Brought me in a few bob.

**FLETCHER**
Yeah, must have done. What did you do with it when you had to leave?

**GROUT**
I ate it.

**FLETCHER**
Oh very nice. I should watch your step if I were you, Jackdaw.

**JACKDAW**
Will we – that be all then, Harry?

**GROUT**
Probably, but hang about . . . oh and Jackdaw?

**JACKDAW**
Yes, Harry?

**GROUT**
We're in conference so do the minding, right?

**JACKDAW**
Yes, Harry.

***He withdraws.***

**GROUT**
Do you want a Bath Oliver?

**FLETCHER**
You got a bath in here an' all?

***Grout offers him a biscuit.***

**FLETCHER**
Oh, biscuit.

**GROUT**
With your cocoa?

**FLETCHER**
No thanks, Grouty. Got to watch the weight, you know what I mean.
***He spoons four heaped spoonfuls of sugar into his cocoa.***

**GROUT**
Well then; Fletch . . .

**FLETCHER**
Well then, Grouty . . .

**GROUT**
They're going to have this boxing match, aren't they?

**FLETCHER**
So I hear. Inter prison championships or something.

**GROUT**
Well then – money to be made.

**FLETCHER**
You mean a flutter?

**GROUT**
Sport means competition, don't it? Which means there's a winner and a loser. Which is all right providing you're on the winner.

**FLETCHER**
Forgive me for saying this, Grouty, but do you need the funds? I mean if you want money all you have to do is go to people and they give it to you.

**GROUT**
Where's the fun in that? We're talking about sport, my son. The speculation, the excitement, the tension, the thrill of the outcome.

**FLETCHER**
Oh the thrill of the outcome, yes.

**GROUT**
That's what I enjoy.

**FLETCHER**
Yeah, yeah.

**GROUT**
That's why I want you to fix the fight.

**FLETCHER**
You what?

**GROUT**
Well that's putting it a bit strong. What I mean is what I want you to do is to feed me certain information so that I get all my thrill of speculation and excitement from knowing that I'm on a certainty.

**FLETCHER**
Feed you what information, Harry? There's seven fights. Wing against wing.

**GROUT**
I know that, but as they all have to train in the same gymnasium, it just needs someone with an experienced eye to run over the form. Someone like yourself. As you know, in this nick I have a bit of a rival. Namely the presumptuous upstart, Billy Moffatt.

**FLETCHER**
That nurk, Moffatt. No contest, Harry.

**GROUT**
Nevertheless he's running a book. Without my seal of approval. So I'd like to take him to the cleaners.

**FLETCHER**
Yes, I sees your point, Harry, but you know me, I'm a loner. I sees myself as

the Randolph Scott of Slade Prison. I don't like being responsible to nobody, not even someone as distinguished as yourself. So I think really the best thing is for me to say straight off, very adamantly, that I decline this flattering invitation. Thanks for the cocoa.

***He starts towards the doorway. There is a very large prisoner standing there.***

**GROUT**

You disappoint me, Fletch.

***Fletcher changes his mind and returns to Grout.***

**FLETCHER**

When do I start?

**4. GYM**

***Lennie is sparring with Larry in the ring. The PTI is watching them. Fletcher walks into the gym.***

**REFEREE**

What are you on, Fletcher? Charity walk, is it?

**FLETCHER**

You know me, Mr Bayliss. I'm not a man what gets involved in the recreational pastime of this prison. When all around me's a frenzy of activity, I'm happy to be on my bunk whittling. But I was lying there, you know, and I was thinking about the honour of the wing, and I realised that it would be a crime if I didn't offer you the benefit of my experience.

***Mackay approaches.***

**MACKAY**

What experience is this, Fletcher?

**FLETCHER**

Oh hello, Mr Mackay. My experience of ringcraft, the noble art. Just telling Mr Bayliss how my know-how is at his disposal.

**MACKAY**

Well, we don't know what to say, do we, lads? We're overwhelmed. All right then, Fletcher. In the ring.

**FLETCHER**

In the ring? What d'you mean, in the ring?

**MACKAY**

Show the lads a thing or two.

**FLETCHER**

I'm offering you my advice. My expertise.

**MACKAY**

Have to show the lads a thing or two. Show 'em the old magic's still there. How else will they believe in you?

***He starts putting gloves on Fletcher.***

**FLETCHER**

The England Squad believe in Don Revie, but he don't get on the park and kick a ball around. Angelo Lundee – he don't spar with Ali. Stays in the corner, muttering words of advice and minding the gumshield.

**MACKAY**

He wants to work for the squad, lads, he has to show willing, doesn't he?

***The prisoners agree. Fletcher is trapped.***

**REFEREE**
Go on then, Fletch, out you come, Larry.
***Larry gets out of the ring. Fletcher climbs in. Fletcher walks up to Lennie who pushes his gloves forward in the prematch gesture.***
**FLETCHER**
Now just go easy, sonny. Don't make me lose my rag. Hey, watch it.
**LENNIE**
Keep your guard up, Fletcher.
**REFEREE**
Seconds out.
***He rings the bell.***
**FLETCHER**
Fire drill, oh – back to the cells everyone.
***He walks to the ropes.***
**MACKAY**
Fletcher.
**FLETCHER**
Oh sir, sorry, sir. Yes, sir.
***He returns to Lennie and starts ducking round him. Lennie just stands there in amazement. Finally he takes one punch at Fletcher. Fletcher falls to the ground.***

## 5. UTILITY ROOM

***It is evening. Jackdaw, followed by Fletcher, comes down the corridor and up to the door. He unlocks it. Grout is sitting on an old deckchair, smoking a cigar, when Jackdaw ushers Fletcher into the utility room.***
**GROUT**
Come in, Fletch. How are you?
**FLETCHER**
I'll live, I suppose.

**JACKDAW**
Should I er – ?
**GROUT**
Yeah, keep an eye.
***Jackdaw withdraws. Fletcher looks around him with some distaste.***
**FLETCHER**
Preferred your other place.
**GROUT**
The less you and I are seen together the better. So what's the form then?
**FLETCHER**
Well there's not much to choose between any of the matchings, Grouty. Anybody's guess who'll win the flyweight, since they're both equally stupid and cowardly. Question of which one bursts into tears first. I think Big Mac's a certainty in the heavyweight.
**GROUT**
Well we all know that.
**FLETCHER**
The other certainty, I must say, is young Godber. 'Course being his second, I've been able to give a bit extra, y'know – phuh phuh.
**GROUT**
Yes, I heard from other quarters, he's well favoured. Good strong boy.
**FLETCHER**
And his opponent, young Nesbitt – he just hasn't got it. No contact.

**GROUT**

Well that's the one then.

**FLETCHER**

You won't get very good odds on Godber.

**GROUT**

No, but I will on Nesbitt.

***Fletcher realises instantly the implications of this.***

**FLETCHER**

Oh now, Harry . . .

**GROUT**

Tell the lad to make it look good. And then go down in the second.

**FLETCHER**

Oh Grouty, please! Not the lad. It means a lot to him.

**GROUT**

Means a lot to me, Fletch. Billy Moffatt will be on your boy.

**FLETCHER**

But why him? Why not nobble Big Mac? Get even better odds on his opponent.

**GROUT**

Don't be daft. Where's the credibility in Big Mac going down? He put four screws in the hospital last year when someone knocked his jigsaw over. Can you see Hermigton beating him?

**FLETCHER**

David beat Goliath.

**GROUT**

With a sling full of shot, not a left hook.

**FLETCHER**

Put some shot in his glove?

**GROUT**

No, no, it's got to be Godber.

**FLETCHER**

But, Grouty, I'm not sure the lad will do it. He's young, he's idealistic. He's still got his scruples.

**GROUT**

If he don't do what I ask, he may not have them much longer.

## 6. FLETCHER'S CELL

***Lennie is doing press-ups on the cell floor when Fletcher enters, diffidently and watches him for a moment.***

**FLETCHER**

Oh, anyone we know?

**LENNIE**

Just a minute, Fletch . . . twenty-four . . . twenty-five . . .

***He collapses, then staggers on to his bunk.***

**LENNIE**

Twenty-five, Fletch.

**FLETCHER**

That's very commendable.

***He gives Lennie a mug of tea.***

**LENNIE**

Thank you. And I did twenty pull-ups on the wall bars before I left the gym.

**FLETCHER**

Twenty? Really?

**LENNIE**

Pull-ups. Yes.

***Fletcher looks at Lennie panting on the bed for a minute and then shakes his head.***

**FLETCHER**

Is it worth it?

**LENNIE**

How d'you mean?

**FLETCHER**

All these press-ups, and pull-ups. All these deep breathing exercises. And this weight-lifting. It's a bit daft in' it? I mean it's just punishment.

**LENNIE**

It's for the boxing, Fletch.

**FLETCHER**

I know, Len, I know. That's my worry, you see.

**LENNIE**

Why?

**FLETCHER**

My concern, my very genuine concern is that you're neglecting your pottery classes. And all those other arts and crafts activities in which you indulged so diligently. And what's happened to your elementary plumbing – that's gone down the drain an' all. You see there's no future in boxing. It's a mug's game. Snout?

***He offers him some.***

**LENNIE**

No, I'd better not.

***He pats his chest.***

**FLETCHER**

Suit yourself. Oh here, that reminds me. I got you some chocolate – your favourite, fruit and nut.

***He gives it to him.***

**LENNIE**

Oh that's ever so kind, Fletch. I'll save it till after the fight.

**FLETCHER**

Suit yourself.

**LENNIE**

You all right, Fletch?

**FLETCHER**

What do you mean, am I all right?

**LENNIE**

Well, the snout, the tea and the chocolate. It's not you, normally you're so mean.

**FLETCHER**

What do you mean – mean?

**LENNIE**

(*Standing up*) I was wondering if my right cross had done some permanent brain damage. I think you ought to go to the MO and have your bumps felt.

***He laughs.***

**FLETCHER**

(*Walking over to Lennie*) Now you listen to me, Godber, you listen to me. Just shut your mouth and hear me out, you cocky young scroat.

**LENNIE**

(*Sitting down*) That's better. That's the old Fletch.

**FLETCHER**

(*Crossing to Lennie*) No, it isn't. It isn't

your old Fletch you see before you but a very troubled man.

**LENNIE**

Oh?

***Fletcher paces the floor for a few moments, then says.***

**FLETCHER**

I'm a cynical old so-and-so . . . well, I don't have to tell you. It's 'cos I've seen it all. You on the other hand haven't seen anything. That's what gives you your naïve charm I suppose. You ain't had all the idealism ground out of you. Yet! But I have to ask you – well *tell* you – what someone has asked me – well *told* me – they were wondering – well they was insisting – if you could see your way clear – not that you have very much choice . . . I don't know how to say this, kid . . .

**LENNIE**

What is it you're trying to say, Fletch?

***Fletcher looks him in the eye.***

**FLETCHER**

Tomorrow night's not going to be your night, Lennie.

**LENNIE**

How?

**FLETCHER**

(*Taking a deep breath*) Harry Grout wants you to take a dive in the second.

***Lennie stares at him blankly.***

**FLETCHER**

Don't look at me in that way, son. You're shocked, of course you are . . . and me . . . I'm ashamed.

***There is a pause before Lennie says, quietly.***

**LENNIE**

I can't do that, Fletch.

**FLETCHER**

I knew you'd say that, Len . . . and I respect you for it. But you have to see the position I'm in.

**LENNIE**

I appreciate that, Fletch. But I just can't do it.

**FLETCHER**

But it means nothing! What does it mean after all! It's a wing against a wing. It's meaningless!

**LENNIE**

I know that.

**FLETCHER**

Then why can't you do this? For me!

**LENNIE**

I've already promised Billy Moffatt to take a dive in the first.

***Fletcher is outraged.***

**FLETCHER**

You've what! You're going to take a dive –

**LENNIE**

Keep your voice down, Fletch.

**FLETCHER**

(*Voice down*) You're taking a dive for Moffatt?

**LENNIE**

Yes.

**FLETCHER**

I don't pretend to understand the younger generation. I really don't.

Would you mind telling me why?

**LENNIE**

They asked me first.

**FLETCHER**

Oh, they asked you first. So you're in the market for corruption, are you? Case of the biggest bidder, is it?

**LENNIE**

Oh come on, Fletch! You know the score. I may be innocent and naïve but I'm not bloody daft. I'm au fait with the realities inside. I'd rather be clobbered in the ring than out of it. It's the easy way out – no skin off my nose.

**FLETCHER**

It's me that's going to get skinned! And not just off the nose neither.

**LENNIE**

'Spose you want your fruit and nut back.

**FLETCHER**

I most certainly do.

***He takes it and starts eating it.***

**FLETCHER**

You've disappointed me you have. You could have been a contender, you could.

**LENNIE**

But you just said . . .

**FLETCHER**

Never mind what I just said, you forget what I just said, it's none of your business what I just said! Things have changed between you and me. I'm disappointed, bitterly disappointed in you. I've never been so let down since my son Raymond broke into his school one night and had a prior peep at the exam papers.

**LENNIE**

Did he?

**FLETCHER**

Yes he did, and he still didn't pass.

## 7. UTILITY ROOM

***It is night time. Grout is still sitting in the same chair. He is talking to Fletcher.***

**GROUT**

Well, I don't know what to make of youngsters today. No moral fibre.

**FLETCHER**

They won't be told.

**GROUT**

Poses a problem though, don't it?

**FLETCHER**

Now wait a minute, Grouty. Godber's still going to lose. We're all on Nesbitt to win, so there's no conflict of interests, is there?

**GROUT**

There's no odds neither. All the big money in this nick's on Nesbitt – wouldn't even get evens.

**FLETCHER**

Why don't we just withdraw gracefully from this one, Harry? It's getting ever so complicated. Why don't you just go back to demanding money with menaces?

**GROUT**

That doesn't satisfy my sporting

instincts, I told you before, I like the excitement, the old adrenalin. Only one thing for it. If they've nobbled Godber we've to make sure that he wins.

**FLETCHER**

How?

**GROUT**

You nobble Nesbitt.

***Fletcher looks in pain.***

## 8. GYM

***Prisoners are coming in to take their seats. Grout and Jackdaw are among them. Grout looks at Moffatt.***

## 9. CHANGING ROOM

***The boxers are getting ready for the fight. Fletcher and Lennie come in.***

**LENNIE**

What's up, Fletch?

**FLETCH**

I want a word.

**LENNIE**

What?

**FLETCHER**

The fix is on.

**LENNIE**

Well I know that, don't I? I'm going down in the first.

**FLETCHER**

Yeah, well don't hang about, 'cos so is Nesbitt.

**LENNIE**

Is he?

**FLETCHER**

Which is serious for all three of us. If you win, you're in trouble with Moffatt. If Nesbitt wins he's in trouble with Grouty. And whoever wins I'm in trouble with both of them. One of us is going to suffer, and it's going to be me twice. It ain't the customs of the fight I'm worried about, it's the outcome of the outcome.

**LENNIE**

Whatever it is it's going to be serious.

**FLETCHER**

That much is certain, my son. In fact the only element of speculation in this fight is which one of you hits the flaming canvas first.

**LENNIE**

What are we going to do?

## 10. GYM

***The boxers enter with their seconds and climb into the ring. The Referee calls the boxers over to him.***

**REFEREE**

All right, lads, let's have a good fight. If you go down take a mandatory count of eight, you break when I say break and you fight fair, right?

**THE BOXERS**

***The boxers touch gloves and return to their respective corners.***

**FLETCHER**
(*Putting gumshield in Lennie's mouth*) Go in and may the best man lose.

***Nesbitt in his corner is also getting his gumshield.***

***The bell rings.***

**VOICE**
(*Offscreen*) Seconds out, round one.

***Grout and Moffat are watching the fight when both boxers go down. Lennie is on the floor apparently knocked out. The referee starts to count. Fletcher, relieved, counts with him.***

***Grout leaves, as do Moffat and the other prisoners.***

## 11. FLETCHER'S CELL

***It is night time. Lennie is on his bunk. Fletcher is brought into the cell by a Warder.***

**FLETCHER**
Thanks very much, James. I'm sorry I don't seem to have any small change.

***The Warder goes and slams the door shut.***

**FLETCHER**
(*To Lennie*) Are you all right?

**LENNIE**
'Course I am. Hardly touched me. What did Grouty say?

**FLETCHER**
Couldn't say anything, could he?

**LENNIE**
He didn't suspect?

**FLETCHER**
He's all right. Bets were void, weren't they? So he didn't gain anything – on the other hand he didn't lose anything. Nor did he lose any prestige to that Billy Moffat.

**LENNIE**
A great idea. Nobody won, and none of us lost.

**FLETCHER**
Er yeah . . . well, that's not exactly true.

**LENNIE**
How d'you mean?

**FLETCHER**
There was somebody who came out of this ahead.

**LENNIE**
You?

**FLETCHER**
Confidentially, I made quite a bit of money off of that bent warder who works in the bakery.

**LENNIE**
How?

**FLETCHER**
I was the only bloke in this nick what bet on a draw. Chocolate?

# 2 MEMORIES

**Sam Kelly** (Warren in the series)

'Can you imagine the joy in speaking the lines and working with those actors for someone who had hardly set foot in a television studio in 1975? That was me playing the illiterate Bunny Warren, a man who was inside because he couldn't read the sign that said "burglar alarm". And who better to be inside with than the brilliant Mr Barker. Don't mistake Ronnie for a comedian, he's a great actor with the skill and generosity that made newcomers like me gain in confidence with each episode, and the knowledge that with good actors around him the show would work and that he would shine. And shine he did! Norman Fletcher is without doubt one of the greatest creations in the history of television.

'Syd Lotterby had used me previously in an episode of *The Liver Birds* and in a one-off sitcom playing, of all things, Cilla Black's boyfriend. To have crossed his mind when casting *Porridge* has helped my career to take off in all directions, both in television and the theatre. Innumerable sitcoms later I give thanks to Syd.

'What do I remember of a fantastic couple of years? The hilarious weekly read-throughs (I deliberately didn't read the scripts beforehand); the rehearsals with Ronnie putting in his little looks, double takes and the odd extra line; Fulton Mackay fussing around on his way towards that marvellous performance. I watched relentlessly, instinctively knowing that I was learning all the time. I watched everyone: Beckinsale, Osoba, Biggins, Ken Jones. I learned things from actors far less experienced than I, and now that Ronnie has retired I can safely say that I stole some of his expressions and "takes" and shamelessly use them to this day.

'Favourite moments are many: Philip Madoc on the mating habits of spiders; Lukewarm knitting while waiting for a visit from his boyfriend; Fletcher wangling a weekend at home in his big bed with his big wife; the food riot (which nearly brought Ealing Studios out on strike); the two episodes with the legendary Maurice Denham as a bent judge; great visiting actors such as Ronald Lacey, Dudley Sutton, Madge Hindle, Patricia Brake and Peter Jeffrey. And a great comic coup was the fey governor who couldn't cope with anything, least of all Norman Stanley Fletcher.

'*Porridge* worked because it was truthful. Despite the laugh, jokes and hilarious characters there was no doubt that these men were in prison. Acting is about being truthful, nothing else, and we were blessed with two writers who knew that and who could write in no other way.'

**Tony Osoba** (McLaren in the series)
'"Disturbing the Peace" is one of my favourite episodes and I vividly recall filming the riot scene on the set at Ealing film studios. The *Porridge* sets were always quite superb – testimony to the brilliance of the designers Tim Gleeson, John Pusey, David Chandler and Gerry Scott. Many people were convinced that we shot the series in a real prison.

'I think the writing beautifully sets up the character of Napper Wainwright and his relationship with Fletcher. The late Peter Jeffrey captured the essence of Wainwright magnificently and later I was privileged to enjoy hooking and slicing my way round the golf course in the company of this delightful man.

'Meanwhile, back at the riot, can you imagine turning a group of thirty people loose in a canteen scene and encouraging them to chuck the food around? What we'd all have given for that to have happened at school dinners! And nobody telling you off. To make sure everything was suitably messy we were supplied with appropriate victuals: vats of mashed potatoes, tureens of mushy peas, etc.

'The downside to all of this delinquent fun was that we ran out of time whilst filming the scene and had to return the following day to complete it. Continuity meant that the costumes couldn't be washed and the set had to remain exactly as it had been left. Even now I recall with nauseous clarity climbing into my costume, still wet in patches with the congealing mushy peas, cracking in other places with hardened mashed potato and squelching around the set, slipping and sliding on unspeakable concoctions formed from our previous day's efforts. And as to the smell, well I won't even begin to describe that. Ah, all in the name of art! Fond memories.'

**Philip Madoc** (Williams in 'Disturbing the Peace')
'The first sight of Machu Picchu, the approach through the Sik and entry into Petra, the advent of sliced bread – could these moments in my life compare with the phone call from Ronnie Barker inviting me to be in *Porridge*? Comparisons are odorous [sic] and the jury is still out – but I can certainly say – without fear of contradiction, that the week spent with Ronnie and that splendid cast made upon me the most indelible of impressions. Ronnie, Richard, Fulton and Brian were perfect and we worked with an impeccable script. In Mr Williams I had the most interesting of parts.

'*Porridge* has always seemed to me to be underpinned with truth, subtlety and delicacy, and Sydney Lotterby was most clearly in tune with it all. I would love to have developed my character in other episodes, but Sydney later told me – unsolicited – that he had himself found the character fascinating, had tried to get hold of the writers (Dick Clement and Ian La Frenais) to suggest that they might like to extend Mr Williams's lease, but they were in America at the time and he failed to contact them. Nevertheless it was an experience just to be in this one episode, "Disturbing the Peace", and I know that whenever it still appears, it continues to provoke much laughter and is sheer enjoyment.'

# 3 SERIES THREE

## MEMORIES



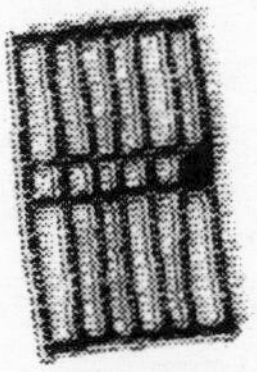

# 3 SERIES THREE

## EPISODE ONE: A STORM IN A TEACUP

### 1. FLETCHER'S CELL

***Fletcher sits at the table reading a tatty paperback. He has a mug of tea. Warren walks in, eating an apple.***

**WARREN**
What are you reading, Fletch?

**FLETCHER**
A book.

**WARREN**
No, I meant what sort of book?

**FLETCHER**
A paperback sort of book, lots of bits of paper all stuck together down the left-hand side.

**WARREN**
Is it a good book?

**FLETCHER**
I won't know that till I've finished it, will I? Which will be some time if I get these continual interruptions.

**WARREN**
I'd read books, if I could read.

***Fletcher, for the first time, looks up, then looks back to his book.***

**WARREN**
Is it a dirty book?

**FLETCHER**
Yes, filthy. Coming back from lunch, I dropped it in a puddle.

***McLaren approaches.***

**MCLAREN**
Reading a book, Fletch?

**FLETCHER**
No, I'm ironing.

***McLaren peers over his shoulder, reading.***

**FLETCHER**
Don't do that. Read over my shoulder. Can't stand that. Height of bad manners, that.

***McLaren lowers his head to read cover.***

**MCLAREN**
*Mandingo* . . . what's that about then?

**FLETCHER**
Curiously enough, it's about your lot. Slaves in the Deep South.

**MCLAREN**
Scots, are they?

**FLETCHER**
Blacks, sonny Jock, blacks. Your – ancestors. Toiling in the cotton fields.

**MCLAREN**
My ancestors are from the West Indies. Or at least half of them.

**FLETCHER**
All the same. Slaves an' that. This lot picked cotton. Your lot picked bananas. Comes down to the same difference. A load of blacks toiling in the fields under a boiling sun picking something.

**WARREN**
I thought slaves were in Roman times. In galleys, rowing like.

**FLETCHER**
Well yes, them, Warren, them was your galley slaves.

**WARREN**
But they was white. I know they was 'cause I've seen all them films. Set in Roman times. And they always had slaves in them. And Rosanna Podesta. Oh and Steve Reeves. Did you see Jason and the Golden Fleas?

**FLETCHER**
*Jason and the Golden Fleece* – fleece would be the word you had in mind, Warren – if you had a mind to have it in, that is.

**WARREN**
Oh what was that other one – I loved it at the time. Oh yes! Jason and the Astronauts.

**MCLAREN**
You dim nurk, Warren. You're thinking of Jason and the Juggernauts. I know that because . . .

**FLETCHER**
(*Interrupting*) Gawd! Listen Philip Jenkinson, if you'll excuse me I think this is where I came in. I remember it was that bit in the picture where Rod Steiger hit Sidney Poitier over the head with a cup of tea 'cos he wouldn't let him read (*Standing up*) his book in peace.

**MCLAREN**
(*Standing up*) Sorry, Fletch – we're just going.

**FLETCHER**
No, carry on – you might as well stay and see the shoot out at the end. With any luck, Jason there might get his argonauts blown off.

***Fletcher leaves with his mug of tea and his book.***

**WARREN**
That's funny. I didn't think they had guns then.

**MCLAREN**
When?

**WARREN**
In the days of Kirk Douglas.

## 2. ASSOCIATION AREA

***Fletcher walks down the stairs with his book and his mug of tea. He goes to the table where Lukewarm is sitting. He looks at Lukewarm and then sits opposite him and starts to read.***

**LUKEWARM**

Reading a book, Fletch?

**FLETCHER**

Oh gawd, don't you start. Just carry on with your balaclava, there might be another war. In fact, there will be if I don't finish this book.

***He takes a sip of tea and puts the mug down.***

**MACKAY**

(*Offscreen*) Harris!

***Mackay walks up.***

**MACKAY**

Stand where you are – stand still!

**HARRIS**

Me, Mr Mackay?

**MACKAY**

Yes, you. Don't move.

***Lukewarm and Fletcher look up at Mackay.***

**MACKAY**

You've been to the medical room.

**HARRIS**

Yes, sir. Just had me dressing changed like.

**MACKAY**

The orderly thinks you may have palmed some pills.

**HARRIS**

Not me, sir.

***Mackay starts to search Harris. Fletcher looks up.***

**FLETCHER**

Never a dull moment.

***He takes a sip of tea, puts the mug down and goes back to reading. Mackay is still searching Harris who looks down. Pills drop out of Harris's trouser leg and he kicks them over the edge. Pills drop down splashing Fletcher.***

**FLETCHER**

Who did that?

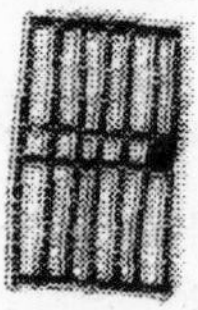

**LUKEWARM**

Did what?

**FLETCHER**

Bleeding sparrows in our roof again? Anything on my face?

***Mackay finishes searching Harris.***

**MACKAY**

Come with me, Harris.

**HARRIS**

'Ere listen, I'm clean. You got no right. This is harassment.

**MACKAY**

(*Walking away*) I'll harass you, Harris – I'm going to strip you down.

**LUKEWARM**

Ooh, some girls have all the luck.

***He turns away. Mackay looks for the voice. Then he indicates to Harris to come and marches him off.***

**LUKEWARM**

He'd whip anything, him. Don't know what he wants with pills.

**FLETCHER**

(*Getting up as he speaks*) Oh come on. You know the racket in here. Always someone who wants to be picked up or zonked out. Inside same as outside, in' it? Can't see it meself. Not my cup of tea, drugs.

***He walks off with his mug of tea and his book.***

**3. CELL**

***Lennie is still in his chef's outfit, washing, when Fletcher enters, carrying his mug of tea and his book.***

**LENNIE**

'Lo, Fletch.

**FLETCHER**

Oh, they've gone, have they?

**LENNIE**

Who?

**FLETCHER**

Warren and McLaren – the black and white minstrels.

**LENNIE**

Oh yeah. Hey, I did the lunches on my own today – did you like it?

**FLETCHER**

Tell me something – what was the name of that pudding?

**LENNIE**

Tapioca.

**FLETCHER**

Oh, tapioca was it?

***He sits down.***

**FLETCHER**

D'you think you could sneak a dollop back here?

**LENNIE**

P'raps. Liked it that much, did you?

**FLETCHER**

No, but I need something to stick down the sole of my shoe with.

**LENNIE**

I'll ignore that. Can't bait me. Tapioca off a duck's back.

***Fletcher takes a sip of tea.***

**FLETCHER**

Tea's cold now.

**LENNIE**

(*Crossing to his bunk*) Tapioca off za duck's back.

***He laughs.***

**LENNIE**

What was the kerfuffle? I heard Mackay nabbed Harris.

**FLETCHER**

Oh that. Thought he'd been pinching pills from the MO's.

**LENNIE**

(*Removing trousers*) Had he?

**FLETCHER**

Probably. Didn't find nothing. Must have stashed 'em.

**LENNIE**

Wonder where?

**FLETCHER**

Why?

**LENNIE**
Wouldn't mind them dropping into my hands. Windfall that.

**FLETCHER**
You don't even knows what they was.

**LENNIE**
Wouldn't matter to the blokes in here. Currency.

**FLETCHER**
Oh I see, you'd sell them, would you? You'd take on the might of genial Harry Grout.

*Lennie thinks.*

**LENNIE**
No, p'raps not. I'd have 'em myself.

**FLETCHER**
Drug addict!

**LENNIE**
Oh come on, Fletch. Your generation has a lot of prejudice about drugs. It's fear through ignorance.

**FLETCHER**
My generation's sensible enough to know that drugs don't do no one no good no how. They're anathema to me, they are.

**LENNIE**
There's even drugs for that.

**FLETCHER**
What?

**LENNIE**
Anathema.

**FLETCHER**
Anathema is an expression, not an ailment.

**LENNIE**
I know, I was only making a joke.

**FLETCHER**
Godber, you have used up your joke ration for the month with that tapioca pudding.

## 4. LANDING

***Harris comes out of Mackay's office, thinking.***

***He climbs up stairs and walks along the landing.***

***Arm comes out from a cell and pulls him inside.***

## 5. GROUT'S CELL

***Crusher has pulled Harris into the cell and he swings him round to face Grouty, who is sitting in his chair with a tray on which are the remains of his lunch.***

**HARRIS**
Oh, hello, Mr Grout, sir.

**GROUT**
Thank you, Crusher. Would you take the tray away.

**CRUSHER**
Yes, sir.

***He picks up the tray and hands it to Spider.***

**SPIDER**
Didn't you like your tapioca?

**GROUT**
Oh that's what it was.

**SPIDER**
Want me to open a box of those crystallised fruits?

**GROUT**
No, I mustn't.

***Patting stomach.***

**SPIDER**
Tins of mandarins then?
They ain't fattening.

**GROUT**
I didn't know we had any.

**SPIDER**
We hadn't but young Tomkiss had a food parcel, didn't he, Crusher?

**CRUSHER**
(*Laughing*) Yeah . . .

**GROUT**
And he gave us some?

**SPIDER**
In a manner of speaking. I know you likes a mandarin.

**GROUT**
I'll have 'em for me tea. On your way.

***Spider leaves, followed by Crusher. Grout crosses to the right of Harris, picks up a napkin ring and puts his napkin into it.***

**HARRIS**
Mandarins eh – rare treat.

**GROUT**
Harris.

**HARRIS**
Yes, sir.

**GROUT**
What did Mackay just do to you?

**HARRIS**
Frisked me over.

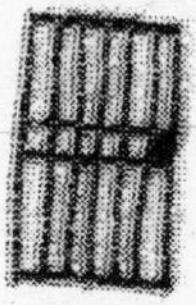

**GROUT**
Why?

**HARRIS**
Dunno.

**GROUT**
Must have had a reason.

**HARRIS**
Oh well, he alleged I took some pills from the MO's.

**GROUT**
Had you?

**HARRIS**
'Course not.

**GROUT**
Dangerous things to do.
Dangerous things, drugs. If they get taken injudiciously, they can be harmful. Leads to addiction. Seen it happen too often.

**HARRIS**
Oh I see. Well, that's a good reason for me not to whip pills, isn't it?

**GROUT**
Oh I agree.

**HARRIS**
I didn't honest.

**GROUT**
Harris, you're a born tea leaf.
It's force of habit. Whip now – think later. That's your motto.

**HARRIS**
Honest – I only went in there to get me bandage changed.

**GROUT**

(*Moving closer*) I see. By the way, how is the arm?

**HARRIS**

Oh well. It's coming on quite nicely –

***He screams as Grout pulls at the arm.***

## 6. FLETCHER'S CELL

***Fletcher is on the top bunk reading. Lennie is standing. They are both startled by the scream.***

**LENNIE**

What was that?

**FLETCHER**

I dunno. Someone's gone on hunger strike and they're force-feeding him your tapioca.

**LENNIE**

(*Going to the door*) No, but it was a terrible scream. Bloodcurdling.

**FLETCHER**

Probably one of your drug addict friends taking the cold chicken cure.

**LENNIE**

Cold turkey.

**FLETCHER**

Yeah, well they use chicken in here, don't they?

**LENNIE**

(*Returning to the bunk*)
You just don't understand, Fletch. Fear through ignorance.

**FLETCHER**

(*Sitting up*) Listen, I'm not ignorant. I'm just more aware of the abuse than you seem to be. I've seen it happen. Saw some of my comrades in arms got addicted to morphine.

**LENNIE**

When was this?

**FLETCHER**

Comrades in arms. Wasn't in the launderette – when I was in the Army.

**LENNIE**

Why did they have morphine?

**FLETCHER**

To ease the pain of the gunshot wounds.

**LENNIE**

Where was you stationed, a rifle range?

**FLETCHER**

You're an impudent nurk, you are, Godber. While you were safely sleeping in your Smethwick crib, some of us was doing our bit for Queen and country. In the steaming Malayan jungle at the height of the terror.

**LENNIE**

You told me you was in the stores.

**FLETCHER**

In Kuala Lumpur.

**LENNIE**

There wasn't any fighting in Kuala Lumpur.

**FLETCHER**
There was in the stores. Anyway, I'm not talking about that. I'm talking about when I lay wounded in hospital.

**LENNIE**
You told me that an' all – four days with a septic toenail, wasn't it?

**FLETCHER**
(*Getting off his bunk*) Oh, it's easy for you, isn't it? Not being there in the heat of it. You heard that scream just now. When I was in hospital that would go on all night.

**LENNIE**
It's your own fault – you should have left the nurses alone, shouldn't you?

**FLETCHER**
Oh shut up. (*Looking at his mug*) I must wash this out.

***He crosses to the washbasin. Grout walks in. Crusher stands in the doorway.***

**FLETCHER**
Oh hello, Crusher – hello, Grouty.

**GROUT**
Hello, Fletch.

**LENNIE**
Hello, Grouty.

**GROUT**
Goodbye, Godber.

***Lennie leaves. Crusher also leaves and shuts the door.***

**FLETCHER**
What's up then, Grouty?

***He puts the mug down on the table.***

**GROUT**
Oh – I just er had a word with Harris.

**FLETCHER**
Oh, I heard you, yes.

**GROUT**
He whipped some pills.

**FLETCHER**
Comes as no surprise.

**GROUT**
Said that when Mackay frisked him, he dropped them over the landing.

**FLETCHER**
Really?

**GROUT**
Immediately under which there were only two people at the time.

**FLETCHER**
Yeah, that's right, me and Lukewarm.

**GROUT**
Well, Lukewarm wouldn't, would he – I mean anything for a quiet life, him. As long as he's got his knitting.

**FLETCHER**
Just a minute – wouldn't what?

**GROUT**
Take advantage.

***He sits down.***

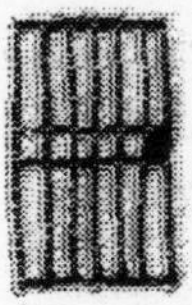

**FLETCHER**
Take advantage?

**GROUT**
Of a windfall. Have a chair, Fletcher.

**FLETCHER**
Oh – thank you very much.

**GROUT**
See, this is the problem, Fletch. I want those pills back where they belong.

**FLETCHER**

In your pocket?

**GROUT**

Dear me no. In the MO's office.

**FLETCHER**

Oh I see. I didn't know you shared my views on the evils of drugs, Grouty.

**GROUT**

It's not that exactly. It's just that despicable pilfering of this nature could mess up my own pill-peddling operation.

**FLETCHER**

Oh I didn't know about that.

**GROUT**

(*Gets out a cigar*) Very few people do. That's one of its virtues. Now unless those pills are returned, Mackay is going to ask the MO to take an inventory to establish what's missing. And if that happens they're going to find that there's more pills missing than they ever imagined.

**FLETCHER**

Oh dear me, yes. Couldn't you replace them from stock?

**GROUT**

I haven't got any stock. I don't keep 'em. I peddle them.

**FLETCHER**

Yes, I see your point.

**GROUT**

Well then, we've got an hour.

**FLETCHER**

Oh, we've got an hour have we? Oh I see, yes.

**GROUT**

Yes. Fortunately the MO's over in the married quarters for an hour or so lancing Mrs Barrowclough's boil.

**FLETCHER**

Now Grouty, you and me know each other. I give you my solemn word – you know it's sacrosanct – that I ain't got the pills.

**GROUT**

The point is you're one of the few people in this nick in a position to acquire some *more* pills.

**FLETCHER**

How?

**GROUT**

Come on! You work the admin block. The Governor, secretaries, typists. Doesn't matter what sort of pills they are. As long as they're back in the MO's office – then I'll get the word to Mackay it's taken care of.

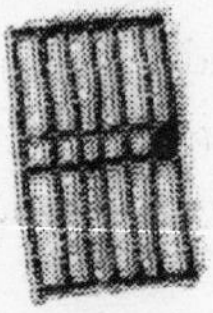

**FLETCHER**

Yeah, well that will solve it. Even supposing I can do what you suggest – what am I looking for?

**GROUT**

Pills is pills, Fletch. Aspirin, allergy pills, slimming pills.

**FLETCHER**

Here – those typists are all on the pill. They're all ravers over there.

**GROUT**

Now steady on Fletch, there are limits. If you whip those and the MO issues them to some poor bloke with toothache, what then?

**FLETCHER**

Stop his teeth getting pregnant, won't it.

***He laughs. Grouty does not react.***

**FLETCHER**

It's a serious matter, isn't it? (*Looking away*) Well, I can't guarantee anything, Grouty. But of course I'll do the best I can.

**GROUT**

(*Rising*) I'm sure you will, Fletch.

***He walks to the door, then turns back.***

**GROUT**

Oh, if there's any codeine while you're there, get a couple for Harris. Apparently his arm's playing him up.

***He leaves. Fletcher is furious. He gets up and goes to the window.***

**LENNIE**

(*Entering*) What were that about?

**FLETCHER**

Grouty wants me to whip some pills for him.

**LENNIE**

Why?

**FLETCHER**

To replace the pills Harris whipped.

**LENNIE**

Well, where are the pills Harris whipped?

**FLETCHER**

Precisely. Where are the peppers that Peter Piper picked? If we knew that, sonny Jim, there'd be no problem, would there?

**LENNIE**

(*Sitting by the table*) Barrowclough has pills.

**FLETCHER**

Does he?

**LENNIE**

All sorts. Nerve pills, indigestion pills. And he's a vitamin freak. He takes so many of 'em, I should think when he makes love he rattles.

**FLETCHER**

Don't think he'll be having a rattle for some time – apparently his old lady has a boil.

***He sits down.***

**LENNIE**

Depends where the boil is.

**FLETCHER**

The boil is in a very nasty place.

**LENNIE**

Where?

**FLETCHER**

Married quarters.

**LENNIE**

Ooh, nasty.

**FLETCHER**

And what is more, it is being attended to by the MO which is why we've still got fifty minutes.

**LENNIE**

We?

**FLETCHER**

Oh come on, Godber, you're supposed to be my mate, aren't you?

**LENNIE**

I'm your mate, Fletch. Always have been, always will be I hope.

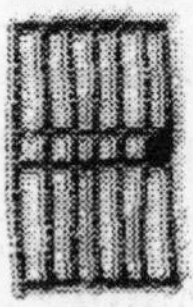

**FLETCHER**

(*Rising*) Then help me get some pills!

**LENNIE**

I would do but for one thing.

**FLETCHER**

What?

**LENNIE**

You told me not to have anything to do with drugs.

***Fletcher raises his arm as if to backhand Lennie, when Barrowclough comes in.***

**BARROWCLOUGH**

Fletcher?

***Fletcher freezes, arm still raised.***

**FLETCHER**

What?

**BARROWCLOUGH**

Raised arms.

***Fletcher looks round for one.***

**FLETCHER**

Raised arm, sir – where?

**BARROWCLOUGH**

(*Pointing*) There.

***Fletcher sees it.***

**FLETCHER**

Oh that. That is not a raised arm, sir. That is a flexed arm. It's me muscles – can't clench, you see.

***He demonstrates.***

**FLETCHER**

Muscular stress. It's due to me nervous condition. I wish I had something for nerves. A pill or something.

**BARROWCLOUGH**

I have pills for my nerves.

**FLETCHER**

Really – what an unbelievable coincidence! Are you telling me you have something which can alleviate the suffering?

**BARROWCLOUGH**

Well, I don't carry them around with me.

***Fletcher lowers his arm immediately.***

**FLETCHER**

Oh don't you. No, I noticed you weren't rattling.

***He sits down.***

**BARROWCLOUGH**

They're prescribed, you see. They're only mild tranquillisers, but they help me cope with the horrors of life.

**FLETCHER**

Yes. How is Mrs Barrowclough?

**BARROWCLOUGH**

Not too good, I'm afraid. As you know, she's not the easiest of women to live with at the best of times, but now that she can't sit down . . .

**FLETCHER**
Oh, we thought that's where it was.

**BARROWCLOUGH**
What?

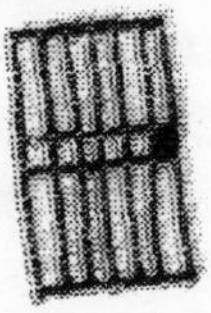

**FLETCHER**
The boil.

**BARROWCLOUGH**
How did you know about my wife's boil?

**FLETCHER**
Oh – it just leaked out.

**BARROWCLOUGH**
We're hoping a hot poultice will help.

**FLETCHER**
You want to slap a dollop of Godber's tapioca pudding on it. That would make her sit up and take notice.

**BARROWCLOUGH**
Oh, that's what it was.

**LENNIE**
I'd like to see you lot do any better.

**FLETCHER**
Well, of course, a lot of these blemishes is caused by lack of vitamins.

**LENNIE**
Oh, I don't think so. I think a boil's more to do with the bloodstream.

**FLETCHER**
Shut your face, Godber. When I want a second opinion I'll go to Harley Street.

**BARROWCLOUGH**
I've always been a great believer in vitamins. I think that's why I have such a good complexion.

**FLETCHER**
(*Standing up*) Yes, that's what I need you know. 'Cos my nerves is caused by vitamin deficiency. You haven't got any to spare, have you, Mr Barrowclough?

**BARROWCLOUGH**
I'll bring you some in the morning.

**FLETCHER**
Oh – too late then, don't bother.

**BARROWCLOUGH**
Well, it's never too late to improve your health.

**FLETCHER**
By tomorrow morning my health might be a lot worse. Got anything for broken kneecaps?

**BARROWCLOUGH**
I don't think I follow.

**FLETCHER**
I shan't be able to either with broken kneecaps.

**LENNIE**
(*Mumbling to himself*) I do me best with the ingredients provided. Chef said my raspberry blancmange was the finest he'd ever tasted.

***They look at him.***

**FLETCHER**
No seriously, Mr Barrowclough, the main problem with my nerves and my lack of vitamins is the terrible indigestion it brings on.

**BARROWCLOUGH**
Oh, really?

**FLETCHER**
Yes, terrible.

**BARROWCLOUGH**
Oh I can help you there.

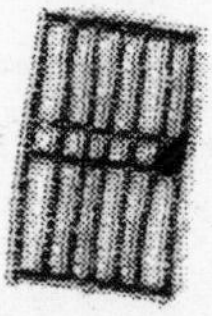

***He produces a packet of Alka-Seltzer from his pocket.***

**BARROWCLOUGH**
Have you got a mug, or something?

***He picks up Fletcher's mug and goes to the washbasin to rinse it when Fletcher interrupts him.***

**FLETCHER**
(*Holding two tablets*) No, don't bother. They're too big.

**BARROWCLOUGH**
What on earth do you mean, too big?

**FLETCHER**
Oh well . . . I mean my condition's too chronic for anything as big as that. I even get indigestion if I eat Rennies too quickly.

**BARROWCLOUGH**
I must say you seem to be in pretty poor physical shape, Fletcher.

**FLETCHER**
Oh, I can put up with it. The thing that really gets me is the blinding headaches.

**BARROWCLOUGH**
(*Taking the tablets back*) Then I suggest you go on sick parade tomorrow. Get a couple of codeine from the MO.

***He leaves. Fletcher follows him to the door.***

**FLETCHER**
That was no flaming help, was it? (*To Lennie*) And nor was you!

**LENNIE**
Not talking to you.

**FLETCHER**
Pardon?

**LENNIE**
Not talking to you.

**FLETCHER**
Just proved yourself wrong. Why do you think you aren't talking to me?

**LENNIE**
Had enough of your derogatory remarks about my culinary prowess.

**FLETCHER**
Has your culinary prowess got any relevance to the urgent matter at hand? No, it has not. When Grouty asks you a favour it is with the clear understanding that the favour will be done. If it isn't, he takes it as a personal affront and sends round his big henchmen to mete out retribution – from Crusher with love.

**LENNIE**
That'll solve your problem then – you'll end up in the hospital. No shortage of pills there.

***Harris walks in.***

**HARRIS**
'Lo, Fletch.

**FLETCHER**
You've got a bleeding nerve, Harris.

**HARRIS**
What?

**FLETCHER**
Showing your face round here.

**HARRIS**
Why?

**FLETCHER**
Cause of all the trouble, ain't you?

**HARRIS**
All right, all right I took 'em. But I haven't got 'em now.

**FLETCHER**
Well, what are you doing here then?

**HARRIS**
I heard you'd got a bit of a problem. You've got to find some pills and I think I know where I can lay me hands on some.

**FLETCHER**
(*Getting up*) Well flaming 'eck, Harris, why didn't you tell Grouty this in the first place?

**HARRIS**
Wouldn't dare. See, er . . . today wasn't the first day I nicked some. But I never knew about Grouty's racket. And if he knew I'd taken some before – ooh dear me – too dire to contemplate, isn't it?

**LENNIE**
What sort of pills have you been taking?

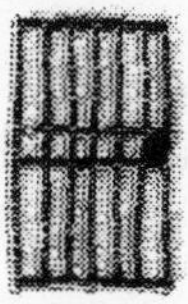

**HARRIS**
Anything. Always a market in here, isn't there? Uppers, downers, twisters, benders.

**FLETCHER**
Let me get this straight. What you're saying is you've still got a previous theft intact, have you?

**HARRIS**
Could be.

**FLETCHER**
So you give 'em to me, and I get them to Grouty pretending I got them elsewhere.

**HARRIS**
'Sright. I think it's a very noble gesture on my part, don't you? Get us both out the clarts, right?

**FLETCHER**
Yes, yes, very noble, Harris. Let's have 'em then.

**HARRIS**
No, no, hold your horses.

**FLETCHER**
What?

**HARRIS**
Depends, doesn't it?

**FLETCHER**
Depends on what?

**HARRIS**
How much?

**FLETCHER**
How much!!!

**HARRIS**
Fair do's. Give you a fair price an' all.

**FLETCHER**

Words fail me.

***He walks to the window.***

**LENNIE**

Has it occurred to you, Harris, that there's more at stake in life than a quick quid? Such as comradeship, honour, and chivalry?

**HARRIS**

No.

**FLETCHER**

Don't try to appeal to his better nature, son, 'cause he ain't got none. There's only one language the Harrises of this world understand and that's the one I intend to use in future negotiations.

**HARRIS**

What's that, Fletch?

***Fletcher moves toward him.***

**HARRIS**

No, no, Fletch . . .

## 7. LANDING

***Several prisoners are in the association area.***

***Barrowclough is walking along the landing. As he passes two prisoners there is a loud scream.***

***Barrowclough looks around.***

***The prisoners do not react.***

***Barrowclough moves on.***

## 8. GROUT'S CELL

***Grout is on his own when there is a polite knock.***

**GROUT**

Come in.

***Fletcher enters.***

**GROUT**

Oh, it's you, Fletch.

***Fletcher puts a small packet in front of Grout.***

**FLETCHER**

There you are, then.

**GROUT**

Already.

**FLETCHER**

Yeah, well, you said it was a matter of some urgency. But just for the record, those aren't the original pills. I did not steal them. I had to get those using all my ingenuity.

**GROUT**

(*Significantly*) Yes, I heard you.

**FLETCHER**

I just hope that this puts me at the bottom of your 'favours to be done by' list.

**GROUT**

Certainly, Fletch.

**FLETCHER**

What a lunch hour. Didn't even have time to finish my cup of tea. And now I've got to get back to work.

**GROUT**
(*Lying on the bed*) Yes, well, no peace for the wicked.

**FLETCHER**
Don't you have work to go to, Grouty?

**GROUT**
No, I'm on light duties, Fletch. They put me in charge of the swimming pool.

**FLETCHER**
That's nice, we ain't got one.

**GROUT**
I know.

**FLETCHER**
Oh – clerical error, was it?

**GROUT**
Something like that – which is why time hangs so heavy on my hands.

**FLETCHER**
Oh dear me. What a shame. Well I'd best be off then. Don't want to interrupt your boredom.

***He walks towards the door.***

**FLETCHER**
Aren't those crystallised fruits over there?

**GROUT**
Yes.

**FLETCHER**
My favourite them.

**GROUT**
Really, mine too. Pass them over will you?

***Fletcher picks up the box. Grout has opened his pyjama case and is putting the pills inside.***

**GROUT**
Any idea what these pills are?

**FLETCHER**
(*Walking to Grout*) Well, you said yourself a pill is a pill.

**GROUT**
No, but you got to be careful with drugs. These could be highly dangerous.

**FLETCHER**
Well – yes, yes – best be on the safe side. Try 'em out in the Governor's cup of tea.

***Grout takes the box of fruits, but Fletcher, unnoticed holds back one fruit. When Grout is not looking, Fletcher puts it in his mouth and leaves.***

## 9. FLETCHER'S CELL

***Lennie is lying on Fletcher's top bunk, reading Fletcher's grubby paperback, when the master himself enters, not in the best of moods.***

**FLETCHER**
What are you doing on my bunk, Godber?

**LENNIE**
More light up here.

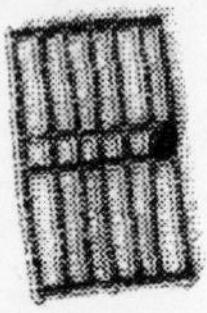

**FLETCHER**

Yeah, to read *my* book by. Give it here.

***He grabs it from him.***

**LENNIE**

I only borrowed it.

***He is swinging himself round on the bunk.***

**FLETCHER**

Lost my place, in't you?

**LENNIE**

(*Getting off the bunk*) That's a good scene, that is. Where the plantation owner gets hold of the nubile young slave girl behind the cotton gin –

**FLETCHER**

Here, shut up, will you! I haven't got that far yet. Blimey, you got that far! You've had a hard afternoon, in't you?

**LENNIE**

I'm entitled. Up at four, me. No joke, you know, frying five hundred eggs at dawn.

**FLETCHER**

You want to make one vast omelette and let 'em get on with it. You could have tidied up a bit. I mean, look at this place. Haven't even washed the mugs out.

***He swishes his tea into the sink, then reacts in surprise.***

**FLETCHER**

'Ere, what's this?

**LENNIE**

What's what?

**FLETCHER**

Look.

***He holds up a small packet of pills and moves to the table. Lennie joins him.***

**LENNIE**

Where's that come from?

**FLETCHER**

It was in the tea.

**LENNIE**

Open it then, have a look.

**FLETCHER**

You know what these are, don't you? These are the original pills Harris got rid of. What are they?

**LENNIE**

(*Picks up two*) Can't be sure. Could be amphetamines. Or maybe Bennies.

**FLETCHER**

Whose?

**LENNIE**

Benzedrine. How did they get in your tea?

**FLETCHER**

They must have fallen from above.

**LENNIE**

Oh – Bennies from heaven.

**FLETCHER**

What?

**LENNIE**

Joke.

**FLETCHER**

Do me a favour.

**LENNIE**

It's funny though, isn't it? When you think of all the trouble you went to and they was under your nose all the time.

**FLETCHER**

Whole thing was a storm in a teacup.

**LENNIE**

What?

**FLETCHER**

Another joke. And better than yours.

**MACKAY**

(*Offscreen*) Move you men!

***Fletcher puts his mug down.***

**FLETCHER**

Mackay.

***He crosses to the door.***

**LENNIE**

(*Indicating pills*) Get rid of those.

***Fletcher returns to the table.***

**LENNIE**

He'll find 'em.

**FLETCHER**

Where?

**MACKAY**

(*Offscreen*) Don't lounge around the landing.

**FLETCHER**

Naffing hell.

**LENNIE**

Swallow them?

**FLETCHER**

Swallow them?

***They grab some pills and start to swallow them.***

***Mackay looks in suspiciously.***

**MACKAY**

What's wrong with you two?

**FLETCHER**

Nothing, Mr Mackay.

**MACKAY**

I can always tell when a man is acting suspiciously. Got something to hide.

***He walks in.***

**MACKAY**

Fletcher?

**FLETCHER**

No, sir.

***Mackay goes over to Lennie.***

**MACKAY**

Godber?

**LENNIE**

No, sir.

***The container that held the pills appears to pass to Fletcher's hand. Mackay's head whips round. He points to Fletcher's hand.***

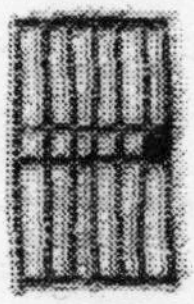

**MACKAY**

All right, Fletcher.

***He lifts Fletcher's right hand and taps it. Fletcher opens it but there are no pills in it. Mackay grabs the left hand which reveals the pills.***

**MACKAY**

What's this?

**FLETCHER**
What's what?

**MACKAY**
I repeat what's this?

**FLETCHER**
Oh it's a thing, sir.

**MACKAY**
A thing that looks like a container for pills.

***He opens it.***

**LENNIE**
Just a couple, like – for Fletcher's . . .

**FLETCHER/LENNIE**
Nerves – indigestion.

**FLETCHER/LENNIE**
Indigestion – nerves.

**FLETCHER**
I gets the indigestion on account of my nerves, and visa versa.

**MACKAY**
Pills are a dirty word in this prison. Nearly caught Harris this morning.

**FLETCHER**
Oh well, a man like Harris, sir.

**MACKAY**
Since the doctor told me what was missing, I'd like to think the wretched fellow ate the whole lot of them.

***Fletcher and Lennie exchange glances. Mackay walks away.***

**FLETCHER**
'Scuse me, Mr Mackay. Out of idle curiosity – what was they then?

**MACKAY**
They were the MO's own pills. Well not exactly his . . . (*Crossing to Fletcher*) They were for his spaniel's bad breath. Carry on.

***He goes out. Fletcher and Lennie look at each other.***

**LENNIE**
How d'you feel, Fletch?

**FLETCHER**
Rough . . . ruff.

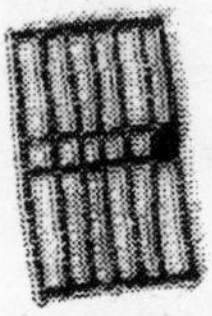

# 3 SERIES THREE

## EPISODE TWO: POETIC JUSTICE

### 1. LANDING

***Harris and Lennie are carrying a bed, supervised by Barrowclough. They start to go upstairs.***

**LENNIE**

Fletch won't like this you know, Mr Barrowclough.

**HARRIS**

He naffing won't. Didn't like you moving in here, never mind a third.

**BARROWCLOUGH**

Fletcher will have no choice in the matter. We're running a prison not a hotel. Prisons are very overcrowded this time of year.

**LENNIE**

Not surprising really. It's bitter out.

***They walk along the landing and into Fletcher's cell with the bed, followed by Barrowclough.***

**BARROWCLOUGH**

Take it in and lean it up against the wall.

***Fletcher is crossing the bridge, singing.***

**FLETCHER**

Some enchanted evening,
You may see a stranger . . .

**VOICE**

Shut up.

**FLETCHER**

Naff off!
You may see a stranger,
Across a crowded room . . .

***He is making his way to his cell.***

### 2. FLETCHER'S CELL

***Fletcher walks in.***

**FLETCHER**

Hello, what's this here?
A stranger in a crowded room.

**BARROWCLOUGH**

I'm just off, Fletcher.

**FLETCHER**

Oh no you're not.

**BARROWCLOUGH**

Pardon?

**FLETCHER**
What is that?
**BARROWCLOUGH**
What is what?
**FLETCHER**
That bed – what is it?
**BARROWCLOUGH**
It's a bed.
**FLETCHER**
What is that bed doing across my already overcrowded cell?
**BARROWCLOUGH**
Well . . .
**FLETCHER**
And why is Harris here? I hope there's no connection between that bed and 'orrible Harris.
**HARRIS**
'Ere, I only brung it 'ere.
**FLETCHER**
Oh good, then you can just brung it out again.
**BARROWCLOUGH**
Fletcher, an alarming rise in crime rates in this country has caused an extra burden on an already overworked penal system.
**FLETCHER**
Oh yes?
**BARROWCLOUGH**
That in turn has meant that prisons have had to stretch their already limited resources to try and accommodate the extra influx of convicted felons.
**FLETCHER**
Oh yes I see, of course.
**BARROWCLOUGH**
Well, as long as you appreciate our difficult position.
**FLETCHER**
I do yes. We've all got to make the best of a difficult situation. Now shift that bed out of here.
**BARROWCLOUGH**
Fletcher, a new arrival is moving in here and that's that, so you may as well accept it as a fait accompli.
***He leaves. Fletcher crosses to the door.***
**HARRIS**
I'll be off too then, Fletch. Bit crowded in here. I hope the three of you will be very happy.
**FLETCHER**
Naff off, Harris.
**HARRIS**
Naff off yourself, Fletch. With knobs on.
***He leaves. Fletcher closes the door.***
**LENNIE**
I'm afraid the whole rhythm of our lives is in some jeopardy, Fletch.
**FLETCHER**
Flaming outrage. Where's my shirt?
***He goes to his bunk.***

**FLETCHER**
What's the word then?
**LENNIE**
Well I had a word with Davey Greener who works in reception. He says there's three come in today. And one of them's a bit of a mystery. Name's Rawley. He was never documented.
**FLETCHER**
How d'you mean?
**LENNIE**
The screw just whipped him off some place. No documentation, no mug shots.
**FLETCHER**
Really?
**LENNIE**
I think they whipped him straight up to the Guvnor.
**FLETCHER**
Maybe he's a celebrity. Maybe a rock star on a drug bust and they took him off for a press conference.
**LENNIE**
He was no rock star. Kind of small and bald and flat-footed.
**FLETCHER**
Might be Elton John.
**LENNIE**
No, no, he walked like a pregnant duck.
**FLETCHER**
'Ere, 'ere, stop that.

**LENNIE**
Stop what?
**FLETCHER**
That. Drawing attention to people's physical peculiarities. I've noticed that about you recently. I was saying to Jacky, young people today are always taking the mick out of folk because they're too tall or too fat or walk with bow legs.
**LENNIE**
Who's Jacky?
**FLETCHER**
You know – bloke in the hobby shop. Fat guy with ears like jug handles.

## 3. GOVERNOR'S OFFICE

***Prison Officer Collinson at the door. Rawley walks in.***
**COLLINSON**
All right, Rawley, step in front of the Governor. Stand still, straighten up. Rawley, sir.
**GOVERNOR**
Thank you, Mr Collinson, that will be all.
**COLLINSON**
Excuse me, sir – you want me to leave you alone? With a prisoner?
**GOVERNOR**
(*Standing up*) It will be all right I think in this case.
**COLLINSON**
If you say so, sir.
***He leaves. They wait for him to go.***

**GOVERNOR**
Steven . . .

**RAWLEY**
Hello, Geoffrey.

**GOVERNOR**
I thought we should have a little chat before we document you. But . . . what can I say?

**RAWLEY**
Perhaps the less said, the better.

**GOVERNOR**
Tragic . . . how's Marjorie taking all of this?

**RAWLEY**
As well as can be expected. And how are you, Geoffrey?

**GOVERNOR**
Oh I'm all right.

**RAWLEY**
And – Muriel?

**GOVERNOR**
Busy as ever. She has her committees, I have my prison.

*Offers Rawley a cigarette.*

**RAWLEY**
Haven't seen you both for such a long time.

**GOVERNOR**
You must come round for dinner. Oh no, of course, you won't be able to. Silly me.

**RAWLEY**
Not unless my appeal comes through, no.

**GOVERNOR**
This whole thing is most embarrassing for me.

*He sits down.*

**RAWLEY**
It's a little worse than that for me. The entire fabric of my life has collapsed.

**GOVERNOR**
Yes, but see it from my point of view. We were at Winchester together. In the Guards together. We're in the same Club.

**RAWLEY**
We won't be for much longer – they've asked for my resignation.

**GOVERNOR**
Nevertheless, our relationship is going to create a bit of a problem.

**RAWLEY**
Is there any reason why people should become aware of it?

**GOVERNOR**
Perhaps not. There isn't anyone from the old school here, thank God.

**RAWLEY**
There's everything else though – officers, Clubmen, Rotarians. In the shower an embezzler came up to me and gave me a Masonic handshake.

**GOVERNOR**

There you are, you see.

**RAWLEY**

I don't want to plead special treatment of course, but couldn't you separate me in a single cell with a few books?

**GOVERNOR**

Fatal. Can't have secrets in here. Cause speculation. Resentment. Best thing is to slip you into a cell with other men.

**RAWLEY**

But I'd be with a bunch of common criminals.

**GOVERNOR**

With due respect, Steven, since the verdict you are a common criminal.

***There is a knock at the door.***

**GOVERNOR**

Come in.

***Mackay enters.***

**MACKAY**

You sent for me, sir.

**GOVERNOR**

Ah Mr Mackay, I want to discuss a delicate situation with you. Please close the door.

***Mackay shuts the door.***

**GOVERNOR**

This is an old friend of mine, Steven Rawley, who will be with us for a while.

**MACKAY**

(*Shaking hands*) How do you do, sir? Will you be staying for lunch?

**RAWLEY**

If my appeal fails, I'll be staying for three years.

***Mackay starts to laugh, then checks himself.***

## 4. ASSOCIATION AREA

***Fletcher is sitting at a table with Lennie, Warren and McLaren. Mackay walks through the gates with Rawley. Rawley is not in prison uniform.***

**LENNIE**

Hey, that's him – the mystery man. Him with Mackay.

**MACKAY**

All right, you men. This is Rawley who's moving in with Fletcher and Godber. I don't know what you've heard about him already, but I want you to treat him just like any other prisoner – understand?

**ALL**

Yes, Mr Mackay.

**MACKAY**

Carry on.

***He leaves.***

**RAWLEY**

Good afternoon.

**LENNIE**

Afternoon. I'm Godber . . . you're in with us.

**RAWLEY**

Oh.

***Fletcher has been staring at Rawley in amazement.***

**FLETCHER**
God preserve us!
**RAWLEY**
I'm sorry?
**LENNIE**
Oh, this is Fletch. He's in with us an' all.
**RAWLEY**
Really.
**FLETCHER**
You don't remember me, do you?
**RAWLEY**
Your face is vaguely familiar, but I can't quite . . .
**FLETCHER**
Middlesex Assizes? Three years ago?
**WARREN**
Oh, did you two do a job together or something?
**FLETCHER**
Do a job? He's the judge who bleeding sent me here!
***Rawley peers at Fletcher anxiously. The others stare at Rawley.***
**FLETCHER**
The Honourable Judge Steven Rawley! In person! How are the mighty fallen!
**RAWLEY**
I'm sorry, I still don't recall you . . .
**FLETCHER**
Why should you? I am merely one of a thousand faces who come before you, while you weigh our lives in the balance of what you call justice!
**RAWLEY**
(*Instantly*) It's Fletcher, isn't it?
**FLETCHER**
Oh, you remember now?
**RAWLEY**
I remember your rhetoric. I remember your endless protestations of innocence.
**FLETCHER**
Which you were deaf to.
**LENNIE**
But you were guilty, Fletch. You've told us that.
**FLETCHER**
That is beside the point, Godber.
**RAWLEY**
It did seem relevant when I passed sentence.
**FLETCHER**
The point is the man was not fit to sentence me, as his presence here indicates.
**WARREN**
He's still a judge. Or he were at the time.
**MCLAREN**
Yeah, but obviously a bent one. When you're sent up it's one thing knowing it's by an upright pillar of society. But Fletcher's been sent down by a fellow con.
**FLETCHER**
Thank you, Jock. He is the same as me. How d'you think I feel being sent down by a crook like me?
**LENNIE**
A judge inside!
**MCLAREN**
What d'they bust you for then?

**RAWLEY**
Bust?

**MCLAREN**
What were the charges against you?

**RAWLEY**
I was indicted on three counts for corruption at common low – party to a criminal conspiracy; forgery of legal documents under the Forgery Acts of 1913–48; and accepting an illicit –

**FLETCHER**
(*Joining in with Rawley*) – payment as an officer of the crown.

**FLETCHER**
That's bribery and corruption, don't camouflage it behind that legal mumbo jumbo.

**RAWLEY**
I have no wish to camouflage anything. As I instructed my counsel, 'Let light be shed on this whole sorry affair. Let's bring it out into the open, let there be no half truths or evasions.'

**LENNIE**
Well, that's refreshingly honest. So you're saying you're guilty then.

**RAWLEY**
I refuse to discuss the matter, pending my appeal.

**MCLAREN**
You're bound to get off. Old school tie, top lawyers.

**RAWLEY**
If they were that good, I'd be out on bail now.

**FLETCHER**
Listen, it's a token stretch. Most of what you call us common folk never get the chance of bail. Some blokes are inside for months pending appeal.

**LENNIE**
The same law sent him down what sent us down, Fletcher.

**FLETCHER**
What are you saying, Godber?

**LENNIE**
What I'm saying is, I think his presence here is very reassuring. It's a vindication of our legal system. It proves that no one is beyond the reach of the law.

**FLETCHER**
I just ask myself for every one of his kind they nobble, how many's getting away with it? The bloke who sent him up is probably worse than he is.

**MCLAREN**
Hear, hear!

**FLETCHER**
Why, do you know him?

**RAWLEY**
(*Making an emotional appeal*)
Don't you think I have a conscience? Can you imagine what it's been like, to live a lie?

**FLETCHER**
'Course we can, we're criminals. does it all the time.

***Barrowclough walks in.***

**BARROWCLOUGH**
(*Approaching the table*) How are you lads improving the sunshine hour?

***Rawley stands, pauses, then sits down again.***

**FLETCHER**
We was just getting acquainted with our learned friend.

**BARROWCLOUGH**
Oh you know who he is then?

**FLETCHER**
We met professionally, so to speak.

**BARROWCLOUGH**
I see. Well you men must treat Rawley no different from any other prisoner.

**MCLAREN**
We will if you will.

**BARROWCLOUGH**
What's that supposed to mean, McLaren?

**MCLAREN**
Dinna show no favours.

**BARROWCLOUGH**
Rawley will get no favours from me. Whatever you were before, you're just a number now. A statistic. A set of fingerprints. A mug shot, like the rest of these men. You'll pay your dues the same way they do – is that understood?

**RAWLEY**
Yes.

**BARROWCLOUGH**
Yes, what?

**LENNIE**
(*Prompting*) Yes, Mr Barrowclough.

**RAWLEY**
Yes, Mr Barrowclough.

**BARROWCLOUGH**
That's better. Now we must see about getting you a job. Could you come this way please, your honour.

***The others react as Barrowclough leads Rawley away.***

**5. CELL**

***It is night time. Lennie is in his pyjamas and is making up Rawley's bed when Fletcher comes in from the showers.***

**FLETCHER**
What are you doing, Godber?

**LENNIE**
Oh, just making his bed up. He couldn't do it himself.

**FLETCHER**
Well, I suggest you let him bleeding learn. Either that, or roll your trousers up and wear a little frilly apron.

**LENNIE**
Oh come on Fletch, go easy on him. He's lonely, he's afraid. Just like I was, me first night.

**FLETCHER**
He's the enemy within. Within my cell, what's more.

**LENNIE**
No, he ain't, Fletch. He *was* a judge. But now he's a con like the rest of us.

**FLETCHER**
Don't you believe it. He's the establishment, he is. And I don't fancy the establishment breathing down my neck all day and all night. I mean you must admit it's a bit unusual, Godber.

**LENNIE**
What is?

**FLETCHER**
Well, when a judge sentences you to five years, you don't expect him to come in with you.

***Rawley comes in, having just returned from the showers.***

**RAWLEY**
Oh you've made my bed up, Godber, that's most kind.

**FLETCHER**
Ovaltine or Horlicks, is it?

**RAWLEY**
Excuse me?

**FLETCHER**
And what colour do you want your brown shoes polished?

**LENNIE**
Leave it off, Fletch.

**FLETCHER**
Where you been – having a nightcap with the Chief Warders?

**RAWLEY**
Look, I have no influence in here. If I had I'd be in a single cell with a few books instead of sharing with people like . . .

**FLETCHER**
Go on say it, people (*Crossing to the table*) like us, say it. Listen, let me tell you something about people like us. We don't make no alibis. We deserve to be here. But compared to you lot, there's something very honest about our dishonesty. Some people like us had no way of getting things, except to take them. People like you, you had it all, but you wanted more.

**LENNIE**
Look, he's a criminal now. Are you saying that right is only open to the poor? Don't you think the rich have a right to be criminals as well?

**FLETCHER**
They better not try it. The unions will be on to them straight away.

**LENNIE**
Don't be stupid.

**FLETCHER**
I'm not being stupid. You're being stupid.

**LENNIE**
I'm not being stupid.

**FLETCHER**
Well one of us is being stupid.

**FLETCHER/LENNIE TOGETHER**
Well, it's not me.

**LENNIE**

I'm just annoyed 'cause you're so inconsistent, Fletch.

**FLETCHER**

I'm not inconsistent.

**LENNIE**

Don't start that again. You are, you're inconsistent in your attitude. Inside is not out there. Inside's another world it is. We're all equal. We only have one enemy, that's the screws. And we only have one purpose in life, that's screwing the system.

**RAWLEY**

(*Sitting down on the bed*) Godber is right. I know we've always been on opposite sides of the fence. You're the sort of people I'd normally cross the street to avoid. But the fence is down now.

**FLETCHER**

I still think the gulf between us is immeasurably wide. I mean him and me, and most of the lads in here, we come from the same background, ran the same streets. They're a little different from your streets. Your streets have rich kids riding round on bicycles waving tennis racquets. Rows of elm trees and hand-carved privet hedges. Don't have no problems on your streets.

**RAWLEY**

Yes we do. I had to spend fifteen hundred pounds last year on Dutch Elm disease.

**FLETCHER**

Yeah? And I bet you went to a private doctor with it though, didn't you?

**RAWLEY**

Look, I know you're bound to feel cynical, I understand your attitude, but we all have one thing in common – we're in trouble.

**LENNIE**

He's right, Fletch.

**FLETCHER**

I'm just clearing the air, letting you know my feelings.

**RAWLEY**

I shall do my best to be as unobtrusive as possible.

**FLETCHER**

Unobtrusive, I see yes. Well get yourself a hammock then.

***He crosses to the bunk.***

**FLETCHER**

Shift your barrow.

***Lennie moves. Fletcher climbs on to the top bunk.***

**LENNIE**

He's a miserable old scroat. Listen, rules of the house. Top bunk's his. Seniority, like. No one reads the paper till he's through with it. It's best to speak only when spoken to, and his is the toothpaste with the marked tube.

**RAWLEY**

I have my own toilet requisites.

**FLETCHER**

Just as well.

**LENNIE**

Never borrow anything of Fletcher's without express permission.

**FLETCHER**

I am not mean, Godber, if that's what you're saying. It's just that I never give anybody anything. What one has one keeps.

**LENNIE**

Oh come on, Fletch. You are mean.

**FLETCHER**

No, I'm not. Thrifty perhaps. Frugal.

**LENNIE**

He unwraps Bounty Bars under water so I can't hear he's got one.

**RAWLEY**

I'll be only too willing to share any of the few things they've allowed me.

**FLETCHER**

Bribery and corruption, he's at it again!

**RAWLEY**

I only meant . . .

**FLETCHER**

Just get yourself to bye-byes, Judge Jeffreys.

**RAWLEY**

Well, let me say that whatever rules you make, I will go along with them.

**LENNIE**

Oh we're very democratic in here – Fletcher decides and we agree.

## 6. LANDING

***Camera shows Prison Officers locking up.***

## 6A. CELL

***It is night time. Fletcher is on the top bunk. Lennie is lying on his bunk. Rawley is sitting reading in his bed. A Prison Officer looks in and closes and locks the door.***

**LENNIE**

(*To Rawley*) Want some snout?

**RAWLEY**

Oh I don't, thank you. Only very occasionally.

**LENNIE**

Currency in here, snout.

**RAWLEY**

Really?

***He looks very depressed.***

**LENNIE**

You all right?

**RAWLEY**

Since that door slammed shut, I've realised what prison is all about.

**LENNIE**

I know the feeling. This is my first stretch, you know. But stir's a state of mind and survival's in your own head. His Highness taught me that. (*Jerking a thumb upwards to Fletcher*) It's only the first twelve months that are the worst . . . ha, ha, ha . . .

***He registers that his joke has gone down like a lead balloon.***

**LENNIE**
. . . Sorry.

**RAWLEY**
Don't feel sorry for me.

**LENNIE**
Oh, but I do. I mean, you've had so much more to lose than the rest of us. Position, respect. It's the classic story of a man who had it all and blew it all away in a moment of weakness.

**FLETCHER**
This is life, not *Peyton Place*.

**RAWLEY**
My weakness was a younger woman. An avaricious, grasping nineteen-year-old go-go dancer.

**LENNIE**
Oh, the younger woman, yes, typical.

**RAWLEY**
Yes, one sees it happen so many times to colleagues. What is it, some middle-aged madness that affects us all? She was a sweet young thing when I first met her. Then over the years she demanded more and more. Trinkets, trips abroad, a car, a maisonette in South Kensington.

**FLETCHER**
I was wrong, this is *Peyton Place*.

**LENNIE**
How did you meet her?

***The lights go out.***

**RAWLEY**
Oh.

**LENNIE**
Half-past ten.

***Rawley looks at his watch.***

**LENNIE**
How did you meet her?

**RAWLEY**
At our regional reunion.

**FLETCHER**
Oh, nice. She was in your regiment, was she?

**RAWLEY**
She was part of the cabaret. She was assisting a magician called the Great Alfredo. While he was making cockatoos disappear, my eyes never left Sandra's long shapely legs.

**LENNIE**
Long and shapely, were they?

**FLETCHER**
Look, where are those legs now? One glimpse of a young thigh through a fishnet stocking and look at you.

**LENNIE**
Well, human weakness takes many forms. Desire, greed, lust – we're all here for different reasons, aren't we?

**FLETCHER**
With respect, Godber, we're all here for the same reason – we got caught.

## 7. LANDING

***Barrowclough is on the upper landing.***

**BARROWCLOUGH**

B 3–76 all correct.

**MACKAY**

B 3 unlock.

***A Prison Officer is in the association area.***

**PO**

B 1–83 all correct.

**MACKAY**

B 1 unlock.

***A Prison Officer is on the landing by the stairs.***

**PO**

B 2–96 all correct.

**MACKAY**

B 2 unlock.

***Barrowclough and the two Prison Officers are opening up.***

## 7A. CELL

***It is morning. Fletcher is brushing his teeth. He looks at the range of toiletries on the judge's table.***

**FLETCHER**

You can tell we have the upper echelons in here. Have you seen these toiletries? Mustang talc for men, Rave D'Amour shaving cream by Jean Marie of Paris, and exhibit C, a badger's hair shaving brush. My God, no wonder you never see a badger these days.

**LENNIE**

(*Cleaning teeth*) Nocturnal animal, the badger.

**FLETCHER**

Pardon, Godber?

**LENNIE**

Nocturnal. Only comes out at night.

**FLETCHER**

'Course they do. They've learnt their lesson, haven't they? If they comes out during the day, people keep making shaving brushes out of them.

**RAWLEY**

You're more than welcome to use any of my things.

**FLETCHER**

No, thank you. And you better not, if you know what's good for you.

**RAWLEY**

Why?

**FLETCHER**

Any idea what effect Mustang will have on the fairies in here? They'd all come up from the bottom of the garden.

***The door is unlocked and Mackay walks in.***

**MACKAY**

Good morning, Rawley. How did you sleep?

**FLETCHER**

(*Poking his head round the door*) Oh listen to this. Oh dear! All this time I been inside, you never asked me how I slept.

**MACKAY**
I know how you sleep, Fletcher. You sleep soundly because you have no conscience, no shame, no guilt.

**FLETCHER**
True.

***He returns to the washbasin.***

**RAWLEY**
All the things which explain my sleepless night.

**MACKAY**
You'll have the weekend to settle in. Saturday today, you will stop work at noon. Then the rest of the day is your own.

**LENNIE**
I'll take you to the football match if you like.

**RAWLEY**
I'm quite prepared to work on. Help kill time, that sort of thing.

**FLETCHER**
'Ere – if you wants to be one of us now, you knocks off when we knocks off.

**MACKAY**
Typical prison mentality.

**FLETCHER**
No. Just a working-class mentality.

**MACKAY**
You see yourself as working class, Fletcher?

**FLETCHER**
I always used to. Till I went to Glasgow one time. Then I realised I was middle class.

**MACKAY**
Fletcher!

**RAWLEY**
All I meant was I rather enjoyed the work you assigned me to.

**FLETCHER**
'Course you do. Central Records. Privilege, that is.

**MACKAY**
No, it's not, Fletcher.

**FLETCHER**
You'll have to admit it's one of the cushiest numbers in this nick.

**MACKAY**
That's perfectly true, but that does not mean it's a privilege.

**FLETCHER**
No, but which would you rather do, Mackay? Central Records or Latrine duty? Can't sit and read the paper in there, can you? Well you can, but it gets very repetitive. 'Now wash your hands, now wash your hands, now wash your hands.' One day inside, he scores a job must trusties don't get.

**MACKAY**
He's an educated man. Isn't it logical we should give him a job which requires a clerical aptitude?

**FLETCHER**

If you don't mind my saying, so, Mr Mackay, leave it off. Since when has logic had anything to do with job allocation round here? Who was making our raspberry blancmange in the canteen yesterday? Riggs – and he's in here for poisoning.

**LENNIE**

Is he really?

**FLETCHER**

Certainly. Cause célèbre he was in his home town of Newcastle-under-Lyme. In fact, all his in-laws are under lime now.

**LENNIE**

Is that why they call him Arsenic Riggs?

**FLETCHER**

No, that's 'cos he once sat on a razor blade, you nurk.

**LENNIE**

He didn't, did he?

**FLETCHER**

Oh God preserve us.

**MACKAY**

I'm sorry, Rawley, that you're forced to share a cell with riff-raff.

**RAWLEY**

No, they've been most kind and considerate.

**MACKAY**

I hope so. Because I'm aware of the situation, Fletcher, between you and ex-Justice Rawley. But there will be no malice. No vindictiveness. No grudges borne from bitter memory.

**FLETCHER**

Grudge? How could I bear a grudge? What has this man ever done to me – except rob me of five years of my life.

## 8. ASSOCIATION AREA/LANDING

***Camera shows a dartboard and a prisoner about to throw a dart, when Rawley enters the cell block. Rawley looks around and then moves along the landing.***

***Harris tries to block his way. Rawley tries to get past him. He attempts to go upstairs but the way is blocked by another hefty prisoner.***

***Finally Rawley manages to get to his cell and goes in. Fletcher is at the table reading. He looks up at Rawley.***

***McLaren, Harris and the other prisoner follow Rawley into the cell. Fletcher shuts his book, picks it up as he stands up and leaves.***

## 9. ANOTHER CELL

***A prisoner is sitting on a bed as Rawley comes in followed by McLaren, Harris and the other prisoner.***

**RAWLEY**
Good afternoon.
***McLaren shoves the prisoner out of his cell.***
**RAWLEY**
Seems rather quiet.
***He turns to face McLaren.***
**MCLAREN**
Oh it is. (*Taking Rawley's mug*) Everyone's at a game or visiting their loved ones. That's why we chose this moment.
**RAWLEY**
Moment for what?

**HARRIS**
Lots of blokes in here got something to settle with you. Blokes with long memories and even longer stretches.
**MCLAREN**
Doing you a good turn. Get it over with all at once.
***He nods to the prisoner who closes the door.***
**MCLAREN**
Then you won't have to live your life with one eye cocked over your left shoulder wondering when it's going to happen. 'Cause it's going to happen now.
***Rawley tries to get up but is pushed back.***
**MCLAREN**
Dinna fret looking for screws, there's not one in sight.
**HARRIS**
What do you think we are, naffing amateurs?
***Rawley stands and struggles to go. Fletcher enters.***
**FLETCHER**
Hello, hello, what's this? *Gunfight at the OK Corral*, is it?
**MCLAREN**
Fletcher, he's got it coming. Now you'd be the prime suspect, so we're doing you a favour. Get yourself across the yard and out of harm's way.
**FLETCHER**
Are you about to inflict damage on my cellmate?
**HARRIS**
On your what?
**FLETCHER**
On my cellmate. The bloke with which I share a cell.
**MCLAREN**
He's no friend of yours.
**FLETCHER**
He don't have to be a friend. But he's one of us now, and we looks after our own, don't we?
**MCLAREN**
What are you saying, Fletch?

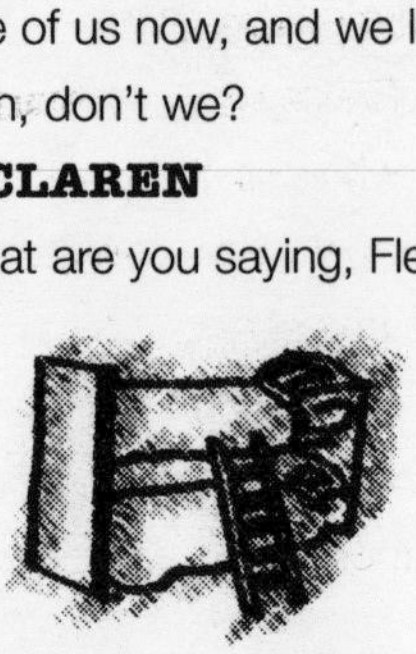

**FLETCHER**
I'm saying if you takes him on, you takes me on an' all. Don't be misled by this bulky torso. It conceals a man of steel. On your way, Judge.

**RAWLEY**
On my way where?

**FLETCHER**
Out the yard. Go and watch the football, you need the fresh air.

***Rawley pauses.***

**FLETCHER**
Don't worry, the word'll go round.
No one will touch a hair of your head.

***Rawley goes.***

**HARRIS**
Naffin 'ell, is that it?

**MCLAREN**
If Fletch says so, that's it. But I'd love to know why. What are you doing siding with the establishment?

**FLETCHER**
You knows me better than that. It's just that I uses my head. (*Holding book up*) What's this?

**HARRIS**
What's what?

**FLETCHER**
No, not what's what – *Who's Who*.
I been looking up Rawley.
Cross-referenced with our dear Governor. D'you know what – they only went to the same school, only went in the same regiment, belong to the same Club. They're lifelong bleedin' oppoes, those two.

**HARRIS**
That makes it worse!

**FLETCHER**
Does it? Do we quench our appetite for blood, or do we agree that what this cell block has always lacked, is a lifelong friend of the Governor?
Think about it.

***He drops book on Harris's toe.***

## 10. LANDING

***The Prison Officers are locking up.***

## 10A. CELL

***It is night time. Lennie is on his bunk. Rawley is sitting in his bed. Fletcher gives Rawley a mug of tea.***

**RAWLEY**
Thank you.

**FLETCHER**
Comfy, your honour?
Want another pillow?

***He walks over to Lennie's bunk and takes his pillow. He goes back to Rawley's bed.***

**RAWLEY**
(*Propping pillow under him*)
Oh, thank you.

**FLETCHER**
Extra blanket?

**RAWLEY**
No, thank you, I'm warm enough.

**LENNIE**
If you're scared of the cockroaches, we can take turns watching out for them.

**RAWLEY**
You're most kind. And let me say again, Fletcher, how much I appreciate what you did for me.

**FLETCHER**
A man in here has a right to prove himself.

**LENNIE**
Here – I said that first.

**FLETCHER**
Yeah. Well, it's hardly original, is it?

**RAWLEY**
You more than anyone, Fletcher, had every right to despise me.

**FLETCHER**
No point in that, your worship. No, let's just sit here and reminisce about happier times. Tell us about you and the Governor for example. That should while away a few hours.

**RAWLEY**
Myself and the Governor?

**FLETCHER**
Yes, well didn't I hear something somewhere that you once knew each other, was it?

***He offers a biscuit.***

**RAWLEY**
(*Taking biscuit*) Known each other for years.

**LENNIE**
Really, what a coincidence.

**RAWLEY**
I hope this doesn't explain your change of attitude, Fletcher.

**FLETCHER**
What?

**RAWLEY**
I trust you're not hoping to profit from my past relationship with Geo . . . the Governor. Because I must warn you that anything I know about him is in the strictest confidence.

**FLETCHER**
Oh, is it?
*(He gets up and removes the pillow).*

**FLETCHER**
I'll have me pillow back then.

***He throws the pillow at Lennie and starts undressing.***

**RAWLEY**
Fletcher. I am grateful. I do appreciate what you did for me today.

**FLETCHER**
Not all that grateful obviously.

**RAWLEY**
Shake?

**FLETCHER**
What?

**RAWLEY**
Shake.

**FLETCHER**
Shake what?

**RAWLEY**
Hands. No hard feelings, that sort of thing.

**FLETCHER**
Why should I have any hard feelings? You're only the bloke that put me in here.

**RAWLEY**
Fletcher, I had no choice.

**FLETCHER**
'Course you did. Several. Could have rejected the jury's verdict. Ordered a retrial. Given me a suspended sentence. Bound me over.

**RAWLEY**
Not in the face of the evidence.

**LENNIE**
And not with your record, Fletch.

**FLETCHER**
I suppose so.

**LENNIE**
You were guilty – you said so yourself.

**FLETCHER**
Yes, you're right. And seeing him in here has made me realise what a big mistake I made. My one regret is that I didn't know then what I know now.

**RAWLEY**
Oh, that's reassuring.

**FLETCHER**
What is?

**RAWLEY**
Remorse.

**FLETCHER**
Remorse! It's nothing to do with remorse! It's just that if I'd known you was crooked I could have slipped you a few bob!

# 3 SERIES THREE

## EPISODE THREE: ROUGH JUSTICE

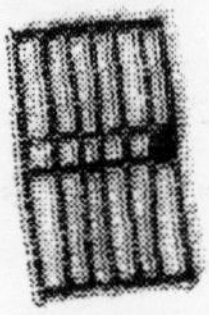

### 1. FLETCHER'S CELL

***Fletcher is writing a letter.***

***Warren comes in tentatively.***

**FLETCHER**

What d'you want, Warren?

**WARREN**

How did you know it was me?

**FLETCHER**

Rear-view mirror. What d'you want?

**WARREN**

I need a letter written. Home, like.

**FLETCHER**

Warren, how long you been inside?

**WARREN**

Nigh on ten months now.

**FLETCHER**

Don't you think you could have taken advantage of the educational facilities and got rid of your illiteracy?

**WARREN**

I'm not illiterate, Fletch.

**FLETCHER**

Forgive me, I thought that was the word what described someone who can't read or write.

**WARREN**

I'm not illiterate. I suffer from dyslexia.

***Fletcher looks puzzled.***

**WARREN**

You don't know what it means, do you?

**FLETCHER**

Dyslexia? Well, it's obviously some sort of acid stomach, isn't it? Though why that should stop you reading or writing, I can't imagine.

**WARREN**

You're wrong. Dyslexia is word blindness, like. I can't make out words when they're written down. They all get jumbled up in my head.

**FLETCHER**

Yeah, well there's plenty of room, ain't there?

**WARREN**

Tragic really. If they'd diagnosed it when I were a lad, I wouldn't be in here now.

**FLETCHER**

Oh here we go. The customary alibi. The hard luck story.

**WARREN**

It's true in my case. I had a real tough break. You see, I couldn't read the sign.

**FLETCHER**

What sign was this?

**WARREN**

The one that said, 'Warning – Burglar Alarm'.

***Fletcher laughs.***

**FLETCHER**

Pardon my laughing. That's much the same excuse as Charlie Gill – he's that burglar in B Wing.

**WARREN**

How?

**FLETCHER**

He's deaf, he didn't hear the dog.

**WARREN**

I didn't know he were short of hearing.

**FLETCHER**

That ain't all he's short of since that Airedale got him.

**WARREN**

I'll come back later I think.

**FLETCHER**

No, hang about.

***He walks over to Warren.***

**FLETCHER**

I'll do it for you. Usual rates. Half a snout a page.

**WARREN**

No, I weren't going to ask you.

**FLETCHER**

What?

**WARREN**

I were going to ask your new celly, Judge Rawley.

**FLETCHER**

Why?

**WARREN**

Take advantage, like. He's a judge. Educated man. Oxford. Public school.

**FLETCHER**

Oh I see – suddenly bowled over by his worship's academic pedigree, you've dispensed with my literary services, have you?

**WARREN**

No offence, like. I just thought he has to be the best person for the job.

**FLETCHER**

Here – letter writing is an art. A gift. What sort of love letter is he going to write? 'My dear Elaine, I am in receipt of your letter of the 6th inst., wherebeit I, the undersigned, hereforward to be referred to as the third party, etc. etc.' What do you want to do, woo her or sue her?

**WARREN**

Well, I just thought –

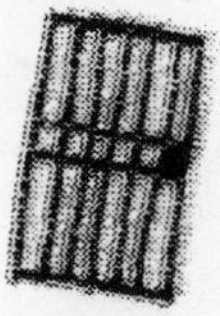

**FLETCHER**

You just thought wrong as usual. Letter writing is a creative art, endowed to a few of us. I mean, how many of you nurks in here have my poetic turn of phrase? For example, here's what I'm writing to my nearest and dearest – just read that. Oh you can't, can you, I'll read it. (*Reading*) 'My Darling, Though we have been driven apart by cruel fate, and an inexcusable misdirection of a jury by a biased judge, who is now sharing a cell with me, I know that our love transcends these grey, grim walls that have driven us apart. You are with me in my heart and this knowledge helps me to wring a few drops of comfort from the limp, damp towel of life. Kiss the baby for me, your own Norman . . .'

**WARREN**

Oh yes, that's beautiful, Fletch.

**FLETCHER**

Yeah, well.

**WARREN**

I'm sorry, Fletch. Will you do a letter for me? When you've got a moment?

**FLETCHER**

When I've got a moment, yes. But first I've got to finish this, get it sent off. Then after that I've got to write to the wife.

***He goes back to the table and sits down. Rawley comes in.***

**RAWLEY**

Oh, good afternoon, Warren.

**WARREN**

Oh, hello, Judge – your Honour.

***He bows.***

**FLETCHER**

Don't call him that. Don't smarm up to him. He is not a judge. He is a former judge, an ex-judge. He has been de-benched. De-wigged.

**WARREN**

He's pending appeal, and you never know . . .

**RAWLEY**

Oh, Warren, that matter you raised with me in the canteen. I'll give it a little thought and speak to you about it later.

**WARREN**

Oh thank you, Judge. See you, Fletch.

***He goes.***

**FLETCHER**

Oh – has he been raising things in the canteen again? What little matter was this then?

**RAWLEY**

Oh, just a legal matter. Something to do with his sister's tenancy of her council house.

**FLETCHER**

Oh, I see. Setting up shop, are we?

**RAWLEY**

Excuse me?

**FLETCHER**

Judge Rawley, QC, is now open for business. What you charging then?

**RAWLEY**

I'm not charging anything.

**FLETCHER**
Well, that's daft to start with. If you have any expertise in here which is in demand, then it's saleable. Rule of the house. It's expected. And any philanthropic notions will be taken as a sign of weakness.

**RAWLEY**
Oh, I didn't realise . . .

**FLETCHER**
No, well, you ain't got the acumen. I'll work out your fees, we'll split 'em fifty-fifty.

**RAWLEY**
I have no intention . . .

**FLETCHER**
You will do.

**RAWLEY**
I will not.

**FLETCHER**
Early days. We could clean up. I mean, there's six hundred blokes in here, all of whom has a legal gripe of one sort of another. We do have an ex-solicitor across the block, but he only knows about mortgages and there's not a lot of call for that in here. One thing we are sure of is that we're always gonna have a roof over our head – albeit with a few slates missing here and there. I tell you where we could score heavy. All the poofs in here are getting a movement together. You know, 'Equal Rights for Homosexuals'. You're the perfect man to represent them. Queen's Counsel, ain't you?

**RAWLEY**
I am not hawking my legal expertise to the highest bidder.

**FLETCHER**
No need to. I do the hawking. You just dispense.

**RAWLEY**
Out of the question. I would be mad to engage in anything of that nature, until I hear the result of my appeal. Within a month I could be back on the bench. One has to preserve some sort of integrity.

**FLETCHER**
Oh integrity is it? I love your high moral tone, despite the disgrace you've wrought on your profession. Do get it into your head, you're now inside. Another world. It's a jungle in here. And you just happen to be fortunate enough to be sharing a cage with King Kong.

## 2. LANDING

***Harris walks along the landing. He goes past two prisoners who sniff the air as he walks by.***

## 2A. CELL

***Lennie is making a model aeroplane. He looks up, sniffing the air. Harris walks in.***

**LENNIE**
Is that you?

**HARRIS**
Me what?

**LENNIE**
That pong.

**HARRIS**
There's a reason for this pong.

**LENNIE**
Well I hope so, Harris. Is it curable?

**HARRIS**
They've moved me back on the naffing farm, haven't they?

**LENNIE**
Nice job, farm. Lots of exercise. Fresh air.

**HARRIS**
Fresh air? I'm swilling out the flaming pigs. You know why, don't you?

**LENNIE**
Well, they try to fit people into their most appropriate function. You and pigs, that makes sense.

**HARRIS**
Watch your lip, Godber.

**LENNIE**
(*Tries to watch lip*) Can't see it from here.

**HARRIS**
I'll tell you why I'm on the farm. 'Cause they've been rejigging jobs round here. To accommodate your naffing VIP.

**LENNIE**
Judge Rawley?

**HARRIS**
That's him. And he only went straight into a clerk's job. Trusty's by right.

**LENNIE**
Has its advantages though, the farm. Don't you get outside trips, like?

**HARRIS**
Oh yes. Only today I went for a trip in the back of a pig truck that hadn't been cleaned for three weeks, slipping about inside. We picked up six new pigs and clipped back just in time for supper.

**LENNIE**
Couldn't you have had a bath?

**HARRIS**
This is what I smell like after a bath. Oh and I'm forgetting the highlight of the day – I caught a glimpse of a woman.

**LENNIE**
A female woman, really? What was she like?

**HARRIS**
Well, porridge does strange things to a man. It's the first time I've been turned on by a fifteen-stone pig breeder.

***Fletcher and Warren walk in.***

**FLETCHER**
What are you on, Harris?

**HARRIS**
Social call.

**FLETCHER**
(*Sniffing*) Dear me, what's that smell?

**HARRIS**
Put me back on the pig farm, didn't they?

**FLETCHER**
Yeah. I heard the pigs held a protest march. Least it takes away the smell of Godber's aeroplane glue.

**WARREN**
I quite like the smell, Harris. Reminds me of home.

**FLETCHER**
Born on a farm, was you?

**WARREN**
No.

***Fletcher looks at Warren and shakes his head.***

**FLETCHER**
Clear off, Harris, go on. It's beginning to smell like a Turkish restaurant on a Monday morning in here.

**HARRIS**
If this cell stinks, it's because of His Worship. Don't know how you stomach a bloke like that.

**FLETCHER**
We know what we can stomach. Naff off, Harris.

**HARRIS**
We'll have him you know. In the end we'll have him.

***He leaves.***

**FLETCHER**
Charmless nurk!

**LENNIE**
Hey, has he whipped my Aerofix? (*Searching for it*) Oh no, here it is.

**FLETCHER**
You're always leaving that around, Godber. I come back last week from the shower and sat on it unbenknownst. I had to be prised out me underpants – talk about a stiff upper lip.

**WARREN**
Come on then, Fletch, let's have me letter.

**FLETCHER**
Let's see the snout first, then.

***Warren gives him a cigarette.***

**FLETCHER**
Cor – who rolls yours? Twiggy?

***He walks across to get an envelope from under his pillow.***

**WARREN**
Is it good?

**FLETCHER**
Fantastic, my son.

**WARREN**
Long as Elaine will like it.

**FLETCHER**
Without question. You see, last night on the box they was showing an old Rita Hayworth film. *Fire Down Below* it was called. Which is exactly what your Elaine will feel when she reads this.

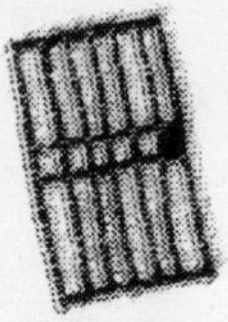

**LENNIE**

Let's have a look.

***Warren walks over to give Lennie the letter.***

**WARREN**

Will you read it for me, please?

**LENNIE**

Who was Rita Hayworth?

**FLETCHER**

(*Sitting on the bed*) Gawd, Godber, you are ignorant.

**LENNIE**

No, I'm just young.

**FLETCHER**

Well, you missed out, my son. Your generation – what have you got? Television – Joan Bakewell and Janet Street Porter.

**LENNIE**

No, since the Olympics, my sexual fantasies are mostly East European gymnasts.

**FLETCHER**

I'm talking about women, my son. Your Rhonda Flemings, your Virginia Mayos. And at the top of that glorious pile of pulchritude was always . . . my Rita.

**LENNIE**

(*Peering at the letter*) Your favourite, was she?

**FLETCHER**

Still is.

**LENNIE**

Is that why you've put Dear Rita instead of Elaine?

**FLETCHER**

I haven't, have I? Give it to me.

***He takes the letter.***

**FLETCHER**

Where's me pen?

***He gets the pen and changes the letter.***

**WARREN**

'Ere, that's not going to look too nice. She'll think I've got a Rita on me mind. She'll get jealous.

**FLETCHER**

Not now she won't.

***He sits down next to Warren.***

**FLETCHER**

I've crossed it out and put Errol Flynn. Do you want me to read it to you?

**WARREN**

Yes, please.

**FLETCHER**

Dear Errol Flynn –

***They all laugh. Rawley comes in carrying a towel and washing things.***

**RAWLEY**

Fletch – oh good evening, Warren.

**WARREN**

Good evening.

**RAWLEY**

Fletch, I just bumped into that middle-aged Teddy Boy – what's his name?

**LENNIE**
Harris.

**RAWLEY**
Yes, very abusive.

**FLETCHER**
Don't you worry about Harris. He's all wind and water. You know what he's in for, don't you? Snatching an old-age pensioner's handbag.

**WARREN**
He never!

**FLETCHER**
At least he tried to. She pinned him down till the cops arrived. She kept hitting him over the head with the handbag.

**WARREN**
And that subdued him?

**FLETCHER**
Not half – it had a brick in it. She was just on her way to do a smash and grab.

**WARREN**
Oh blimey.

**RAWLEY**
Well, he was most abusive.

**FLETCHER**
Take no notice of Harris.

**RAWLEY**
But he threatened me.

**LENNIE**
Don't you worry, your Honour. If anyone comes on strong, you know we'll always back you up.

**FLETCHER**
Yeah, we'll see you all right.

**RAWLEY**
You already have. And I would like to say how grateful I am to you. You men have every right to despise me. Especially you, Fletch, since I sent you here in the first place. But you have shown me only kindness and compassion. I feel a bond with you men – I know it has been forged in adversity, but I think it will remain with me for the rest of my life.

**FLETCHER**
'Ere leave it off, Judge. Go on like this, you're going to make us forget our scruples and start liking you.

**RAWLEY**
No, I mean this. Who'd have thought a few months ago that I could so much as talk to you? Now I find that I respect – more than that – I trust you.

**LENNIE**
You mean that?

**RAWLEY**
Most sincerely.

***He turns to pick up the towel. His expression changes.***

**RAWLEY**
Just a moment.

***There is a pause.***

**RAWLEY**
Which one of you stole my watch?

**FLETCHER**
You what?

**RAWLEY**
My watch. It was there when I went to the showers, it's not there now.

**LENNIE**
'Ere – hold your horses. What's happened to this most sincere trust you felt for us?

**RAWLEY**
That was before one of you stole my watch.

**FLETCHER**
(*Standing up*) We don't rip each other off. We're mates, oppoes. We have a code.

**RAWLEY**
But I'm still an outsider.

**FLETCHER**
That's true. Give him his watch, Len.

**LENNIE**
That's not funny, Fletch. I'm no petty sneak thief. Give him his watch, Warren.

**WARREN**
Pardon? I haven't got his naffing watch. I only come in here for me letter, which I haven't had read yet.

**LENNIE**
See what you've done, Judge. Stirred up mistrust among people who trust each other implicitly. Go on, Fletch, give him his watch.

**FLETCHER**
(*Waving the letter*) Talk to me like that, Godber! You watch it, my son, or I'll darken your outlook.

**WARREN**
(*Snatching the letter*) Don't scrunch it.

**RAWLEY**
I'm sorry, I'm sorry. I was being stupidly hasty. One should never make accusations without firm evidence.

**WARREN**
Never bothered the law in my home town.

**FLETCHER**
What's that supposed to mean?

**RAWLEY**
But I swear to you, my watch was there when I went to take my shower.

**FLETCHER**
Harris. Harris – how long was he here before I came in?

**LENNIE**
Long enough. He could have palmed it when I was glueing this aileron on.

**WARREN**
Come on then. (*Starting to go*) Let's gerr'after that nurk.

**FLETCHER**
Hold on, hold on, you know the crafty git will have stashed it by now.

***A bell rings. It is the prelude to lock-up.***

**LENNIE**
Lock-up. Timed his exit well an' all. Can't go nowhere now.

**WARREN**
I'll have to be off home, Fletch. Should I not say nowt?

**FLETCHER**
Yeah, shtum, Warren. Me and Judge will have words regarding the possibility of further procedure.

### 3. PRISON

***It is night time. Prison Officers are on their rounds.***

### 3A. CELL

***It is night time. Rawley and Lennie are in bed. Fletcher is standing by the window.***

**RAWLEY**
We cannot take the law into our own hands. I shall report the theft to the proper channels.

**FLETCHER**
Listen, we ain't going to set upon Harris. We're going to conduct a civilised investigation. We're all familiar with the working of the law, and we're fortunate in this instance to have a guest Judge.

**RAWLEY**
What?

**FLETCHER**
Yes, one thing is certain, you do knows your law.

**RAWLEY**
You mean, you want me to preside at a hearing?

**FLETCHER**
At a trial, my son.

**RAWLEY**
But do we have enough to go on?

**LENNIE**
Yes. Harris's reputation.

**RAWLEY**
I know he's objectionable, but is he a known thief?

**FLETCHER**
You should know better than to ask questions like that. We might tell you things which would prejudice your impartiality, know what I mean.

***He gets up on his bunk.***

**LENNIE**
Innocent till proven guilty, like.

**RAWLEY**
Of course, of course. Least I know about Harris the better.

**FLETCHER**
'Sright. Why should you want to know about him? A despicable nurk like that what would sell his Granny's Wintergreen.

***He sees Rawley's look of dismay.***

**FLETCHER**
Oh sorry, let that be stricken from the record, your Honour.

**LENNIE**
Are you going to prosecute, Fletch?

**FLETCHER**
Certainly. Should be interesting, see the other side of the fence, like.

**RAWLEY**

But do you know enough about legal procedure?

**FLETCHER**

Been up enough, ain't I? Look, when you chooses your living breaking the law, it pays to know the laws you're breaking. And I've had enough first-hand experience with counsels. Clever men, most of them. Although my last one weren't too bright, as my presence in this nick indicates.

**RAWLEY**

As the presiding Judge at your trial, Fletcher, I thought your counsel argued eloquently against – impossible odds.

***Lennie laughs.***

**FLETCHER**

(*Lifting up the mattress*) Godber! Listen, my counsel, Spence, that's him, he was a loser going in. And I ain't referring to the evidence. I'm talking about his attitude. He sent me this letter when I was on remand in Brixton. Listen I'll read it to you 'cos I kept it.

***He gets it off the top of his cupboard.***

**FLETCHER**

And you know what the pompous git says – I couldn't believe it. This was written to me while I was on remand in Brixton. 'Dear Mr Fletcher – '

**LENNIE**

It's good this.

**FLETCHER**

'I should like you to know that myself and my staff shall dispose ourselves with the utmost vigour and dedication in refuting the charges against you. Investigators will pursue a tenacious enquiry into unearthing evidence and testimony. Researchers will work into the night assembling and collating the facts at our disposal, on which I shall marshal a defence which has left no stone unturned, no avenue unexplored and which will culminate in your honourable and justifiable release. In the meantime, please proceed with your escape plan.'

## 4. BOILER ROOM

***A table and chairs have been positioned to make a court room.***

**RAWLEY**

This is most irregular, I cannot say I'm happy about these proceedings, Fletcher.

**FLETCHER**

Yeah, well happiness is relative, isn't it? I mean this is nick, who's happy – know what I mean?

**WARREN**

Hey up – here comes the accused.

***He moves down the stairs.***

**FLETCHER**

Under escort, is he?

**WARREN**

Yeah. Black Jock's got him in a half-nelson.

**FLETCHER**

All right your Honour, sit down. Court is convened.

***A protesting Harris is propelled in by McLaren.***

**HARRIS**

Here, here, what's going on then? You got no flaming right . . .

**FLETCHER**

Silence in court.

**HARRIS**

You what?

**FLETCHER**

Listen, Harris, we are here to pursue the course of justice and find you guilty.

**RAWLEY**

Fletcher, please. None of us heard that. Well, if we did it's stricken from our minds.

**HARRIS**

What is?

**MCLAREN**

The fact that you're guilty.

**HARRIS**

Guilty – guilty of what? Now listen, I'm . . .

**FLETCHER**

No you listen, Harris – shut up. A watch has disappeared from our flowery dell and you are the prime suspect.

**HARRIS**

Why me?

**FLETCHER**

Because otherwise it's us three and we're above suspicion. Right?

**HARRIS**

No, it's not flaming right.

**MCLAREN**

Shut up.

**RAWLEY**

I must protest these –

**FLETCHER**

Just stay out of this for the moment, your Honour, d'you mind? Thank you. Now, Harris, let me put your mind at rest. You shall get a fair trial. We have a qualified Judge with a long though slightly blemished record. We have an eye-witness.

**HARRIS**

Who?

**LENNIE**

Me.

**FLETCHER**

And I am going to prosecute you. But to ensure absolute fair play, you will be defended.

**HARRIS**

Oh.

**FLETCHER**

By Warren.

**HARRIS**

By Warren!

**WARREN**

What's wrong with that?

**HARRIS**

He's flaming illiterate, he is.

**MCLAREN**

Shut up.

**HARRIS**

Naffing hell – doesn't a man have a right to speak?

**MCLAREN**

In your case, only when spoken to.

**FLETCHER**

If you're innocent, Harris, what you in such a state about, then?

**HARRIS**

Wouldn't you get into a state if Warren was defending you?

**WARREN**

Here, Harris, I didn't volunteer for this job, I don't like you.

**HARRIS**

(*To Rawley*) Do you hear this, do you hear this?

**FLETCHER**

It's all right, Harris, he don't have to like you to defend you. You think any of our counsels liked us?

**LENNIE**

That's a good point, that is.

**FLETCHER**

Right, Harris, how do you plead . . .?

**RAWLEY**

Excuse me, Fletcher.

**FLETCHER**

What?

**RAWLEY**

Excuse me . . .

**FLETCHER**

Oh yes, be my guest.

**RAWLEY**

All right then, Harris, how do you plead? Guilty or Not Guilty?

**HARRIS**

Not Guilty.

**FLETCHER**

I see – a liar as well as a thief.

**WARREN**

(*Rising*) Objection.

**RAWLEY**

All right then, Warren, go on. What is your objection?

**WARREN**

Er – I don't know.

***He sits down again.***

**HARRIS**

Flaming heck. You were objecting to the fact that I was called a liar and a thief!

**WARREN**

No, I wasn't. We all know you're a liar and a thief, Harris.

**RAWLEY**

That remark will be struck from the record.

**FLETCHER**

This is all getting out of hand. I'd like to call my first and only witness, Leonard Arthur Godber. Take the stand, would you please.

***Lennie moves forward.***

**LENNIE**

I swear to tell the truth, the whole . . .

**FLETCHER**
Never mind all that, we've got about ten minutes before the screws tumble us. Just tell us about the events of last night, Mr Godber.

**LENNIE**
Well Mr Rawley took his watch off prior to going to the showers. At the time I was in our cell utilising my spare time in a constructive manner, i.e. making a model of a Flying Fortress.

**RAWLEY**
(*Writing*) Not so fast, Mr Godber.

***Lennie looks at Fletcher.***

**FLETCHER**
Hurry up, then.

**LENNIE**
Harris come in. Then Mr Fletcher and the defending counsel entered the room telling the accused to naff off.

**HARRIS**
Which I did.

**LENNIE**
Which he promptly did.
Shortly afterwards the watch was found not to be there and has not been seen since.

**RAWLEY**
Counsel for the Defence – that's you, Warren.

***Warren looks.***

**RAWLEY**
Do you wish to cross-examine this witness.

**WARREN**
Pardon?

**RAWLEY**
Do you wish to ask him any questions?

**WARREN**
No, I were there, I know what happened.

***Lennie goes back and sits down.***

**HARRIS**
Flamin' heck – they're all in it together – this isn't justice.

**MCLAREN**
I've warned you.

**RAWLEY**
Let him speak. He has that right.

**HARRIS**
Thank you, Judge. Now you know as well as me that this is a mockery. They all know that this is flaming hearsay. No one can prove nowt. Like where's your evidence?

***McLaren drags Harris back.***

**RAWLEY**
Please, please. I have to agree with him. One man's word against another does not constitute legal evidence. This case would not stand up in a court of law, upon which these proceedings are supposedly modelling themselves. In the absence of evidence, there is no prima facie case and I am forced to dismiss the accused.

**HARRIS**
Thank you, your Honour.

**FLETCHER**
Now hang about, Judge – whose side are you on?

**RAWLEY**
I'm sorry, Fletcher, you insisted on a proper enquiry.

**MCLAREN**
Judge – your Honour – would a signed confession help?

**RAWLEY**
Do we have one?

**MCLAREN**
I could soon get one.

**HARRIS**
He's threatening me.

**RAWLEY**
Please, please, I must protest.

**FLETCHER**
You've had your go, Judge, it's best you stay out of this, know what I mean? McLaren, please. Now then, Harris, we don't want no unpleasantness. So wherever you stashed the watch, go git it out. All right? If you traded it, go trade it back. We just wants that watch back. If not, the consequences to your good self are too dire to contemplate.

**HARRIS**
Have I definitely been found Not Guilty?

**FLETCHER**
Yes.

**HARRIS**
All right – I'll go and get it.

*He hurries off.*

**FLETCHER**
See what I mean?

## 5. CELL

***It is night time. Lennie is putting the finishing touches to his model when Fletcher comes in.***

**FLETCHER**
Aye, aye.

**LENNIE**
Evening, Fletch. Look, almost finished.

**FLETCHER**
Oh yes, very good. How you going to get it in the bottle then?

**LENNIE**
Going to hang it on the ceiling. When I was a kid I had planes all over me bedroom. Me dad made them – from the war, like. Hurricanes, Spitfires, Messerschmitts. That's how I know what shape a Flying Fortress was. Me dad told me.

**FLETCHER**
Pity he didn't tell you about what shape Rita Hayworth and Rhonda Fleming was an' all.

**LENNIE**
No, he didn't talk much about women.

**FLETCHER**
Didn't he? Was he all right your dad? Not one of them, was he?

**LENNIE**
My dad – he didn't know they existed in them days.

**FLETCHER**

Oh yes. Your poofter just wasn't so blatant then. In my father's day they used to horsewhip them, you know. Now they've become fashionable. What worries me is they might make it compulsory.

**LENNIE**

Hey, seen the Judge?

**FLETCHER**

No, but I heard he had a call to see the Governor.

**LENNIE**

What'll that be about?

**FLETCHER**

Have to ask him, won't we?

**LENNIE**

Here, you don't think he'll blow the gaff do you? About our Kangaroo court?

**FLETCHER**

Nah. He's learned we takes care of our own. He'll respect that.

**LENNIE**

Specially since Harris gave him his watch back.

***Rawley walks in.***

**RAWLEY**

Hello, Fletch – Lennie.

**LENNIE**

Hello, your Honour.

**RAWLEY**

I'm glad you're both here because I want to thank you, and tell you that I now realise a lot of what you say is true. There are grave abuses of justice. There is often one law for the poor and oppressed, and another law for the rich and powerful. And the poor usually suffer while the rich get off with clever lawyers. I shall remember that lesson when I leave here.

**FLETCHER**

Which won't be for some time though, will it?

**RAWLEY**

Oh no. I'm going out tonight.

**LENNIE**

You're what – going out?

**RAWLEY**

Yes.

**FLETCHER**

Your appeal came through?

**RAWLEY**

Certainly. I'm rich and powerful. I have clever lawyers.

***He goes. Fletcher and Lennie react. Fletcher sits on the table.***

## 6. PRISON LANDING

***Barrowclough comes out of Fletcher's cell followed by two prisoners carrying a bed.***

***As they walk along the landing they pass Judge Rawley, now in civilian clothes.***

***Barrowclough stops and says goodbye to him.***

***The Judge then moves along the landing. He looks down to the association area and sees Fletcher. He turns and starts to go downstairs.***

## 6A. ASSOCIATION AREA

***It is night time.***

***The prisoners are reading and playing cards, including Fletcher, Lennie, Warren and McLaren.***

***The chatter fades away as Rawley approaches. He is now accompanied by Mackay.***

**MACKAY**

All right, you men! Fletcher, Godber – the Governor has kindly allowed Mr Rawley to bid you a fond farewell.

**FLETCHER**

Oh, it's Mister now, is it?

**MACKAY**

Certainly. If the appeal court judges say his nose is clean, that's good enough for me. They are, after all, men of the highest integrity, in the land.

**FLETCHER**

What are you talking about? He's *one* of them!

**MACKAY**

Precisely. And he's innocent. Which proves my point.

**FLETCHER**

(*Confused – thinks*) Just a minute.

**LENNIE**

Get out of that. You can't, can you?

***Fletcher glares at him, defeated.***

**MACKAY**

(*To Rawley*) As brief as possible, if you wouldn't mind my laud – the van is waiting.

***He moves away from the group.***

**RAWLEY**

(*A little uncomfortable, clears his throat*) Er, gentlemen, it's just that I wanted to say goodbye – and to thank you once more; and to promise you something. Whatever I can do to improve the system, I shall do. This has been a frightening experience for me . . . but thanks to you men, a rewarding one.

***There is a moment's silence.***

***Their attitude is not clear.***

**FLETCHER**

(*Gets up and shakes hands*) Listen, you got a break. No one holds that against anybody.

***There is a murmur of agreement with Fletcher's sentiments.***

***Lennie and Warren shake Rawley's hand. Others give him a clap on the shoulder and make 'no hard feelings' sounds.***

**LENNIE**

(*Shaking hands*) You behave yourself now. Don't want to see you back, do we?

**RAWLEY**

Thank you, thank you . . .

***He shakes hands with Warren and McLaren.***

**RAWLEY**

Bunny . . . Jock . . . Oh, one more thing. Fletcher I'd like you to have this.

***He offers his watch.***

**FLETCHER**

No, I don't want your watch. No need for that. 'Sides, only reason they allow watches in this nick is to remind us how slowly the time passes.

**RAWLEY**

But perhaps you could trade it. It's valuable.

**FLETCHER**

(*Taking it*) Oh, ta very much then.

***He sits down.***

**MACKAY**

(*Adopting the tone he reserves for visitors*) Time's up, Mr Rawley – mustn't keep the van-driver waiting, must we? He'll be wanting his tea.

**RAWLEY**

Once again then, goodbye . . . my friends.

***He turns to leave.***

**LENNIE**

Here, Judge. When we get out, we'll come and look you up.

**FLETCHER**

Yeah, talk about old times, re-establish our friendship, meet your family . . . Bring our wives round to meet *your* wife.

***There is a chorus of agreement from the lads.***

**RAWLEY**

(*His face registering the awful truth*) You will? Oh. That will be . . . awfully nice . . .

***He goes.***

**MCLAREN**

Off he goes – free as a bird.

**FLETCHER**

And free to go and find himself a bird, an' all.

**LENNIE**

While we remain behind to carry on vegetating.

**FLETCHER**

True, Lennie, true. But I like to think we've all learnt a little from his visit, albeit short. I think we may all have gained something as a result.

**LENNIE**

*You* have – you've gained his wristwatch.

**WARREN**

Needn't have bothered with that trial. Waste of time.

**FLETCHER**

Not in my case, Bunny. As Lennie so rightly remarks, in my case I have gained time – in the shape of this genuine gold-plated, fourteen-jewelled gents wristwatch, in full working . . . just a minute.

***He rattles it to his ear. Then, with a deft movement, opens the back to the watch.***

**FLETCHER**

Where's that Harris, I'll murder him – it's got no bleeding works in it.

***He gets up and throws the watch.***

# 3 SERIES THREE

## EPISODE FOUR: PARDON ME

### 1. ASSOCIATION AREA

*Prisoners are sitting at tables, reading, playing cards, etc. Fletcher and Blanco are playing Monopoly. Fletcher has just rolled the dice and picks up a 'Chance' card. He laughs . . .*

**FLETCHER**
Would you Adam and Eve it – 'Go to Jail, Go directly to Jail. Do not pass go, do not collect . . .'

**BLANCO**
(*Putting card at the bottom of pile*) I know the flaming words. Just get on with it.

**FLETCHER**
All right, all right, then.

**BLANCO**
I could recite every card on the whole flaming board if I wanted. Been playing every day for donkey's years.

**FLETCHER**
(*Giving him the shaker*) No need to be so grumpy though, Blanco, is there? Go on, your toss.

*Blanco tosses and makes his move.*

**FLETCHER**
Four and three. Seven.

**BLANCO**
I know, I can count. I may be old but I've still got all my faculties.

*He accidentally, on purpose, flicks a hotel on to the floor.*

**BLANCO**
Oh, I've lost a hotel – reach me it, will you, Fletch?

**FLETCHER**
Leave it off, Blanco. I mean, none of us was born yesterday. I know that ploy of old.

**BLANCO**
Ploy?

**FLETCHER**
While I'm down there picking up your hotel you help yourself. I lose Bond Street and Kings Cross in the process.

**BLANCO**
That's a lie. Listen, Fletch, I'm not like

you lot. You take cheating as a way of life. But I'm an older man with an older man's sense of values, and if you don't give a rats about my sciatic nerve, I'll get the hotel meself!

**FLETCHER**

Hey, hey, hang on. I'm sorry, Blanco, honest, I'm sorry. You're right, we're all so corrupt in here, we forget there's the odd honest soul.

**BLANCO**

Yes, you do.

**FLETCHER**

I'll find it for you.

***He bends down to look for the hotel.***

***Blanco adds two more properties to his street.***

**FLETCHER**

I don't see it.

**BLANCO**

Oh look, it's only there.

***He bends down to retrieve the hotel from beneath his feet. Fletcher swiftly helps himself to some more money from the bank. Blanco straightens up.***

**BLANCO**

Now, let's have no more talk of cheating, let's just get on with the game.

**FLETCHER**

Right, my son.

**BLANCO**

Your toss.

***Fletcher throws.***

**FLETCHER**

Odd number – three. I'm staying in the nick.

**BLANCO**

My go.

**FLETCHER**

Come on then, seven and you'll land on my hotels.

***Blanco throws.***

**BLANCO**

Ten! Missed you.

***With glee he moves on to 'Chance'. Fletcher eyes Barrowclough approaching.***

**FLETCHER**

Watch it, watch it, Barra.

***Blanco turns to look. Fatally, as Fletcher takes a 'Chance' card from his pocket and puts it on top of the pack. Blanco turns back and goes to pick up the card.***

**FLETCHER**

No, no, that's your Raquel Welch – Community Chest. Come on, get on with it, this one's the Chance pile. Pick up your card.

***Blanco does so.***

**BLANCO**

'Go back three spaces.'

***Fletcher counts back, moving Blanco's piece on to Vine Street.***

**FLETCHER**
Oh dear, one, two, three – that's Vine Street with hotels. Ten hundred pounds.
**BLANCO**
What!?
**FLETCHER**
Ten hundred pounds, but I'll accept one thousand pounds, thank you very much.
**BLANCO**
Oh, me back.
**FLETCHER**
Never mind your back, just give us the money.
***Barrowclough approaches Lennie who is sitting reading.***
**BARROWCLOUGH**
Are they still playing?
**LENNIE**
Four days now. Could make the *Guinness Book of Records*.
**BARROWCLOUGH**
They're cheating each other into a stalemate, that's why.
***He walks across to Blanco.***
**BARROWCLOUGH**
All right, you two. I think it's well nigh time you wrapped up this marathon. Lock-up in five minutes.
**LENNIE**
There's other people in here would like to use that board. You do tend to monopolise that game. Gerrit?
**BARROWCLOUGH**
What? Oh I see, yes, very witty, Godber.
**LENNIE**
I thought so.
**BARROWCLOUGH**
Very sharp.
**LENNIE**
Quick as a flash, really. Do you know what's brown, lives in the ocean and attacks young mermaids?
**BARROWCLOUGH**
No, I can't say I do, Godber.
**LENNIE**
Jack the Kipper.
**FLETCHER**
Do you hear this? Palace of Varieties, isn't it?
**BARROWCLOUGH**
(*Thinking*) Jack the Kipper . . .
***He resumes his round.***
**FLETCHER**
Come on then, we'd better write all this down.
***He and Blanco start wrapping up the game, making a plan of where they have got to. Lukewarm approaches them.***
**LUKEWARM**
Oh, here you are. Now come on, you're a very naughty old person. You promised me you were going to wash your work shirt – so you'd look presentable for the Parole Board.
**BLANCO**
I'm going to, aren't I? In a minute.

**FLETCHER**

Come off it, Lukewarm. Seventeen-year stretch, you think the Parole Board's going to be swayed by a clean shirt? It's his clean record that counts.

**LUKEWARM**

Silly to jeopardise it for the sake of a drop of soap and water though, isn't it?

**BLANCO**

Look, I've got two on Piccadilly.

***He turns to Lukewarm.***

**BLANCO**

I'll come in a minute.

**LUKEWARM**

See you do. I'm going to get the tea now. I've got your mug.

***He leaves.***

**BLANCO**

Worse than me daughter, nagging.

**FLETCHER**

I though he was your daughter.

**BLANCO**

Still, he does keep the cell spotless.

**FLETCHER**

Well, you soon won't have to worry about that. You're on your way out, ain't you?

**BLANCO**

No – nothing's certain. Nothing's definite.

**FLETCHER**

'Course it is. A doddle. A mere formality. Even Mr Barrowclough would bet on that, and you know how middle of the road he is on every flaming issue. If you ask for a yes or no, he says, 'It depends what you mean by yes or no.'

**BARROWCLOUGH**

What was that, Fletcher?

**FLETCHER**

I was saying, sir, you are unwilling to commit yourself on issues. Like to hedge your bets, sit on the fence, know what I mean?

**BARROWCLOUGH**

I do not. I'm as positive in my opinions as the next man!

**FLETCHER**

Oh well then, you'd agree Old Blanco's release is a formality this time round?

**BARROWCLOUGH**

Oh . . . well, I wouldn't like to say. I mean, one has to consider both sides.

**FLETCHER**

Oh – you sure you're not sure, are you?

**BARROWCLOUGH**

Oh positive.

***He goes.***

**FLETCHER**

Naffin' heck.

**LENNIE**

It's a disgrace he hasn't been free and clear years before now.

**FLETCHER**

You're on your way, Pop. Even genial Harry Grout's giving odds on.

**BLANCO**

I won't bank on nowt, Fletch. Too accustomed to disappointment.

**FLETCHER**

You know what your trouble's been? Always insisting you was innocent. You see that's where you make your mistake. For the Parole Board, it's better to be guilty and ashamed than innocent and defiant.

**BLANCO**

That's true. You have to show them how you've reformed.

**FLETCHER**

Right. In other words, you have to prove you've changed. That you ain't as despicable as what you once was. That's why parole's a piece of cake if you once was an alcoholic or a junkie, or dressed up in women's clothes.

**LENNIE**

So what about a bloke like me who only had the one lapse into petty crime. Who otherwise came from a decent home and had an 'O' Level in geography. What are my chances?

**FLETCHER**

I think your best bet is to buy yourself a cocktail dress and matching handbag. Naff all!

**2. PRISON**

***It is night time. Prison Officers are on the prowl.***

**2A. FLETCHER'S CELL**

***It is night time. Fletcher and Lennie are lying in their beds.***

**LENNIE**

Fletch?

**FLETCHER**

Huh?

**LENNIE**

Fletcher, do you think Blanco's a cert for parole this time?

**FLETCHER**

Need the beds, don't they?

**LENNIE**

What was he originally sent up for?

**FLETCHER**

Now, son, been inside long enough to know you don't ask that. Take people for what they are, not what they was.

**LENNIE**

I know that, Fletch, but come on.

Nothing you could say about Blanco would put me off the old boy. He's one of the nicest human beings in here. He's kind and gentle and helpful. Don't make no difference to me what he's done.

**FLETCHER**

He done his wife.

**LENNIE**

What?

**FLETCHER**

Done her in. Locked her in a deep freeze.

**LENNIE**

And we knock around with a bloodthirsty old scroat like that?

**FLETCHER**

See! That's why you don't ask.

**LENNIE**

I'm sorry, I'm sorry. That was an irrational outburst. Any roads . . . long time ago, wasn't it?

**FLETCHER**

Oh you mean it's okay to refrigerate your old lady as long as it's way back in 1959?

**LENNIE**

I mean, he's obviously changed. Had time to repent, like.

**FLETCHER**

The point is that he's never repented. Always claimed he never done it. Said she had a lover, and that it was the lover who killed her.

**LENNIE**

And was it?

**FLETCHER**

It's very probable 'cos he disappeared very smartish – he never hung around long enough to be asked.

**LENNIE**

'Spose there's no way of ever knowing now. So long ago.

**FLETCHER**

Right. And a wife can't testify against her old man, so there's no point calling on the wonders of modern science.

**LENNIE**

How do you mean?

**FLETCHER**

No point defrosting her and asking what really happened. Cor it's like an icebox in here.

**3. CELL**

***Fletcher is sitting at the table doing a crossword. Lennie enters.***

**LENNIE**

Here.

**FLETCHER**

What?

**LENNIE**

Know summat you don't for once.

**FLETCHER**

That'll be the day.

***Lennie looks over Fletcher's right shoulder.***

**LENNIE**
Well, I know thirteen across for a start.

**FLETCHER**
(*Irritably*) Look, Godber, if you wouldn't mind. Height of bad manners, that is.

**LENNIE**
Anyhow, it's Rook. 'Type of Bird'. R blank blank K. Rook.

**FLETCHER**
Not necessarily.

**LENNIE**
R blank blank K! What else could it be but Rook?

**FLETCHER**
It could just be – Rilk.

**LENNIE**
Rilk?

**FLETCHER**
Yes, Rilk.

**LENNIE**
No such bird.

**FLETCHER**
That is where you are wrong. See, Godber, you're not as smart as you thought you was.

**LENNIE**
What's a flaming Rilk, then?

**FLETCHER**
The Rilk is a migratory bird from the Baltic shores of North Finland. Its most distinguishable feature is that it flies backwards to keep the snow out of its eyes . . . ask me another, Magnus?

**LENNIE**
I bet it's Rook.

**FLETCHER**
Too obvious, Rook. Look it's R I L K – Rilk. So what's this piece of knowledge you're aching to tell me?

**LENNIE**
Oh yes. First Parole Board results are through.

**FLETCHER**
And?

**LENNIE**
They've turned down Gibson who's in for car theft – and okayed Mal Brown who's in for manslaughter. I mean, that's barmy, isn't it?

**FLETCHER**
Not really. Just reflects society's current sense of values.

**LENNIE**
How d'you mean?

**FLETCHER**
Takes only one minute to create a life. Takes ten to make a car. And about five minutes for it to fall to pieces.

***He walks across to the door and sees Blanco and Lukewarm approaching along the landing.***

**FLETCHER**
Hey up, Nat Mills and Bobbie.

**LUKEWARM**
Well the old devil did it this time.

**FLETCHER**
What – worked his parole?

**LUKEWARM**
Yes – sailed through. It was that clean shirt that did it.

**FLETCHER**
Told you, didn't I? Doddle. Come on in.

***They all go into the cell.***

**FLETCHER**
He did it, Len. Sit down, Blanco. We're all very glad for you, ain't we, Len?

**BLANCO**
Ta, Fletch.

**LUKEWARM**
Surprise, surprise.

***Produces some Jaffa cakes. Lukewarm and Fletcher stand. Blanco and Lennie sit.***

**LENNIE**
Been a few changes, though. Since 1959.

**FLETCHER**
I flogged a hot car in 1959. Ford Zodiac it was. Two-tone Ford Zodiac with wing mirrors. Took the wife to Butlins on the proceeds. We won a bronze medal in the 'Tea for Two' cha-cha.

**LENNIE**
I were in Junior School in 1959. Sitting next to Ann Podmore. She was left-handed.

**FLETCHER**
Bet you got on the right side of her then.

**BLANCO**
I remember 1959 only as the year I were sent away for something I didn't do.

**FLETCHER**
Here, listen mate, you're casting a gloom on the whole proceedings. I mean, we're only trying to be festive, which does befit, dunnit?

**BLANCO**
Reckon?

**FLETCHER**
And here, now you're going out, you can level with your mates. Was you innocent all this time?

**BLANCO**
I was that. Listen, Fletch, I know you'd like to think I've been screwing the system all this time. But truth is, system's screwed me for seventeen years. That's why I've come to a decision.

**FLETCHER**
Decision?

**BLANCO**
Aye. For all these years, I've stood me ground. Claiming me innocence. If I accept parole you know what I'm doing, don't you? Admitting me guilt.

**FLETCHER**
(*Leaning towards Blanco*) Blanco, parole wipes the slate clean. It says you're free and clear.

**BLANCO**

It's not a pardon. It says you've done your bird for what they sent you up for in the first place. That's not good enough.

***He stands up.***

**BLANCO**

It says we'll let you out now and don't be a bad lad again. Well, I were never the bad lad they said I were in the first place. So they can take their parole – and SHOVE IT!

***He turns on his heel and leaves them.***

## 4. PRISON ALLOTMENT

***Camera shows a spade digging. Fletcher and Blanco are in the prison allotment.***

**FLETCHER**

You haven't, have you?

**BLANCO**

I have.

**FLETCHER**

Told 'em to stuff it?

**BLANCO**

Aye.

**FLETCHER**

What did Guv'nor say, then?

**BLANCO**

Put the wind up his clappers, I know that.

**FLETCHER**

You could be on the streets now, you know. Free. Queueing up at the Labour Exchange. Standing in the rain waiting for a bus. Couldn't you?

**BLANCO**

Waited long enough. Bit longer won't make no difference. Fetch me the scraper, will you?

**FLETCHER**

Rhubarb's coming on a treat.

**BLANCO**

Can't wait to get your hands on my rhubarb, can you? Thought I'd bequeath that if I got out, did you? In lieu of Monopoly debts?

**FLETCHER**

Don't be daft.

**BLANCO**

And me strawberries. Well, I'm still here, right? And this is still my allotment.

**FLETCHER**

We'd've looked after it, you know that. Till you came back inside.

**BLANCO**

Reckon you would.Just like life, prison. Makes plans and do naff all about it. Look at this place.I were going to do so much. Caulies, I thought. And spring onions, and big ripe runner beans.

Maybe even raspberries and goosegogs . . . never got round to it. In all that time.

**FLETCHER**

Didn't one Governor once let you grow grapes?

**BLANCO**

Aye, one time. I read all about vines. Knew I could grow grapes here, even in this neck of the woods. I did an' all. Bloody marvel, it were. Seeing those ripe juicy beauties, up here . . . then they made me pack it in.

**FLETCHER**

Why?

**BLANCO**

Grapes make wine, don't they?

**FLETCHER**

Do they? Always used potato peelings and anti-freeze myself.

**BLANCO**

Didn't tumble till we'd got about a dozen bottles put down.

**FLETCHER**

Nice drop, was it?

**BLANCO**

In the wine stakes, I don't suppose it was a classic. But to a man who hadn't had a drink for eleven years – Chateau Slade were the finest drop I ever supped . . .

**FLETCHER**

If you weren't such a stubborn old mule, you could be out there now supping champagne.

**BLANCO**

Got me pride.

**FLETCHER**

Freedom's pride.

**BLANCO**

Want both, Fletch.

**FLETCHER**

Have to see what we can do then.

***Fletcher walks away.***

## 5. ASSOCIATION AREA

***Barrowclough comes down stairs. He walks along the area and is surprised to find Fletcher, Lennie and Lukewarm sitting there.***

**BARROWCLOUGH**

Saturday, and you're all indoors!

**FLETCHER**

Crow, sir.

**BARROWCLOUGH**

I beg your pardon?

**FLETCHER**

These are the central headquarters of our campaign – Crow . . . C–R–O–W.

**BARROWCLOUGH**

Which stands for what?

**FLETCHER**

The Campaign for the Release of Old Webb. You know – Blanco. We wanted to make it the Campaign for the Release and Pardon of Old Webb, but that would've spelt Crapow

– which sounds a bit rude when you're petitioning the Home Office.

**BARROWCLOUGH**

The Home Office?

**FLETCHER**

Well, eventually the Home Office. The Governor first.

**LENNIE**

See, Old Blanco doesn't want to go out free and guilty. So we have to make sure he goes out free and innocent.

**LUKEWARM**

Which is what Crow is all about.

**LENNIE**

Already got three hundred signatures.

**BARROWCLOUGH**

But what are you petitioning for?

**FLETCHER**

There's two ways we can spring him. First, we can demand a retrial.

**BARROWCLOUGH**

After all this time! I should think the Judge, the jury and most of the witnesses are nearly all dead by now.

**FLETCHER**

Yeah, well that may be to the old boy's advantage, know what I mean? Secondly, the Governor has the right to request a pardon from the Home Office, under Sub-section twenty-three, Part three, Paragraph D, Penal Code (*Giving Barrowclough the book*) as amended by the Act of 1972.

**BARROWCLOUGH**

Really?

**FLETCHER**

Oh yes, well-known fact that is. But we're going for the retrial. That's what this petition's all about.

***Warren comes in with a sheet of paper in his hand.***

**WARREN**

Hey, look at this, Fletch. I've done the mailbag room and got sixty-three signatures.

***He sits down.***

**LUKEWARM**

Oh, lovely.

**LENNIE**

Give 'em here, Warren.

***He takes the sheet.***

**BARROWCLOUGH**

Just a minute. Sixty-three? There's only forty fellows work in the mailbag room.

**FLETCHER**

Just goes to show the strength of their feelings, don't it?

**BARROWCLOUGH**

There are twenty-three Xs on this sheet, Warren.

**WARREN**

Lot of folk in this nick can't write.

**BARROWCLOUGH**

How can you be sure that these Xs are the genuine article?

**FLETCHER**

Don't be daft, Mr Barrowclough. Look at the difference in the handwriting. Look here – one bloke's spelt X with a Y. I'll cross him off.

**BARROWCLOUGH**

Well, I have to say it's a praiseworthy effort. My only fear is the Governor's attitude. He has an automatic resistance to any notion proposed by you lot.

**FLETCHER**

You could maybe help us there, Mr Barrowclough, sir. Add some weight to our pitch, like.

**LENNIE**

Give us the credibility we apparently lack.

**BARROWCLOUGH**

How?

**FLETCHER**

Well, you're a humanitarian, ain'tcha? You're no hardnose.

**WARREN**

You've played fair with us.

**LENNIE**

Always have done.

**LUKEWARM**

Always seen our point of view.

**FLETCHER**

Your example has brought reason and compassion into a world where too often only violence prevails.

**ALL**

Yes.

**BARROWCLOUGH**

Well, as you know, I consider you men are in here to be helped, not punished. I try to understand, not condemn. I respect your rights and if you have a just cause, I'll back it to the hilt.

**FLETCHER**

Never doubted it, sir, so would you just add your Monica here.

***He offers Barrowclough the sheet.***

**BARROWCLOUGH**

What?

**LENNIE**

Just cause, sir.

**FLETCHER**

Here's a pen.

**LENNIE**

Here, that's my pen.

***He takes it.***

**LENNIE**

That's where it went.

**FLETCHER**

Shut up.

***He takes the pen back.***

**FLETCHER**

Here you are, Mr Barrowclough.

**BARROWCLOUGH**

Oh no, you don't. No blinking fear. I'm up for promotion next month. I'm not jeopardising that by being party to a prisoners' conspiracy!

***He goes.***

**LUKEWARM**
Well, I never.
**LENNIE**
Hardly the humanitarian we reckoned, is he?
**FLETCHER**
No, but give him his dues, he's smarter than we thought.
**LENNIE**
Pity, though. Get his signature and a few more screws might've followed.
**FLETCHER**
No bother.
***He reaches for the pen and starts to write.***
**FLETCHER**
H.J. Barrowclough . . .
**WARREN**
Can you really forge Barra's signature?
**FLETCHER**
'Course I can. How d'you think we got the new requisition for ping pong balls last week?
**LENNIE**
You'll be for it if they trace it back to you, Fletch.
**FLETCHER**
They're more likely to trace it back to you, it's your pen.
***He puts the pen in front of Lennie.***

## 6. GOVERNOR'S OFFICE

***The Governor and Mackay are standing by the desk.***
**MACKAY**
It means trouble, sir, with a capital T. We've got to stamp it out from the word go.
**GOVERNOR**
All right, they'd better come in.
**MACKAY**
(*Walking over to the door*) All right, Mr Barrowclough, wheel 'em in.
***Barrowclough enters with Fletcher, Lennie, Warren and Lukewarm.***
**BARROWCLOUGH**
Left, right, left. Left, right, left.
**MACKAY**
Stand still in front of the Governor.
**BARROWCLOUGH**
The petitioners, sir.
**GOVERNOR**
Now listen, you men, I'm not in favour of prisoners' pressure groups.
**BARROWCLOUGH**
They have the right, Governor, under sub-section thirteen which clearly states that in the event of –
**GOVERNOR**
Don't spout the Penal Code at me, Barrowclough.
**FLETCHER**
Let us say straight off, sir, how much we appreciate you seeing us. May I present, sir, for your perusal and consideration (*Placing petition on the desk*) our petition for the retrial of Old Man Blanco, sir.

*The Governor looks at the sheets of signatures.*

**GOVERNOR**

Do we have this many men here?

**LENNIE**

The petition, sir, is a sincere expression of the feeling in Slade Prison. And the fact they have responded in this way is a tribute to your enlightened administration.

**GOVERNOR**

Is it?

**FLETCHER**

Oh most certainly, sir. All them blokes out there, burly felons, putting their names to a piece of paper. In, as the lad puts it, a less enlightened administration, they'd have torn the place apart by now.

**MACKAY**

Is that a threat, Fletcher!

**FLETCHER**

Not a threat, sir. Observation. Based on several years of first-hand experience of the mood of the incarcerated male.

**GOVERNOR**

The mood is this strong?

**FLETCHER**

Growing stronger every minute . . . and uglier, sir. Present company excepted of course.

**MACKAY**

Sir, what is the point of this? The authorities have been compassionate enough to offer Webb a parole. He should accept it and be grateful for it.

**FLETCHER**

Not enough, Mr Mackay. Had to clear his name, see?

**MACKAY**

Then the man's a stubborn old fool.

**BARROWCLOUGH**

No, no, no. Stubborn, but not foolish. Something quite heroic about all this.

*He trails off catching Mackay's incensed look.*

**BARROWCLOUGH**

But, as you say, the man's a fool.

**GOVERNOR**

The case was too long ago, Fletcher, for a re-trial.

**FLETCHER**

There's ways and means, sir. This petition's only the first step in making this a national issue.

**GOVERNOR**

National?

**LENNIE**

We want to make Old Blanco a national hero. We want to touch the conscience of the nation. We want the spotlight of the mass media on the old fella.

**GOVERNOR**

Mass media!

**FLETCHER**

Yeah, make him a corse celebre . . . Get him on the telly, in the papers. You might be a celebrity yourself, Governor. Might get on the *Michael Parkinson Show* – or if the worst came to the worst, Esther Rantzen.

**MACKAY**

There's no way in the world that this petition could escalate into a national issue.

**FLETCHER**

Oh in itself, no, Mr Mackay, you're right of course. That's why we need the hunger strike.

**GOVERNOR**

Hunger strike – what hunger strike?

**FLETCHER**

Old Blanco's. But don't worry, Gov, a man of his age and his state, shouldn't last more than a week.

***There is a moment's silence while this is digested.***

**GOVERNOR**

All right, you can leave this here.

**FLETCHER**

I think we should discuss this further.

**MACKAY**

On your way . . . Fletcher.

**GOVERNOR**

Yes, get back to your cells.

**FLETCHER**

Sir.

***Barrowclough escorts the prisoners out of the office, closing the door behind them.***

**GOVERNOR**

A hunger strike . . .

**MACKAY**

Typical of Fletcher's devious mentality, sir. Turning the old man into some kind of martyr.

**GOVERNOR**

The last thing a prison needs, Mr Mackay, is a martyr . . .

**7. LANDING**

***A Prison Officer unlocks the gates. Fletcher and Lennie come into view.***

**LENNIE**

What you think, Fletch?

**FLETCH**

Keep 'em crossed, son.

**LENNIE**

Did seem to cause a bit of panic, like.

**FLETCHER**

Which was the intended effect. They'll just have to scratch around for an alternative now, won't they?

**LENNIE**

Pardon?

**FLETCHER**

They'll have to scratch around for an alternative.

***He moves on.***

**LENNIE**

No – pardon.

**FLETCHER**

Granted.

***He goes.***

## 8. GOVERNOR'S OFFICE

***The Governor is sitting at his desk. Mackay is still standing. There is a tentative knock on the door.***

**GOVERNOR**

Yes?

***Barrowclough walks in.***

**BARROWCLOUGH**

Could I just have one more word, sir?

**MACKAY**

Have you left those men out there without an escort?

**BARROWCLOUGH**

No, no, Mr Collinson's taking them back to their cells.

**MACKAY**

Just as well – last week we lost a typewriter.

***He checks the outer office.***

**GOVERNOR**

What is it, Mr Barrowclough?

**BARROWCLOUGH**

(*Crossing over to the desk*) There might be a solution to this problem, sir. Which I'm sure you're aware of, given your knowledge of the Penal Code.

***The Governor looks at Mackay for help but Mackay looks equally puzzled.***

**GOVERNOR**

Er . . . refresh my memory, Mr Barrowclough.

**BARROWCLOUGH**

Sub-section twenty-three, part three, paragraph D.

**GOVERNOR**

Ah! Yes . . . yes . . . good old sub-section twenty-three, paragraph G.

**BARROWCLOUGH**

D, sir, paragraph D.

**GOVERNOR**

D, yes! Of course. Er, jog my memory again, will you, Mr Barrowclough?

**BARROWCLOUGH**

Well, as you know, sir, under special circumstances the Governor of a prison has the right, if his discretion feels it's warranted –

**GOVERNOR**

Yes?

**BARROWCLOUGH**

To request the Home Office for a prisoner's pardon.

**GOVERNOR**

A pardon?

**BARROWCLOUGH**

That's right, sir.

**MACKAY**
A pardon?
**GOVERNOR**
It would certainly put paid to the news of a hunger strike being splashed across the newspapers.
**BARROWCLOUGH**
Well, all round, by and large, it does seem a good idea.
**GOVERNOR**
Yes, well I'm paid to come up with ideas in situations like this. I'll submit a recommendation to the Home Office. Can we get rid of all this nonsense –
***He starts to push aside the petition when something catches his eye.***
**GOVERNOR**
Just a minute . . . your signature's on this thing, Mr Barrowclough.
**BARROWCLOUGH**
(*Looking for his spectacles*) Oh no, sir, some mistake, sir.
***Mackay picks up the petition.***

**MACKAY**
Look man – look at that. Is that not your signature?
**BARROWCLOUGH**
(*Takes the petition*) Must be a forgery, sir.
***He looks at it.***
**BARROWCLOUGH**
No, that is my signature. I must have signed it.

**9. CELL**
***Fletcher is in his cell when Lennie walks in with an envelope.***
**LENNIE**
So miracles do happen, then. Off out today, is he?
**FLETCHER**
Yes, free pardon. 'Course they're all claiming credit for it. The Governor's happily going round saying he thought of it; Barrowclough's miserable because he thinks he thought of it. Funny thing is, *we* know who really did think of it, don't we?
**LENNIE**
Yes, me.
**FLETCHER**
What you talking about, Godber?
**LENNIE**
Only joking.
**FLETCHER**
Joking – I've not got over that Jack the Kipper yet.
**LENNIE**
Hello – Lukewarm.
***Lukewarm enters.***

**LUKEWARM**
Gentlemen, may I present the best-dressed man in Slade Prison.
***He stands aside and Blanco enters, dressed in a seventeen-year-old light grey suit now a mite too large for him.***
**FLETCHER**
Oh yes. Very elegant. Where d'you nick that – War on Want?
**BLANCO**
I think it were Fifty Shilling Tailor's.
**FLETCHER**
You were robbed.
**BLANCO**
January Sale, 1959.
**LENNIE**
Back in fashion then.
**FLETCHER**
I think in '59 I wore Italian pin stripes. And a shirt with a Billy Eckstein collar.
**LENNIE**
I wore short grey flannel shorts.
**FLETCHER**
All right.
**BLANCO**
I wore this suit to my wife's funeral.
**FLETCHER**
Hardly black, is it?
**BLANCO**
Couldn't afford another suit. Only just finished paying for that damn freezer. Terrible to think she finished up inside it. Mind you I suppose it were fitting in a way, 'cos all her life she were a cold woman.
***Barrowclough puts his head round the cell door.***
**BARROWCLOUGH**
Don't be long, Mr Webb. Bus is waiting.
***He goes.***
**FLETCHER**
Thank you.
**BLANCO**
By gum, d'you know how good that sounds? Mr Webb.
**FLETCHER**
When you goes out there, hold your head up high, my son.
**BLANCO**
I will that, Fletch.
***There is a pause.***
**BLANCO**
I'm not very good, you know, at expressing gratitude. But I know what you done . . . and I'll not forget it.
***He shakes Fletcher's hand.***
**FLETCHER**
You're going out now. All that matters.
**LENNIE**
Got a lot of living to make up for. Don't waste your time nattering with the likes of us.
**BLANCO**
I don't want much from life.

**FLETCHER**
I know, but it's good to know that justice has been done – albeit a bit late. This pardon's for your family name, for your children and your grandchildren. That's why we done it. So's you can walk out of here and look any man in the face without shame or guilt. Life's taken a lot from you, me old mate, but all you need back from it is your pride, right?

**BLANCO**
Right, Fletch.

**LENNIE**
Tarra, Blanco. Keep your nose clean.

**BLANCO**
So long – same to you, son.

**FLETCHER**
Oh and one more thing, of course.

**BLANCO**
What?

**FLETCHER**
You sue the Government for every penny they've got.

**BLANCO**
Too bloody true, I will.

**LUKEWARM**
(*Stands up and gives him cigarettes*)
Ta, ta Blanco – I'll miss you.

**BLANCO**
Thanks for looking after me. I'll try and get that scented notepaper that you want.

**FLETCHER**
Here listen – We knows you didn't do in your old lady, which means some other bloke did. And you paid the penance. But don't you go out there harbouring thoughts of revenge.

**BLANCO**
I know him what did it. It were the wife's lover. But don't you worry, I shan't waste my time looking for him – he's dead.

**FLETCHER**
Oh that's all right then.

**BLANCO**
That I do know. It were me that killed him. Cheerio.

***He leaves. The others exchange looks of consternation.***

# 3 SERIES THREE

## EPISODE FIVE: A TEST OF CHARACTER

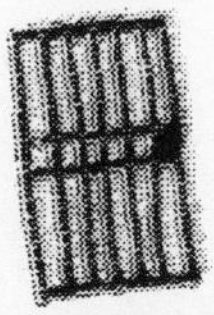

### 1. STUDIO
### FLETCHER'S CELL

***It is night time. Lennie is sitting at the table studying, textbooks in front of him. He is deep in concentration. Fletcher walks in singing.***

**FLETCHER**

There's just one place for me
Near you
And forever I'll be
Near you –

***He crosses the cell and puts his towel on the end of his bunk.***

**FLETCHER**

Times when we're apart
I can't hear my heart.

**LENNIE**

Naff off, Fletch.

**FLETCHER**

(*Still singing*) Say you'll never stray
More than just one bunk away.

**LENNIE**

Naff off, Fletch.

**FLETCHER**

I beg your pardon, Godber?

**LENNIE**

You heard.

**FLETCHER**

Shall I tell you something? Prison's coarsened you, my lad.

**LENNIE**

Yeah well, it's hardly finishing school, is it?

**FLETCHER**

Nevertheless when you first come in here, you did retain some vestiges of old world courtesy – such as respect for your elders.

**LENNIE**

When I first come in here, you taught me the value of peace and quiet. I'm in accordance with that now.

**FLETCHER**

Meaning?

**LENNIE**

Meaning – Do not disturb.

**FLETCHER**

Suit yourself. Not another word.

**LENNIE**

Thanks, Fletch.

***He goes back to his books. There is a pause.***

**FLETCHER**

(*Putting a shirt on*) No, not another word. Not a single, solitary word will emit from my lips forthwith . . . forthwith my lips are sealed, sealed are forthwith my lips . . . I have sealed forth my lips with . . .

**LENNIE**

Fletch!!

**FLETCHER**

What?

**LENNIE**

You weren't going to say nowt.

**FLETCHER**

I'm not, am I? Honest. Schtum, right. With a capital Scht.

***Lennie goes back to reading. A few moments later, Fletcher goes over to him, cupping his hands.***

**FLETCHER**

Here, Len.

**LENNIE**

Oh, naffin' heck!

**FLETCHER**

No, no, this won't take a minute.

**LENNIE**

What?

***Fletcher holds his hands in front of Lennie.***

**FLETCHER**

Guess what I've got in my hand.

**LENNIE**

I don't care, Fletch, go away, won't you?

**FLETCHER**

No, it's a good one this. Have a guess. What have I got in my hands? Go on then.

**LENNIE**

Okay. A cockroach.

**FLETCHER**

No.

**LENNIE**

I give up.

**FLETCHER**

You've got two more guesses.

**LENNIE**

A walnut.

**FLETCHER**

A walnut! Where could I get a walnut?

**LENNIE**

All right – it's a naffin' giraffe with a harelip wearing purple Y-fronts!

***Fletcher looks at Lennie and then opens his cupped palms ever so slightly, peering. He sniffs.***

**FLETCHER**

You've been peeping!

**LENNIE**

Oh God, give me strength!

**FLETCHER**

Didn't you like that – I thought it was funny. Maybe I told it wrong. Let's try it again.

**LENNIE**

Fletcher, naff off! I've asked you nicely. I have an exam and I need to study.

**FLETCHER**

I have no objection to that. Just go and do it somewhere else, right?

**LENNIE**

Where, for instance?

**FLETCHER**

Education Room for one. That would seem the most appropriate.

**LENNIE**

There's a lecture in there tonight. The Accident Prevention Officer is speaking on industrial safety.

**FLETCHER**

That's been cancelled.

**LENNIE**

Has it?

**FLETCHER**

Yeah. On his way here the Accident Prevention Officer fell off his bike. He's in Carlisle General now.

**LENNIE**

I wish you were.

**FLETCHER**

Listen, Godber – there are two people to a cell you know. And it's very unsettling for a social misfit like me to have someone sat here who wants to better himself.

**LENNIE**

Yeah, well when I get out of here I may have another 'O' Level. What will you have to show for it? Just another stretch done!

***Mackay appears.***

**MACKAY**

Oh yes, oh yes.

**FLETCHER**

(*Getting on his bunk*) The Town Crier.

**MACKAY**

What's going on here? A heated exchange, is it? Raised voices.

**FLETCHER**

Oh here it is, Mother Superior.

**MACKAY**

Watch your lip, Fletcher.

**FLETCHER**

My lips are sealed, sir. Forthwith my lips are sealed.

**LENNIE**

If only that were true.

**MACKAY**

What's the problem?

***He walks across to Lennie.***

**MACKAY**

Godber?

**LENNIE**
I'm trying to study, Mr Mackay. You're always encouraging education, rehabilitation – only there's nowhere in this naffing nick conducive to it.

**MACKAY**
I'm afraid that won't cut much ice with an ageing recidivist like Fletcher.

**FLETCHER**
Ageing what?

**MACKAY**
Recidivist. A person who pays his penance for performing a crime, goes out and straight off performs another one.

**FLETCHER**
Oh – you means a professional.

**MACKAY**
No – I mean an habitual criminal. Something which you may not have been if you'd stuck in to your education like laddo here.

**FLETCHER**
Yeah, well I never finished school, did I? Never got as far as exams. What was it called – School Certificate in them days.

**MACKAY**
I can imagine.

**FLETCHER**
Always playing truant.

**MACKAY**
Oh yes.

**FLETCHER**
Well it was the war. We was always on the bomb sites, collecting shrapnel and that. Learning about sex in the air-raid shelters during their off-peak hours. So eventually they sent me to a special school with other kids who were always playing truant. But we never learned nothing.

**MACKAY**
And why not?

**FLETCHER**
No one ever turned up for school.

**MACKAY**
See me, I had to leave school at fourteen. Help bring a living wage into the house. Hard times in those days in the Lanarkshire coalfields. My father was an unemployed miner but there were still eight children to provide for.

**FLETCHER**
Eight kids eh? He wasn't unemployed the whole of the time then?

**MACKAY**
Did I hear you correctly, Fletcher?

**FLETCHER**
No you didn't, sir.

**MACKAY**
Let me tell you something, not one of our family neglected education. Not one. Even under the most difficult circumstances like Godber here. I've had to pass exams, you know. (*Picking a book up*) *The Aspects of*

*the Reformation.* What's the subject you're studying, Godber?

**LENNIE**

History. 'O' Level like. Already got one 'O' Level before I come inside. Geography.

**MACKAY**

That's the spirit, laddie. You stick in. And I'm telling you, Fletcher, no I'm ordering you – you do nothing to hinder this lad's concentration, otherwise get out.

**FLETCHER**

I just come in from work – I'm entitled.

**MACKAY**

You're entitled to nothing in here except to obey the sound of my voice. When's the exam, son?

**LENNIE**

Two days' time.

**MACKAY**

Right, so make yourself scarce, Fletcher. Is that clear!

***He exits.***

**FLETCHER**

(*Calling after him*) All right, all right, I'll go out for the evening! Give us the keys, I'll let meself in. So. Can't stay in me own flowery dell in case it upsets his nibs' concentration here.

**LENNIE**

You can if you're quiet. It's not much to ask, Fletch. Means a lot to me, this exam does.

**FLETCHER**

History, is it?

**LENNIE**

Yes.

**FLETCHER**

History and geography, huh!

**LENNIE**

What d'you mean, huh?

**FLETCHER**

Well they got no application have they in real life?

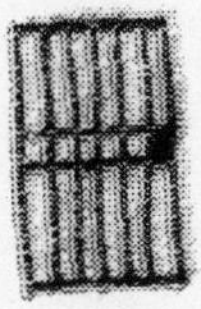

**LENNIE**

The point is not what exam I get, the point is that I got an exam. That's what's going to impress any future employer. That I had enough diligence and application to pass an exam even under the most adverse circumstances imaginable.

**FLETCHER**

It's not easy studying in the nick.

**LENNIE**

All I'm saying is, it's worth a try and I'm trying.

**FLETCHER**

Oh well, far be it for me, et cetera.

***He settles back with a satsuma. Lennie studies his books. Fletcher looks at him, there is a pause.***

**FLETCHER**

Quiet enough for you, then?

**LENNIE**
Thank you.

**FLETCHER**
You won't know I'm here.

***A few moments of rare silence, then Warren comes in.***

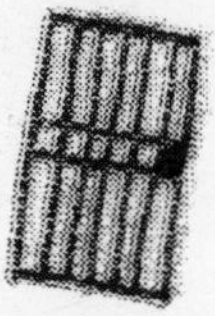

**WARREN**
Evening, lads.

**LENNIE**
Oh gawd.

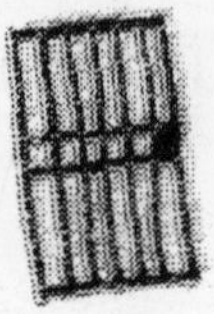

**FLETCHER**
Ssshhhh.

**WARREN**
What's up?

**LENNIE**
Naffin' heck.

**FLETCHER**
I didn't ask him round!

**LENNIE**
It's impossible.

**WARREN**
What's up?

**FLETCHER**
Seat of learning in here, this is. Professor Godber's studying for his NBG.

**WARREN**
Oh he's always at that lark, is Len.

**LENNIE**
(*Slamming the book shut*) Cobblers to it. I give up.

***He goes across to his bunk.***

**WARREN**
I know knowledge.

**FLETCHER**
You know knowledge? You can't even read.

**WARREN**
Maybe not, but I get it from the telly. Schools programmes, *University Challenge*, *Sale of the Century*. I learn things and I digest them with my memory. Shall I give you an example?

**FLETCHER**
No.

**WARREN**
Right. Apparently. Are you listening, Fletch? If every Chinaman in China jumped up and down – at the same moment, like – it would cause a tidal wave which would engulf America.

**FLETCHER**
Really.

**WARREN**
Straight up. (*Doubtfully*) Or is it Australia?

**FLETCHER**
Hey – that could be used as a secret weapon. They could hold the threat of that one over President Carter's head. One jump up and down all at the same time and whoosh! World domination.

**WARREN**
Yeah.

***He pauses.***

**WARREN**
But they wouldn't though, would they?

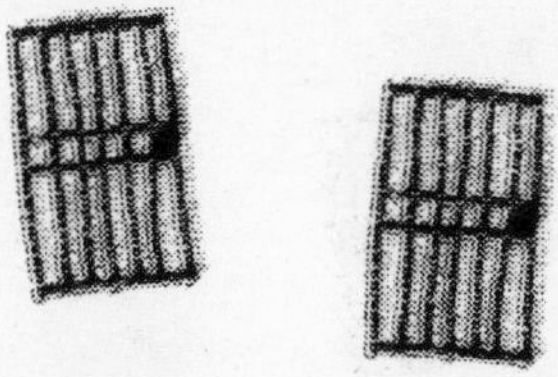

**FLETCHER**
Well, they might you know, knowing the Chinese. If anyone could pull it off they could. 'Cos they're regimented. Do everything by numbers. Look at the menu in a Chinese Restaurant. Never work in England.

**WARREN**
We could, if we put our minds to it.

**FLETCHER**
Not a snowball's. The British working man wouldn't demean himself by jumping in the air, in case he spilt his tea.

**WARREN**
Still, that is knowledge, isn't it?

**FLETCHER**
Oh yes. May I enquire where you got this fascinating piece of information, Warren?

**WARREN**
Someone read it to me once from a magazine in this chiropodist's waiting room.

**FLETCHER**
Oh dear. What was wrong with you – toothache?

**WARREN**
No, I was there with me feet, you see.

**FLETCHER**
Naturally.

**WARREN**
I've always had these feet, like. It's a good chiropodist, though. They're very quick.

**FLETCHER**
Do they do them while you wait?

**WARREN**
Eh?

**FLETCHER**
I mean – or do they say leave 'em with us, they'll be ready Thursday. Soled and heeled.

**WARREN**
Get off – you're pulling my leg, Fletch.

**FLETCHER**
I wouldn't dare. Your foot might come off.

**WARREN**
No, listen, I've got some more knowledge. Even better. It's about planets.

**FLETCHER**
Oh planets – that'll be nice. Even better! You should write all this down, Len.

**LENNIE**
I've chucked the towel in.

**WARREN**
Now, does anyone have a football?

**LENNIE**
No, we ain't gotta football.

**WARREN**
Never mind, we can use something else. Can I borrow one of your satsumas, Fletch?

**FLETCHER**
My satsumas?

**WARREN**
And I've got my ping-pong ball.

**FLETCHER**
What's all this about, Bunny?

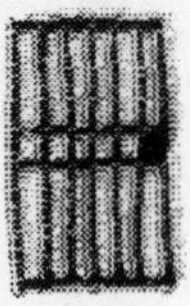

**WARREN**
I'll show you, I'll show you.

***Fletcher gives him a satsuma.***

**FLETCHER**
I want that back. Unbruised.

**WARREN**
Yes.

***He takes the chamber pot and places it on the shelf.***

**WARREN**
Now, we don't have a football but we can use this Jerry to be the sun. 'Course it should be round like a football 'cos the sun's round.

**FLETCHER**
That wouldn't be any good if it was round, would it?

**WARREN**
Why not?

**FLETCHER**
You wouldn't be able to sit on it. You'd keep rolling off.

**LENNIE**
Just let him get on with it.

**FLETCHER**
It's all in the sun tomorrow – that's true. Get on with it.

**WARREN**
So pretend the Jerry's a football but it's really the sun.

**FLETCHER**
I am, I am.

**WARREN**
Now this ping-pong ball is supposed to be the planet Mercury, and that goes right here. Excuse me, Fletch. Because it's nearest the sun.

**FLETCHER**
I'll get a chair in the shade then.

***He moves over and sits down.***

**WARREN**
Now – one, two, three, four (*Pacing steps out*)

***Bumps into Fletcher.***

**WARREN**
Oh, excuse me, Fletch, you're sitting where the Earth goes.

**FLETCHER**
(*Getting up*) Am I – oh dear. Have I got any on my trousers?

**WARREN**
Now this satsuma is the planet Earth, and that goes here. Now.

**LENNIE**
You left out Venus.

**WARREN**
You what?

**LENNIE**
Venus comes between Mercury and the Earth.

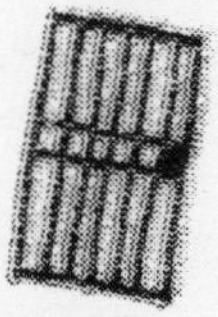

**FLETCHER**

(*Stamping foot*) Yeah, about here.

**WARREN**

Oh, that's right. And Venus is smaller than the Earth so we need something smaller than a satsuma.

**LENNIE**

Your brain.

**WARREN**

Fletch, you got a prune?

**FLETCHER**

Curiously enough I'm fresh out of prunes. They got all wrinkled, so I chucked 'em out. Why don't you skip Venus?

**WARREN**

If you like. (*Pointing to the three objects*) sun . . . Mercury . . . skip Venus . . . Earth. Now, on this scale, not counting the sun, how far away from this cell where we are would the nearest star be? Lennie?

**LENNIE**

Is this one of these trick questions?

**WARREN**

No, no.

**LENNIE**

(*Getting up*) 'Cos if it is I'll stuff you, Warren.

**WARREN**

No it's not – straight up.

**LENNIE**

All right. Let's get this straight. That's the sun, Mercury, Earth. On that scale . . .

**WARREN**

On that scale.

**LENNIE**

Where would the nearest star be . . .

**LENNIE/WARREN TOGETHER**

. . . to where we are now.

**WARREN**

That's right.

**LENNIE**

I would imagine, er yes, I would reckon, like, well, let's see, then . . . I'll say the recreation yard.

**WARREN**

Wrong. Fletch?

**FLETCHER**

Recreation yard must be wrong. Got to be the Married Quarters, hasn't it? Thereabouts.

**WARREN**

You're wrong as well.

**FLETCHER**

Not by much I bet.

**WARREN**

Johannesburg!

**FLETCHER**

Never – never in a thousand years.

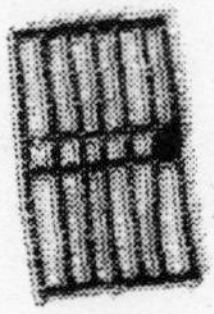

**WARREN**
It is. The nearest star would be in Johannesburg . . . (*Doubt sets in*) Or is it Australia?

***Lennie walks to the table and picks up his books.***

**LENNIE**
I don't believe it, I just don't believe it. You lot will drive me round the ruddy twist.

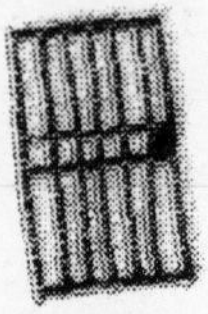

**WARREN**
What's wrong, that's learning that is.

**LENNIE**
Oh yes, and what have I learned today then? The sun is a chamberpot which is really a football, and America will drown given the unlikely probability that six hundred million Chinese jump up and down in unison!

***He throws the ping pong ball and gets out.***

**WARREN**
What have I said?

**FLETCHER**
(*Moving chamber pot*) Finished with the sun have you?

**WARREN**
It's the exam, is it? The strain, like?

**FLETCHER**
Won't open no doors though.

**WARREN**
History?

**FLETCHER**
At this point in time, yeah – it happens to be history. You know what he's like. Been through every course in this nick like a dose of salts.

**WARREN**
He gets discouraged so easy. Look how quick he jacked in elementary Spanish.

**FLETCHER**
Yeah, elementary it was an' all. After four weeks all he knew was the Spanish for 'bread' and 'donkey'. That's not going to get you far in Spain, is it? Unless you want to live on donkey sandwiches.

**WARREN**
I think he gives things in 'cos you undermine his confidence.

**FLETCHER**
Oh it's my fault, is it?

**WARREN**
Yes. It's tough enough to study inside, but you distract him.

**FLETCHER**
Hold your horses, Bunny. If Godber passes that exam it will be due in no small part to yours truly.

**WARREN**
How?

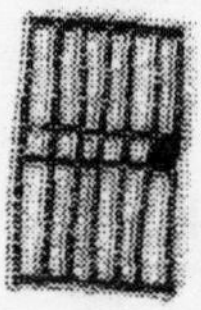

**FLETCHER**
How? I've been tutoring him, in' I? Up all night sometimes. Learning him about the Second World War, as told by someone what lived through it – me.

**WARREN**
Is he studying World War II then?

**FLETCHER**
Does it matter? A war is a war, it's all history, in' it?

**WARREN**
Just saying, Fletch – thing like this exam means a lot to young Len. To himself like. And if he puts a lot of store on this exam, then fails – well –

**FLETCHER**
What – could turn him a bit sour, you mean?

**WARREN**
Shatter his confidence, like. He'll think stuff it – go back to thieving.

**FLETCHER**
Well then let us agree that you and I and the lads should unite in the rehabilitation of Lennie Godber.

**WARREN**
If we can.

**FLETCHER**
Before he takes this exam we'll go over the questions with him. Make sure he passes so he can pursue a life of honesty and integrity.

**WARREN**
But how can we go over the questions?

**FLETCHER**
There's only one way – you and me have got to go down the Education Room and nick the exam papers.

## 2. EDUCATION ROOM

***Like all prison rooms, it is furnished with only the basic essentials. It has some desks and some shelves lined with textbooks. A wall displays a prospectus of educational programmes, and Ministry of Labour courses, prison rehabilitation schemes and the like. On another wall there is a map of the world. Off this room is a small, private office with a desk, a filing cabinet and a duplicating machine. Barrowclough and a prisoner (Spraggon) are in the main room. Spraggon is sitting at a desk.***

**BARROWCLOUGH**
This, er, manuscript of yours, Spraggon.

**SPRAGGON**
Always wanted to write. Always felt I had it in me. Literary bent, like.

**BARROWCLOUGH**

Yes, well, it's very interesting . . . brutal, but interesting.

**SPRAGGON**

It would mean a lot to me. If I become a writer. Nobody in my family's ever been famous, except for me cousin Ernie.

**BARROWCLOUGH**

Your cousin Ernie Spraggon was a notorious tearaway.

**SPRAGGON**

Still famous, though, wasn't he? He got into the top ten.

**BARROWCLOUGH**

(*Horrified*) Top ten most wanted men, yes!

**SPRAGGON**

Made a name for himself, but. Couldn't go in a post office without seeing a photo of our Ernie.

**BARROWCLOUGH**

(*Walking over to Spraggon*) Look, er, writing could be your escape – if you'll pardon the expression – and I would be the last one to discourage that. But I think we should start with some grammatical essentials. For example, on page one, the first paragraph – there's a 'k' in knuckleduster. And also in kneecaps.

**SPRAGGON**

Kneecaps?

**BARROWCLOUGH**

Yes, the ones you break with a cricket bat at the top of page two.

**SPRAGGON**

Look, I know I ain't put much grammar in there. I know my spelling leaves a lot to be desired, like, but I didn't want to interrupt me stream of self-conscious, did I? See, I write with me gut.

**BARROWCLOUGH**

Yes, I noticed that.

## 3. ASSOCIATION AREA

***The camera shows the association area.***

***McLaren, Warren and Fletcher are walking along the landing and down the stairs. They are all carrying balls. They pass Mackay at the bottom of the stairs.***

**MACKAY**

What have you men got there?

**FLETCHER**

Balls, Mr Mackay.

**MACKAY**

Why the different sizes?

**FLETCHER**

That's life, sir.

***They start to go. A prisoner near Mackay laughs.***

**MACKAY**

What are you grinning at Sowerby? Get your hair cut. You too, Jones.

***Jones is completely bald. He reacts. Mackay reacts and starts to go.***

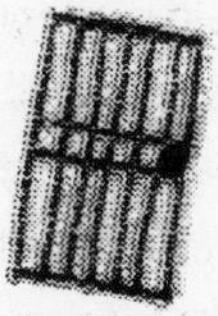

## 4. EDUCATION ROOM

***The door opens and Fletcher enters, followed by Warren and McLaren. They are carrying a football, a tennis ball and a ping-pong ball.***

**FLETCHER**

Oh 'scuse me. Hello, Spraggs, not disturbing you, am I?

**SPRAGGON**

No, you're all right.

**FLETCHER**

Wouldn't want to interrupt the literary flow. I've heard about your aspirations in that direction. All very glad to hear you're going to lay down the sword and pick up the pen. As are lot of battered nightwatchmen round your way.

**BARROWCLOUGH**

What is it, Fletcher? What do you men want?

**FLETCHER**

Looking for the Education Officer, sir. The one with the brains, you know.

**BARROWCLOUGH**

Mr Kingsley's taking a class. I'm just helping him out with some of his more bru – er basic pupils.

**MCLAREN**

We want you to settle an argument.

**WARREN**

An intellectual argument.

**BARROWCLOUGH**

Can't it wait? I'm dealing with Spraggon.

**FLETCHER**

Spraggs is used to waiting. Been waiting parole for four years.

**BARROWCLOUGH**

All right, what is it then?

**FLETCHER**

Well, me and the lads was sitting around our cell as one does discussing the wonders of the universe.

**BARROWCLOUGH**

You were what?

**FLETCHER**

Yeah, this great and wondrous galaxy what still enthralls man with its magnitude and mystery. Anyway, Warren has a theory what me and McLaren are disputing.

**BARROWCLOUGH**

What theory?

**FLETCHER**

Now, must get this right. I'll show you, Mr Barrowclough. You see this football, well it represents the sun.

***He puts it on the desk.***

**WARREN**

It hasn't got a handle, like the Jerry, but at least it's round.

**FLETCHER**

Now don't confuse things, Warren. This ping-pong ball represents the planet Mercury and goes here.

***He places it on Spraggon's desk.***

**FLETCHER**
We're going to skip Venus 'cos we ain't got a prune. Follow? Now this is the Earth. (*Holding up ball*) It doesn't bruise easily like a satsuma. It also bounces. That's gravity. McLaren, show us where this goes.

**MCLAREN**
There's not enough room in here, Fletch.

**FLETCHER**
Oh. Could you step in the corridor, Mr Barrowclough. Galaxy won't fit in this room it seems.

**BARROWCLOUGH**
Well it will, if you will just adjust the proportions.

**FLETCHER**
No – it has to be on this scale.

**BARROWCLOUGH**
Excuse me, Spraggon. I think I can see what they're trying to do. It does seem silly not to . . .

***Going out of the room.***

**SPRAGGON**
Yeah, go on, like.

***Barrowclough is followed by Fletcher and McLaren. Warren quickly goes through to the inner office and tries the filing cabinet. It is locked. He returns to Spraggon.***

**WARREN**
Hey, Spraggs, where does the Education Officer keep the keys?

**SPRAGGON**
Keys for what?

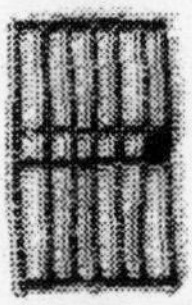

**WARREN**
Filing cabinet through there.

**SPRAGGON**
Hey, hey, hey. He's my tutor, old Kingsley. And Barra. They may be the screws, but they're okay. Before I met them I didn't know a semicolon from an apostrophe. When me book's published, I might dedicate it to Barra 'cos he trusts me, and you're asking me to betray that trust, right? Well, naff off!

**WARREN**
Tell us where the keys are and there's an ounce of snout in it for you.

**SPRAGGON**
In that drawer.

***Warren goes quickly to desk, then freezes as Barrowclough re-enters, followed anxiously by Fletcher.***

**FLETCHER**
Listen, we don't need to go back in there . . .

**BARROWCLOUGH**
If a job's worth doing it's worth doing well. I've got just the thing.

***He opens a desk drawer and takes out two large red apples.***

**BARROWCLOUGH**
There we are – just the thing we need.

(*As he passes Spraggon*) Jupiter and Saturn.

***They leave the room again. Warren quickly gets the keys from the drawer and goes into the inner office. He unlocks the filing cabinet, rifles through the documents inside until he finds a sealed official envelope. He takes it out and closes the filing cabinet. He returns the keys to the desk and puts the envelope in his pocket as the others return.***

**BARROWCLOUGH**

I know Alpha Centauri is the nearest star. Astrology is a bit of a hobby of mine.

***Fletcher looks at Warren who nods OK.***

**FLETCHER**

Really, yeah, well . . .

**BARROWCLOUGH**

Now on this scale, let's see. I wouldn't have thought it was Johannesburg.

**FLETCHER**

Yeah, well you know where to find us if you work it out – let's face it we can't get away.

**BARROWCLOUGH**

Just a minute – could I have my –

***Fletcher and McLaren simultaneously take large bites out of the apples.***

**BARROWCLOUGH**

– Oh well, never mind.

**MCLAREN**

Sorry to take your valuable time, Mr Barrowclough.

**FLETCHER**

Much appreciated.

***Fletcher goes out followed by Warren and McLaren. When they have left, Barrowclough shakes his head disappointedly.***

**BARROWCLOUGH**

Do you know I think that they enacted that whole, elaborate charade . . . simply to steal my apples.

## 5. CELL

***Lennie is studying when Fletcher enters, smug in the knowledge of his secret. He is followed by Warren, equally smug.***

**FLETCHER**

Still hard at it, are we?

**LENNIE**

(*Groans*) Trying, yes.

**FLETCHER**

Know what they says. All work and no play makes Jack a dull beanstalk.

**LENNIE**

D'as a favour, Fletch.

**FLETCHER**

(*Winks at Warren*) Already have, my son.

**LENNIE**

All right, you left the cell for half an hour. But did you have to come back so soon?

**FLETCHER**
Knew you'd miss me, little flower. Knew you'd be worried if I didn't come back before nightfall.

**LENNIE**
Where've you been?

**FLETCHER**
Down the Education Room.

**LENNIE**
(*Surprised*) What for?

**FLETCHER**
Thought we'd enrol in something, didn't we, Warren?

**LENNIE**
(*More surprised*) For what?

**FLETCHER**
Trigonometry.

**WARREN**
What's that?

**FLETCHER**
Gawd, thick as two short planks.

**LENNIE**
Go on then, tell him.

**FLETCHER**
Tell him what?

**LENNIE**
What trigonometry is.

**FLETCHER**
Well, if he doesn't know by now –

**LENNIE**
– then it's time someone told him, isn't it. Go on?

**FLETCHER**
Don't come it with me in that sarky tone, Godber.

**LENNIE**
Look, Fletch. I will be the first person in this nick to admit I owe you a lot. But one of the reasons I so desperately want to pass this exam tomorrow is so's I have a chance of not ending up like you.

**FLETCHER**
I'll have to think about that a minute. It's an insult, isn't it?

**WARREN**
Ungrateful, that's what. If he only knew . . .

**LENNIE**
(*Back to book*) Knew what?

**WARREN**
Knew how much Fletch cares.

**FLETCHER**
(*Grieved*) No, no, don't bother him.

**LENNIE**
Cares about what?

**WARREN**
Cares about you, that's what.

**FLETCHER**
(*Never appreciated*) One day perhaps . . .

**WARREN**
No, you tell him, Fletch. Tell him what you just done for the benefit of his nibs here at great personal risk to yourself.

**FLETCHER**
You played your small part, Warren. And McLaren. Though it makes you wonder why we took such terrible risks.

**LENNIE**

(*Leaving book*) What terrible risks? On my behalf? Listen, the only thing I ask you to do on my behalf is give me half a flaming chance to pass the exam!

**FLETCHER**

Which is precisely what we have done, Godber!

**WARREN**

We're only going to make sure you passes it, aren't we?

**LENNIE**

How?

**FLETCHER**

By going over the questions with you so you can prepare the appropriate answers.

**LENNIE**

(*Patiently*) In that case, it would be useful to have the appropriate questions.

**FLETCHER**

You've got 'em.

***From inside his jacket he has taken the envelope and throws it in front of Lennie.***

**LENNIE**

(*Picks it up curiously*) What's this?

**FLETCHER**

(*Airily*) Tomorrow's exam paper. Now shift yourself 'cos we gotta get it back where it come from.

**LENNIE**

(*Not taking it in*) The exam paper?

**WARREN**

(*Chuffed*) Yeah, we did it, didn't we?

***Lennie hurls the envelope down as if he was scalded.***

**LENNIE**

No!

***He stands up. Fletcher and Warren exchange puzzled looks.***

**FLETCHER**

What do you mean – no?

**LENNIE**

I mean NO. I don't want to cheat. I want to pass this exam honestly!

**FLETCHER**

Well, of course you do. But honesty is only something you can afford once you made it. And passing this exam is going to help you make it.

**LENNIE**

Don't you understand? I've cheated all me life. For the first time in my life I want to do something straight.

**FLETCHER**

Look – once you've passed this exam, no one's going to know *how* you passed it.

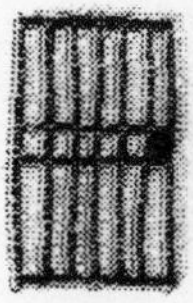

**LENNIE**

*I* will. Look, if I fail, I fail. But I'm not going to pass through cheating.

***Fletcher decides to use the persuasive rationale.***

**FLETCHER**

Len, Len. No, no, listen, will you? Lennie, my son, cheating isn't a crime.

***He says this as if it were an obvious, irrefutable truth. Lennie looks at him as if to say – what are you talking about?***

**FLETCHER**

'Course it isn't. Cheating is – getting away with it. World of difference. I mean, everyone cheats.

**WARREN**

(*Going to sit beside Lennie*) Listen, Len, you know when you play draughts with Fletch and he says he thinks one fell on the floor and could you pick it up, so you bend down only when you straighten up you find the board's rearranged – that's all cheating is.

**FLETCHER**

That's right.

**WARREN**

Oh, so you admit it?

**FLETCHER**

Name of the game, isn't it? Getting away with it. It's not what you do in life – it's what you get caught doing.

**WARREN**

And if you don't get caught . . .

**FLETCHER**

You're away, ain'tcha? Home and dry.

**LENNIE**

No.

**FLETCHER**

Listen, Godber, you watch your favourite television programme – *Kojak* – Telly Savalas, you think he's such a great actor. Well you know why he's always opening filing cabinets and looking at his shirt cuffs? Eh? 'Cos his lines are written all over the place.

**WARREN**

(*Rising*) And that's cheating.

**FLETCHER**

Right. But who gives a rat's? Listen, son, cheating is only another word for conning. Putting one over. And if that was a crime, the whole country would be doing porridge. I tell you what would be a crime. You turning down this golden opportunity we are handing you.

**WARREN**

We took a big risk to get that for you, Len.

**LENNIE**

All right, I appreciate your efforts. You want my thanks – thanks. But I'll do it my way.

***He lays down the envelope, stands, walks to his bunk and lies down.***

**FLETCHER**

If you do it your way, you ain't honest, you're dumb. 'Cos if you do it your way – you'll fail.

**LENNIE**

There comes a point in everyone's life

when the only person you're cheating is yourself. It's like cheating at patience.

**WARREN**

Fletcher does that an' all.

**FLETCHER**

Come on, Warren, what's the use? Let's leave him.

***He and Warren make to leave the cell. Fletcher pauses.***

**FLETCHER**

You're at the crossroads of life, Godber. You make your own breaks, son, 'cos when you get out there, people are going to give you precious few. You can go up for a job one day with all the qualifications in the world and get pipped by some nurk who's never passed an exam in his life. But he's got the right accent, plays for the local rugby club and he ain't never been in no nick!

***Fletcher throws the envelope to the floor, turns and leaves the cell with Warren.***

***Lennie sits at the table looking at the envelope lying there. He wrestles with his conscience. Then he glances back to the open cell door. He picks up the envelope, pauses for a moment, then slowly opens the flap.***

***At that moment, Warren peers into the cell through a crack in the door. He smiles.***

## 6. ASSOCIATION AREA

***Prisoners are sitting around playing cards, draughts, etc. Fletcher and Warren are sitting at a table.***

**WARREN**

Lennie should be out of his exam soon.

**FLETCHER**

Yeah, I wonder how he got on? Mind you, you must never let him know that you know.

**WARREN**

'Course not. Guvnor will be pleased when he passes 'cos Slade Prison's got a terrible academic record, Fletch.

**FLETCHER**

Oh I don't know. Chap got his 'O' Level in Spanish last year – what's his name – Gomez. Hey here he comes.

***Lennie comes down to them.***

**FLETCHER**

Hello then, son. How did the exam go?

**LENNIE**

Some questions were a bit tough, but it weren't as bad as I thought it were going to be.

**FLETCHER**

No, I'll bet it wasn't.

**LENNIE**

I think my essay was pretty fair. Me spelling's a bit dodgy like, but they can't have any complaints about the factual content and that's what counts most, isn't it?

**FLETCHER**

Oh yes, that's what counts. Anyhow, asides from your essay, what about the more technical questions then? The dates?

**LENNIE**

I'll just keep me fingers crossed. But I will admit to being quietly confident.

**FLETCHER**

Quietly confident, say no more.

**LENNIE**

I'll tell you one thing, though. Pass or fail, at least I have the satisfaction of knowing I did it on me own.

**FLETCHER**

You what?

**LENNIE**

I did it on me own efforts.

**WARREN**

Your own efforts!!

**FLETCHER**

Er, Godber, would you like to rephrase that? Bearing in mind that some of us may know a little more than what you thinks we do.

**LENNIE**

I'm just saying I did it my way. With no help from no one.

**FLETCHER**

Listen, Godber, there are many sorts of crime and we're all here for most of them. But the one thing I can't abide is hypocrisy!

**WARREN**

That's the worst offence of all in my book an' all.

**LENNIE**

So?

**FLETCHER**

So cut out the holier-than-thou attitude, Godber, you steaming hypocrite. He saw you through the crack in the door – Warren saw you look at those papers.

**LENNIE**

Yeah I clocked them, but it didn't make no difference.

**FLETCHER**

How can you say that!

**LENNIE**

Who actually lifted them?

**WARREN**

Me.

**LENNIE**

Next time, pick someone who can read.

**FLETCHER**

What?

**LENNIE**

You nicked the Biology papers.

# 3 SERIES THREE

## EPISODE SIX: FINAL STRETCH

### 1. VISITING ROOM

***Barrowclough is walking down the rows of visitors and prisoners. Ingrid is visiting Fletcher; Mrs Godber, Lennie and Jarvis (a tough unpleasant-looking inmate) is being visited by his brother.***

**INGRID**

I know it's only Feb, but if you book your holiday now it's ever so cheap. So me and Barbara, you don't know Barbara, she's my friend at work – we fancy going to Rimini. That's on the Adriatic. We thought Italy because your money goes much further there. That's 'cos the lira's the only European currency what's as bad off as the pound.

***Fletcher has been listening with little interest. He casts dubious looks at Barrowclough, who seems to be hovering nearby.***

**INGRID**

It's either Rimini or Portofino – which is supposed to be rather smart. I believe Rex Harrison goes there.

**FLETCHER**

Anyhow, the riot is set for Tuesday, we're going to barricade ourselves in with half a dozen screws as hostages with which we can bargain for better living conditions.

***Barrowclough has heard this. As he was meant to. He takes the bait, whipping round on Fletcher.***

**FLETCHER**

(*Got him*) I knew he was earwigging.

**INGRID**

What?

**FLETCHER**

Listening to every word he was, of our supposedly private conversation.

**BARROWCLOUGH**

I was doing no such thing, Fletcher.

**FLETCHER**

Yes, you were, Mr Barrowclough. Shouldn't be allowed, hovering.

**BARROWCLOUGH**

It wouldn't be necessary if we could

trust you people not to pass each other contraband.

**FLETCHER**

Oh I see, it's contraband now, is it? Hear that!

***He has a packet of cigarettes in front of him.***

**FLETCHER**

Here, check this. She's brung me half a pound of hashish in there, she has.

***With this, he throws the packet across the table towards Barrowclough, but it falls on the floor.***

**BARROWCLOUGH**

There's no need to take that attitude, Fletcher.

***He bends to pick up the packet. As he does so, the entire row of visitors flick contraband across the table to their loved ones. It disappears instantly – just before Barrowclough straightens up, handing over the packet.***

**BARROWCLOUGH**

Here you are – now just carry on.

**INGRID**

Where was I?

**BARROWCLOUGH**

Rimini or Portofino.

***He moves on.***

**INGRID**

Oh yes, well we was thinking of May before it gets too touristy –

**FLETCHER**

Listen, girl, has it not occurred to you that it's a bit tactless in front of your old dad. This conversation about foreign climes.

**INGRID**

Oh.

**FLETCHER**

I mean you know –

**INGRID**

(*Sympathetically*) You've passed the halfway mark, Dad. Less to do than's already done. With parole, only another year – just under.

**FLETCHER**

Oh, is that all – that's nothing, just a mere bagatelle, isn't it?

**INGRID**

Getting rough, is it?

**FLETCHER**

Oh you know me, I'll survive. It's just every time I see you or Marion or Raymond I realise you're all grown up a bit more. Without me.

**INGRID**

I grew up before you come in, Dad.

**FLETCHER**

Oh you had. Grew up too soon, you did. You somehow bypassed puberty.

**INGRID**

No, I didn't. You bypassed my puberty by going into Maidstone.

**FLETCHER**

Nevertheless it has to be said, you was wearing a 36D in Junior School.

**INGRID**

Not my fault, that's nature.

**FLETCHER**

All right, all right put 'em away. forewent my parental responsibilities during your most formative years. Same with young Marion.

**INGRID**

Oh she'll be all right. Don't you worry, Marion will always end up on her own two feet.

**FLETCHER**

If she ever gets herself off her back.

***Ingrid looks shocked.***

**FLETCHER**

No, no, I didn't mean that to sound like it did. I mean, she's a lazy little so-and-so, that's all. She still work at Woolies?

**INGRID**

She don't need to, Dad. 'Cos her boyfriend Ricky's ever so well off. He's got three cars. He gave her one for Christmas.

**FLETCHER**

I'll bet he did. Did she get a present as well?

**INGRID**

Dad!

**FLETCHER**

Well . . .

**INGRID**

If she marries Ricky, she'll want for nothing.

**FLETCHER**

If. What's he do, this Ricky?

**INGRID**

He runs these cheap charter aeroplane trips.

**FLETCHER**

What's it called? Gullible's Travels?

**INGRID**

No – Sunset Tours. It was him what put me and Barbara on to Rimini.

**FLETCHER**

What I'm trying to say is, his three cars was bought from the deposits scraped together by the likes of you.

**INGRID**

Dad! I hate to hear you talk like this. You never give no one the benefit of the doubt. You're getting so cynical in your old age.

**FLETCHER**

Listen, it ain't no bed of roses in here.

**INGRID**

You've got nothing to bleat about. You chose to live outside the law, so you accept the consequences. What was it you told young Lennie? If you can't do the time, don't do the crime!

**FLETCHER**

How d'you know I told young Godber that?

**INGRID**

He told me in one of his letters.

***She turns to look at Lennie and waves. Lennie waves back.***

**FLETCHER**

Oh – so you've been keeping in touch, have you?

**INGRID**

Only pen pals.

**FLETCHER**

Yeah well, but he's going out next week, isn't he? Won't need no stamps on your letters then, will you?

**INGRID**

Subject to his parole board.

**FLETCHER**

Oh he'll smarm his way past that lot with his naïve charm, his boyish smile and his one flaming 'O' Level in geography. Probably get lost as soon as he's outside the gates.

**INGRID**

That's why you're so grumpy! He's going out and you're going to miss him.

**FLETCHER**

Miss him? That's not the point. His going out reminds me that I ain't going out. I'm staying in. While he's out I'll still be in, won't I?

**INGRID**

Won't be too long, Dad. Tell you what, soon as your release date is set I'll get in touch with Ricky and he can book you some lovely holiday in the sun.

**FLETCHER**

Yeah, well after Marion and you, why not me and your mam? Then apart from young Raymond he'll have done the whole family.

## 2. PRISON YARD

***Barrowclough comes out followed by several prisoners. They file out and walk away.***

***Jarvis calls out to Godber.***

**JARVIS**

Godber!

***Godber waits until Jarvis catches him up. They walk along together. Barrowclough is watching the prisoners. More prisoners come out of the door, including Fletcher. The prisoners are walking away. Godber and Jarvis start fighting. Barrowclough is locking the door when he notices the fight.***

**BARROWCLOUGH**

Stop that – just a minute!

***Fletcher is walking along. He spots the fight.***

***Barrowclough runs to break up the fight.***

## 3. MACKAY'S OFFICE

***Lennie and Jarvis are standing side by side in front of Mackay. Barrowclough is in attendance.***

**MACKAY**
What's all this about then?

**LENNIE**
What's all what about, Mr Mackay?

**MACKAY**
Brawling in the yard.

**LENNIE**
Weren't brawling, sir.

**JARVIS**
Just fooling around. Playful high spirits, sir.

**LENNIE**
We were just re-enacting a big moment from last Sunday's football on the telly. The bit where Peter Shilton dived at Charlie George's feet.

**MACKAY**
I don't recall Charlie George smashing a dustbin lid over Peter Shilton's skull. Not even in the action replay.

**LENNIE**
He would have done if he'd had one handy.

**MACKAY**
Don't be funny with me, Godber.

**LENNIE**
Not trying to be, sir.

**MACKAY**
You were brawling.

**LENNIE**
Wasn't sir, honest. Got me parole board next week. Daft to jeopardise that, wouldn't I?

**MACKAY**
You would indeed, sonny.

**JARVIS**
Len's my mate, sir. Him and me are like that.

***He holds up two crossed fingers.***

**MACKAY**
(*Questioningly*) Mr Barrowclough?

**BARROWCLOUGH**
(*Uncertain*) Well, I was some distance away, but it did seem to be a vicious altercation.

**LENNIE**
Oh, from a way's away it could easily have been misconstrued. If you'd been close up you could have seen we were smiling.

***He smiles briefly by way of demonstration.***

**JARVIS**
Straight up, sir.

**MACKAY**
You're no stranger to violence, Jarvis. Your only interest in football was supervising violence at the Stretford End. It's no coincidence that since your imprisonment football hooliganism has declined.

**JARVIS**

Didn't know no better then, sir. But thanks to people like Len . . .

**LENNIE**

It's true, sir. Look . . .

***He turns to Jarvis and says, challengingly.***

**LENNIE**

Manchester United are rubbish compared to Villa.

**JARVIS**

(*Evenly*) You could be right, Len.

**LENNIE**

Doesn't that prove it, sir?

***Mackay looks towards Barrowclough, as if to say can you believe these two?***

**LENNIE**

I admit we got a bit boisterous in the yard.

**JARVIS**

That's true. But to me, sir, Len's family.

**LENNIE**

(*Touched*) D'you mean that, Jarvis?

**JARVIS**

Cross me heart.

**LENNIE**

Well, I'm touched. You don't know what that means to me.

**MACKAY**

I'm in two minds, Mr Barrowclough. Should I give them solitary confinement or announce their engagement?

## 4. ASSOCIATION AREA

**BARROWCLOUGH**

Back to your cells. And think yourselves damned lucky!

**LENNIE/JARVIS TOGETHER**

Thank you, Mr Barrowclough.

***They walk along the landing. Barrowclough watches them and then walks off.***

***Jarvis and Lennie are walking along.***

**LENNIE**

Got out of that then.

**JARVIS**

Bloody did.

**LENNIE**

Did well in there, us. Abbott and Costello.

**JARVIS**

Morecambe and Wise.

**LENNIE**

We were daft though. Having a go in front of the screws.

**JARVIS**

Should have found somewhere private.

**LENNIE**
We will do. (*Stopping*) 'Cos I'm going to punch your lights out, musclehead!

***He goes.***

## 5. FLETCHER'S CELL

***It is night time.***

**FLETCHER**
(*Appalled*) I thought I knew you, Godber.

**LENNIE**
If someone provokes you, what you s'posed to do, back off?

**FLETCHER**
If you're up for parole next Monday, most certainly, yes.

**LENNIE**
He made certain remarks.

**FLETCHER**
What remarks?

**LENNIE**
Never you mind. Suffice to say I found them insulting and offensive.

**FLETCHER**
If my release was in the balance here, ain't an insult in the world that would prevent me from turning the other cheek.

**LENNIE**
Have to draw the line somewhere.

**FLETCHER**
Wrong. You could bring in the question of the virtue of my old woman; call me a poof; even tell me I molest goats – water off a duck's back to me – or in this case, off a goat's back.

**LENNIE**
P'raps you haven't the same pride as what I do.

**FLETCHER**
Oh, it's the old pride stakes, is it? The old self-respect.

**LENNIE**
It matters.

**FLETCHER**
Self-respect is something you preserve on the outside. No such thing inside – you forfeited that when you were sent down. Anyhow, people's opinion in here matters naff all.

**LENNIE**
Not doing it for them. Doing it for me.

**FLETCHER**
I was talking to my daughter today.

**LENNIE**
Ingrid?

**FLETCHER**
Yeah, your pen pal. She says, you know, I don't give anyone the benefit of the doubt. Thinks I'm cynical. She's probably right. I just thought someone like you could just about make it out there but . . .

**LENNIE**
But what?

**FLETCHER**
You obviously ain't got the bottle.

**LENNIE**
If I hadn't got no bottle, would I be taking on Jarvis?

**FLETCHER**
That ain't bottle, that's stupidity. Tell you what does take bottle in life – knowing when to turn the other cheek. Like Gary Cooper in *High Noon*, Alan Ladd in *Shane*, or . . . Gregory Peck in *The Big Country*, Glenn Ford in *The Fastest Gun Alive*.

**LENNIE**
I've seen those pictures.

**FLETCHER**
Then you know what I mean.

**LENNIE**
Just answer me one question.

**FLETCHER**
Gladly.

**LENNIE**
How come all them films ended in the worst fights you ever seen? Teeth and whiskers all over the place.

**FLETCHER**
I'll tell you why, sonny Jim. Because Hollywood had to pander to the public's insatiable thirst for senseless violence.

**LENNIE**
No, you're wrong. Those films raised a moral question which had to be answered by the last reel. A man has to do . . .

**FLETCHER**
(*Joining him*) . . .what a man has to do – yes, yes, oh blimey it's Batman, is it?

**LENNIE**
There is a basic truth there though.

**FLETCHER**
Let me ask you one question.

**LENNIE**
Go on.

**FLETCHER**
(*Going over to Lennie*) Would Gary Cooper and all them others have done what they done had they been up for parole next Monday? And would they have walked into the final shoot-out so willingly had they known their adversary was Reggie, the Red Menace, Jarvis? You see, there's two sorts of violence inside. One that's born out of frustration and despair, and one that comes from the likes of Reggie Jarvis. A man full of Mancunian macho 'cos he's got five years to do and nothing to lose. You've got everything to lose. Unless freedom ain't everything. Then, well . . .

**LENNIE**
Listen, Fletch, I appreciate your concern but it's just something I have to do.

**FLETCHER**
I'll make one final appeal to your sense, Godber. Then I'll wash my hands of it.

**LENNIE**
Go on then.

**FLETCHER**

There are three good reasons why you shouldn't take on Jarvis. A – you could jeopardise your parole; and B – it offends civilised sensibilities.

**LENNIE**

What about C?

**FLETCHER**

C – it's obvious, ain't it? C – he'll bleedin' murder you!

## 6. RECREATION ROOM

***A few prisoners are playing cards or smoking. The TV is off. Fletcher sits playing dominoes with Warren.***

**FLETCHER**

Knock.

***He puts a matchstick in the kitty.***

**WARREN**

Four–five.

**FLETCHER**

Knock.

**WARREN**

Double five.

**FLETCHER**

(*With rising irritability*) Knock.

**WARREN**

Five–one.

***Barrowclough comes in.***

**BARROWCLOUGH**

Excuse me, Fletcher.

**FLETCHER**

Oh dear me, interruption – void game.

***He throws all his dominoes on the table and withdraws his matchsticks.***

**WARREN**

I only had one to play.

**FLETCHER**

Well, that's hard luck, me old son. But we can hardly continue playing when Mr Barrowclough has something to say, can we?

**BARROWCLOUGH**

There was no need to break up your game, Fletcher.

**WARREN**

See!

**FLETCHER**

(*Pity!*) Too late now. Showed me hand, ain't I?

***Warren disgustedly throws his remaining domino in. Barrowclough examines their respective hands.***

**BARROWCLOUGH**

Oh, you'd have beaten him hollow there, Warren.

**FLETCHER**

(*Mixing the dominoes*) Matter of opinion. So what's the problem then?

**BARROWCLOUGH**

Just a word in your ear.

***Fletcher indicates Warren.***

**FLETCHER**

Oh. Try this one – it's further away from *him*.

**BARROWCLOUGH**

Oh, Warren's all right, he's a friend.

**FLETCHER**

Friend of whose?

**BARROWCLOUGH**

Godber's.

**FLETCHER**

What *about* Godber?

**BARROWCLOUGH**

Him and Jarvis –

**FLETCHER**

What about Jarvis?

**BARROWCLOUGH**

You know.

**FLETCHER**

Do I?

**BARROWCLOUGH**

You were there – after visiting – in the yard.

**FLETCHER**

Was I? Where was this then?

**BARROWCLOUGH**

I must say, you're not much of a conversationalist, Fletcher.

**FLETCHER**

What's you on about, Mr Barrowclough?

**BARROWCLOUGH**

(*Darkly*) Something's brewing.

**FLETCHER**

Oh good. Two sugars.

**BARROWCLOUGH**

You know very well what I mean.

**FLETCHER**

Do I? Oh good.

**BARROWCLOUGH**

I'll say no more.

**FLETCHER**

Yes, I think you've said enough.

**BARROWCLOUGH**

As long as we understand each other.

**FLETCHER**

Perfectly, Mr Barrowclough.

**BARROWCLOUGH**

Good.

***He goes off. Fletcher starts to select dominoes for a new game.***

**WARREN**

What were all that about?

**FLETCHER**

Godber and Jarvis had a barney in the yard. The screws know about it – want it stopped before it goes any further. If it does, bad for all of us, specially the lad. My down, double six.

**WARREN**

I didn't hear him say all that.

**FLETCHER**

Read between the lines, son. Your go.

**WARREN**

(*Peering at his dominoes*) Would you believe it – I'm knocking.

**FLETCHER**
In the kitty. Six–two.

***Lennie approaches.***

**WARREN**
Oh, look, look, it's Lennie.

**LENNIE**
Hello, Fletch, Warren.

***He sits down.***

**FLETCHER**
Never mind him – have you got a two?

**WARREN**
No, but it's a void game, isn't it? Interruption, like.

***He tries to gather the dominoes but Fletcher stops him.***

**FLETCHER**
Naff off.

**WARREN**
That's what you did when Barra came up.

**FLETCHER**
Barra's a screw – different, ain't it?

**LENNIE**
What did he want?

**FLETCHER**
The topic was senseless violence, the prevention of.

**LENNIE**
If he wants to stop that, he should get the telly fixed. It's been bust for a week.

**WARREN**
Jarvis broke that.

**FLETCHER**
Only because he couldn't get a good picture of his favourite programme – *The Magic Roundabout*. I tried to tell him – I said if Florence and Zebedee appear a little blurred, you fix it by adjusting the fine tuner with a delicate twist of the wrist. You don't chuck the set against the wall – mind you, that usually does the trick.

***Jarvis enters. Only Warren notices.***

**WARREN**
Change the subject, change the subject.

**FLETCHER**
What's wrong with you? Got a sore throat?

**WARREN**
I said change the subject.

**FLETCHER**
Yeah – and I saw your lips move.

***Warren tries to warn them about Jarvis with a subtle indication of head but Jarvis is already upon them. He thumps the TV set twice.***

**FLETCHER**
Are you knocking again?

**JARVIS**
Godber . . .

**LENNIE**
Hello, Jarvis.

**JARVIS**
Score to settle, right?

**LENNIE**
Any time.

**JARVIS**
Up to you.

**LENNIE**
Ready when you are.

**JARVIS**
What's wrong with now?

**LENNIE**

Why not? Telly's broke.
(*Getting up*) Nothing else to do.

**WARREN**

I think I'll go t' lavatory.

***He starts to leave.***

**FLETCHER**

(*Getting up*) You sit down – nothing's going to happen so just hold your horses. Or hold whatever you have to hold.

**JARVIS**

None of your business, Fletch.

**FLETCHER**

It's everyone's business, Jarvis.

***He goes over to them.***

**FLETCHER**

A happy nick is a placid nick. Cause a rumpus, you naff it up for all of us.

**JARVIS**

Listen, my gripe's with him. But I'll stuff the both of you if you want.

***Fletcher, backs off to beside the TV set.***

**FLETCHER**

Shut your face, toilet mouth.

**WARREN**

That's reminds me (*Getting up*) I really do have to go to the lavatory.

**JARVIS**

I'm going to have you for that.

***Everyone in the room reacts to the tension. Jarvis walks up to Fletcher. Fletcher quickly picks up the TV set which he holds threateningly above his head. Mackay comes in.***

**MACKAY**

(*Offscreen*) Everybody freeze!
What's going on here?

**FLETCHER**

Oh we was just trying to fix the telly, Mr Mackay.

**MACKAY**

With the set above your head?

**FLETCHER**

Yeah, I was just trying the vertical hold.

**WARREN**

(*Amazed*) Hey, look – we got a picture.

***Sure enough, to everyone's astonishment, the set starts to work. All the prisoners, except Fletcher, immediately sit down, cross their legs and start watching the programme. Mackay turns up the sound. Then walks off as they all sit enjoying the TV.***

**7. CELL**

***Fletcher is in his cell darning his socks when Warren walks in.***

**WARREN**

Fletch.

**FLETCHER**

What are you doing? I told you to tag Godber. To never let him out of your sight.

**WARREN**
That's what I've come to tell you. It's all right, he's on duty. And Jarvis is in the yard with some of his cronies.

**FLETCHER**
Well, we'd better tail Godber when he comes out of the cookhouse. It's the weekend now. This is when it's going to happen, in' it?

**WARREN**
I had 'opes you'd've talked Len out of it. If anyone could, you could.

**FLETCHER**
Well, I ain't. Which is a testimony to his pigheadedness.

**WARREN**
Maybe we should look on the bright side. Maybe the fight won't be tumbled. And maybe Len'll do all right. I mean, he knows a bit. He made the boxing squad.

**FLETCHER**
The boxing squad. Oh yes, the noble art. The Queensbury Rules, the fairplay and the gumshield, and all that rubbish. While Lennie is still shaking hands Jarvis will have fractured his groin with his No. 9 prison issue boot, won't he?

**WARREN**
Could we nobble him? Drugs like?

**FLETCHER**
There is some animal tranquilliser on the farm. How much do you need to tranquillise an animal like Jarvis? Not to mention the problem of who goes and sticks a hypodermic in his backside without him noticing. No, there's only one thing for it, you know – I'll have to take on Jarvis myself.

**WARREN**
You? (*Laughs*) D'you think you can put Jarvis out of action?

**FLETCHER**
No, you nurk. But it's Saturday morning now, ain't it? If I fight him and we're discovered, it's automatically the cooler for forty-eight hours and he won't come out till after Len's been up for his parole Monday morning.

**WARREN**
But hang on, if you're discovered you'll go to the cooler an' all.

**FLETCHER**
Yeah, well.

**WARREN**
You're going to blot your copy book.

**FLETCHER**
Yeah, well. Few weeks' remission won't do me any harm. But listen, I'm going to need your help Warren, 'cos I wouldn't last two minutes with Jarvis. The moment anything happens, you fetch the screws and you move like greased lightning. Right?

**WARREN**
Hey, wait a minute, Fletch. If I tip off the screws that makes me a snitch.

**FLETCHER**
If you don't tip them off, son, that makes me a corpse.

**8. PRISON YARD**

*A group of prisoners are playing pitch and toss, including Jarvis. The Prison Officers are chatting. Fletcher and Warren come round the corner of the building and see Jarvis.*

*They look at him, then at a Prison Officer.*

*Fletcher is walking across the yard and he sees a group approaching. When he reaches them he speaks.*

**FLETCHER**

Jarvis!

**JARVIS**

Oh hello, Fletch. You want in?

**FLETCHER**

You what?

**JARVIS**

Want to join in, like?

**FLETCHER**

Jarvis? I thought you and me had some unfinished business. From the television room, remember?

**JARVIS**

Oh that, don't be daft.

**FLETCHER**

I mean what I said, Jarvis.

**JARVIS**

No, you didn't. I know what you were doing – trying to protect the kid.

*Jarvis turns back to the game.*

*Fletcher moves into Jarvis.*

**FLETCHER**

Jarvis!

**JARVIS**

What?

**FLETCHER**

You know when I called you toilet mouth?

**JARVIS**

Yeah.

**FLETCHER**

I ain't taking it back.

**JARVIS**

Well, you're right, me old mate.

My language is a bit colourful.

Me wife's always on at me about it.

I try you know, but I can do sod all about it.

*He returns to the game.*

*Fletcher turns and starts to move away. But an idea strikes him and he turns back. Fletcher returns to Jarvis and taps him on the shoulder.*

**FLETCHER**

Jarvis.

**JARVIS**

Now what?

**FLETCHER**

Talking about your wife . . .

**JARVIS**

What about my wife?

**FLETCHER**

You're luckier than most of us. I mean, when a bloke's doing a long stretch, you know, his old lady's out looking for nooky, in' she?

**JARVIS**

Speak for yourself.

**FLETCHER**

I am. That's why I'm saying you're luckier than most. I 'eard your old lady's only been unfaithful to you twice.

**JARVIS**

Twice?

**FLETCHER**

Once with the milkman and once with the Household Cavalry.

***Jarvis thinks, then laughs.***

**JARVIS**

Huh, huh, huh – good one that, Fletch.

**FLETCHER**

Oh gawd.

***He turns and starts to leave.***

***Crusher walks past Jarvis who calls out to him.***

**JARVIS**

Here, Crusher.

**CRUSHER**

What?

**JARVIS**

Listen to this.

***He laughs at the group and turns back to Crusher.***

**JARVIS**

I heard that your old lady's only been unfaithful to you twice.

***Crusher says nothing.***

**JARVIS**

Once with the milkman and once with the Household Cavalry.

***The camera shows the back of Jarvis's head and Crusher's fist punching it. Jarvis falls backwards.***

***Suddenly the whole group starts fighting.***

***Prison Officers start running about blowing whistles.***

***The fight rages on. Fletcher walks off.***

**FLETCHER**

All right then, I owe you one.

***The Prison Officers run up to the group and break the fight up.***

**9. CELL**

***Fletcher is busying himself with his back to the cell door, when Lennie walks in.***

***He has a smile on his face and is about to enjoy imparting some news when Fletcher, without turning around, says.***

**FLETCHER**

Congratulations.

**LENNIE**

(*Taken aback*) What?

**FLETCHER**

Congratulations. On getting your parole.

**LENNIE**
I was just about to tell you that.

**FLETCHER**
Well, I knows, don't I?

**LENNIE**
How?

**FLETCHER**
It pays me to, don't it?

**LENNIE**
But I only left the board an hour ago.

**FLETCHER**
Son, son. I works the admin block, don't I?

**LENNIE**
Oh yes, of course.

**FLETCHER**
(*Walking over to Lennie*)
Anyhow, well done.

***They shake hands.***

**FLETCHER**
Tomorrow morning then.

**LENNIE**
Yeah, I'd better get packed up. It's only when you move that you realise how much stuff you got.

**FLETCHER**
Yeah.

**LENNIE**
'Ere, the Governor was ever so nice about it. He let me ring my mum.

**FLETCHER**
I know.

**LENNIE**
How?

**FLETCHER**
I listened in on the extension.

**LENNIE**
Fletch!

**FLETCHER**
I wanted to share in your elation.

**LENNIE**
Oh I see.

**FLETCHER**
She was chuffed. Your mum.

**LENNIE**
Quite emotional really. For her. Wish I could tell me dad . . . if I only knew where the old bastard was.

**FLETCHER**
Well look at it another way. Your dad's absence meant he never knew you went in in the first place.

**LENNIE**
I suppose so. Come in handy today, he did.

**FLETCHER**
How?

**LENNIE**
Well I told the parole board that I thought my father's desertion was a contributory factor towards my temporary diversion from the straight and narrow. Not in so many words though.

**FLETCHER**
You're learning, ain't you?

**LENNIE**
(*Sitting*) Thanks to you, Fletch.

**FLETCHER**
Yeah, well.

**LENNIE**
If it hadn't been for you, I'd've messed this parole up, you know.

**FLETCHER**
True.

**LENNIE**
I mean, the fact that you risked solitary confinement and loss of your own remission . . . well, I mean . . . well, that's real friendship.

**FLETCHER**
Look, there was no way I was going to let you jeopardise your parole, son.

**LENNIE**
I realise that now. But I never realised it meant so much to you.

**FLETCHER**
'Course it did. I had three to one on you getting out.

***Lennie thinks about this, then decides not to believe it.***

**LENNIE**
You don't fool me, Fletch. You did that out of the kindness of your heart.

**FLETCHER**
If you believe that, then you are a stupid sentimental nurk.

**LENNIE**
No I'm not.

**FLETCHER**
Well, you're certainly stupid. As your behaviour over the Jarvis affair demonstrated only too clearly.

**LENNIE**
I promise you, Fletch, I did have a reason for reacting like I did. Jarvis came up to me and made an obscene remark.

**FLETCHER**
(*Putting envelope down*) Did that affront your Brummagen sensibilities then?

**LENNIE**
Yes, it did. 'Cos the remark concerned what he'd like to do to your daughter Ingrid.

**FLETCHER**
What?

**LENNIE**
To put it delicately, he indicated his carnal desires towards her, then reckoned that he fancied his chances, on account of her sexual proclivities.

**FLETCHER**
(*Licking envelope*) Well, she's always had those. Ever since she was thirteen. So – you was defending my family's honour, was it?

**LENNIE**
Seemed a good reason – I owe a lot to you, Fletch. I'd've never made the distance without you.

**FLETCHER**
(*Sitting*) Look, don't make me out to be no hero.

**LENNIE**
I wasn't. Father figure maybe.

**FLETCHER**
I ain't been no great shakes as a dad. 'Fact I ain't been no great shakes as anything.

**LENNIE**
You have to me. And I won't let you down, Fletch. I ain't coming back.
**FLETCHER**
Oh we all say that. But you'd better mean it, Godber. You've got your life before you. Out the last twenty years I've spent eleven of 'em doing porridge. That ain't life, that's marking time. I'm not moaning. What's done's done. But it's a terrible waste.
**LENNIE**
I won't be back. Given the breaks.
**FLETCHER**
Make the breaks. No alibis. No ifs and buts. You can make it. You're not stupid, and you're not evil. You're a good lad. Well, nuff said. Hope you're leaving me your snout.
**LENNIE**
Only right.
***He gives Fletcher the tobacco from his box.***
**FLETCHER**
Chocolate?
**LENNIE**
Fruit and nut.
***He hands Fletcher the chocolate.***
**FLETCHER**
(*Looking in box*) Other bit. (*Lennie gives him it*) And first thing you do when you go out, you do for me.
**LENNIE**
What?
**FLETCHER**
As soon as you get off the train at New Street, Birmingham, you go straight into a pub and order a pint of best bitter and drink to your old mate.
**LENNIE**
I'm not going to Birmingham. I was thinking of Rimini actually, with a friend. We thought May 'cos it's not so touristy then. Or perhaps Portofino . . .

**10. CELL**

***Fletcher is lying on his bunk reading a newspaper.***

**10A. PRISON LANDING**

***Mackay comes upstairs. He pauses and then looks around, moves on. Mackay walks along the landing and stops outside Fletcher's cell. He goes in.***

**10B. CELL**

*Mackay enters.*
**MACKAY**
Fletcher?
**FLETCHER**
Good afternoon, sir.
**MACKAY**
Good afternoon, sir?
**FLETCHER**
Your title, in' it, sir?
**MACKAY**
True. I did not expect to hear it so readily from your lips.
**FLETCHER**
Why make waves, eh? Only ten months to do if I keep my nose clean.

**MACKAY**

Throwing in the towel, are we Fletcher?

**FLETCHER**

I just want to get home.

**MACKAY**

(*Moving nearer*) I've noticed a certain change in your attitude since laddo's release. Our customary ill-feeling seems to be missing. You seem to have lost a lot of that brash Cockney lairyness. Or are you just acknowledging that the system always wins.

**FLETCHER**

Nobody wins, Mr Mackay. That's what's so tragic.

**MACKAY**

Normally I would have hesitated about putting a sprog in here, Fletcher.

**FLETCHER**

Oh yes. Got some company coming in, have I?

**MACKAY**

In the past you have not been the healthiest of influences on first-time offenders. But now I don't think I have too much to fear. (*Crossing to the window*) Got a young lad called Nicholson moving in.

**FLETCHER**

Not a Scot, is he? I mean, we do draw the line somewhere.

**MACKAY**

(*Turning to Fletcher*) No, he's from Sunderland.

**FLETCHER**

Dangerously near.

**MACKAY**

He's a tearaway. Lashes out. Doesn't think. I have a feeling that the new quiescent Fletcher might be just what he needs.

**FLETCHER**

Whatever you think, Mr Mackay.

**MACKAY**

(*Moving nearer*) So you'll keep an eye on him?

**FLETCHER**

Be difficult to ignore him in a room this size.

**MACKAY**

No, but perhaps you'll show him the ropes, show him what you've learnt.

***He walks towards the door.***

**FLETCHER**

What have I learnt, Mr Mackay?

**MACKAY**

(*Crossing over to Fletcher*) That there's no point to bucking the system.

**FLETCHER**

Oh yes. Glad to, Mr Mackay. Sir. I'll watch out for him. I shall simply tell him three things. Bide your time (*Holds up one fingers*), keep your nose clean . . . (*Two fingers*) and don't let the bastards grind you down . . .

***Fletcher puts up the third finger.***

# 3 MEMORIES

**Colin Farrell** (Norris in 'Happy Release')

'Before being cast in "Happy Release", the fifth episode in series two, I had performed very little in front of a live TV audience. At that time I was mainly a theatre person and, in classical or modern works, considered that comedy was probably my forte. Faced with a live audience in a TV studio, however, I felt a complete plonker.

'I hated it. Should I time my lines in reaction to the audience, or totally ignore them? Should I compromise my angle to the camera in order to give the studio audience a better view? None of the stagecraft – or such camera craft as I possessed at that time – learned over the previous dozen or so years, seemed to apply and after two or three unhappy experiences, I made up my mind that TV comedy shows involving anybody other than the technicians and my fellow actors on the studio floor, were simply not my bag. Then along came Sydney Lotterby with an offer that I would have been mad to refuse.

'Nasty Norris was a character that leapt off the page at me. Instinctively, I knew how I would play him, and heard his whining tone of voice from the moment I read the first words. It was a peach. What's more, I would get the chance to work with the likes of Ronnie Barker and the wonderful Fulton Mackay, not to mention Sydney Lotterby – one of the very best of our TV comedy directors.

'Much of the action takes place in the prison sick ward because Fletcher has broken his leg. My character is across the ward complaining of an ingrowing toenail. In rehearsals, I was amazed to find that the old man in the bed opposite was being played by a friendly young chap much the same age as myself. It was, of course, David Jason. David used to come in hours before the rest of the cast to be fitted with layers of latex wrinkles and make-up, topped with a convincing grey wig. He was unrecognisable.

'Whoever had the courage and imagination to cast him in that role deserves a medal. His was a semi-regular character in the series and it gave him a marvellous kick-start to a highly successful career; but it would never happen today. Nowadays you are expected to turn up to a casting session looking exactly like the character you might be playing, and I can't imagine David would fancy travelling up to White City covered in latex!

'I think "Happy Release" must be the most repeated episode of the whole series; in fact, I've come to rely on it to pay off my overdraft at least once a year, and I need hardly say that I learned more about playing TV comedy from Ronnie and Sydney and the rest of that fantastic team, in a few short days, than almost any time before or since, so when the offer came to go into Yorkshire Television's *In Loving Memory*, where Dame Thora Hird continued my education, I felt equal to the task.'

**Christopher Biggins** (Lukewarm in the series)
'In 1974 I was a young actor – twenty-six years old, in fact, and terribly starstruck. When I went to visit Syd Lotterby, the director and producer of a new sitcom set in prison, I had no idea that it was written by Dick Clement and Ian La Frenais, and starred my all-time favourite comedy actor, Ronnie Barker.

'When my agent, Gillian Coffey, rang and told me I had got the part of Lukewarm, I was over the moon; I immediately rang my parents who were thrilled. So I suddenly became part of history by being involved in one of the most popular and, thank God, most repeated sitcoms ever.

'My first day was nerve-racking and yet so exciting. Ronnie was enchanting, as were the rest of the cast, and after the read-through one knew we were on to something rather special. Ronnie was incredibly generous and if during rehearsals he felt one of his lines was better off said by another actor, he would give it over with no complaints. It was so good to work with a star who was considering the whole product; it was a lesson I took on and, hopefully, have always tried to repeat in my career. I have come across the opposite in other stars I've worked with – not everyone's like Ronnie.

'One of my fondest memories was in the episode "Men Without Women". Fletcher wrote a letter on behalf of all the inmates to their respective wives telling them of their love of the fairer sex. When the wives were travelling to the prison on the bus, one of the wives started reading out aloud the contents of the letter, when suddenly all the women realised that their letters were the same. But one of the biggest laughs in a studio I've ever heard was when Lukewarm's boyfriend brought out the same letter – it was a moment of comic genius.

'After the first series had been completed, Ronnie gave all the regulars a silver tankard with the inscription, "Slade Prison 1974" together with our character's name; he gave mine an initial so it read "Lukewarm. P". I will always treasure it.

'I remember vividly the day word reached me of the tragic death of Ronnie's co-star, the multi-talented Richard Beckinsale. I was making a film, *The Tempest*, directed by Derek Jarman, on the northeast coast. It was bitterly cold and I was having a rest in my room late one afternoon when the telephone rang: it was a journalist from the *News of the World* asking whether I'd like to comment on the death of Richard. I was stunned and devastated; what a world star he would have been if he hadn't died so young, and how proud he would have been of his daughter, Kate.

'I, in turn, am very proud to be associated with one of the most glorious television sitcoms ever, starring two huge stars and a cast you would give your eye teeth to work with, written by two literary geniuses and held together by a brilliant producer. Nearly thirty years on nothing comes near its brilliance. Thank you, Syd.'

**Cyril Shaps** (Jackdaw in 'The Harder They Fall')

'My memories of *Porridge* are of rehearsals which demonstrated how inventive Ronnie Barker was throughout. His improvisations, his brilliant technique and, above all, his constant good humour were an inspiration.

'We shared a love of gardening and, in particular, rockeries. I mentioned this to him and he said he would like to see mine, which was in full bloom at the time. I invited him to tea after the day's rehearsal and he agreed immediately. We had a very happy session together.'

# CHRISTMAS SPECIAL

## NO WAY OUT

### 1. ASSOCIATION AREA

***The camera shows a fairy on top of a Christmas tree. Lennie walks in to the association area with two mugs of cocoa. He hears prisoners singing carols.***

***Lennie walks round the catwalk and stops to watch the choir. One of the singers is Lukewarm. He looks up and notices Lennie. Lennie leaves.***

### 1A. FLETCHER'S CELL

***Fletcher is pasting a newspaper cutting of a topless girl on to a piece of card, on which he has written 'Merry Xmas'. Lennie enters.***

**LENNIE**

What's that – you making a Christmas card?

**FLETCHER**

Yes – it's for my brother George. I cut it out the paper.

**LENNIE**

Not very seasonal, is it?

**FLETCHER**

It is for George – he's only allowed it once a year.

**LENNIE**

Can you hear the carols?

**FLETCHER**

Yeah – shut the door, will you?

**LENNIE**

Don't you like it?

**FLETCHER**

They've been at it for two hours – and they only know four carols. And the words of one of them are a bit suspect. Shepherds washed their socks by night!

**LENNIE**

Don't you find it rather moving? All those blokes, some of them real tearaways, united in a common exultation of this great occasion.

**FLETCHER**

Don't be daft. They're singing, my son, to drown the noise of Tommy Slocombe's tunnelling.

**LENNIE**

Tunnelling?

**FLETCHER**

That's the great occasion round here. Not the coming of our Lord, the going of Tommy Slocombe.

**LENNIE**
Nobody ever tells me nothing.

**FLETCHER**
It wasn't thought an event suitable for publication. It's a secret between Tommy, six baritones, twelve tenors and soprano.

**LENNIE**
Have we got a soprano?

**FLETCHER**
Oh there's lots of sopranos in here, my son. And a few of those baritones need watching an' all. Don't let those deep gruff voices fool you. 'Come over 'ere, son.'

**LENNIE**
Where is the tunnel?

**FLETCHER**
Where's the choir?

**LENNIE**
Just outside cell twenty-eight.

**FLETCHER**
About three feet under cell twenty-nine then. Give us a biscuit.

**LENNIE**
Well, I like the singing. At least it brings an air of festivity into our otherwise monotonous existence. There's ever such a lot to look forward to – there's the carol service, and the concert coming up. And the tree.

**FLETCHER**
Useful, the tree.

**LENNIE**
Useful?

**FLETCHER**
For stashing Christmas contraband. All those dingly danglies hide a multitude of sins. And even that Christmas fairy on the top has got two ounces of tobacco shoved up her tutu.

**LENNIE**
No wonder she looks uncomfortable. Where did that come from?

**FLETCHER**
The Governor's office. It was his present for Mr Mackay. Welsh George made a nifty switch when he was in there doing the floors.

**LENNIE**
He must have left something to take its place.

**FLETCHER**
He did. An identical gift-wrapped box, which Mr Mackay will doubtless open on Christmas Day.

**LENNIE**
What's in it?

**FLETCHER**
Well, I'll tell you one thing – if he uses it for putty all his windows will fall out.

***He gets up.***

**LENNIE**
What's Christmas like inside, Fletch?

**FLETCHER**
Slightly less 'orrible than any other day.

I mean, the Governor don't dress up as Santa Claus and give us all bottles of after-shave, you know.

**LENNIE**

But we get turkey, don't we – do we, do we get turkey?

**FLETCHER**

They call it turkey, but not seeing it carved we don't know, do we? If it is, the one we had in our block last year must have been a funny shape. Twenty-eight legs and no breast. Like Lulu and the Young Generation.

***He sits down.***

**LENNIE**

Hey, that's good – can I use that in my after-dinner speech? By the by, we get pudding as well, don't we? Xmas pudding like, with cream?

**FLETCHER**

Oh yes – that artificial whipped cream. You'd be better off shaving with that though. And, of course, the wheeler-dealers make a few bob at Xmas time. Slade Prison's Mister Big, genial Harry Grout, has granted a few franchises. Young Terry Maidment is making himself a fortune, flogging mistletoe to the poofters.

**LENNIE**

Just like the outside then. People have forgotten the real meaning of Christmas. It's just a commercial exercise.

**FLETCHER**

What do you expect? Goodwill to all men – what? From Mackay? As much chance of getting that as you have finding a partridge up a pear tree.

**LENNIE**

Still the actual day should be a bit brighter though, shouldn't it?

**FLETCHER**

Won't be this year.

**LENNIE**

Why not?

**FLETCHER**

Because of that flaming tunnel. That tunnel spells disaster for us all. That Tommy Slocombe's only chosen to make his break on Christmas Eve. Dear, dear never get through the traffic.

**LENNIE**

(*With a smile*) Oh – he's only got six more digging days to Christmas then.

**FLETCHER**

It's not funny, sonny Jim. We're all going to be implicated in this escape. Whether we like it or not.

***He gets up.***

**LENNIE**

But Slocombe's such a despicable nurk. I don't see why anyone would lift a finger for him.

**FLETCHER**

It so happens young Slocombe is the brother-in-law of a big villain in the smoke. A man who is also a colleague of genial Harry Grout. Now he's obviously got the word to Harry – 'Get our kid away for Christmas.' So Harry's running this caper. Which means if any of us are asked to assist we are in no position to refuse. Otherwise, one morning we might find something else hanging on the Xmas tree. Us.

**LENNIE**

I'm not going down no tunnel, I suffer from claustrophobia.

**FLETCHER**

Do you?

**LENNIE**

It dates back to the time when I was stuck in a chimney for two hours.

**FLETCHER**

Oh dear, how was that?

**LENNIE**

I was going to turn over this big house in Sutton Coldfield. The chimney was my only means of access.

**FLETCHER**

Oh yeah, and you got stuck, did you?

**LENNIE**

Yes, it was terrifying. What made it worse was my intended victims came home from the pictures, and saw my legs sticking out of the fireplace. I managed to run off though.

**FLETCHER**

Did they give the police a description?

**LENNIE**

Yeah, luckily I was covered in soot. They're still looking for a tall, blue-eyed Negro in a black suit.

**FLETCHER**

Yeah – well that might excuse you tunnelling duties. But when Slocombe's well out of it we'll all be well in it. You, just as much as anybody else. The point is, it's disturbing the equilibrium of prison life.

**LENNIE**

The equilibrium?

**FLETCHER**

Yeah, them and us, it'll tilt the balance of power which exists between the law and the villain. With this escape we shall have pushed the system too far.

**LENNIE**

There's nothing we can do though, is there? I mean, what can we do?

**FLETCHER**

I know what I'm going to do. I intend to be well out of it.

**LENNIE**

How?

**FLETCHER**

I'm going away for Christmas.

**LENNIE**

Where to, Majorca?

**FLETCHER**

No – everyone goes to Majorca, don't they? No, I thought I'd try the prison hospital this year for a change. A, because it's the nearest thing to a holiday in here, and B, because I shall be far removed from any retaliations by the screws over this escape fiasco.

**LENNIE**

You'll never get in the infirmary, not with that doctor. What's supposed to be wrong with you?

**FLETCHER**

It's my knee, isn't it?

**LENNIE**

I never knew there was anything wrong with your knee.

**FLETCHER**

No, well I've been keeping it up my sleeve. Or more precisely, my trouser leg.

**LENNIE**

What's the matter with it?

**FLETCHER**

Cartilage. I've lived with the pain for years. But recently, being on my feet all day in the damp weather, it has escalated the pain to an unbearable degree.

**LENNIE**

Which knee is it?

**FLETCHER**

Eh?

**LENNIE**

Which knee is it?

**FLETCHER**

This one . . . or is it this one?

## 2. PRISON CLINIC

**DOCTOR**

Am I hurting you?

**WARREN**

(*Happily*) Yup.

**DOCTOR**

Sorry.

**WARREN**

You got your job to do.

**DOCTOR**

It's a pretty bad burn.

**WARREN**

(*Still happily*) Yeah, I know.

***The Doctor looks up at Warren.***

**DOCTOR**

What are you so pleased about?

**WARREN**

Well, Doc, if you're going to hurt yourself in here, might as well make sure it's nothing trivial. I mean there's no way I can go back to work with this hand, is there?

**DOCTOR**

I'm reluctantly forced to admit there isn't.

**WARREN**

I think I could just about make it to the infirmary though, if somebody opens the door for me.

**DOCTOR**

(*Resolutely*) You're not going to the infirmary. You're confined to your cell for three days.

**WARREN**

You can't manage in a cell on your own with your hand tied up like this.

I know it seems silly to lie in the infirmary with a bandaged hand. But, on the other hand . . .

**DOCTOR**

Neither of your hands is going to find its way into the sick-bay, is that understood?

**WARREN**

You don't like people getting in your infirmary, do you?

**DOCTOR**

And mess up all those crisp white sheets, certainly not. Next! (*To Warren*) Now just hold this dressing in place for a few moments, then I'll get you bandaged up.

***Fletcher enters, limping and wincing. Just the quickest of looks from the Doctor, then –***

**DOCTOR**

Out of here, Fletcher.

**FLETCHER**

I got my white card.

**DOCTOR**

Out, out, out.

**FLETCHER**

I'm sick!

**DOCTOR**

Out!

**FLETCHER**

I'm entitled.

**DOCTOR**

Years of medical practice have enabled me to tell at a glance if a man's sick or not. You're a perfect specimen of manhood, Fletcher.

**FLETCHER**

It's not that I've come about, it's my knee.

**DOCTOR**

What's wrong with your knee?

**FLETCHER**

Just ask me to stand on one leg.

**DOCTOR**

What?

**FLETCHER**

Ask me to stand on one leg.

**WARREN**

Go on, ask him. No harm in that.

***The Doctor's curiosity gets the better of him.***

**DOCTOR**

All right, stand on one leg.

***Fletcher raises a leg and then collapses on the floor as the other one buckles beneath him. He looks at the Doctor accusingly.***

**FLETCHER**

And you call yourself a doctor!

**DOCTOR**

Get up, Fletcher.

**FLETCHER**

I don't know if I can.

***He raises himself with difficulty, keeping the weight off one foot.***

**DOCTOR**

Sit in the chair. What is it?

**FLETCHER**

I'll show you.

***Dramatically and carefully he rolls up his trouser leg. The Doctor watches. Warren cranes forward to***

***see. Fletcher uncovers a knee . . . a perfectly normal knee . . . and gestures towards it.***

**FLETCHER**

There then!

**DOCTOR**

There what?

**FLETCHER**

It's a knee.

**DOCTOR**

I know it's a knee, Fletcher. I learned that in medical school.

**FLETCHER**

But you didn't learn about this kind of knee. You see the old trouble has flared up again.

**DOCTOR**

What old trouble? Laziness?

**FLETCHER**

Cartilage. And before you say anything, it's all on my medical records.

***He points towards a filing cabinet.***

**FLETCHER**

You check your files, you'll see I have an official history of knee trouble.

**DOCTOR**

I don't believe you.

**FLETCHER**

Have to check though, won't you?

***The Doctor turns towards the file shaking his head.***

**DOCTOR**

I don't know why I'm doing this.

**FLETCHER**

You're doing it because you know that there's one chance in a million that one day one of us will be telling the truth.

***The Doctor opens the filing cabinet and first of all removes a Christmas cake.***

**FLETCHER**

What's that then?

**DOCTOR**

It's a Christmas cake. I get one every year.

**FLETCHER**

What for?

**DOCTOR**

The patients in the infirmary.

**WARREN**

But you never *allow* any patients in your infirmary.

**DOCTOR**

That's true. I always take it home for the wife.

***The Doctor goes through the files as Fletcher turns to Warren.***

**FLETCHER**

Hey, that's a turn-up for the book, ain't it – in prison.

**WARREN**

What?

**FLETCHER**

A file with a cake in it – get it, get it?

**WARREN**

Oh, yes. You're a very witty man, Fletch.

**FLETCHER**
Here, are you a mason?
***The Doctor has found Fletcher's record and is reading it.***
**DOCTOR**
My God, it's true – Maidstone Jail 1967. Cartilage.
**WARREN**
Very common with footballers that. That and groin strain.
**FLETCHER**
Little chance of groin strain in here.
**DOCTOR**
All right, I accept you have an official record of surgery on your left knee. But this was years ago.
**FLETCHER**
Yeah, and I've lived with the pain ever since. Now I don't complain, do I, Bunny?
**WARREN**
No, he don't complain. Even though we've seen him crawl in from work some days like a wounded bloodhound on his hands and knee.
**FLETCHER**
(*Heroically*) Please – I'm not after sympathy.
**DOCTOR**
What is it you are after?
**FLETCHER**
Well . . . every so often, when the pain becomes unbearable, I have to lie down with my leg up – just for a week or two.
**DOCTOR**
(*Playing along*) You think a week in the infirmary would do the trick?
**FLETCHER**
Maybe a week.
**DOCTOR**
Let me tell you something, Fletcher. Of all the penal institutions in the north of England, my infirmary has the lowest record of admissions. Donaldson, who's doing a five stretch for grand larceny and embezzlement, has more chance of getting a Barclaycard than you have of getting in my infirmary.
**FLETCHER**
On your head be it.
***The Doctor makes up his mind. He starts to fill out a form.***
**DOCTOR**
Fletcher, I know you, and I know you're going to make an issue out of this, and waste a lot of my valuable time with your stupid nonsense, so here's what I'm going to do. I'm going to cut it out before it goes any further.
**FLETCHER**
Amputate? Now, hang on . . .
**WARREN**
That should get you in the infirmary.
**DOCTOR**
I'm sending you to a civilian hospital. For X-ray and specialist examination. You'll be there and back in a day. Then the matter will be irrevocably closed.
***Fletcher realises he is losing the battle.***

**FLETCHER**

Why waste the taxpayers' money? I tell you, I know my knee. All I need is to rest up for a day or two.

**DOCTOR**

(*Giving Fletcher the card*) On your way, Fletcher. You're a liar and a malingerer.

**FLETCHER**

Harsh words, Doctor. In this season of peace and goodwill to all men. I hope your conscience pricks you, that's all.

**DOCTOR**

You can say a little prayer for me on Christmas morning. Next.

**FLETCHER**

Yeah, I will. You don't mind if I say it standing up, do you? I can't kneel down, I've got a bad knee.

***He walks across to leave and shakes Warren's hand.***

**FLETCHER**

All the best.

**WARREN**

Aaaagh!

## 3. CELL

***Fletcher is in his cell. Lennie walks in. In the distance we hear the choir, now singing 'O Come All Ye Faithful'.***

**LENNIE**

Hey, Fletch –

**FLETCHER**

Shut the door!

**LENNIE**

Harry Grout's coming to see you.

**FLETCHER**

(*Surprised*) What?

**LENNIE**

Straight up. Grouty. On his way.

**FLETCHER**

What did I tell you? Gawd blimey, I knew it. This will be some little favour pertaining to Slocombe's moonlight flit – hello, Harry!

***Fletcher's change of expression is explained by Grout's arrival.***

**GROUT**

Hello, Fletcher.

**FLETCHER**

This is a rare privilege. You don't often drop in on people. Usually you get people to drop in on you. And if they don't you get other people to drop things on them.

***Lennie laughs.***

**GROUT**

You always were a bit of a joker, Fletch.

**FLETCHER**

Yes, I was. Up to now. What brings you to my humble abode, Grouty?

**GROUT**

I wanted to get out of my cell just for a while.

**FLETCHER**

Change of air?

**GROUT**

No, a couple of warders are putting up my Christmas decorations.

*Lennie laughs. Grout takes a coin from his pocket and flicks it to Lennie.*

**GROUT**

There you are, son. Go to the pictures or something.

*Lennie gets the point.*

**LENNIE**

Oh – thank you.

*He goes.*

**GROUT**

Shut the door.

*Door crashes heavily.*

**GROUT**

Sit down, Fletch.

**FLETCHER**

(*Sitting down*) Oh, thank you very much. Like the smell of a nice cigar. Wish I had something festive to offer you, Grouty.

**GROUT**

Not in the festive mood, Fletch. There's a tunnel being dug. You've heard, I suppose?

**FLETCHER**

Only when they leave off singing.

**GROUT**

Slocombe's a relative of friends of mine on the outside, and they want him sprung.

**FLETCHER**

Oh, isn't his dad Billy the Ponce Slocombe? Yes, the one that got out of Brixton in '72. Where did he end up?

**GROUT**

Apparently he emerged on some Caribbean Island where the authorities took advantage of his criminal experience.

**FLETCHER**

How?

**GROUT**

Made him Chief of Police.

**FLETCHER**

Well, he did have a bit of style, the old man.

**GROUT**

Trouble is, it's beholden to me to accomplish the disappearance of his idiot offspring.

**FLETCHER**

Delicate, Grouty.

**GROUT**

Extremely.

**FLETCHER**

If only I could help in some way.

**GROUT**

You can, my son.

**FLETCHER**

Oh gawd.

**GROUT**

You're having a little day trip tomorrow, aren't you?

**FLETCHER**

Only to get my knee X-rayed.

**GROUT**

Still you'll be on the outside. And we have friends on the outside who could take advantage of that.

**FLETCHER**

How?

**GROUT**

There'll be a package. Someone. Somewhere. Sometime. No sweat.

**FLETCHER**

I'll be under escort, Grouty. I'm not just getting the bus down there and doing a bit of last-minute Christmas shopping at the same time, you know.

**GROUT**

It's only a small package. A blank passport. Inky Stevens needs one to give Slocombe a more acceptable identity.

**FLETCHER**

Wouldn't it be safer for him to pick up his new passport on the outside?

**GROUT**

Normally, yes. But the finest forger in the country's Inky Stevens, and he's on the inside, isn't he?

**FLETCHER**

Yes, yes . . .

**GROUTY**

I won't be ungrateful, Fletch.

***He stands up.***

**FLETCHER**

Oh good.

**GROUT**

Be something extra in your Christmas stocking for this. Besides your bad knee, that is.

***He laughs at his own joke. When he opens the door, the choir can be heard again. They are now halfway through 'God Rest Ye Merry Gentlemen'.***

***Grout reacts with pleasure.***

**GROUT**

Oh, I like this one.

***He joins in.***

**GROUT**

'Great tidings of comfort and joy, comfort and joy . . .'

***He gestures to Fletcher to join him. Fletcher does so, his expression conveying anything but comfort and joy.***

**FLETCHER**

'Great tidings of comfort and joy . . .'

## 4. PRISON YARD

***Barrowclough and Mackay walk up to a waiting minibus and Barrowclough gets in.***

***Fletcher approaches with a warder.***

**MACKAY**

Haven't you forgotten something, Fletcher?

**FLETCHER**

What?

**MACKAY**

Your limp – ha, ha . . .

**FLETCHER**
Oh, yes, mock the afflicted.

**MACKAY**
You're not sick, as the X-rays will soon prove.

**FLETCHER**
Well look, let's call the whole thing off then. Seriously. I can live with pain a few years longer. Hospitals is busy enough this time of year. Yeah, I'll just hobble back to my cell.

***He turns and limps away.***

**MACKAY**
Get in, Fletcher. Mr Barrowclough has his Christmas shopping to finish.

***Fletcher gets in the bus and Mackay shuts the door. The bus starts to move.***

## 5. HOSPITAL BUILDING

***The camera shows the sign 'X-ray', then the hospital building.***

**FLETCHER**
(*Voiceover*) All right, doc, you're the expert. I can take it. Give it to me straight . . .

**DOCTOR**
(*Voiceover*) (*Gravely*) I am afraid I have bad news for you, Mr Fletcher.

**FLETCHER**
(*Voiceover*) You have?

**DOCTOR**
(*Voiceover*) Yes . . . you have a perfectly healthy knee.

## 6. HOSPITAL ANTE-ROOM

***It is a bare room, with a few tables, chairs and magazines. Fletcher and Barrowclough are sitting on chairs with cups of coffee. On the chair beside Barrowclough are several gift-wrapped packages. The camera shows a young Nurse holding up an X-ray photograph of a healthy knee.***

**NURSE**
You've really got quite an attractive knee, Mr Fletcher.

**FLETCHER**
Not as attractive as yours, nurse. Yeah, I bet *they're* going to have a happy Christmas, ain't they?

**BARROWCLOUGH**
Now, that will do, Fletcher. You're old enough to be the girl's father.

**FLETCHER**
No, impossible, I never been round this way before.

**NURSE**
The main thing is, it's a healthy knee.

**FLETCHER**
Those X-rays prove nothing, you cannot photograph pain.

**NURSE**

When did your knee trouble start?

**BARROWCLOUGH**

Two days ago, when he thought he'd wangle the infirmary for Christmas.

**FLETCHER**

No, it does not. Goes back ten years.

***As the Nurse leaves Hospital Porter passes by pushing a trolley. Another girl, dressed in civilian clothes but wearing a hospital white coat over them comes up to the men.***

**SANDRA**

Can I get you gentlemen some more coffee?

**FLETCHER**

No, no, let's just get back to where we come from.

**BARROWCLOUGH**

(*Rising*) Well, I'd like another cup of coffee. It's all milk, isn't it? I only get half and half at home.

**FLETCHER**

Half and half?

**BARROWCLOUGH**

Milk and water.

**FLETCHER**

Oh yeah.

**BARROWCLOUGH**

If it's not too much trouble, Miss. Very sweet of you to ask.

**SANDRA**

(*To Fletcher*) You sure you don't fancy some?

**FLETCHER**

Not coffee, no thank you.

***She gives them a dazzling smile and leaves.***

**BARROWCLOUGH**

Charming girl.

***He sits down.***

**FLETCHER**

Look at you. Chapel hat pegs, ain't it? More sex-starved than me. How much longer are we going to sit around this draughty corridor, then?

**BARROWCLOUGH**

What's the matter with you, Fletcher? You seem very ill-at-ease. Relax. Enjoy yourself, it's Christmas. Have a biscuit.

**FLETCHER**

It's your attitude that's unsettling me. 'Have a biscuit' – God Almighty. Next thing we know we'll have Mr Mackay tucking us up in bed at night.

**BARROWCLOUGH**

Now, Fletcher! Mr Mackay's no different from anyone else. Outside the grey grim walls of our institution you'll find that he can be an amiable man.

**FLETCHER**

(*Incredulously*) Amiable?

**BARROWCLOUGH**

On Tuesday he stroked a dog. He did. I saw it with my own eyes. The Governor's boxer.

**FLETCHER**

What happened?

**BARROWCLOUGH**
It bit him.

**FLETCHER**
(*Amused*) Oh dear.

**BARROWCLOUGH**
Oh yes. He had to have an injection in case he caught rabies.

**FLETCHER**
What, the dog did – yes, he would.

**BARROWCLOUGH**
It's nothing to laugh at.

**FLETCHER**
Depends on your sense of humour, doesn't it? Look, I'm like the Governor's dog, ain't I? Conditioned to mistrust in an atmosphere of mutual contempt. I'm relaxed when we get back to the nick, you lock me up and we go back to hurling insults at each other.

**BARROWCLOUGH**
You're spoiling my day out, Fletcher.

**FLETCHER**
Oh, forgive me.

**BARROWCLOUGH**
Don't you think I sometimes get as sick of Slade Prison as you do? Today's been a break for me.

**FLETCHER**
Why? What would you have been doing today back at the prison, Mr Barrowclough?

**BARROWCLOUGH**
I was off duty today. I just volunteered for this trip.

**FLETCHER**
You could have stayed at home. Spent the day with your lady wife.

**BARROWCLOUGH**
That's really why I volunteered.

***Sandra returns carrying a tray with coffee. Barrowclough is instantly on his feet.***

**BARROWCLOUGH**
Here, let me take that.

**SANDRA**
I brought an extra cup just in case.

**FLETCHER**
Ta very much.

**BARROWCLOUGH**
You must forgive our friend here. He's a little morose. Not his usual self.

**SANDRA**
May I say something to your friend here?

**BARROWCLOUGH**
Certainly, my dear, by all means. The young lady wishes to address you, Fletcher.

**SANDRA**
It's just that . . . well, we're all very well aware in here of . . . what you are. And we realise it can't be a very happy time of year for you. So – with your permission (*To Barrowclough*) the radiologists and me have just got a little something here.

***She produces a package the size of a large, stiff Christmas card.***

**SANDRA**

It's not very much but I think it's the thought that counts.

**BARROWCLOUGH**

What a very nice thought. Isn't that nice, Fletcher?

***Fletcher gets up and takes the package.***

**FLETCHER**

Oh . . . oh, very nice of you, Miss. I can't say I'm not touched. In fact I'm deeply moved. Should I open it now?

**SANDRA**

(*Grabbing his arm*) No!! Not before Christmas Day.

***She winks at Fletcher.***

**FLETCHER**

Oh yes. Yes, of course.

**SANDRA**

Spoil the surprise, wouldn't it?

**FLETCHER**

(*Nervously*) Oh yes . . . oh no . . . Oh.

## 7. CELL

***It is night time. Inside Fletcher's cell Grout is tearing open the envelope which contains a Christmas card and inside that a passport.***

**GROUT**

Well done, my son.

**FLETCHER**

Give me palpitations I can tell you. Right under Barrowclough's nose! Fortunately he was put off his guard by the day out, her legs and a couple of large Johnny Walkers.

**GROUT**

Smart bird that Sandra.

**FLETCHER**

Who is she, does she work there?

**GROUT**

'Course not. Come up from the smoke. All it took was a bit of nerve and a white coat.

**FLETCHER**

My nerve nearly went.

**GROUT**

Not you, Fletch, you're a dab hand. I'm only sorry your knee got a clean bill of health, Fletch. But p'raps I could do you a favour in that direction.

**FLETCHER**

How?

**GROUT**

Couple of my lads could have a go at it. Damage it beyond medical dispute.

**FLETCHER**

Er, I think I'll pass on that one, Grouty. Much as I appreciate your kind consideration.

**GROUT**

Please yourself. I just thought I'd mention it, because you see I would like to elicit the help of you and the lad a little further.

**FLETCHER**

Ain't I done my bit, Grouty?

**GROUT**

You see, it's the tunnel.

**FLETCHER**

Hang on a bit. The kid's got claustrophobia. And look at the size of me. A ferret I ain't.

**GROUT**

Nothing physical. Just want you to join the choir. They've come up against a very stoney bit, and we need all the fortissimo we can get.

**FLETCHER**

Oh, my pleasure, Grouty. Enjoy a good sing. Used to do a lot of it down in Maidstone when we worked on the prison farm. Church hymns mostly. Favourite one with the boys was 'We plough the fields and scatter'. A lot of 'em did, an' all. Right, that's everything then, is it?

**GROUT**

Not quite. Just one tiny thing.

**FLETCHER**

Oh, please, Harry, aren't I doing my share? Smuggling, singing . . .

**GROUT**

It's essential to the success of our venture.

**FLETCHER**

Well?

**GROUT**

We need a bicycle.

**FLETCHER**

Oh certainly, what colour?

## 8. PRISON LANDING

***Barrowclough waits for Warren, then walks along the catwalk behind him. Lukewarm sees Barrowclough and moves to the radiator. He taps it. The radiator answers (it replies to taps). Lukewarm moves towards the tables and starts singing 'The First Noel'. Other prisoners start to join in.Barrowclough and Warren walk round the catwalk as the men are singing. As he sings, Lukewarm is watching Barrowclough.***

## 9. CELL

***Fletcher and Lennie are about to leave the cell when Warren and Barrowclough walk in.***

**FLETCHER**

What's this, Mr Barrowclough? Lunchtime, in' it?

**BARROWCLOUGH**

Lunch can wait. I have something very serious to say to you three.

**LENNIE**

Why us three?

**BARROWCLOUGH**

Because it was you three who were in

the yard today when I arrived at work – you three who involved me in a pointless discussion on the outcome of the Cup Final in 1962. That's why I'm asking you three one pertinent question . . . Where-is-my-bicycle?!!

***There is a pause while the three prisoners look at each other in outraged innocence.***

**FLETCHER**
What bicycle was this, then?

**BARROWCLOUGH**
The one I cycled to work on.

**LENNIE**
You got a bicycle, then?

**BARROWCLOUGH**
I've had one for a month or so. Ever since the medical officer advised me to take more exercise.

**WARREN**
I had a bike once.

**BARROWCLOUGH**
So did I! And I want to know what's become of it.

***Lennie frowns as if trying to understand.***

**LENNIE**
Let me get this straight, Mr Barrowclough. You are saying that prior to our conversation you were the owner of a bicycle?

**BARROWCLOUGH**
That's right, yes.

**LENNIE**
And that since our conversation you are the former owner of a bicycle?

**BARROWCLOUGH**
That's what I'm saying, yes.

***Fletcher sits down at the table. He tries hard to get to the nub of the matter.***

**FLETCHER**
Let me get this straight, Mr Barrowclough. You are saying that you arrived at work as a cyclist and you'll be leaving as a pedestrian?

**BARROWCLOUGH**
Yes, yes, yes!

**FLETCHER**
Are you assuming there's a connection between our discussion on the '62 Cup Final and the disappearance of your alleged bicycle?

**BARROWCLOUGH**
There's nothing alleged about it. Green it was.

**WARREN**
When did you last see your bicycle?

**BARROWCLOUGH**
When I got off it.

**FLETCHER**
You sure you had it with you when you got off it?

***Barrowclough produces his cycle clips.***

**BARROWCLOUGH**
Why do you think I wear these?

**WARREN**
To stop things falling out of your trousers?

**LENNIE**
If we were talking to you, how could we have palmed your bike?

**BARROWCLOUGH**
It was a well-known diversionary tactic.

**FLETCHER**
If you ask me, lads, this whole thing sounds very dodgy.

**BARROWCLOUGH**
Dodgy?

**FLETCHER**
It has all the classic elements of an insurance swindle.

**BARROWCLOUGH**
How dare you!

**FLETCHER**
(*Rising*) How dare you accuse us of being bicycle thieves.

**LENNIE**
I saw that film. It was a beautiful example of early Italian neo-realism.

**BARROWCLOUGH**
You're as impossible as ever. I thought at this time of year . . . oh well, that's just my naïve trust in human nature. I should have known better. Warren – follow me.

**WARREN**
Where to?

**BARROWCLOUGH**
Back to your cell. I'm going to conduct a thorough search. And if I find anything resembling a bicycle pump in your trousers, you're for it!

***Fletcher reacts as they exit.***

## 10. MACKAY'S OFFICE

***It is a tiny office with a gas fire, racks of keys and a grubby calendar. Barrowclough, clipboard in hand, faces Mackay who is sitting behind his desk.***

**MACKAY**
Pull yourself together, Barrowclough. It's your own fault. You should never turn your back on them, not for a minute.

**BARROWCLOUGH**
I've always thought that the best way to encourage trust was to show them trust.

**MACKAY**
They're criminals, man.

**BARROWCLOUGH**
They're also human beings.

**MACKAY**
All right – but criminal human beings. And they too often take advantage of your lack of control. You lack discipline. You're gullible.

**BARROWCLOUGH**
I sometimes give the men the benefit of the doubt.

**MACKAY**
Never do that! It's rule one! Any time a prisoner makes a request, a prison officer must ask himself – 'What is he up to?' Even the simplest request must be

treated with deep mistrust and suspicion. A prisoner ties his shoelace – question! What is he concealing in his sock?

**BARROWCLOUGH**

I know all that of course – but I never thought they'd steal a bicycle. They can't conceal that in their sock.

**MACKAY**

Oh come on, man! You know what these people are like! Did we ever find any trace of our billiard table?

**BARROWCLOUGH**

We found the red ball.

**MACKAY**

They'll have dismantled your bike in an instant. If we have as much luck as we did with the billiard table, maybe you'll get back your rear light.

**BARROWCLOUGH**

It seems so pointless.

**MACKAY**

There's always a point. My antennae tell me there's something going on. Think – have they asked you anything, any seemingly innocent favours?

**BARROWCLOUGH**

No, no, no. Well, they asked me one thing, but it was completely innocent.

**MACKAY**

(*Suspiciously*) What?

**BARROWCLOUGH**

They asked me to help with their choir at the carol service. There can't be any harm in that.

**MACKAY**

And you trusted them? Haven't I just told you – once you turn your back on them, you're finished.

**BARROWCLOUGH**

Oh, I won't do. I'll be conducting.

**MACKAY**

I think I'll conduct a little enquiry. Who's running this Glee Club?

***They exit.***

## 11. ASSOCIATION AREA

***The prisoners' choir, including Fletcher, Lennie, Warren and Lukewarm, are grouped round singing.***

**CHOIR**

'Good King Wencelas looked out
On the feast of Stephen
When the snow lay round about,
Deep and crisp and even.
Brightly shone the moon that night. . .'

***Mackay and Barrowclough come from the office doorway and along the catwalk.***

**CHOIR**

'Though the frost was cruel.'

**MACKAY**
Silence.
**FLETCHER**
'When a Scotsman came in sight, hollering . . .'
**MACKAY**
That will do, Fletcher.
***Lukewarm looks towards radiator from which can be heard 'clink, clink, clink'. Lukewarm starts to move towards the radiator.***
**MACKAY**
Stand still.
***Lukewarm freezes.***
***Mackay walks to the centre of the room.***
**MACKAY**
What's that noise?
**FLETCHER**
Central heating, sir.
***Mackay moves to the radiator and kicks it twice.***
***The radiator replies.***
**FLETCHER**
Oh – didn't know you was a plumber, Mr Mackay. Think you've mended it.
**MACKAY**
All right – come on, back to your cells.
**WARREN**
We need more rehearsal, don't we?
**MACKAY**
There won't be any more.

**LENNIE**
Christmas, isn't it?
**MACKAY**
You've forfeited your right to Christmas.
**LENNIE**
How?
**MACKAY**
Through a series of incidents, culminating in the disappearance of Mr Barrowclough's bicycle.
***He walks among the prisoners.***
**MACKAY**
I can't prove anything of course, but don't think that technicality will affect my judgement in the least. You were put in here to keep crime off the streets. But I'm not having you bringing it into my prison. You will be advised to remember that we have a solitary confinement area, with which you will become only too familiar if you continue to practise the contemptible habits which brought you here in the first place. Clear? Right – back to your cells the lot of you. Move!
***Prisoners file past Barrowclough and Mackay.***
**FLETCHER**
I suppose you realise you've stifled at birth what could have been the start of a religious revival in here.
**MACKAY**
Out, Fletcher.
***Lukewarm stops to shake Barrowclough's hand.***

**LUKEWARM**

In spite of all, Merry Christmas, sir. (*Taking his hand again*) And a very happy Christmas to Mrs Barrowclough.

**BARROWCLOUGH**

Right, now come on – move it along . . . (*Hesitantly*) Lukewarm . . .

**MACKAY**

(*To Barrowclough*) That is the only attitude they respect. The only attitude that will wipe out this wave of insubordination and petty theft.

**BARROWCLOUGH**

I suppose you're right . . . d'you think you could countersign my report?

***He hands Mackay the clipboard.***

**MACKAY**

Very well . . . (*Feeling for his pen*) That's funny, I seem to have mislaid my pen. (*Feeling other pocket*) Where's my wallet . . . Mr Barrowclough, I've been mugged!

**BARROWCLOUGH**

But that's not possible, sir. We've only been here a minute. We came in here at . . . (*Automatically checks his watch*) . . . Where's my watch!

## 12. CELL

***Lennie is making a paper chain, when an indignant Fletcher enters.***

**FLETCHER**

It's on the bulletin board, it's official.

**LENNIE**

What is?

**FLETCHER**

Christmas is cancelled. It says on the board, 'There'll be no Xmas Eve, Xmas Day or Boxing Day. Just the 24th, 25th and 26th December.'

**LENNIE**

Oh well, no point in finishing this chain.

***He puts down the paper chain.***

**FLETCHER**

I told you, didn't I?

**LENNIE**

About the equilibrium being disturbed?

**FLETCHER**

Disturbed, it's upside down, my son. Marvellous, isn't it? Tick along all year, keeping your nose clean, and through sheer intimidation we all get dropped in the yuletide clarts. And then that bleeding Lukewarm, talk about daylight robbery!

**LENNIE**

Not his fault, Fletch, be fair. He was under Grouty's instructions like the rest of us. They needed Mackay's wallet to keep topping up the getaway car.

**FLETCHER**

They didn't need Barrowclough's Timex though, did they? Force of flaming habit that was. The whole thing's been a mockery. Ill-conceived, badly organised and doomed to fail –

*Grout enters, Fletcher does not miss a beat.*

**FLETCHER**

– oh hello, Grouty. I was just saying what a shame your brilliant strategy should come to naught.

**GROUT**

Know what they say, the best-laid plans . . .

**LENNIE**

Should I – er, go to the pictures?

**GROUT**

No, sit down, sonny – no secrets now. Bad business. My friends in the smoke are bound to bear malice.

**FLETCHER**

Oh no – they'd never be so heartless, Grouty.

**GROUT**

Why not? I would.

**LENNIE**

Excuse me, Mr Grout, but couldn't you reactivate the tunnel at a later date?

**GROUT**

No, it was off course anyhow. He's an idiot that Slocombe. He nearly come up in the laundry last week.

**FLETCHER**

So the tunnel's now defunct then?

**GROUT**

Except for storing contraband, yes.

**FLETCHER**

I have a glimmer of an idea, Grouty. Which may solve all our problems.

**GROUT**

Oh yes?

**FLETCHER**

If the screws was to find that tunnel, it would do two things. One, it would tilt the balance of power back in their favour, 'cos they'd be chuffed at their own perspicacity. And two, they'd think that was the intended escape route.

**LENNIE**

But it was.

**FLETCHER**

It was, but it ain't now. It's a red herring. Then while the screws are still full of self-congratulatory ardour, you get Tommy away in a dustcart or something. That should please your pals in London.

**GROUT**

Here, here, you have had a thought, haven't you, Fletch.

**FLETCHER**

Save your face, Grouty.

**GROUT**

That it would.

**LENNIE**

It'll appear to be a perfectly executed plan.

**GROUT**

You're not wrong, son. Tip the Governor off?

**FLETCHER**

No – I think Mackay should find it. In fact if you give me the blueprints I might arrange for him to drop right in it.

## 13. PRISON YARD

***Mackay is walking down the steps to the prison yard.***

**MACKAY**

Fletcher, I'm told you wanted a word with me.

***Fletcher moves to the foot of the steps.***

**FLETCHER**

Just a seemingly innocent stroll, Mr Mackay. Away from prying ears. Know what I mean.

**MACKAY**

Oh yes.

***They move away together.***

**FLETCHER**

I know you see me in the role of adversary, Mr Mackay, but we're both old hands at this game – there's you and us. But we both know that neither of us must push the other too far.

**MACKAY**

That's true.

**FLETCHER**

Thereby we maintain a tolerable rhythm of life. We must season our mutual contempt with mutual respect.

**MACKAY**

What are you getting at, Fletcher?

***They stop.***

**FLETCHER**

Over this way, Mr Mackay, don't want to get too near the eavesdropping nurks.

***They move on.***

**MACKAY**

You were about to say?

**FLETCHER**

I was about to say I don't like to see your authority undermined.

***Mackay stops.***

**MACKAY**

And?

**FLETCHER**

Nothing specific. I just wanted to articulate these views. Can we go a bit further?

**MACKAY**

If there's any point.

**FLETCHER**

It would be a step in the right direction.

***They move on again.***

**MACKAY**

I wish you could be a little more specific, Fletcher.

**FLETCHER**

Oh I've gone far enough.

***He stops and stamps his feet.***

**FLETCHER**

Getting a bit parky, isn't it?

**MACKAY**

I'm a very busy man, Fletcher. I didn't come out here to discuss the weather.

**FLETCHER**

Nor did I, Mr Mackay.

**MACKAY**

I don't think this conversation's having any useful purpose at all.

**FLETCHER**
Well, hang about and we might discover something to your advantage.

**MACKAY**
Fletcher, I think you're trying to divert my attention. I'm not falling for it.

**FLETCHER**
No, you're not, are you?

***Mackay turns and moves away.***

**FLETCHER**
I'm only trying to explain my position.

***He moves and falls through a gaping hole.***

***Mackay turns and walks back to the hole. He looks down in amazement.***

## 14. PRISON INFIRMARY

***Fletcher is lying in bed with his knee bandaged up, eating his Christmas lunch.***

***The door is unlocked by a prison officer and Lennie enters, carrying a box of cigars and a package.***

**LENNIE**
Morning, Fletch.

**FLETCHER**
Morning, my son.

**LENNIE**
They've reinstated Christmas.

**FLETCHER**
I know, I'm eating it.

**LENNIE**
Here you are. Merry Christmas.

**FLETCHER**
Cuban cigars!

**LENNIE**
They're from Grouty.

**FLETCHER**
Where did he get these?

**LENNIE**
Some things we never know, Fletch. Where did B Block get their goose? That's one from me. Bit mundane after cigars, but I knitted them myself.

***Fletcher finishes unwrapping the package.***

**FLETCHER**
Oh very nice . . . I'll wear the other one when I get the bandages off.

**LENNIE**
They're mittens. Grouty says he's very sorry that his directions were eighteen inches out, but that's typical of Slocombe's prowess as a surveyor.

**FLETCHER**
I'm not bothered. What I set out to do's all come to roost, in' it?

**LENNIE**
Ensconced in the hospital, right. The screws are so chuffed with finding the tunnel – you should see them out there wha-hey . . .

*Mackay walks in.*

**MACKAY**

Compliments of the season, Fletcher.

**LENNIE**

See what I mean?

**MACKAY**

Pardon?

**LENNIE**

Nothing.

**MACKAY**

All right, Godber, cut along. Don't want to miss your Christmas lunch.

**LENNIE**

See you, Fletch.

**FLETCHER**

In due course, son.

**LENNIE**

Yeah. I'll send you a get-well-slowly card.

*Mackay laughs. Lennie leaves.*

**FLETCHER**

Well, Mr Mackay, you look a little . . . flushed – is that the word?

**MACKAY**

Just been to the Governor's sherry party. Everyone was in high spirits. Except the doctor . . . you've got his cake.

*Fletcher reacts.*

*Mackay holds up a package.*

**MACKAY**

Look at this – a present from the Governor. Pipe tobacco, I imagine.

**FLETCHER**

I'd open that when you get home if I was you, when you're on your own.

**MACKAY**

Oh, I will.

**FLETCHER**

Yeah, I shall look forward to that.

**MACKAY**

Fletcher, I wanted to say that I appreciate what you were up to in the yard.

**FLETCHER**

Oh?

**MACKAY**

(*Laughing*) All right, Fletcher. Just between you and me.

**FLETCHER**

I don't know what you're inferring, Mr Mackay.

**MACKAY**

Of course you don't, officially. But as you said we're both old hands at the game. Like to ask you just one question. What became of the soil that was excavated from the tunnel?

**FLETCHER**

No, wait a moment. Whatever you're assuming about our relationship, do not assume that you have a new informer in your back pocket. There's you and us, and I'm still on the side of us.

**MACKAY**

It's a harmless question, for future reference. I just want to know how they disposed of the soil.

**FLETCHER**

Can't help you.

***Mackay produces a bottle of Scotch.***

**MACKAY**

Scotland's finest.

**FLETCHER**

With a couple of nips out of it, I see.

**MACKAY**

Still an unexpected treat.

**FLETCHER**

Bribe, is it?

**MACKAY**

Christmas present.

***Fletcher looks at the bottle.***

**MACKAY**

Come along, Fletcher. Just between you and me.

**FLETCHER**

Is that door closed?

**MACKAY**

And there's no one out there.

**FLETCHER**

Christmas present.

**MACKAY**

Christmas present.

**FLETCHER**

You want to know where they put the soil?

**MACKAY**

Simple as that.

**FLETCHER**

I'll tell you then.

**MACKAY**

I thought you might.

**FLETCHER**

They dug another tunnel and put it down there.

***Mackay laughs with satisfaction and starts to go. Then he realises he has been done. He looks back to Fletcher who is about to have a drink.***

**FLETCHER**

Happy Christmas.

***He drinks.***

# CHRISTMAS SPECIAL

## CHRISTMAS TRAILER

### FLETCHER'S CELL

***Lennie and Fletcher are sitting at the table.***

**LENNIE**

I'm looking forward to it. There's the carol service, and the concert coming up. And the tree.

**FLETCHER**

Useful, the tree.

**LENNIE**

Useful?

**FLETCHER**

For stashing Xmas contraband. Even the fairy on the top has got two ounces of tobacco stuffed up her skirt.

***Barrowclough enters.***

**FLETCHER**

Hello, Mr B., what brings you here?

**BARROWCLOUGH**

Important message from the Governor. Christmas is cancelled.

**FLETCHER**

You what?

**LENNIE**

You what?

***Mackay enters behind Barrowclough.***

**MACKAY**

Oh yes. It's official. There will be no Xmas Eve, Xmas Day, or Boxing Day. Just the 24th, 25th and 26th December.

**LENNIE**

He can't do that – it's traditional.

**BARROWCLOUGH**

He's done it.

**MACKAY**

It's on the bulletin board. It's just not going to *happen*.

***He chuckles.***

**MACKAY**

Carry on!

***He and Barrowclough continue on their rounds.***

**FLETCHER**

That's rubbish, that is. Take no notice. We shall be here, shan't we, Lennie?

**LENNIE**

Yeah.

**FLETCHER**

I mean – where can we go?

# CHRISTMAS SPECIAL

## THE DESPERATE HOURS

### 1. ASSOCIATION AREA

*Camera shows the well area and the prisoners. A warder walks across.*

*McLaren and Tulip are watching. The warder walks past a prisoner, who watches and then nods to McLaren. He receives the nod, in turn nods to Tulip and moves away. Tulip is sitting reading a newspaper. He receives the nod and, in turn, nods to the prisoner at the end of the table. The prisoner receives the nod. He then nods to Warren. Warren receives the nod and leaves. McLaren comes to the gates and nods.*

*Fletcher receives the nod and shakes his head. The camera reveals that he is standing outside the door marked 'WC'. The door opens and Mackay comes out. He reacts to Fletcher and then leaves. Fletcher then nods, gets a label from his pocket and sticks on the door 'Gentlemen only'. He then goes in. McLaren, Warder unlocking gate. Warren joins McLaren and they walk through the gate and depart.*

*McLaren and Warren go in through the WC door.*

### 2. SHOWER ROOM

*Fletcher and Tulip are near the sink. Lennie is near the second cubicle. McLaren and Warren walk in.*

**FLETCHER**

McLaren, Warren . . . I have gathered you here as representatives of your respective cell blocks.

**WARREN**

What's this all about, Fletch?

**FLETCHER**

A minute, please. As you know, the festive season is almost upon us.

**MCLAREN**

With all the high spirits and jollity which that entails.

**FLETCHER**

Now come on, Jock, that's the wrong attitude going in, that is. Let me ask you all what is the real meaning of Christmas? Aside from the shepherds and the swaddling an' that. What comes to mind then?

**LENNIE**
Chestnuts roasting on an open fire.

**FLETCHER**
What? Oh yes, very good.

**MCLAREN**
What about Mackay roasting on an open fire?

**FLETCHER**
No, that's Guy Fawkes night.

**WARREN**
Crackers. Holly.

**LENNIE**
Treetops glistening and children listening –

**FLETCHER**
That will do, Godber. You can leave out the Perry Como. I'm talking about what the likes of us associate with Christmas. Aside from robbing a postman.

***They look at each other.***

**TULIP**
What?

**FLETCHER**
Drink.

**WARREN**
Drink?

**FLETCHER**
Drink, yes. That's what everyone does at Christmas, gets drunk. Bombed. Plastered. Elephant's trunk. Legless. Brahms and Liszt as the proverbial newt.

**LENNIE**
(*To McLaren*) I've never understood the derivation of that expression myself. Are newts known to be heavy drinkers?

**FLETCHER**
(*Irritated by the interruption*) Time is somewhat precious. We are running a security risk. Time is somewhat precious.

**LENNIE**
Sorry, Fletch, I was just saying . . .

**FLETCHER**
Yuh, well.

**TULIP**
What are we here for, Fletch?

**FLETCHER**
Wine tasting.

**TULIP**
Wine tasting?

**FLETCHER**
Yes, unbeknownst to all and sundry and out of charity to our fellow inmates, young Godber and me have been fermenting illicit liquor since last July. We done this so it would reach its peak maturity at this festive season.

**MCLAREN**
Fletch, you're a marvel, you're a naffing marvel, you know that?

**FLETCHER**
Yuh, well.

**LENNIE**
I helped him as well.

**WARREN**
And are you dishing this stuff out, like?

**FLETCHER**
I knew I shouldn't have used that word,

charity, Warren. This is a business transaction. You are here to obtain a free sample – sip – and place an order for your fellow felons. Godber . . .

***Lennie moves to the second cubicle, stands on the toilet bowl and takes from the cistern two bottles of colourless fluid.***

**FLETCHER**

We are offering two selections. We have five-star in the white bottle and the two-star in the blue bottle.

**PRISONER**

(*Putting his head round the door*) Oi!

***Tulip, Fletcher, Warren and McLaren rush to the urinals. Lennie goes to the second cubicle and sits down.***

***The warder enters and walks round looking at them. He leaves.***

***The prisoners return to their original places and the conversation continues.***

**FLETCHER**

Now as I was saying, the two-star is the Vin Ordinaire, though let me tell you it ain't that ordinaire. The five-star is our special reserve, we'll sample that first.

***Lennie is carefully pouring some of the five-star into a bottle cap.***

**LENNIE**

I'd like to warn you gentlemen, that this should be sipped delicately, like a fine liqueur. It should not be smashed down the throat by the mugful, all right.

***Lennie passes the cap first to Tulip. He takes a cautious sip and passes it to Warren.***

***He sips and passes it to McLaren who also sips for a moment. Then they react with anguished gasps.***

**FLETCHER**

I thought they'd like it, Len.

**WARREN**

You ought to have washed the bottle out first.

**MCLAREN**

Fletcher, are you sure this stuff is fit for human consumption?

**FLETCHER**

No, I'm not. That's why you three nurks is testing it for me.

**TULIP**

This stuff's evil, Fletcher.

**FLETCHER**

Don't forget it's got another week to mature. Lennie, the two-star. I should warn you gentlemen that this one isn't quite so smooth. Be careful otherwise not only will you lose the flavour and the bouquet, you will probably lose your power of speech as well.

***Lennie has given them the cap of the two-star. Warren holds it. They sniff it cautiously.***

**MCLAREN**

(*Sniffing it*) Smells like embrocation.

**FLETCHER**

There is a hint of that, yes.

**TULIP**

You could poison the whole prison, Fletcher.

**FLETCHER**
It's not very easy to get the right ingredients in here you know. I got the potato peelings, and the orange pips. No bother. But normally I would never have used boot polish.
***There are howls of protest from the others.***
**FLETCHER**
Only a joke, only a joke.
**WARREN**
(*With the cap near his lips*)
You sure?
**FLETCHER**
'Course I am.
***Warren drinks.***
**FLETCHER**
It was anti-freeze.
***Warren splutters it out.***

## 3. PRISON GOVERNOR'S OFFICE

***Venables is checking the morning mail when there is a knock at the door.***
**VENABLES**
Come in.
***A trusty enters carrying a tray of coffee and biscuits. He is a small, inoffensive man named Keegan with a Yorkshire accent.***
**KEEGAN**
Morning, Guv'nor.
**VENABLES**
Morning, er, er . . .
**KEEGAN**
Keegan, sir . . .
**VENABLES**
You're new aren't you, Keegan?
**KEEGAN**
I'm not new to prison, sir, I'm just a new trusty. Mr Mackay's Christmas box 'cause I'm going out soon, like.
**VENABLES**
Good, good. Well, don't fall back into your old ways.
**KEEGAN**
No chance of that, sir. Not since t' wife passed away.
**VENABLES**
Oh I'm sorry. When was this?
**KEEGAN**
A few weeks before I came inside.
**VENABLES**
Poor woman, what happened?
**KEEGAN**
I murdered her.
***Venables is slightly taken aback.***
**VENABLES**
Well, see that it doesn't happen again.
***Keegan leaves as Mackay comes in.***
**MACKAY**
Morning, sir.
**VENABLES**
Close the door, Mr Mackay.

**MACKAY**
Sir?
*Closes the door.*
**VENABLES**
This new trusty – what's his name . . . Keegan?
**MACKAY**
No complaints, I hope, sir.
**VENABLES**
The man's a murderer.
**MACKAY**
Oh. Yes, sir. But crime of passion. Crime passionelle – that's French. Not a criminal type. His sort of murderer makes a model prisoner. Do their porridge, no bother, full remission. According to Home Office figures, seventy-five per cent . . .
**VENABLES**
I'm not interested in statistics, Mr Mackay. Just don't want my morning coffee served to me by a wife murderer. All right?
**MACKAY**
Very good, sir.
***Venables crosses to the desk.***
**MACKAY**
Replace him, sir.
**VENABLES**
Now to the business in hand. I have always found Christmas to be a very difficult time.
**MACKAY**
Yes, sir. So open to abuse. Contraband, bartering, smuggling. There isn't a Christmas cake comes inside that isn't laced with marijuana.
**VENABLES**
What are we doing about that?
**MACKAY**
I've taken precautions, sir. I've put Mr Barrowclough on to sampling all food parcels.
**VENABLES**
Has he anything to report?
**MACKAY**
He's still too stoned to tell me, sir.
**VENABLES**
What about drink?
**MACKAY**
Always a problem, sir. They're so ingenious at hiding it, as you know, sir. I remember once they concealed it in a fire extinguisher. A fact we only discovered because a fire broke out in the education room. It was only a small fire, but after we used that particular extinguisher, it became a raging inferno.
**VENABLES**
Disgraceful. Well, as you know, Mr Mackay, I am a staunch teetotaller, and I am strongly opposed to drinking, legal or illegal.
**MACKAY**
Yes, sir.
**VENABLES**
So let us be especially vigilant this Christmas and hope that we get through it with a minimum of incident.

**MACKAY**

I'll drink to that, sir.

**VENABLES**

Hardly an appropriate remark, Mr Mackay.

**MACKAY**

Sorry, sir.

**VENABLES**

All right, carry on.

***Mackay starts to go.***

**VENABLES**

Oh, and you'll see about replacing er . . .

**MACKAY**

Keegan, sir. Yes, sir.

**VENABLES**

(*Drinking his coffee*) Incidentally, how did he kill his poor wife?

**MACKAY**

Poison, sir.

***Venables looks at his coffee cup with grave misgivings.***

## 4. ASSOCIATION AREA

***As the gate is unlocked by the warder, two prisoners come out and Fletcher and Lennie go in. They stop.***

**FLETCHER**

Hello, hello,

***Camera reveals a Prison Officer searching through the bedclothes in Fletcher's cell.***

**FLETCHER**

I think we've got burglars.

**LENNIE**

Who hasn't?

***They move on.***

## 4A. FLETCHER'S CELL

***Fletcher and Lennie enter to discover Barrowclough in the process of turning over their cell.***

**FLETCHER**

(*Indignantly*) What's this then?

**BARROWCLOUGH**

You're not being singled out, Fletcher, we're doing the whole block.

**LENNIE**

Harassment. Despicable infringement of civil liberties.

**FLETCHER**

If you told us what you was looking for, we might be able to save you all this bother.

**BARROWCLOUGH**

Drink.

**FLETCHER**

Drink? You mean alcohol? The demon rum, mother's ruin?

**BARROWCLOUGH**

That's what I mean, yes.

**FLETCHER**

I'm a strict teetotaller, Mr Barrowclough.

**BARROWCLOUGH**

(*Sceptically*) Really, Fletcher.

***He walks across the cell.***

**FLETCHER**

(*Following him*) Oh yes. Never touch tea, never have. I tell you something, the pathetic state of this country today has got more to do with tea than alcohol.

**BARROWCLOUGH**

How?

**FLETCHER**

Because we invented the tea break, that's where the rot set in.

**BARROWCLOUGH**

You're in no position to point the finger, Fletcher, when you've never done an honest day's work in your life.

**FLETCHER**

Oh that's very nice. He's added slander now to breaking and entering.

**LENNIE**

They've been turning us over all week. D'you know what they did last night? They come in the Hobby Shop where we was making soft toys for orphan children. I saw Mr Barrowclough with me own eyes, disembowelling my panda.

**BARROWCLOUGH**

Don't you think I felt bad about that? Just as I felt bad about sampling your food parcels.

**FLETCHER**

I heard you felt pretty good afterwards, though. (*To Lennie*) They found him standing in a bucket of sand and singing the 'Desert Song'.

**BARROWCLOUGH**

(*Embarrassed*) Yes, well, I suggest you men get this cell tidied up.

***He leaves. Fletcher raises his voice for the departing Barrowclough's benefit.***

**FLETCHER**

Oh very nice, exit the red shadow. (*Crossing to the door*) That's charming, ain't it? You don't find nothing, but no apologies, no retraction. As you say, Len, a total infringement of civil liberties. An unjustifiable act of mistrust and suspicion.

**LENNIE**

They didn't find nowt, though.

**FLETCHER**

'Course not, we hid it too well. Shut the door and fetch your mug.

***Lennie does so. Fletcher, plays barman, fetching a mug and putting a towel across his arm. He moves to the right of his bunk.***

**FLETCHER**

Good evening, sir. And what will it be?

**LENNIE**

The usual.

**FLETCHER**

Care for a drink first?

**LENNIE**
Why not.
**FLETCHER**
Large one?
**LENNIE**
Mind your own business.
**FLETCHER**
Thank you.
***He unscrews screw from bedstead and pours from it into the mug. Lennie puts a finger over the hole.***
**LENNIE**
Have one yourself.
**FLETCHER**
(*Taking drink*) Oh thank you, sir. When.
***Lennie puts his finger back over the hole.***
***They drink.***
**FLETCHER**
(*Putting screw back on*) Prisoners one, system nil.
***Mackay enters.***
**MACKAY**
Not necessarily, Fletcher.
**FLETCHER**
Oh my gawd . . . time gentlemen please. Haven't you got no cells to go to?

## 5. GOVERNOR'S OUTER OFFICE

***Mrs Jamieson, the Governor's secretary, sits at her desk. Barrowclough is sitting on a bench, waiting to see Venables. He is holding a cake. Mackay opens the door and marches Fletcher and Lennie in.***
**MACKAY**
Left, right, halt, face the front. Good morning, Mrs Jamieson, Mr Barrowclough . . .
**MRS JAMIESON**
Good morning, Mr Mackay.
**FLETCHER**
Good morning, Mrs Jamieson – you're looking very . . .
**MACKAY**
Quiet, Fletcher. Is the Governor in?
**BARROWCLOUGH**
I'm waiting to see him, he's indisposed.
***He indicates the corridor.***
**FLETCHER**
In the where?
**MRS JAMIESON**
He's not feeling too well. Ever since he sampled the Christmas pudding.
**LENNIE**
(*Offended*) Here, I made that. Nothing wrong with it.
**FLETCHER**
That's what you said about your Hungarian gluelash.
**MACKAY**
The word Fletcher is 'goulash'.

**FLETCHER**

I chose the word advisedly, Mr Mackay. Seeing as most of us were stuck in the bog.

***Venables walks in. He looks wan and pale and walks cautiously towards his office.***

**MACKAY**

Attention.

**FLETCHER**

Bless you.

**MACKAY**

Morning, Governor.

**VENABLES**

Morning, Mr Mackay.

**MACKAY**

Not too good I hear, sir. Sorry to hear it.

**VENABLES**

Not too good at all. That prisoner we replaced, Keegan – you didn't put him in the kitchen, did you?

**MACKAY**

No, sir.

**VENABLES**

I wondered if he was extracting some terrible revenge. I'd better have some more of that vile stuff, Mrs Jamieson. Right, Mr Barrowclough, you can come through, but I warn you, I've not got long.

***He goes through into his office, followed by Barrowclough.***

***Mrs J. gets a bottle of medicine and starts to pour it into a glass.***

**FLETCHER**

(*To Lennie*) See what you done? A stricken Governor. What sort of Christmas is he going to have then?

**MACKAY**

What sort of Christmas are you two going to have?

**FLETCHER**

Chuffed, aren't you?

**MACKAY**

Your own fault, Fletcher. You know the penalties for brewing illicit hooch.

**FLETCHER**

Wasn't illicit hooch. It was a health drink.

**MACKAY**

Poppycock!

**FLETCHER**

No, it is not poppycock. We couldn't get the poppies. Mind you in here there's no shortage of . . .

**MACKAY**

Fletcher!

**FLETCHER**

Just saying, health drink. Me and four hundred of the lads saved up a wine gum each. Then we crushed them in a press in the woodwork shop. The resultant extract is a remedy for all known ills.

**LENNIE**

You should give the Governor some, Mrs Jamieson.

**MACKAY**

I think the Governor's sick enough.

***Mrs J. stands up, crosses to the***

*door and goes into the office. All look at her legs appraisingly. Mackay notices Fletcher and Lennie.*

**MACKAY**

Stop it, you two.

**LENNIE**

I've always been attracted to older women. When I was a lad, I always wanted to be seduced by my aunty Pauline. She was very sophisticated. Worked in a dress shop in Smethwick and wore Evening in Paris behind her ears.

**FLETCHER**

Oh, behind the ears, yes, sure sign.

**LENNIE**

I nearly was once.

**FLETCHER**

What?

**LENNIE**

Seduced. I went round her house and the radio was on and she said, 'Lennie, it's time you learned how to do the foxtrot.' Well, even at the naïve age of fourteen, I thought to myself, 'Foxtrot? In the middle of the day? Yum, yum.'

*Mackay, despite himself, is fascinated by the story. Fletcher notices this.*

**FLETCHER**

Should you go on in front of Mr Mackay? Edinburgh Presbyterian you know. Sex is only allowed when Hearts beat Celtic.

**MACKAY**

I am not interested in Godber's carnal reminiscences.

*He walks over and sits down.*

**FLETCHER**

Well I am, so what happened, Len?

**LENNIE**

Nothing.

**FLETCHER**

What?

**LENNIE**

Nothing happened. I mean, she held me very close like, but for an hour we just danced round the living room floor accompanied by the Northern Dance Orchestra.

**FLETCHER**

Big room, is it? Godber, your stories have a habit of tailing off like that. You are the master of the anti-climax.

**LENNIE**

I can't half foxtrot though.

*Mrs Jamieson returns and sits at her desk. There is a knock on the door.*

**MACKAY**

Come in.

*The door opens and a trusty enters carrying a tray with coffee and biscuits. It is Reg Urwin. He seems a little disconcerted to see the room so full.*

**URWIN**

Oh . . . hello, lads.

**FLETCHER**

Hello, Reg.

*Urwin indicates his left arm.*

**FLETCHER**

Something wrong with your arm?

*Urwin indicates the red band.*

**FLETCHER**

Oh, trusty now, are we?

**URWIN**

Er, yes. Replaced Keegan, thanks to Mr Mackay.

**MACKAY**

If a man keeps his nose clean, I don't forget.

**URWIN**

Should I come back later?

**MACKAY**

(*Rising*) Not at all, lad – don't be thick. Take the Governor his coffee. Chop, chop.

*Urwin goes through into the other office.*

## 6. GOVERNOR'S OFFICE

*Barrowclough is standing by the desk while Venables signs papers. Urwin moves towards the desk with the coffee.*

**URWIN**

Your coffee, sir.

**VENABLES**

Oh, thank you, er . . .

**URWIN**

Urwin, sir. With a 'U'. I'm the new trusty.

**VENABLES**

That's a privileged position, Urwin.

**URWIN**

I know it is, sir. That's why I've been so well behaved the last few months. So that I could get this job. So that I could get ahead with my plan.

*But a look of anguish has crossed over Venables' face.*

**VENABLES**

(*Standing*) I'm afraid your plan will have to wait, Urwin.

*He makes a dash for the door.*

## 7. OUTER OFFICE

*Fletcher and Lennie react with interest as Venables dashes through.*

**MRS JAMIESON**

Oh, Mr Venables – have you got time to sign . . .

**VENABLES**

No!

*He leaves. Then he comes back.*

**VENABLES**

I'll take it with me.

**FLETCHER**

Pity it wasn't in triplicate.

*Venables goes.*

## 8. GOVERNOR'S OFFICE

*Barrowclough and a puzzled Urwin wait.*

**URWIN**

Where's he gone?

*He moves to the door.*

**BARROWCLOUGH**
It's just that he has a bit of an upset tummy.

**URWIN**
Yes, but he was instrumental in my plan, he was.

**BARROWCLOUGH**
What plan is this, Urwin?

**URWIN**
(*Distractedly*) I suppose a screw's just as good. Yeah, I don't see why not.

**BARROWCLOUGH**
I said, what is your plan?

**URWIN**
I want to get out of here.

**BARROWCLOUGH**
That's what we all want, Urwin.

**URWIN**
Yes, but you don't want me to get out as soon as what I do. That's why I'm taking you hostage.

***He produces a home-made gun from his pocket and points it at Barrowclough's back. Barrowclough turns and stares incredulously.***

**URWIN**
It's a gun. And it works. And it's loaded.

**BARROWCLOUGH**
Now just a moment, er . . .

**URWIN**
Urwin. With a 'U'.

**BARROWCLOUGH**
Urwin, why don't you put that gun down?

**URWIN**
What, so you can pick it up?

**BARROWCLOUGH**
You should think very carefully about what you're doing.

**URWIN**
Oh I have done. Now here's what I'd like you to do. First, would you draw them blinds. Second off, would you get me an 'elicopter.

***Barrowclough stares at him in astonishment.***

**URWIN**
Well go on.

***Barrowclough walks across to the window.***

## 9. OUTER OFFICE

***Mackay, Fletcher and Lennie are waiting.***

**FLETCHER**
Listen, the Governor's obviously got other things on his mind, why don't we all come back in the New Year, Mr Mackay, round about April.

**MACKAY**
Fletcher, I'm in no hurry. I've waited long enough for this moment.

**FLETCHER**
Well, in that case, let's take a seat.

*They move to the bench.*

**MACKAY**

Fletcher – how dare you?

**LENNIE**

I don't mind waiting. It's almost worth getting busted these days, just for a glimpse of Mrs Jamieson's lovely . . .

**MACKAY**

Godber.

**LENNIE**

Smile.

**MACKAY**

(*Crossing to Mrs J.*) I apologise for these two.

**MRS JAMIESON**

That's all right, Mr Mackay, working in prison I've learnt to turn the other cheek.

**LENNIE**

And a very attractive cheek, too.

***The connecting door opens and a pale-looking Barrowclough pokes his head through.***

**BARROWCLOUGH**

Eh, Mrs Jamieson, I want to get in touch with the nearest RAF station.

**MRS JAMIESON**

I don't know where that is.

**BARROWCLOUGH**

Well, the Fleet Air Arm or Air Sea Rescue. Anyone who can get me a helicopter.

**FLETCHER**

My word, you're being a bit lavish with your Christmas presents, aren't you, Mr Barrowclough?

**BARROWCLOUGH**

What?

**FLETCHER**

You'll need a lot of coloured paper to wrap that up.

**MACKAY**

Quiet, Fletcher. Is there a problem, Mr Barrowclough?

**BARROWCLOUGH**

Yes, Mr Mackay, something's come up.

**MACKAY**

Come up?

**BARROWCLOUGH**

Yes, I'm being held at gunpoint by Urwin here.

***He gestures over his shoulder.***

**MACKAY**

You're what?

***Urwin appears behind Barrowclough, brandishing the gun.***

**URWIN**

It's true, look.

***Mrs Jamieson gives a little scream.***

**URWIN**

Don't panic, missis. Just get on the blower.

**FLETCHER**

Here, Reg, you gone off your rocker?

**URWIN**

Shut up, Fletch.

**FLETCHER**

As you say, my son.

***Mackay decides the time has come for him to take charge.***

**MACKAY**

All right, Urwin. Give me that gun.

***He starts to move.***

**URWIN**

You make a move and Barrowclough gets it.

***Mackay advances slowly.***

**MACKAY**

I said, give me that gun.

**BARROWCLOUGH**

Shut up, Mackay! This is no time for stupid heroics.

**MACKAY**

We can't let these people intimidate us.

**BARROWCLOUGH**

That's all very well for you to say, but it's my head the gun is pointing at.

**URWIN**

You just naff off, Mackay. I've got two hostages, him and her, so put the word out right?

***Mackay looks at Mrs Jamieson, then at Barrowclough.***

**BARROWCLOUGH**

Go on man, do as he says.

***Mackay moves reluctantly towards the door.***

**MACKAY**

Very well. Don't panic, Mrs Jamieson, soon have you out of this. And don't you panic, Mr Barrowclough.

**FLETCHER**

(*Crossing to the centre of the room*) Mr Mackay?

**MACKAY**

Yes?

**FLETCHER**

Can we panic?

**MACKAY**

You two come along with me.

***Fletcher and Lennie move quickly to the door.***

**URWIN**

No – they stay. I can use them. Now naff off, Mackay.

***Mackay leaves.***

***Mrs Jamieson looks up from the phone directory.***

**MRS JAMIESON**

I've found the number for RAF Topcliff.

**URWIN**

Get them then.

***She starts to dial. Fletcher and Lennie exchange glances.***

**FLETCHER**

Listen, Reg, you don't really need us. We're only littering up the place. We'll just be getting back to our cells if it's all the same to you. Busy day ahead.

**URWIN**
No, I need you two. Lock that door, Godber.
***Lennie locks the door.***
**URWIN**
Now both of you, move that filing cabinet up against it.
***They start to move towards the cabinet.***
**MRS JAMIESON**
I have them on the line, Mr Barrowclough.
**BARROWCLOUGH**
Er . . . should I . . . talk to them in there?
***He indicates the inner office.***
**URWIN**
Yeah, go on.
***Barrowclough goes through into the other office. Urwin stays in the doorway covering both rooms.***
**LENNIE**
Er . . . is that all you wanted us for, Reg. To move the cabinet?
**URWIN**
Yeah.
**LENNIE**
Oh well . . . we'll be getting off then.
**FLETCHER**
Yeah, give us a hand to shift this, Len.
***They start moving the cabinet but Urwin stops them.***
**URWIN**
Hey, hey! Think I'm crackers or something?
**FLETCHER**
Possibly, Reg. Your behaviour ain't exactly that of a rational man.
**URWIN**
I know what I'm doing. Give me that key.
***Lennie gives him the key. He goes to the doorway.***
**URWIN**
We'll just sit tight and wait.
***There is a pause.***
**MRS JAMIESON**
I have a dental appointment in half an hour.
**URWIN**
Then you'll have to bleedin' cancel it.

## 10. INNER OFFICE

***Barrowclough is standing at the desk, talking on the phone. Urwin watches him.***

**BARROWCLOUGH**
Hello? Yes, this is Prison Officer Barrowclough from Slade Prison . . . well, thank you Flight Sergeant, but don't you think I ought to speak to the Commanding Officer . . . yes, I know there's only two shopping days left till Christmas, but there is some urgency here.
***Urwin crosses to the desk and grabs the phone from Barrowclough.***
**URWIN**
Here. This is Reg Urwin. I'm in charge.

I've got the gun. Listen, I'm holding a man and a woman as hostage. I don't care how you do it, but I want a chopper here in half an hour. And wait a minute –

***Fletcher and Lennie are standing in the doorway listening.***

**URWIN**

– I also want ten thousand quid in used notes. Otherwise I'm not responsible for my actions.

***He puts the phone down and turns to Barrowclough.***

**URWIN**

That's the way to talk to those people. If they ring back and they're still stalling, make believe I'm going to kill you.

**BARROWCLOUGH**

I'll try to remember that.

## 11. OUTER OFFICE

***Lennie is standing by the window. Mrs Jamieson gets up from her desk and goes to the cabinet. She opens a drawer.***

**LENNIE**

Bearing up?

**MRS JAMIESON**

Pardon?

**LENNIE**

Under the strain, like.

**MRS JAMIESON**

Oh I'm keeping myself busy.

***Both move towards the desk.***

**MRS JAMIESON**

Doing some of those jobs one's always putting off. Helps keep my mind occupied otherwise I might go to pieces.

**LENNIE**

Not you, Mrs Jamieson.

***He sits on the edge of the desk.***

**LENNIE**

I think you're holding up extremely well. Typically British, if I may say so. Stiff upper lip. Calm under crisis, that sort of thing.

**MRS JAMIESON**

That's sweet of you to say so.

**LENNIE**

To be quite honest, it doesn't surprise me. I've always admired you, Mrs Jamieson. From afar, like.

**MRS JAMIESON**

Oh why?

**LENNIE**

You remind me of my aunty Pauline.

***Fletcher comes through into the room and reacts to Lennie's line.***

**FLETCHER**
(*At door*) Oh yes. Do I really?

**LENNIE**
(*Crossing to the bench and sitting down*) Oh, I was just –

**FLETCHER**
(*Walking over to Lennie*) I know just what you was justing. (*Quietly to Lennie*) You horny little beast.

**MRS JAMIESON**
He was trying to keep my spirits up.

***There is a knock at the door.***

**FLETCHER**
Come in. Oh, of course, you can't, can you? Give us a hand to shift this, Lennie.

***Urwin comes to the doorway.***

**URWIN**
'Ere, wait a minute, wait a minute, who is it?

**FLETCHER**
Wait a minute, wait a minute, who is it?

**MACKAY**
(*Offscreen*) It's Mr Mackay. I've brought the coffee you asked for.

**FLETCHER**
(*To Urwin*) It's Mr Mackay with the coffee we asked for.

**URWIN**
All right, let him in. But watch it.

**FLETCHER**
All right, you can come in. But watch it.

***They move the filing cabinet away from the door and open the door.***

***Mackay is there with a tray of coffee mugs. He passes it through and Mrs Jamieson takes it.***

**MACKAY**
Is everything all right in there, Fletcher?

**URWIN**
Everything's all right, so naff off, Mackay.

***Mrs Jamieson takes the tray to the inner office.***

**MACKAY**
I can't believe a thing like this is happening in my prison. And at Christmastime.

**FLETCHER**
All right for you lot out there. Just remember it's us what are going through this terrifying ordeal.

**URWIN**
That'll do, Fletch. Lock the door, give me the key and put the cabinet back.

**FLETCHER**
Mr Mackay, one last thing. Could you do me a favour?

**MACKAY**
What, Fletcher?

**FLETCHER**
I left my socks soaking in the basin, could you wring them out for me?

***Mackay glares and closes the door.***

*Fletcher locks it and gives the key to Urwin. They start moving the cabinet back.*

## 12. INNER OFFICE

*Barrowclough and Mrs Jamieson are serving the coffee.*

**BARROWCLOUGH**

Here we are, Urwin.

*Urwin crosses to the desk, sits down and puts his feet up.*

**URWIN**

Ta.

*He takes the coffee. Fletcher and Lennie walk in.*

**BARROWCLOUGH**

Fletcher, Godber, help yourself to sugar.

**FLETCHER**

(*Picking mug up*) Well, I must say this is nice, very nice. Never thought I'd be served coffee by a screw.

**LENNIE**

(*Crossing from the desk to the chair*) In the Governor's office, too.

**BARROWCLOUGH**

Barriers tend to come down in situations like this.

**FLETCHER**

You don't mind if I sit then.

**BARROWCLOUGH/URWIN (TOGETHER)**

No, that's all right.

**BARROWCLOUGH**

Urwin?

**URWIN**

Go ahead.

*Fletcher sits down. Lennie invites Mrs Jamieson to sit and then does so himself on the arm of the chair. Barrowclough remains standing.*

**FLETCHER**

Thanks, Reg. Here's to you. Wherever you ends up.

**LENNIE**

Where will you go, Reg?

**URWIN**

Somewhere a long way away where they don't ask too many questions and don't care who I am as long as I can pay for it.

**LENNIE**

Oh you mean somewhere corrupt where they turn a blind eye if you grease their palm.

**FLETCHER**

Isle of Wight?

**URWIN**

I was thinking of South America or Mexico, somewhere like that.

**FLETCHER**

Oh yeah, funny country Mexico. Very . . . Mexican. Apparently all the dogs limp.

**MRS JAMIESON**

I didn't know that.

**FLETCHER**

Oh yes, well-known fact. It's something to do with the food.

**LENNIE**

Food?

**FLETCHER**

Bloke gets up in the morning, contemplates his hideous breakfast and kicks the dog.

**URWIN**

Really? And I'd always rather fancied Mexico.

**FLETCHER**

Contrary to travel brochure myth, they're not a happy people you know. I suppose any country which has tequila as its national drink is bent on self-destruction.

***Urwin finishes his coffee.***

**URWIN**

I appreciate your advice, Fletch. Maybe I'll think of somewhere else.

**BARROWCLOUGH**

You won't be going anywhere, Urwin.

***He picks up Urwin's mug.***

**URWIN**

What?

**BARROWCLOUGH**

Don't you think we have well-rehearsed precautions for emergencies like this? Don't you worry, Mrs Jamieson, you and I will not be going South of the Border down Mexico way.

**URWIN**

What you on about?

**BARROWCLOUGH**

Didn't it puzzle you that I was being so polite, handing out the coffee? That was because one of those mugs was laced with a powerful tranquilliser which acts very swiftly, and in a few moments, Urwin, in a few moments you will be happily asleep in the land of nod.

***There is a loud snore from Fletcher who is now fast asleep, an empty mug of coffee in his hand.***

## 13. ASSOCIATION AREA/LANDING

***Camera shows feet walking on the landing. A senior Police Officer is marching along. He meets up with the Governor. They cross the bridge together and walk along the landing, round a corner and in through a door.***

## 14A. MACKAY'S OFFICE

***Mackay is brewing tea as Venables enters with the Senior Police Officer.***

**VENABLES**

Any word yet?

**MACKAY**

Not yet, no, sir. But everything's under control. The rest of the prison is quiet – all in the cells locked up. Cup of tea, sir?

**VENABLES**

No, no. So they've no idea what's going on?

**MACKAY**

(*Crossing to desk*) They know something's up. They probably think someone's gone over the wall.

**VENABLES**
As long as we keep the lid on this thing.

**MACKAY**
(*Looking at his watch*) That stuff should have worked by now. I put enough in to knock out a rhinoceros.

**VENABLES**
I still can't believe that this is happening here. Where did he get the gun?

**MACKAY**
Probably made it. He's spent a lot of time in the machine shop has Urwin, and now one can see why.

***The phone rings.***

**MACKAY**
Aha!

***He picks up the receiver.***

**MACKAY**
Everything all right, Barrowclough . . .

***His expression changes.***

**MACKAY**
I see . . . yes, Urwin. Mr Urwin. Very well. I'll remember that.

***He puts the phone down.***

**VENABLES**
What's happened?

**MACKAY**
Urwin says thank you for the coffee, it perked him up. Fletcher on the other hand is sleeping like a rhinoceros.

## 14B. INNER OFFICE

***Fletcher's head is on one side, facing a stuffed trout which is mounted on the wall. He is still asleep.***

***The phone rings in the outer office.***

**MRS JAMIESON**
Hello . . . Just one moment.

***Urwin moves to the door.***

**URWIN**
Is that for me?

**MRS JAMIESON**
(*At her desk*) I'm afraid not.

***She walks to the door.***

**MRS JAMIESON**
It's your wife, Mr Barrowclough.

**BARROWCLOUGH**
Oh dear. How does she sound?

**MRS JAMIESON**
Same as usual.

**BARROWCLOUGH**
Oh dear. (*To Urwin*) May I?

**URWIN**
Be my guest.

***Barrowclough goes across to the phone.***

**BARROWCLOUGH**
Perhaps she hasn't heard yet.

***He stands at the desk and picks up the phone.***

**BARROWCLOUGH**

Hello, dear . . . what? No, I haven't forgotten but I think I should tell you there's a chance I may be late this evening . . . Now just a minute, Alice . . . Alice, if you'd give me a moment to explain . . . I know I've been late three times this week already, but I'm being held at gunpoint as a hostage . . . I *know* we're supposed to be going round to Mrs Wainwright's at eight . . . yes, yes, it's rude and inconsiderate, but I may be going abroad in a helicopter . . . Alice, I don't believe you've heard a word . . . at gunpoint, yes! There's Mrs Jamieson, two prisoners and myself . . .

***He sits down and turns away.***

**BARROWCLOUGH**

What do you mean, 'Oh is that woman with you!' . . .

***Mrs Jamieson goes back to the outer office.***

**BARROWCLOUGH**

Well, of course she's going too, neither of us has much say in the matter. Of *course* I'm not glad! Alice, this is pointless. I'll try and call again, but if I don't I suggest you watch the six o'clock news.

***He replaces the phone and is suddenly aware that Lennie and Urwin have taken this all in and have put two and two together.***

**URWIN**

(*Crossing and sitting on the arm of Lennie's chair*) Here Barra, your old lady reckons that you and Mrs Jamieson have got a little thing going, does she?

**BARROWCLOUGH**

Certainly not.

**URWIN**

I bet she didn't believe all those late shifts you've been working.

**LENNIE**

Now, Reg, this thing between Mr Barrowclough and Mrs Jamieson is sheer speculation.

**BARROWCLOUGH**

(*Getting up*) There is no 'thing' Godber. Our relationship is purely professional.

***Mrs Jamieson comes in and walks across to the desk.***

**MRS JAMIESON**

Should I clear these cups up, Mr Barrowclough?

**URWIN**

(*Crossing over to her*) No need to be so formal, love. We know all about you and him.

***Mrs Jamieson blanches and bristles towards Barrowclough.***

**MRS JAMIESON**

Henry, how could you!

**BARROWCLOUGH**

Dorothy, I never said a word.

**MRS JAMIESON**

Well, it never came from my lips!

***She storms out, taking the tray. Fletcher wakes up, stretching himself, unaware at first of his whereabouts. He starts on seeing the fish, then looks around him, and notices Lennie.***

**FLETCHER**
Where am I?

**LENNIE**
(*Getting up and going over to Fletcher*) We're in the Governor's office, remember?

***Fletcher gets to his feet and launches straight into his defence.***

**FLETCHER**
Oh yes, sir, about Mr Mackay's allegations, Godber and me weren't drunk, we never drink. Sometimes we chew on the occasional sock, but . . .

***Lennie is trying to stop him.***

**LENNIE**
Fletch, Fletch . . . The Governor isn't here! Don't you remember?

***He points to Urwin.***

**FLETCHER**
Hello, Reg, you the new Governor? What are you doing here?

**URWIN**
I'm hijacking Barrowclough, don't you remember?

**FLETCHER**
How could I nod off in the middle of that?

**BARROWCLOUGH**
The coffee you drank was drugged.

**FLETCHER**
Drugged?

**LENNIE**
It was meant for Reg, but Barrowclough messed it up.

**FLETCHER**
I do feel a bit queer.

***He sits down.***

**LENNIE**
Could be dangerous, Fletch. Those drugs on top of all the booze we had.

**BARROWCLOUGH**
Thank you, Godber, I'll remember that.

**FLETCHER**
So will I, my son.

***Suddenly Mrs Jamieson comes back with a transistor radio.***

**MRS JAMIESON**
Listen, we're on *The World at One.*

***Urwin stands up and Lennie moves to the radio. They all listen.***

**VOICE**
(*Offscreen*) A government spokesman said that the Home Secretary could not be reached for comment regarding the situation at Slade Prison.

Details are still confused, but it appears that the Governor's secretary, Mrs Dorothy Jamieson . . .

***Despite the situation, she is pleased at hearing her name on the radio, and Lennie gives her a little 'that's you' look.***

**VOICE**

(*Offscreen*) and a Prison Officer . . . are being held at gunpoint by three desperate prisoners.

**FLETCHER**

Three!

***He stands up, holds his head and sits down again.***

**VOICE**

(*Offscreen*) They are demanding transportation and a large sum of money. In the City today, shares suffered a further decline when . . .

***Urwin turns the radio off.***

***Mrs Jamieson takes it back into the outer office.***

**FLETCHER**

(*Walking to the desk*) Here, what's this about three desperate men?

**BARROWCLOUGH**

They said that details were confused.

***He sits down.***

**FLETCHER**

Oh, yes, but next thing, they'll be issuing names.

**LENNIE**

What's my family going to think?

**FLETCHER**

What's my wife going to think?

**BARROWCLOUGH**

I hope she shows a little more consideration than mine.

**URWIN**

(*Getting up*) Hey, hey, hey. Never mind your naffing families, what about me? It's on the wireless so everybody knows about it. So why am I still stuck here, where's my helicopter?

***Fletcher takes charge, the pacifier.***

**FLETCHER**

Reg, Reg . . . a word of caution. I don't want you to build your hopes too high, my son.

**URWIN**

What d'you mean?

**FLETCHER**

I think you should get used to the idea that they may not play ball. Put yourself in their shoes. They have to demonstrate to an anxious public that they ain't going to bow down to every nutter with a gun and fly him off to sunnier climes.

**URWIN**

Here, I'm no nutter.

**FLETCHER**

I'm taking the Establishment viewpoint, Reg. Nothing personal.

**LENNIE**

'Nother thing – ten thou's a lot of money.

**BARROWCLOUGH**

Doesn't seem an excessive amount for a Prison Officer with twenty-three years' unblemished service.

**URWIN**

(*Sitting at the desk*) Let me get this straight. What you're saying like, is they're calling my bluff. They haven't been taking me seriously?

**BARROWCLOUGH**

(*Triumphantly*) Right. And there's nothing you can do about it now.

**URWIN**

There is one thing I could do.

**BARROWCLOUGH**

What?

**URWIN**

I could always shoot you.

***He points the gun at Barrowclough.***

**BARROWCLOUGH**

Yes, yes, I suppose you could do that.

**FLETCHER**

Wouldn't advise it, Reg. Any wave of public sympathy you might attract would go right out of the window if you was to maim a screw.

**LENNIE**

Listen to Fletch, and just keep cool.

**FLETCHER**

That's the ticket, son. 'Cause I have been through this before, you see.

**URWIN**

Have you?

**BARROWCLOUGH**

(*Disbelievingly*) Really, Fletcher?

**FLETCHER**

Yeah. First nick I was in. There was this bloke called Popplewell. He was a trusty like you, Reg. That's how he come to be on an outside work party. Repainting the Governor's house. Well, the next thing we knew he was barricaded in there with Mrs Bailey.

**BARROWCLOUGH**

Mrs Bailey?

**FLETCHER**

Yeah. Mrs Bailey, the Governor's wife, Mrs Bailey. That was her name. The Governor's name was Bailey, and she was married to him so she was Mrs Bailey. Follow all that, so far?

***He looks round at Lennie and raises his eyes.***

**LENNIE**

I suppose you called him Old Bailey?

**FLETCHER**

(*To Lennie*) Do you want to tell the story, Godber?

**LENNIE**

I'm sorry, I was just . . .

**FLETCHER**

(*Moving back to Urwin*) Yeah well.

**LENNIE**

Please go on, Fletch.

**FLETCHER**

Don't know if I can now. I've lost the thread.

**URWIN**

(*Pointing gun*) Get on with it.

**FLETCHER**

All right, all right. Well now, before you could say Jack Robinson the house was surrounded by the screws, and the law, and of course there was newspapers and television cameras. If I remember rightly, even Fyfe Robertson turned up but he soon cleared off. Anyhow, for three days all sorts of people made appeals to Popplewell, like the Chaplain, and the psychiatrist. But there was never a word from him or Mrs Bailey. Remember Mrs Bailey?

**BARROWCLOUGH**

What happened?

**FLETCHER**

On the fourth day Mrs Bailey let him go.

***He sits down.***

**LENNIE**

You mean she was holding him. Why?

**FLETCHER**

Why? Well, I think to use a catchphrase what was prevalent at the time, Len . . . she'd never had it so good.

## 15. OUTER OFFICE

***The camera shows the clock on the wall which says half-past four. Mrs Jamieson is putting files in the filing cabinet. Fletcher and Lennie walk in from the Inner Office.***

**FLETCHER**

You all right, Mrs Jamieson?

**MRS JAMIESON**

What is happening in there?

**LENNIE**

Oh, we've won a little victory. He's extended his deadline till five o'clock.

**MRS JAMIESON**

Oh good, then I'll probably have time to finish this before he shoots us all. Or must I expect a fate worse than death?

**FLETCHER**

Is there a fate worse than death?

***Mrs Jamieson thinks about it for a moment.***

**MRS JAMIESON**

No, I don't suppose there is.

**FLETCHER**

That's the spirit. Here listen, are those prisoners' files?

**MRS JAMIESON**

Yes.

**FLETCHER**

Fish Urwin's out for me, would you?

**MRS JAMIESON**

Why?

**FLETCHER**

Might help, who knows? Have a quick shifty, Len.

***He goes back into the inner office, while Lennie and Mrs Jamieson move to the filing cabinet.***

## 16. INNER OFFICE

***Urwin is sitting in the chair and Barrowclough is sitting at the desk.***

**URWIN**

Listen, I'm getting bloody angry, now. When are we going to get some action around here?!

**BARROWCLOUGH**

I'm still waiting to hear from the Governor.

**URWIN**
Well, I can't wait much longer, remember that.

***Fletcher feels the onus is on him to cool Urwin down.***

**FLETCHER**
Here, Reg, you seem kind of tense.

**URWIN**
I got to get out, Fletch. Can't take any more.

**BARROWCLOUGH**
That's exactly how I feel.

**URWIN**
You feel like that after half a day. I've been in stir half me life.

**BARROWCLOUGH**
But you're up for parole soon, Urwin.

**URWIN**
Parole – they won't give it to me. Not a snowball's. They never have and they never will. And I just got to get out of here.

**FLETCHER**
But why this way, Reg?

**URWIN**
Because if I stay inside much longer, I'm going to top myself.

**FLETCHER**
Suicide. You wouldn't do that, would you?

**URWIN**
Tried it once before.

**FLETCHER**
Oh yes? How d'you make out?

***Urwin stares at Fletcher for a moment.***

**URWIN**
I failed, didn't I? Typical. I was in a supermarket. Trying to steal a tin of pork luncheon meat. Suddenly I thought, 'Is this what my life has come to? Stealing luncheon meat?'

**FLETCHER**
You tried to kill yourself in a supermarket. How?

**URWIN**
I just put me head down and charged towards the glass doors.

**FLETCHER**
What went wrong?

**URWIN**
(*Motions doors opening*) Electric. I ran head first into an off-duty cop . . . he booked me for nicking a tin of pork luncheon meat.

**FLETCHER**
Always one about when you don't want one. What you should realise, Reg, is you're one of those people who doesn't get the breaks. Not even with glass doors. Today's typical. Obviously you've been planning to

hijack the Governor for months. The day you choose he gets the runs.

**LENNIE**

(*Offscreen*) Er, Fletch . . .

***Fletcher goes through to the outer office.***

## 17. OUTER OFFICE

***As Fletcher comes in, Lennie hands him Urwin's file.***

**LENNIE**

Look at this.

**FLETCHER**

(*Reading the file*) Would you Christmas Eve it.

**LENNIE**

Three times in the past two years, Urwin's been recommended for psychiatric treatment.

**FLETCHER**

Only he never got it, did he? The system did this to Reg. I've got to talk to him. Mrs Jamieson, would you come through here a minute, please.

***He opens the door for her.***

## 18. INNER OFFICE

***Fletcher walks in, holding the file, followed by Mrs Jamieson.***

**FLETCHER**

Sit down, love. Reg, can you come through and have a word with me and Godber? Private, like.

***Urwin looks a little doubtful.***

**URWIN**

I dunno.

**LENNIE**

Come on, Reg. These two can't get up to nowt.

***He casts a look in their direction.***

**LENNIE**

Well, they can, but I don't think they'd want to with us in the next room.

**URWIN**

Okay then.

***Lennie goes across to the desk with the file.***

**LENNIE**

Read this, Mr Barrowclough. It should interest you.

***Lennie returns to the Outer Office.***

## 19. OUTER OFFICE

***Fletcher escorts Urwin to the bench.***

**FLETCHER**

Here, Reg, sit down. You trust me, don't you?

**URWIN**

Maybe.

***He sits.***

**FLETCHER**

Well, I got to tell you, son. You ain't going to make it.

*Lennie moves in behind Fletcher.*

**URWIN**

Got to make it, Fletch. I'm a three-time loser.

**FLETCHER**

I swear to you there ain't no way. They got all the arguments on their side. Worst thing that could happen is if they say okay.

*He sits.*

**FLETCHER**

'Cause you know you'd never make it to that helicopter. They've got blokes out there could shoot a fly's eyebrows off at four hundred yards. And if flies had anything else they could shoot them off an' all. Know what I mean? And say you got to Mexico. Where next? Look at you. You think you're going to check into the Acapulco Hilton looking like that?

**LENNIE**

They'd never let you in without a tie.

**FLETCHER**

Reg . . . me and lad could have jumped you over the last few hours. But we didn't. You know why?

**URWIN**

Why?

**FLETCHER**

Because that would have dropped you in even further than what you is now. They have to see that you chucked in the towel yourself. Voluntary, like. Look, I won't lie to you. They're going to throw the book at you. But I've been reading your file. You've got some kind of case . . . if you give yourself up.

*Urwin considers, then shakes his head negatively.*

**URWIN**

No, Fletch. I'm going through with it.

**FLETCHER**

Think, Reg.

**URWIN**

No . . .

*He stands up.*

**URWIN**

I'm going the distance.

*Fletcher stands up.*

**FLETCHER**

In that case, you leaves me no choice. I'm going to have to take that gun off of you.

**URWIN**

You're what?

*He backs off, brandishing the gun. Lennie stares at Fletcher astonished. He holds out his hand.*

**FLETCHER**

Give me the gun.

**URWIN**

Stay where you are, Fletch.

*Fletcher starts to walk towards him – John Wayne never did it better.*

**FLETCHER**

Reg, you're my mucker, you ain't going to shoot me.

**URWIN**

Don't bank on it!

**LENNIE**
Hey, Fletch, give over. He's serious.
**FLETCHER**
Not to worry. Reg and me is mates.
**URWIN**
Don't push it – mate!
***Fletcher reaches out a hand. The gun is in Urwin's hand. Fletcher very deliberately pushes a finger into the barrel of the gun.***
***Fletcher gently takes the gun from Urwin and puts it in the desk drawer. Urwin crumples into the chair.***
**FLETCHER**
(*Arm round Urwin*) Now, Reg, on your feet, son. Don't let go. Don't pack it in. Now's the time you have to be in control.
**URWIN**
What's the point?
**FLETCHER**
Every point. Mustn't let Barra think we overcame you. You go in there and tell him this was your decision. And Len and me will back you up.
**LENNIE**
He's right, Reg. It's your only chance.

**URWIN**
You'd back me up?
**FLETCHER**
'Course we will, like I said we're still on the side of us. There's still them and us.
**URWIN**
But you two could be heroes. For what you two have just done you could probably get a free pardon.
***Fletcher stands up and looks at Lennie.***
**FLETCHER**
Well – what d'you think, Len?
**LENNIE**
'Tis Christmas after all.
**FLETCHER**
Goodwill to all men and all that swaddling. (*To Urwin*) On your way, son.
**URWIN**
Maybe you're right.
***He gets up and starts to go, then stops and turns.***
**URWIN**
But I'm still calling the shots, aren't I?
**FLETCHER**
'Course you are. Main thing is, you didn't shoot the shots.
***Urwin walks through to the inner office.***
**URWIN**
(*Offscreen*) Mr Barrowclough . . .
***Lennie walks over to the door and shuts it.***

**LENNIE**

Fletch, you are a ruddy marvel. I've never seen anything like it.

**FLETCHER**

What – oh, the gun, yes well . . .

***He gets the gun from the drawer.***

**LENNIE**

No, no, don't denigrate what you just done. I never seen anything like it. Not even in *Kojak*.

**FLETCHER**

Yeah well, I had an advantage over Lollipop head, didn't I, I knew the gun weren't loaded.

**LENNIE**

Wasn't it?

**FLETCHER**

No . . . I been working in the machine shop with Reg. He's been making that gun for months, it's only a toy.

***Lennie takes the gun.***

**LENNIE**

You knew that all along?

**FLETCHER**

Yes, but as I just said, if I'd mentioned it I'd've dropped him deeper in the clarts.

***He takes the gun.***

**LENNIE**

Looks very authentic to me – are you sure it's a toy?

**FLETCHER**

'Course I am. Look.

***He points the gun towards the ceiling and pulls the trigger. There is a bang followed by a shower of plaster falling on their heads.***

## 20. CELL

***Fletcher is putting up a pathetic paper chain when Barrowclough enters. He clears his throat.***

**BARROWCLOUGH**

Evening, Fletcher.

***He walks over to the bunk.***

**FLETCHER**

Oh hello, Mr Barrowclough.

**BARROWCLOUGH**

This is very nice. Is Godber about?

**FLETCHER**

No, he wanted to prove that his Christmas pudding was not the cause of the Governor's indisposition. So he ate three helpings to vindicate his reputation.

**BARROWCLOUGH**

Three!!! Oh I see, where is he then?

**FLETCHER**

Still in the bog. Two more to go.

***He moves to the table and picks up the paper chain.***

**BARROWCLOUGH**

How are you feeling then, after our terrible ordeal?

**FLETCHER**

I'm all right, Mr Barrowclough. But me and the lads are still a bit concerned about Reg Urwin.

***He stands on the chair to pin up the paper chain.***

**BARROWCLOUGH**

I have been assured that Urwin will be undergoing psychiatric treatment. He will not be punished so much as helped.

**FLETCHER**

(*On chair*) Yeah well, not before time.

**BARROWCLOUGH**

And I had a word with the Governor and in appreciation of your conduct the charges against you and Godber will be dropped.

**FLETCHER**

(*Getting down from chair*) Charges! Oh you mean those unfounded allegations about us making booze. Well good, only right and proper.

**BARROWCLOUGH**

'Nough said.

**FLETCHER**

Yeah, we don't get our booze back though, do we? (*Picking up the paper chain*) Hold this.

***He moves the chair.***

**BARROWCLOUGH**

In . . . in . . . in return, of course, I would like to think that you could forget certain things that may have been revealed during those desperate hours.

***He moves towards Fletcher.***

**FLETCHER**

(*On chair*) Like what?

**BARROWCLOUGH**

The rather delicate matter of Mrs Jamieson and myself. I'd like it to go no further.

**FLETCHER**

(*Getting down*) I don't know what you're on about, Mr Barrowclough.

**BARROWCLOUGH**

That's the spirit, Fletcher.

**FLETCHER**

If you're trying to tell me there's something I'm supposed to forget, I think you're overlooking the fact I was asleep most of the time. I didn't hear anything.

**BARROWCLOUGH**

You mean . . . you didn't know about myself and Mrs Jamieson?

**FLETCHER**

No, sir. Just don't worry . . . I do now, Henry . . .